UNDERSTANDING SPONSORED SEARCH

This book addresses the underlying foundational e̶ ███ g-
ical, of sponsored search. As such, the contents ar̶ ███ e-
mentation aspects of technology. Rather than focu ███ at
causes the how. Why do certain keywords work wh ███ k
well when others that are similar do not? Why does ███ do
we measure what we do in keyword advertising?

This book speaks to that curiosity to understand why we do what we do in sponsored search. The content flows through the major components of any sponsored-search effort, regardless of the underlying technology or client or product. The book addresses keywords, ads, consumers, pricing, competitors, analytics, branding, marketing, and advertising, integrating these separate components into an incorporated whole. The focus is on the critical elements, with ample illustrations, and with enough detail to lead the interested reader to further inquiry.

Jim Jansen is an Associate Professor at the College of Information Science and Technology at The Pennsylvania State University. He has authored and coauthored more than 200 research publications, with articles appearing in a wide range of journals and conferences. He is the author of *Understanding User-Web Interactions Via Web Analytics*, coauthor of *Web Search: Public Searching of the Web*, and coeditor of *Handbook of Research on Weblog Analysis*. Jansen is a member of the editorial boards of eight international journals and serves on the research committee for the Search Engine Marketing Professional Organization (SEMPO). He has received several awards and honors, including an ACM Research Award and six application development awards, along with other writing, publishing, research, and leadership honors. He is also a Senior Fellow at the Pew Research Center with the Pew Internet and American Life Project.

Understanding Sponsored Search

Core Elements of Keyword Advertising

JIM JANSEN

The Pennsylvania State University

CAMBRIDGE UNIVERSITY PRESS
Cambridge, New York, Melbourne, Madrid, Cape Town,
Singapore, São Paulo, Delhi, Tokyo, Mexico City

Cambridge University Press
32 Avenue of the Americas, New York, NY 10013-2473, USA

www.cambridge.org
Information on this title: www.cambridge.org/9781107628366

First published 2011

Printed in the United States of America

A catalog record for this publication is available from the British Library.

Library of Congress Cataloging in Publication Data
Jansen, Bernard J.
    Understanding sponsored search : core elements of keyword advertising / Jim Jansen.
       p.   cm.
    Includes bibliographical references.
    ISBN 978-1-107-01197-7 – ISBN 978-1-107-62836-6 (pbk.)
    1. Internet advertising.   2. Internet searching.   3. Keyword searching.   4. Search
    engines.   5. Branding (Marketing)   6. Consumer behavior.   I. Title.
    HF6146.I58J37   2011
    659.14′4–dc22   2011010612

ISBN 978-1-107-01197-7 Hardback
ISBN 978-1-107-62836-6 Paperback

Contents

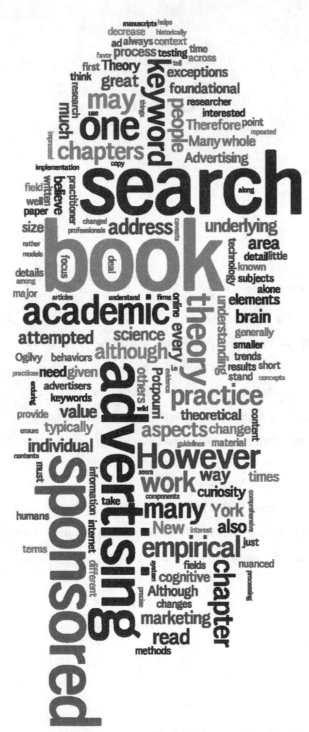

Word cloud generated by Wordle

Preface

As Asimov mentions in his *Guide to Science* [1], curiosity may be a basic human attribute. It is a drive that compels us to learn, discover, describe, and understand the world around us. It is this compelling drive that has driven me to write this book on sponsored search.

I've had the privilege of having many discussions with some top-notch, and often young, search engine marketing professionals from well-known online marketing firms, as well as professionals from lesser-known firms. I'm typically impressed (very impressed, actually) with their depth and breadth of knowledge about the mechanisms and tactics of sponsored search. Many times, they have provided interesting and perceptive insights on techniques for keyword selection, methods for composing ad copy, and other aspects of implementing keyword advertising campaigns.

However, I have always sensed an underlying curiosity from these professionals, pointing to a possible knowledge absence, regarding the foundational and underlying elements of sponsored search. Why does one select certain keywords (other than that historically they seem to work)? Why does one choose particular terms for one's ad copy (other than that historically they seem to work)? Why is this bidding process the way it is? Why look at certain metrics and not at others?

In other words, *why* do we do what we do?

This book is for those who are curious about such things.

I am one of these people, as I am curious why things are the way they are with sponsored search, which is the process in which advertisers pay to have their advertisements appear on a search engine results page in response to a query from a searcher. Sponsored search is also commonly known as keyword advertising.

There is also a great practical benefit in understanding the theoretical foundations of what one does. Doing something just because it worked in the past will generally produce good results – until the context, situation, or environment changes. Then, all the historical data and results are of little value. However, an understanding of the theory and models of a given area provides us with continuity during turbulent times [2], as theory is more stable and enduring.

Therefore, theory is of value to both the academic and the practitioner.

Potpourri: As an academic researcher, I used to be amazed by the number of scholarly articles on advertising that would lament the rift that exists between academic advertising researchers and advertising practitioners.

I used to be amazed, but no longer.

There is typically little effort expended to ensure that academic research is impactful to practitioners. Unfortunately, this is true in many academic fields and will remain so until the reward system changes (i.e., from publication to impact).

For the content in this book, nearly every chapter has been reviewed by both a researcher and a practitioner to increase the possibility that the material will be of value to both.

Also, theory helps us avoid ultimate relativism, where each individual case is unique in terms of attributes and context. Theory aids in finding the generalities among these individual cases, highlighting the trends and commonalities.

Theory helps us see the forest in the trees.

The contents of this book address the underlying foundational elements, both theoretical and methodological, of sponsored search. As such, the contents are less affected by the ever-changing implementation aspects of technology. Rather than focusing on the how, we examine what causes the how.

- *Why* do certain keywords work whereas others do not?
- *Why* does that ad work well when others that are very similar do not?
- *Why* does that keyword cost a given amount?
- *Why* do we measure what we do?

This book speaks to that curiosity to understand why we do what we do in sponsored search.

So, this is not a how-to book for pay-per-click, keyword advertising, or sponsored-search efforts. There are many such books, manuscripts, articles, Web sites, and blogs that address in great detail the mechanical aspects of implementation. Many are quite good and are a must-read for anyone in the profession. However, these publications are continually updated, as their half-life is generally short given the rapid pace of change in the interfaces and algorithms of advertising platforms and technology.

The theory of sponsored search is more enduring because keyword advertising is a business of people.

I'm of the belief that the Internet, Web, and search engines have changed (and are changing) people's behaviors but have had little effect on people's thinking, or more accurately, their cognitive processing of the world around them. People may now communicate faster, process information in smaller chunks, and buy products and services differently, along with many other changes in behaviors. The metaphors they use may have changed. However, I find it hard to believe that cognitive processing developed over millions of years has altered much at all.

Therefore, many of the theoretical perspectives in this book deal with people. Sponsored search is a people venture, with informational and technical aspects.

> **Potpourri**: Although I do not believe that there has been any change in the way people think, I am open to the possibility. In fact, there is some evidence that we may have undergone a radical transformation in the way people think, although it appears to have had nothing to do with the Internet.
>
> What is the evidence of this change?
>
> In the last 20,000 or so years, the average size of the human brain has decreased by about 10 percent [3]. That's right! Going by brain size, Cro-Magnon had the best brain-to-body ratio. Modern humans have less brain per body mass.
>
> This decrease in brain size began about the time that humans transitioned from hunter-gatherer cultures to agricultural communities.
>
> Researchers believe that this decrease in brain size is the result of the more complex social structure of humans, which reduces the need for aggression and other cognitive processes to survive in the wild.
>
> In others words, we domesticated ourselves! This domestication might have caused a smaller brain, which may have resulted in a change in the way humans think.
>
> It has been observed that domesticated animals (i.e., dogs, cats, sheep, cows, etc.) have smaller brains than their wild counterparts.
>
> However, the Internet appears to have had no effect on this reduction in human brain size, as far as we can tell.

What is the relationship between theory and practice?

There is an old academic joke that goes like this. "What is the difference between theory and practice?" The punch line is: "In theory, they aren't that different. In practice, they are quite different." (Note: Academic jokes typically are not particularly funny.)

Like many jokes, it has an element of inherent truth. Theory and practice are different, as any account manager of a sponsored-search campaign will tell you. Every advertiser, every product, and every campaign has caveats and exceptions that the practitioner deals with on every account. However, there are some general trends, behaviors, and guidelines. Theory explains the principles and constructs underlying these guidelines and trends.

Therefore, in this book, we deal with theories and models that have provided the grounding for the techniques that empirical testing and practice have shown to work – or not work – in sponsored search. The methods of practice are typically the result of repeated testing among many advertisers across many verticals. In this book, we aim to provide insight into these practices.

We deal with the fundamentals that provide understanding. Do not, however, take away from this that I am against the empirical. Exactly the opposite, as I am an empirical researcher myself.

Keyword advertising is, by nature, an empirical field. Many wonderful advertisers have been proponents of taking nothing at its face value, always testing [4, 5, 6, 7]. This is a position with which I completely agree. However, the theories presented in this book have withstood repeated empirical evaluation. They explain much of keyword advertising, although there are always caveats and exceptions for individual accounts, campaigns, keyphrases, and ads.

> **Potpourri**: Although some may consider theory the "higher ground," I fully acknowledge that it all depends on the situation, and there are times when one can only solve a problem or leverage an opportunity via empirical research.
>
> One classic example of this is the invention of paper, with the credit going to Ts'ai Lun, around A.D. 105, although the word "paper" comes from papyrus, invented by the Egyptians, which was the first paper-like substance.
>
> The reason that paper is an empirical invention is that there is no "theory" that takes one from "I need a cheap, portable, durable, flexible, and versatile material to write on" to "therefore I need to pulverize wood, mix it with water, and let it dry." One can only get from the *need* to the *solution* via empirical methods [8].

What subjects does this book not address?

The book does not address affiliate marketing or contextual advertising in any great detail. These are forms of online advertising related to keyword advertising concepts, but they are distinct from the keyword-triggered advertising of sponsored search.

Who is the book written for?

The book is written for those interested in understanding the fundamentals of sponsored search, which includes:

- those just *beginning* in the sponsored-search area
- those who are *skilled* in the mechanics of keyword advertising

The material presented here will be of great interest and value to those starting out in the area of sponsored search, providing a framework within which to connect the pieces inherent to this system. Such an introduction to the foundational elements can greatly accelerate the process of becoming skilled in this rather intricate area of online advertising. If this describes you to some degree, then this book is for you.

From my own experiences, however, I believe that one must work in sponsored search for some time, becoming immersed in the subtleties, before one really understands its problems and issues. At this stage, one can only realize how nuanced the area is and how much there is still to learn. At such a point, a return to the foundational aspects is needed to reground oneself in the core concepts of the field. Otherwise, you get lost in the weeds! If this is generally your state of expertise, then this book is for you also.

How do you read this book?

The book is designed both to be a complete read and to serve as a reference for workshops, seminars, or courses. As a reference, one can use the whole book or individual chapters. I have attempted to be comprehensive, covering each of the major facets of sponsored search. So, depending on one's background, there may be some areas with which one is not familiar. Each chapter is stand-alone. If there is a section that you do not understand fully, you can skip a chapter at first and then return later to reread.

What academic fields are addressed?

My focus is, of course, sponsored search, but I delve deep into the academic fields of information science, consumer behavior, and advertising, along with aspects of computer science, cognitive science, marketing, and statistics. However, I've avoided the nuanced jargon that academics favor and that is sometimes required when the precise meaning of a term is needed. Instead, I have sacrificed preciseness for an easier flow of content. Interested readers are welcome to dig deeper into the academic literature for the meticulous details. The chapters contain comprehensive references. In fact, I have attempted to provide published research to support common practices in the field. The book also has an extensive glossary of terms both addressed in the book and those one hears in the practice of sponsored search.

So, although I focus on some weighty academic subjects, I have intentionally kept my writing light and conversational. There are some mathematical formulas, but these are accompanied by straightforward explanations. Each chapter contains selected items of interest (labeled **Potpourri**), a highlight of the major takeaways (if you like, you can read just these before wading into the whole book), and a subsection that relates the theoretical discussion to practice. The more experienced readers can certainly skip Chapter 1, which lays out the context of the rest of the book, although it is a short read and will not take much time. So, I encourage you to take the few minutes to read it.

How is the book organized?

I have partitioned the subject of sponsored search in rather precise chapters. I am not in favor of the books on Web subjects that come across as "random walks on the Internet" or "look at the Web pages that I browsed." The separate chapters are somewhat artificially walled, but I have simultaneously attempted to integrate the chapters into a coherent whole. Therefore, although the chapters are stand-alone, the book is a consistent work.

To make each chapter stand alone, there are a few instances where I must repeat a concept across multiple chapters. In these situations, I refer back to the chapter where the concept was introduced in full. Although this approach introduces some repetition, it also facilitates reader concentration on an individual chapter, without having to digest the entire book.

As much as my academic nature will permit, I have attempted to keep the book short, direct, and to the point. However, at times, an aspect may be nuanced and require several examinations to drive the point home.

Although the book is written in an easy-to-follow tone, I have taken great pains to ensure that every word counts. The downside of such an approach is that details and exceptions might not be given their fair due. However, other manuscripts and information sources are available that address these details and exceptions. Many of these sources are listed in the references.

The content flows through the major components of any sponsored-search effort, regardless of the underlying technology or client or product. The book addresses keywords, ads, consumers, pricing, competitors, analytics, branding, marketing, and advertising, integrating these separate components into an incorporated whole. The focus is on the critical elements, with ample illustrations, and with enough detail to lead the interested reader to further inquiry.

In sum, I have attempted to address the curiosity. The *why*.

References

[1]   Asimov, I. 1965. "Chapter 1: What Is Science?" In *Asimov's Guide to Science*. New York: Basic Books, pp. 3–16.

[2]   Shapiro, C. and Varian, H. R. 1999. *Information Rules: A Strategic Guide to the Network Economy*. Boston, MA: Harvard Business Press.

[3]   McAuliffe, K. 2010. "The Incredible Shrinking Brain." *Discover*, September. pp. 54–59.

[4]   Caples, J. 1997. *Tested Advertising Methods*, 5 ed. Rev. by Fred E. Hahn. Upper Saddle River, NJ: Prentice Hall.

[5]   Hopkins, C. 1924. *Scientific Advertising*. New York: Cosimo Classics.

[6]   Ogilvy, D. 1963. *Confessions of an Advertising Man*. London: Atheneu.

[7]   Ogilvy, D. 1983. *Ogilvy on Advertising*. Toronto: John Wiley and Sons.

[8]   Hart, M. H. 1992. The *100: A Ranking of the Most Influential Persons in History*. New York: Citadel Press.

Acknowledgments

Thanks! Merci! Danke! Spasibo! Gracias! Xie xie! Arigato! Dyakooyu!

There are many folks who have made this book possible and who deserve thanks and much more than the small token of appreciation that I offer here. Many of their efforts have made the content of this book clearer and sharper than my initial attempts and thus more valuable to readers. These folks deserve credit for their efforts and assistance, and I deeply appreciate their contributions:

The kind folks at Cambridge University Press who were open to the idea and concept of this book, especially Lauren Cowles and David Jou. Both Lauren and David were just wonderful during the entire process. A big thanks also to the folks at Newgen Publishing and Data Services! Great job!

The three anonymous reviewers of this book's proposal who supported the concept of this book and provided initial feedback and guidance. Their quick response, enthusiastic encouragement, and wonderful suggestions were great early motivators for getting me started on this journey.

Brooke Randell, independent copy writer, who performed expert proofing and content review of the entire book. Brooke was a former student of mine who has now moved on to better things! We'll continue to hear more good things about her.

Rianna Jansen, my daughter, who did the final copyediting prior to submission. She corrected the many mistakes of grammar that I interjected into the manuscript with my continual fiddling up to the last moment. Her efforts significantly improved the readability of the final content.

Thanks also to the subject-matter experts who reviewed individual chapters. Nearly every chapter was reviewed by both an academic and a practitioner. The chapter reviewers were

- Brad Geddes, CertifiedKnowledge.org
- Daehee Park, Acxiom
- Dietmar Wolfram, University of Wisconsin, Milwaukee
- Don Turnbull, independent consultant and researcher
- G. Allen Westra, Upper Iowa University
- George Michie, Rimm-Kaufamn Group

- Lu Zhang, Penn State University
- Nico Brooks, Two Octobers
- Sebastien Lahaie, Yahoo! Research
- Shelby Thayer, Penn State University
- Theresa Clarke, James Madison University

I list the affiliations of the reviewers as a courtesy. However, the reviews provided were not the opinion of their respective institutions but only those of the individual reviewer.

I thank Gord Hotchkiss and Ian Everdell, both of Mediative (formerly Enquiro), for the use of a search engine results page heat map for this book. Gord did one of the initial eye-tracking studies in the area. So, I am extremely thankful.

My thanks to Clay Davis, who provided me with the idea for the Seven Words You Can't Say on Television.

I have interacted with many search engine marketing firms and agencies over the years, which added greatly to my understanding of the field of sponsored search and the techniques of keyword advertising.

I've been fortunate to have a great relationship with IMPAQT, which has been a fantastic supporter of search engine marketing education. So, a special thanks to Richard Hagerty, IMPAQT CEO, who has truly been great!

Thanks also are in order to the other search engine marketing and related agencies that have been gracious enough to give me their time, expertise, or assistance, which include:

- Acronym Media
- AskHowie.com
- Atlas Solutions (now part of Microsoft)
- bjTheory
- BlitzLocal
- Bloom Marketing
- CertifiedKnowledge.org
- ClickEquations
- Google AdWords
- Google Research
- GSI Commerce
- iProspect
- Mediative (formerly Enquiro)
- Pepperjam (now part of TrueAction)
- Razorfish
- Rimm-Kaufman Group
- Seer Interactive
- TrueAction (part of GSI Commerce)
- WebMasterWorld.com
- Wordstream
- Yahoo! Research
- Yahoo! Search Marketing
- Yodle

Finally, I owe a big thanks to the many experts in the field of sponsored search, both academic and practitioner, with whom I have collaborated over the years in research, education, consulting, or expert witnessing. Your insights and knowledge have proven invaluable.

Naturally, the errors, omissions, and mistakes contained in the pages of this book are mine and mine alone.

Word cloud generated by Wordle

Notes on Terminology

Within any complex field, such as sponsored search, that spans many domains of study, the jargon of the field can quickly become overloaded (i.e., the same term can have multiple meanings), inaccurate (i.e., a term can have nuanced meanings depending on the context, and the context may be different in a given case), and sloppy (i.e., several terms for the same thing or concept). Therefore, as Antisthenes reminds us, the study of words is at the foundation of education.

In this book, I have striven to use the same term for the same concept throughout, to be as accurate as possible in discussion, and to be as precise as possible in usage of terminology.

However, the nuances of meaning are often dependent on context and convention. Therefore, there are several issues of terminology that we must address.

Searcher versus Potential Consumer

- A *searcher* is a person who submits a query to a search engine, engages the results, or browses Web pages.
- A *potential consumer* is a searcher who may make a purchase or is engaged in a possible e-commerce transaction.
- A searcher engaged in a search process may at some point transition to be a potential consumer. The point of this transition is key to the concept of sponsored search.

Consumer versus Potential Customer

- A *consumer* is a person within a market segment.
- A *customer* is a person who has a realistic possibility of converting (i.e., purchasing, signing up for a newsletter, etc.).
- A consumer may at some point become a potential customer. In fact, this is the *goal of sponsored search.*

Keyphrase versus Keyword

- A *keyword* is a word selected by an advertiser that links a searcher's query to an advertisement.
- A *keyphrase* is a set of two or more keywords.

Keyword versus Term

- A *keyword* is a word selected by an advertiser that links a searcher's query to an advertisement.
- A *term* is a word selected by a searcher for use in a query.
- A *query* may contain one or more terms.

Advertisement versus Sponsored-Search Result

- An *advertisement* is a commercial message to a consumer.
- A *sponsored-search result* is an advertisement that appears on a search engine results page.

Search Engine as Business versus Search Engine as Technology

- A search engine is a *business*, especially within the domain of sponsored search.
- A search engine is a *technology* that provides a searching service, which can be a general-purpose search engine, a niche search engine, or a social media service that provides searching capabilities.
- At times, one must view the search engine as a business and at other times as a technology. The *viewpoint depends on the context* of the discussion.

Sponsored Search as Process versus Sponsored Search as Platform

- Sponsored search is a *process* involving a search engine technology, the business aspect of the search engine as a company, a searcher who may become a potential customer, and an advertiser.
- Sponsored search is a *technology* for advertising provided by a search engine.
- Depending on the context, one must view sponsored search as a process and other times as a platform. The *viewpoint depends on the context* of the discussion.

Advertiser versus Business

- An *advertiser* is an entity that pays for a commercial message.
- A *business* is an entity that can engage in advertising for some commercial purpose.
- Sometimes, the advertiser and business can be the *same entity*.

Business versus Organization

- A *business* is an entity that can engage in advertising for some commercial purpose.

- An *organization* is an entity that can engage in advertising for some noncommercial purpose.

Advertiser versus Bidder

- An *advertiser* is an entity that pays for a commercial message.
- A *bidder* is an entity that engages in a sponsored-search auction.
- Depending on the *context*, one must view an entity as an advertiser in the sponsored-search process and other times as a bidder in a sponsored-search auction.

Search Engine as Auction Technology versus Search Engine as Auctioneer

- A search engine *provides* a sponsored-search technology for advertising.
- A search engine acts as an *auctioneer* in a sponsored-search auction.
- Depending on the context, sometimes the search engine is the sponsored-search technology and other times the auctioneer. Its *goals are different* for each role.

Rank versus Position

- *Rank* is the numerical label for an advertisement in a sponsored-search listing.
- *Position* is a slot for an advertisement in a sponsored-search listing.

Keyphrase Bid versus Maximum Cost-Per-Click

- A *keyphrase bid* is the amount that an advertiser is willing to pay to a search engine for serving its advertisement, typically for a click.
- *Maximum cost-per-click* is the maximum amount that an advertiser pays for a click on an advertisement.
- The maximum cost-per-click is *equal to or less than* the keyphrase bid.

Sponsored-Search Effort versus Sponsored-Search Campaign

- A *sponsored-search effort* is one or more sponsored-search campaigns by an advertiser.
- A *sponsored-search campaign* is a set of keyphrases, bids, and advertisements cognitively linked to a topic by an advertiser.

Web versus Internet

- *Web* is a browser-based, typically HTTP and HTML communication medium, which is a layer of user application that sits on the Internet (note capital I) hardware and software network.
- *internet* (note lowercase i) refers to any communication medium that is not browser-based, typically apps and software that facilitate user communication and transactions on the Internet (note capital I) hardware and software network.

Word cloud generated by Wordle

1

A Context for Sponsored Search

Context is the surroundings, circumstances, environment, background,
or settings which determine, specify, or clarify the meaning of an event.
Wiktionary, 2010 [1]

You must always consider the context within when a given phenomenon occurs
to derive any meaning from it. As the Wiktionary quote states, the context is what
clarifies the meaning of an event [1].

Let's Place Ourselves in the Proper Context

You are the owner of a small- to medium-size business that sells some product or
service. Pick any product or service that interests you. We will use a framing shop as
an example throughout this book. Our framing shop is called Faster Frames.

You have a brick-and-mortar storefront, but you decide that you also want to sell
your product (or service) online to better serve the potential customers in your immediate area and to potentially market to an audience beyond your specific geographical
area. What do you do?

Well, first you need some sort of virtual storefront. Traditionally, this has been
a Web site, either built in-house or contracted out to a company that provides this
service. However, it can also be a virtual presence on a number of social media platforms where some aspect of business occurs. For our framing shop, we have created
a nice Web site showing our frames and our framing service.

What now?

It is rare for a brick-and-mortar store to have large numbers of potential customers
just walk in. Most often, one has to do some marketing to alert the potential consumer
base that the business exists. Certainly, if your product, pricing, performance, place,
and people provide value to consumers, marketing is much easier, as your business
will probably have a good brand image with the potential customer base. However,
there are typically competing businesses that offer similar (or identical) products in
one's geographical area. So, even the top companies typically have to engage in some
sort of marketing and advertising efforts. This is certainly true for our framing shop,
as there are several national competitors, as well as numerous local franchises and
several mom-and-pop stores.

The situation is even more competitive in the virtual world. There could potentially be dozens, hundreds, even thousands of companies competing in the same market. You may even find that many of these companies have been competing with your brick-and-mortar store in your own geographical area.

So whether you want to or not, you are competing in the online world!

Given that framing is a service as well as a product, as long as we have a shipping and receiving service, there is no reason we cannot compete nationally for the high-end market.

Each of these competing businesses has some sort of online presence, a virtual storefront. It is rare for a Web site to have large numbers of potential customers just randomly arrive at their site. Just as in the brick-and-mortar world, businesses must do some marketing to get new customers to their online storefronts. Certainly, given the competitive marketplace, this is true for our framing shop.

Marketing on the Web hinges on a few key technology services. Social media sites are important as commercial marketing outlets and are especially important as viral marketing. However, the big marketing guns in the online world are the search engines. Of course, the social media sites and the search engines may be the same entities.

How do these Search Engines Impact the Business?

For years, search engines have been the major gateways to the Web. With their legions of software agents indexing Web pages, acres of computers for storing terms and metadata from these Web pages, and intuitive interfaces for searching, these search engines are the workhorses of the Web. They are critical navigational elements that enable people in their role as potential consumers (along with many other roles) to leverage the vast content on the Web. In other words, the major Web search engines are value enhancers. The information on these Web sites would be of little value if few people could find them.

> **Potpourri**: Although it is now obvious that search engines and the techniques they employ are critical tools for using the Web, it was not always so clear-cut.
>
> The original manuscript discussing the highly important Google ranking algorithm was rejected by the Special Interest Group on Information Retrieval (SIGIR) Conference, which is the leading information retrieval conference in academia.
>
> In defense of the SIGIR reviewers, the paper was not clearly written, which is an example of the important relationship between function and form. One cannot neglect either.
>
> A version of the paper was eventually published in an academic journal and has subsequently become one of the most highly cited papers in the information-retrieval field (see [2]).

Why has the Web had such a big impact?

One reason may be the theory of affordances [3], which posits that people view the world in terms of both object shapes (i.e., including spatial relationships) and object possibilities for action (i.e., affordances). This perception of object possibilities helps drive people's action (i.e., perception drives action). Sometimes these affordances are what designers intended. At other times, people bring their own affordances to a technology, which has certainly occurred with the use of the Web.

So for our virtual business, we have to get our Web site indexed by the major search engines. Luckily, this is fairly easy to do. Sometimes, we have to do nothing. Other times, we may have to request the search engine to index our site. Given that we are somewhat technically suave, we quickly get the Web site for our framing shop indexed by major search engines.

Once indexed, though, our real challenge begins. The screen space on any computer or computing device is limited. There is only so much space (or screen real estate) to show information. So, when a searcher submits a query to a search engine, there are only so many results that a search engine can display. Let's say this number of results is ten.

Actually, ten is an exaggeration, as there are typically fewer than ten results that appear above the fold (the portion of the screen that first appears to the user where the user does not have to scroll down). Most users do not scroll down [4].

So, a potential customer submits a query that relates directly to your business. Although you might imagine that one of the results would be for your site, there is no guarantee. It is rare for a business to have a market alone to itself. Rather there may be from dozens to hundreds to thousands of businesses (all with viable products for the potential customer) competing for one of those ten result slots.

Your business wants to be one of these ten slots on the first page of results, which is where most of the consumer traffic is; actually, you want to be at the top of this list. With each business equally viable, the search engine uses a variety of factors to rank which businesses get one of those ten slots. However, you have only a limited idea of what factors the search engine uses for ranking, so it is somewhat of a crapshoot.

What other options does your business have to get on this page of results? One answer lies with sponsored search (a.k.a. keyword advertising, paid search, pay-per-click). Sponsored search is the process in which advertisers pay to have their advertisements appear on a search engine results page in response to a query from a searcher. In sponsored search, advertisers pay search engines for traffic from the search engine to their Web sites. With sponsored search, major Web search engines have significantly altered online commerce.

Potpourri: Sponsored search can come in various forms; the most common is pay-per-click.

The Search Engine Marketing Professional Organization (SEMPO) defines pay-per-click as a model of online advertising in which advertisers pay only for each click on their ads that directs searchers to a specified landing page on the advertiser's Web site.

Let's say that our framing shop does not show up in the top ten for the query "frame shops" in our area. Then, we are really going to depend on sponsored search as an advertising medium.

How Do We Leverage Sponsored Search to Market Our Business?

The major search engines have sponsored search platforms where one can establish an account within a short amount of time. There are a couple of implementations of sponsored search. We are going to assume that we signed up for the version where we pay the search engine when someone clicks on one of our ads (referred to as pay-per-click). We might sign up for accounts on multiple search engines. We sign up for a sponsored search account on a major search engine for our framing shop.

Our goal in this sponsored search effort is the same as in all advertising endeavors. We aim to acquire new customers at a cost that permits us to make a profit on the products and services that we sell to these customers.

Once Done with this Administration, What Do We Do?

The first step is to select some words that we believe potential customers will use when they would want to find our business on the Web. Using the search engine's sponsored search platform, we then add these keywords to our account. Typical keyphrases for our framing shop could be "frames," "framing," and "custom framing."

We decide what advertisements we want to appear when a searcher enters one of these keywords. Using the search engine's sponsored search technology, we create the advertisements on our account, linking ads to the keywords that we selected.

Let's assume that we create the following ad for our framing shop:

> Faster Frame
> $50 Off Custom Framing Coupon
> FASTER FRAME Satisfaction Guaranteed
> www.fasterframe.com

Once we have a sponsored search account established and running, our ads can appear on Web pages, cell phones, tablets, and many other devices. These ads can take potential customers to our Web site or provide them a means to click the ad and call our business or visit some other site related to our business, such as one of our social media sites.

Okay, How does the Search Engine Make Money?

The search engine company does not provide this marketing service for free. We offer to pay the search engine a set amount for each keyphrase, which is called a bid. It is called a bid because there may be (and probably are) several other businesses wanting to show their ads for the same keywords that we want to show our ads. Each business offers a bid, and the laws of supply and demand take over. The more businesses that want to bid on a certain keyword, the higher the bid price to get your ads to show on the search engine results page (SERP), with the critical resource being screen real estate.

The bid price is the maximum amount that we will pay the search engine when someone clicks on our ad. Generally, what we actually pay is the same as the bid price. Sometimes lower. Never higher.

This bidding process thus involves some decisions on the part of each business – namely, what cost the business is willing to shoulder for its advertisements. This is rather difficult to determine at first, but once we get some historical data, we can fine-tune our bids and budget. For our framing shop, we will set a maximum bid price of $1.00 per click.

So, we have our account set up, our keywords entered, our ads crafted, and our bids set. We are ready to roll with our sponsored search effort! We activate our account, and typically within minutes, our ads are set to appear.

It is really that simple. One could be running a sponsored search campaign in a matter of minutes. However, there are a lot of complex questions, assumptions, and issues underlying this seemingly simple setup.

This book addresses those complexities.

> **Potpourri**: Sponsored search is a poster child for the concept of technological innovation, which consists of three stages, in a self-reinforcing cycle.
>
> The three stages are: (1) a creative and feasible idea, (2) a practical implementation and application, and (3) the diffusion of this technology throughout society [5, p, 27].
>
> It is really quite amazing that in the period of less than one decade, sponsored search grew from conceptualization to a multibillion-dollar enterprise, directly affecting millions of businesses and billions of people. It has shaped the Web as we know it.
>
> In addition to its direct impact, it probably has had second-order effects of several billion dollars more [6].

What are these Complex Questions, Assumptions, and Issues?

Let's start with the seemingly simple step of selecting keywords. Which keywords do we select? How many do we select? Why would we select these? The selection of keywords is a critical step in the sponsored search process, and there are literally thousands of guides, checklists, and tools to aid us. However, there are limited documents that address the underlying theories and models to inform us what these guides, checklists, and tools are based on, or why certain keywords work and others do not. In this book, we examine these underlying theoretical aspects.

It is a similar case with advertisements. Advertisements in sponsored search systems are typically short, with just a few lines of text (with maybe other elements, such as a small image). Like with keywords, there are numerous checklists and suggestive guides to craft sponsored search advertisements. But why do these suggestions work? Why do certain ads get the potential customer's attention whereas others do not? What causes potential customers to click on certain ads but not click on others that appear for the same keyword?

What about the bidding? It would seem, at first glance, to be a simple process of deciding how much the business would like to spend. In actuality, our bids are part of a complex and intricate online auction process, with multiple competing interests (i.e., ours, our competitor's, and the search engine's).

These are some of the issues with major components of sponsored search. There are other related components to consider:

- Customer Component: How can we determine what the customer is really after? How will the customer behave when shopping online? What causes the customer to make a purchase?
- Marketing Component: How does our business engage in the sponsored search process? What are the business's overall goals and objectives?
- Advertising Component: How can we leverage sponsored search to achieve the objectives of our advertising efforts?
- Branding Component: What is the image that we want for our business in the online marketplace? Can we leverage sponsored search to increase our brand worth?

Conclusion

It is for the understanding of these issues that this book is written. No tactics, no checklist, and no implementation advice will address these questions. For this, we must venture into the place of theory and models.

Let's begin.

References

[1] Wiktionary. 2010. Context. Retrieved January 15, 2011, from http://en.wiktionary.org/wiki/context.
[2] Brin, S. and L. Page . 1998. "The Anatomy of a Large-Scale Hypertextual Web Search Engine." *Computer Networks and ISDN Systems*, vol. 30(1), pp. 107–117.
[3] Gibson, J. J. 1977. "The Theory of Affordances." In *Perceiving, Acting and Knowing*, R. Shaw and J. Bransford, Eds. Hillsdale, NJ: Erlbaum.
[4] Jansen, B. J. and Spink, A. 2003. "An Analysis of Web Information Seeking and Use: Documents Retrieved Versus Documents Viewed." In *4th International Conference on Internet Computing*, Las Vegas, NV, pp. 65–69.
[5] Toffler, A. 1970. *Future Shock*. New York: Random House.
[6] Johnson, C. H. 2009. *Google's Economic Impact United States 2009*. Mountain View, CA: Google.

Word cloud generated by Wordle

2

Modeling the Process of Sponsored Search

> This is an opening shot of changing the search engines
> from white pages to yellow pages.
> **Bill Gross,**
> 1998 as quoted in: Sullivan, D., *The Search Engine Report* [1].

In our framing shop example of setting up our sponsored-search account, we touched on a process by example without a real appreciation for the underlying complexity of the technology and human interaction inherent in sponsored search. What is the technology that makes the whole process work? What is the business model of sponsored search? Who are the major actors in sponsored search? What are the goals and motivations of these actors? For answers to these and other questions, we examine the sponsored-search model.

It is important to develop a generic model of the sponsored-search process. A model is a representation of a complex natural process, simplifying but still embodying the essential attributes. In other words, a model allows us to peel away the unnecessary to get at the critical elements.

Adding some flavor to our model, it is worthwhile to begin with a brief introduction of the beginnings of sponsored search, which will shed light on how we got to where we are. Bill Gross [1] was right that the introduction of advertising in the search engine results page was to change everything. Finally, we end this chapter with some of the conceptual jargon of sponsored search.

Historical Review of the Early Years of Sponsored Search

The first attempt at something like sponsored search was by the search engine OpenText in 1996 [2]. However, the experiment did not go well for a variety of reasons, perhaps the main one being the desire of searchers to not commercialize the searching process. In fact, the company got so many complaints that OpenText removed the feature within a matter of weeks.

Potpourri: To illustrate how early the concept of sponsored search was introduced, the very first occurrence of Web advertising that I could document occurred on October 27, 1994, when Hotwired signed fourteen banner advertisements to display on their site [3, p. 6]. On that day, the Web became a real commercial medium [3].

Supposedly, AT&T was the first company to have their banner ad displayed, although other companies also can lay claim to the fame, including Club Med, MCI, Volvo, and Coor's Zima.

Disclaimer: Other Web-based magazines (a.k.a., Webzines) lay claim to being the first to market with banners ads, including Global Network Navigator, Virtual Journal, Synapse, Medio, and Chaos Control. All, however, were in the 1993 or 1994 timeframe.

Regardless, Rick Boyce, Hotwired's director of business in 1994, is credited with pioneering the idea of banner ads as a major business concept for online companies.

Here (supposedly) is something close to what that first banner ad looked like (Figure 2.1).

Figure 2.1. Image of first banner advertisement.

It reminds me of one of the cheesy roadside billboards that one sees along interstates in the United States promoting those tourist traps just beyond some state line.

On February 21, 1998, GoTo.com launched a sponsored-search model in which the search engines ranked "Web sites based on how much the sites are willing to pay to be placed at the top of the search under a real-time competitive bidding process [2]." Advertisements for these Web sites appeared on the search engine results page, and the ad displayed based on the searcher was actively seeking at the time.

The conceptualization was relatively straightforward, with a transparent ranking factor (i.e., money), advertisers bidding on exact phrases, and editors checking for relevance. This concept is a first-price auction, where the top bidder gets the top advertising position. GoTo.com also provided nonsponsored listings, provided by Inktomi.com.

Potpourri: GoTo.com was the rebranded search engine, World-Wide Web Worm, which was the first Web search engine.

Created in September 1993 by Oliver McBryan at the University of Colorado, the World-Wide Web Worm is the grandfather of all Web search engines. It started it all!

In contrast to OpenText's experiences, by July 1998, GoTo.com had more than 1,000 advertisers paying between one cent and one dollar a click [4]. This time, there were few outcries against the sponsored-search model.

> **Potpourri**: One of the first patents on sponsored search was filed by GoTo.com on May 28, 1998 [5].
>
> Bill Gross is often credited with creating the business model, although other people are also mentioned as deserving credit, including Scott Banister, Vice President of Ideas at IdeaLab at the time, and Jeffrey Brewer, Goto.com CEO at the time.
>
> The names listed on the original patent are Darren J. Davis, Matthew Derer, Johann Garcia, Larry Greco, Tod E. Kurt, Thomas Kwong, Jonathan C. Lee, Ka Luk Lee, Preston Pfarner, and Steve Skovran.

By 2010, spending on online advertising, primarily sponsored search, exceeded that of spending on print advertising [6]. This is an amazing accomplishment in just twelve years! It parallels and rivals the dramatic rise to prominence of the search engines themselves as gatekeepers to information on the Web.

Why was Sponsored Search Successful?

It is critically important to understand why sponsored search was successful in 1998, while it was unsuccessful just two years previously. It is said that many technologies are ahead of their time. A more accurate statement may be that successful technologies require the right context. In 1998, the context on the Web was ripe for a change, specifically a new revenue model for Web sites, a new advertising model for businesses, and a new frame of reference for people using the Web.

Obviously, much had changed in the two years between the experience of OpenText and that of GoTo.com. As GoTo.com CEO Jeffrey Brewer stated, "Quite frankly, there's no understanding of how any service provides results. ... If consumers are satisfied, they really are not interested in the mechanism [4]."

One reason why searchers may have been more accepting of sponsored search is that it combated the nonrelevant manipulation of search results (a nice way of saying spam) that was occurring at the time.

Second, banner ads (the main online advertising format at that time) were proving ineffective for advertisers [7]. Banners were becoming commonplace and the novelty was wearing off as clicks dropped from between 10 and 40 percent to about 1 percent in 1997 [3, p. 7]. In 1996, click-through rates were around 7 percent on average, declining to approximately 0.6 percent in 1999 [8]. Seeing this decline in click-through rates, Procter and Gamble (P&G) stunned the industry by announcing they would pay only a $5 cost per thousand rate for banner advertisements [3].

Finally, the concept of click-through rates (CTR) was really coming into its own as an online advertising metric. However, P&G was one of the first companies to insist on paying only CTR for Internet advertising, although it eventually altered its stance by supporting a hybrid impressions-and-clicks model [3]. Specifically, in 1996, P&G

made a deal with Yahoo! in which P&G would pay only for click-throughs and not for impressions [9].

The concept of CTR has stuck with the sponsored-search model from its beginning through today, even though many have been critical of its value as metric. According to even early research, CTR has little value as an indicator for return on investment (ROI) optimization because their correlation-to-conversion rates are often low [3].

So, there were a variety of environmental, situational, and commerce factors coming together in mid-1998 that allowed the concept of sponsored search to be accepted by searchers, advertisers, and online businesses.

How did Sponsored Search Evolve?

Figure 2.2 shows a screenshot of the GoTo.com sponsored-search listings. Note that the bid price is listed as part of the search result.

The concept of sponsored search was really quite revolutionary. That a word has a monetary value is truly insightful. Up until that time, search was increasingly viewed as a commodity, even a cost, with search engines basically focusing on developing portals [10]. Sponsored search refocused the search engines back to their core competency of searching and retrieval. Additionally, with advertisers paying only when a potential customer clicked on a sponsored result, it permitted accountability and metrics with online advertising, which was a strategic advantage relative to other forms of solely pushed, impression-based advertising mediums (e.g., television, radio, or print).

Again, given that the advertiser did not pay unless a searcher clicked on the sponsored result, the search engine was servicing the ad at no cost until it was clicked on. This laid the foundation for distribution of risk, another aspect of online advertising. The concept of sponsored search really was a game changer for the Web.

Potpourri: When GoTo.com's sponsored search model was first introduced, many industry analysts were skeptical. Here are some quotes about the process at the time:

"It's kind of strange." – Brett Bullington, executive vice president of Excite [2].

"I have questions about whether a consumer cares about this [model] or not." – Kate Delhagen, analyst with Forrester Research [2].

"They thought it was tainting the search." – Mark Kraatz, manager of corporate Web systems for Open Text (commenting on OpenText's experience with paid listings [2]).

"I'm not sure it's really providing value to the user, in the long term. I think they want some independent sorting." – Rajive Mathur, Lycos search manager [1].

In fact, the whole concept of advertising on the web was questioned. For example:

"In the larger picture, advertising is almost irrelevant for the success of the Web." Jakob Nielsen (1997) Why Advertising Doesn't Work on the Web. Retrieved March 9, 2011 from http://www.useit.com/alertbox/9709a.html

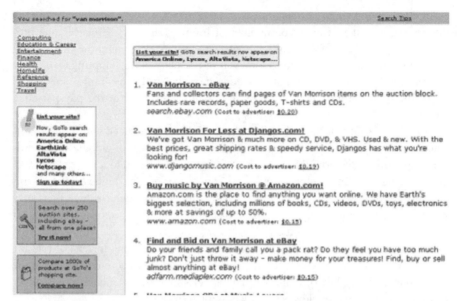

Figure 2.2. Search engine results page from GoTo.com.

GoTo.com (renamed Overture in 2001) faced a challenge, however, which was volume of traffic. Namely, they did not have much of it.

A key component of the sponsored-search platform is getting enough searchers to come to the site, submit a query, and then possibly click on the advertisements. This has been an enduring aspect of sponsored search advertising platforms – one has to get a large volume of traffic (i.e., a cost) to the site by offering free searching and then monetize a portion of this traffic with the sponsored-search results (i.e., revenue).

This is, of course, a balancing act. A search engine has to monetize the greatest amount of traffic possible, but do it in a way that does not decrease the overall amount of traffic to the search engine. That is, if the searchers that come to the site to conduct free searching are turned off with monetization efforts, they may go away, given that switching costs with searching is near zero.

So in a way, each search engine's sponsored-search platform is both cooperating with its own organic search service and in competition with that same organic search service! It was that way in the beginning and is still the same today.

To get traffic, Overture entered into agreements with large Web portals of the time (e.g., CNN, Yahoo!, Microsoft) to serve advertisements on their Web sites (i.e., monetizing their existing traffic). Overture also purchased existing Web search engines, AltaVista and AlltheWeb.com.

Potpourri: Yahoo! acquired Overture in 2003 and was later subsumed with Microsoft's Bing sponsored-search platform in 2010, effectively taking Overture out of the sponsored-search business.

Personally, I find it sad.

But, the world moves on.

In 2000, Google launched its first advertising effort, Google AdWords, although the pricing was at first based on number of impressions [11]. However, the program was quite successful, enrolling approximately 350 clients in the first month. Google's first sponsored-search auction was in February 2002, adopting Overture's pay-per-click revenue model, but they continued their sales-by-impression model in parallel [12] before finally dropping it altogether in favor of the pay-per-click model.

Additionally, Google's sponsored-search model was introduced with some significant changes relative to the Overture model. First, developers of Google's AdWords platform changed the pricing scheme from a first-price auction to a more stable second-price auction. In a single-item second-price auction, the highest bidder wins but only pays the second-highest bid price plus some small delta, which is a fancy word for additional amount. (Note: We'll discuss the significance of this in Chapter 8 where we cover bidding practices.)

Second, Google also changed the standard allocation scheme. Instead of ranking advertisements by bid price alone, they computed a quality score derived from the bid amount and the click-through rate. These factors were later enhanced with other factors such as keyword relevancy and landing-page quality.

Click-through rate measures the rate at which Web searchers click on an ad's hyperlink. When combined with Google's other quality-based criteria, this approach serves to penalize advertisers that use deceptive practices or have poor Web sites. Additionally, it ensures that no advertiser can just buy their way to the top spot while getting no clicks (or it at least makes it more expensive). In other words, Google factored in the concept of relevance to the sponsored-search process, creating a synergy between advertisers and searchers.

This introduction of relevance also aided in the acceptance of sponsored search by the Web community. It suggested that search engines cared about providing good search results and not just about the money. It also fit well with Google's brand image at the time, including point number 6 of its company philosophy, "You can make money without doing evil [13]".

Potpourri: In its most straightforward definition, relevance denotes how well a result on the search engine results page meets the need of the searcher.

However, beyond this, the concept of relevance can get very nuanced, very fast.

The seminal academic paper on relevance is *Relevance: A review of and a framework for the thinking on the notion in information science* [14].

Using this approach, Google protected the user's search experience while also increasing their profits, because users were more likely to click on relevant advertisements. These two auction mechanism changes helped make Google's auction more stable and more profitable than the original first-price auction.

Potpourri: Overture (later known as Yahoo! Search Marketing) updated its pricing scheme to second-price after Google in 2002 and implemented quality-based bidding in the form of its Quality Index in early 2007.

So, Google's sponsored-search model consisted of four synergistic components, improved on over the years, and now characteristic of most sponsored-search models, which are as follows:

- *Self-service* (the advertisers set the price, create the advertisement, monitor the traffic, etc.)
- *Pay-per-click* (the advertiser only pays when searchers click on their ads, instead of paying when the ad is shown)
- *Auction-based pricing* (the set of advertisers in a market vertical determine how much traffic from a given keyword is worth)
- *Relevance* (an advertisement is only shown when triggered by a keyword from the searcher)

Google also had one other factor that Overture did not – search volume! Google had a lot of it.

From its founding in 1998, Google had aggressively and solely focused on search and improving search quality. However, search is a costly endeavor and by itself does not make any money. Yet, Google was quite good at search, so they had garnered a large searcher base. The introduction of sponsored search provided a way to monetize this search traffic in a manner consistent with their core search mission. Additionally, the use of click-through rate was consistent with Google's brand image as a relevant engine. So, unlike the OpenText experience, there was little public outcry against Google commercializing the search process.

Yahoo! Search Marketing and Google AdWords remained the dominant players in the sponsored-search area for several years, although some smaller players attempted to and did enter the market at various times. However, the core elements of sponsored search have generally remained unchanged.

Potpourri: Why has search traffic gone through such a consolidation?

One possible explanation is the Matthew Effect.

Based on verses in the Christian Bible, the Matthew Effect basically means that once someone has a lot of something (i.e., like a lot of search traffic), they get more of it.

We see the Matthew Effect in a lot of economic concepts, such as the bandwagon effect (i.e., once a lot of people do something, more and more people start doing it).

In this brief historical account of the formative years of sponsored search, we have focused on the aspects that lay the groundwork for our foundational understanding. Naturally, there are many aspects, insights, and events not covered here.

For historical accounts of sponsored search, see [15, 16, 17]. For a nice overview of Google and online commerce, see [18]. For a discussion of the evolution from an economic and communication perspective, see [10].

What has been the Effect of Sponsored Search?

The impact of sponsored search can almost not be overstated. It provides the 'air' for the rest of the Web ecosystem to function. It services as the circulatory system that brings the "lifeblood" (i.e., cash) to the other components of the Web. It is the "Rainmaker" that carries the other underperforming Web systems. It is the "court square" where the Web community conducts their business.

Sponsored search has defined the Web!

Sponsored search has played a critical role in supporting access to many free services (i.e., spell checking, currency conversion, flight times, desktop searching applications, etc.) provided by search engines that have rapidly become essential to so many Web users. Without the workable business model of sponsored search, it is doubtful that the major Web search engines could finance anything close to their current infrastructures. These infrastructures provide the capability to crawl billions of Web pages, index several billion documents (e.g., textual, images, videos, news papers, blogs, and audio files), accept millions of Web queries per day, and present billions of links per week, all while servicing most of these queries in a fraction of a second. It is a truly amazing process!

Sponsored search has also provided a workable business model for meta-search engines, which is extremely beneficial for searches needing high recall and requiring a thorough coverage of a topic.

Sponsored search provides an effective method for overcoming the inherent biases or unintended consequences in the technical implementation of Web search engines by allowing content providers to move their links to the first page of results at a relatively low cost. In doing so, sponsored search has become vital to the success of many businesses.

It is fair to say that without sponsored Web search, the Web search engine market – indeed the Web! – would look far different than it does today.

However, in addition to being a business model for the search engines, sponsored search is a great branding, marketing, and advertising platform for businesses. In fact, the reason sponsored search is such a good business model for the search engines is that it is a good marketing medium for businesses (or any entity) that want to get products in front of people.

Let us examine the core process via a model of sponsored search.

Conceptual Model of Sponsored Search

Sponsored search is continually evolving into an ever-more complex process for satisfying both the desire of potential consumers for relevant information and the need for targeted traffic for advertisers.

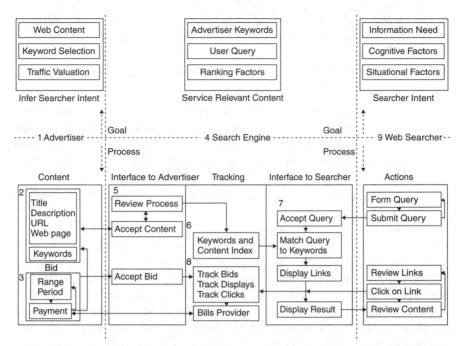

Figure 2.3. The participants, goals, and process of sponsored search on the Web.

Although the payment process and ranking have undergone several incarnations, the other major elements of sponsored search have remained essentially the same throughout its existence [19]. These elements are as follows (see Figure 2.3):

1. *Advertiser*: an entity (e.g., business, person, or organization) interested in generating user traffic to a particular Web site for some specific purpose and is willing to pay for such traffic.
2. *Advertiser Content*: a set of keywords (representing concepts) along with the associated uniform resource locators (URLs) pointing to a particular Web site, title, and description contained within an advertisement.
3. *Advertiser Bid*: offer of payment for specified keywords that are a monetary valuation of traffic to a particular Web site by a provider.
4. *Search Engine*: an information-searching platform that serves advertiser content on the SERP, relevant Web sites, or e-mail interface in response to searcher queries.
5. *Search Engine Review Process*: a method utilized by a search engine to ensure that advertiser content is relevant to the targeted keyword on contextual material.
6. *Search Engine Keyword and Content Index*: a mechanism that matches advertiser's keywords to searcher's queries.
7. *Search Engine User Interface*: an application for displaying advertiser content as links in rank order to a searcher. Typically, the interface displays the sponsored links with nonsponsored links on a SERP, within e-mail, or alongside content on a Web page.

8. *Search Engine Tracking*: a means of matching keywords to queries, gathering advertiser content, bidding, metering clicks, and charging providers based on clicks for their displayed links.
9. *Searcher*: an individual that submits a query and potentially clicks on a sponsored link within a relevant advertisement.

Figure 2.3 presents the sponsored-search process as an aspect of information searching rather than strictly an advertising venue. In this framework, the potential customer is performing the role of Web searcher. And this framework is activated with every single search! Think about that for a minute. Think of the traffic on the search engines, with millions and millions of queries. For each one, every time, the sponsored-search process, including the auction for keyphrases, occurs. It is really a phenomenon!

As stated by Geddes, "Every search result has three different entities trying to reach their goals. Some times these goals get in each other's way, leading to poor search results. Other times, they work in conjunction, leading everyone toward success. It is important to examine [the search engine's goal], the advertiser's, and the searcher's goal for each search result" [20, p. 15]. This describes a relationship that is symbiotic, mutually beneficial to all parties involved. In commercial endeavors, we aim for symbiotic marketing that aims to develop mutually beneficial relationship with the customer. Showing relevant content is good for the customer and, consequently, good for the advertiser and for the search engine. In fact, one can show that it can be more profitable for the search engine to not show a nonrelevant advertisement, leaving the ad space unoccupied, than to take the advertiser's money and show such advertisement [21].

Along the upper half of Figure 2.3, the three major participants (advertisers, search engines, and searchers) have mutually supporting goals. The Web searcher has some need bounded by affective, cognitive, and situational factors, which is what brings the searcher to the search engine and motivates the searcher to submit a query.

Advertisers craft terms and search phrases (i.e., keywords) that they believe:

1. are likely to be submitted by searchers;
2. will be applicable to their Web content;
3. will link their content to the underlying intent of the searcher.

These advertisers also tailor to the presentation of the ad to conform to demographically targeted searchers, with possibly several presentation variations linked to particular sets of queries within a given advertising effort.

> **Potpourri**: The first Google AdWords advertisement was for *Live Mail Order Lobsters* and was posted less than thirty minutes of the Google AdWords platform going live in 2000 [22].

These listings are known as ads or sponsored results, to differentiate them from the nonsponsored listings, (a.k.a., algorithmic or organic) on the SERP. The search engine can also serve these sponsored results on a vast network of Web sites that are deemed relevant to some searcher action, such as searching on one of these Web sites.

This is not to be confused with contextual advertising, sometimes referred to as content targeting (think: banner ads). The idea of the contextual-advertising approach is that visitors to these Web sites will also be interested in certain ads that are like the content on the Web site.

Search engines provide the mechanism for the sponsored-search process to occur, shown in the lower half of Figure 2.3, although the advertiser and the searcher are two major components of this process also.

The pay-per-click model is the most common payment method, although others such as pay-for-impression, pay-per-action, and pay-per-call also exist. Advertisers pay the search engine when a user clicks on their link when serviced on the SERP or another Web site. The advertiser can tailor this matching algorithm from exact targeted matches to very loose matches to account for various spellings as well as term usage. The search engine matches the searcher's query to the keywords that the advertiser bid on.

The advertiser pays the search engine via a bid on the keyword. A bid usually includes a maximum price per keyword and can include a period of activation, language, and geographical limitations, among an increasing host of other factors. The bid is the maximum price that the advertiser is willing to pay per click on an ad for a given keyword. For ads serviced on other Web sites, the search engine splits the revenue per click with the Web site owner, although the price advertisers pay per click for these links is typically lower than those on the SERP.

Potpourri: Education and training in sponsored search can be difficult, and it is even more difficult to get meaningful practical experience in the area. One endeavor that has done much to address this issue is the Google Online Marketing Challenge.

The Google Online Marketing Challenge (or GOMCHA, an acronym first used by Daehee Park, as a student at Penn State) began in 2008 as a worldwide, in-class learning exercise for undergraduate and graduate students in keyword advertising.

Working in teams and supervised by a professor, students design, develop, implement, and manage keyword advertising campaigns for small to medium-size enterprises.

Lee Hunter, as a Google employee, got the whole GOMCHA program running, with Jamie Murphy, as a professor at the University of Western Australia, serving as the academic lead.

GOMCHA is run as both a learning exercise and as a worldwide competition (http://www.google.com/onlinechallenge/).

Multiple advertisers may want to pay a search engine for the same term or phrase. In these cases, ranking (i.e., which result goes on top) is handled by an electronic auction that determines the order of the ads. In practice, the highest bidder generally gets the topmost rank; the next highest bidder gets the next rank, and so on. Various search engine sponsored-search platforms also factor in other elements into their ranking scheme, such as which sponsored result gets more clicks. This approach helps address the concern that search engines will present less relevant content to the searcher solely for profit and serves to bubble relevant ads to the top of the listing.

In practice, the link with the most clicks will generally produce the most profit for the search engine. Therefore, there is a monetary value for all participants in the sponsored-search process to strive for relevant content being presented to a searcher. This is one of the factors that has made sponsored search so successful. The searcher is interested in relevant content, and there is a disincentive for the advertiser or search engine to game the system by showing nonrelevant content.

> **Potpourri**: Web search engines employ a variety of techniques to provide results to searchers. These techniques are collectively known as information retrieval, defined as automatically locating unstructured electronic content stored in a computer in response to a query. Typically, the results are ranked to the degree in which they match the query.
>
> The classic academic work on information retrieval is *Information Retrieval* [23].

The point of sponsored search is to provide a mechanism for advertisers to get searchers to visit their Web sites. When a searcher submits a query, reviews the results on the SERP, and clicks on a sponsored link, the searcher's browser displays the provider's Web page pointed to by the link. The search engine tracks this click, along with all the other clicks within a given period. At the end of this period, the search engine bills the advertiser, providing various statistics concerning the outcomes of the advertiser's campaign.

From an analysis of these statistics, the advertiser can alter bids, maximum costs per period, and keywords in real time. Advertisers can also change terms or phrases, the price they are willing to bid, the degree of term matching, and even how much they pay in a given time period. By engaging in and "buying" key search phrases, these advertisers become active participants in the information-searching process.

> **Potpourri**: *Information searching* refers to people's interaction with information-retrieval systems, ranging from adopting a search strategy to judging the relevance of information retrieved [24].

This accounting is one reason that sponsored search is so popular with businesses and organizations. In many forms of advertising, there is little accountability in terms of the cost resulting from impressions (i.e., how many times and when a particular advertisement is shown).

Naturally, the searcher is presented with a variety of results, not only sponsored ones. In the first few years of sponsored search, there was some resistance to these advertisements and there will probably always be some resistance. However, in their lab study, Jansen and Resnick [25] reported that searchers with commercial queries are unconcerned whether the results were sponsored or nonsponsored. Their primary concern is relevance. In fact, when searchers did view and evaluate links in response to given queries, the ratings of the sponsored links were identical to the nonsponsored links. Additionally, Jansen [26] shows that sponsored and nonsponsored links are equivalent in terms of relevance.

In sum, sponsored search is a viable revenue model for search engines, a workable advertising medium for businesses, and appears to provide relevant content to Web searchers.

The Language of Sponsored Search

Our model provides a framework for investigating the foundational underpinnings; however, we must also clearly understand some of the terminology of sponsored search in order to delve deeper into the elements of sponsored search. We introduce these concepts here and then explore them in greater detail in further chapters.

Although this review may seem basic to the expert, it is often good to return to the clear and clean process to reground oneself in the area.

Let us start with the search engine results page (SERP), shown in Figure 2.4.

A SERP is the entire page and all content shown by a search engine in response to a searcher clicking a search or submit button or, if the search engine provides automated searching, by typing in the query. The space on the SERP is known as the screen real estate. To see the entire SERP, a searcher may have to scroll on the browser to the bottom portion of the SERP.

Potpourri: Why do search engines list the advertisements in a separate listing?

One of the major reasons was a complaint to the Federal Trade Commission (FTC) filed by Commercial Alert in July 2001 against AltaVista, AOL Time Warner, Direct Hit Technologies, iWon, LookSmart, Microsoft, and Lycos [27]. The complaint alleged that the confusion caused in consumers who saw mixed paid and unpaid results in a combined listing constituted fraud in advertising by the search engines.

After that, by convention, the sponsored results are listed separately, or at least labeled as sponsored if they are integrated with organic results.

The fold is defined as an imaginary horizontal line across the browser that separates the portion of the SERP that the searcher sees when the browser first opens from the part the searcher has to scroll to see.

The content on the SERP that the searcher sees without scrolling is referred to as "above the fold." The content on the SERP that a searcher has to scroll to see is known as "below the fold." So, the fold is that line that separates the two portions of the SERP based on the act of scrolling or not.

Types of search results

The shown SERP (see Figure 2.3) has two types of result listings in response to the submitted user's query. The nonsponsored (or organic) results take up the bulk of the screen real estate. The organic results are composed of result summaries that the

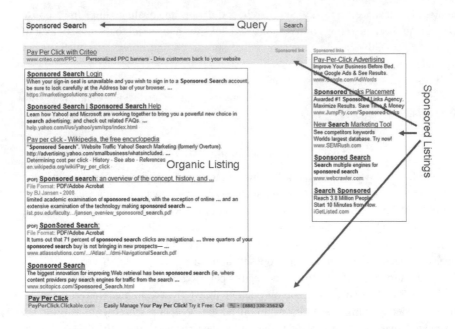

Figure 2.4. Sample search engine results page showing the location of organic and sponsored listings.

search engine crawls, stores, indexes, and ranks based on its own proprietarily algorithm. Web site owners typically do not pay to appear in this index, and it is these results that usually bring in most of the traffic to the search engine.

Potpourri: Getting a result summary for your Web site to appear in the organic results listing is a process known as *search engine optimization*, as one is optimizing the Web page for a search engine's ranking algorithm.

The other type of search result on the SERP is the advertisement that one typically pays for. The sponsored-search results, as shown, typically appear in three locations. They can appear on the right side of the SERP (known as east, also known as the right rail), above the organic listing (known as north), or below the organic listings (known as south).

Potpourri: Web site owners have little control over where their results appear in the organic listing because they have little control over how a search engine indexes Web pages. Search engines can, and do, change their indexing.

One of the most infamous major indexing changes occurred with Google just before the busy Christmas shopping season in 2003. Online businesses that had invested significant money and effort in getting their Web sites ranked higher in the organic listings suddenly found themselves out of the top listings.

> This indexing change was so infamous, it was dubbed "Florida," in honor of where it was first noticed. A series of changes to Google's index, and the resulting search engine optimizations efforts that such changes require, was dubbed the Google Dance.
>
> Once Google started updating its index nearly continuously and streamlined the process, the effects were not so dramatic, and phrases like Google Dance were rarely used.

Although not shown in Figure 2.4, the sponsored results can also appear intermingled with the organic results; this is known as an integrated-results listing [28].

> **Potpourri**: There have been from time to time position papers and even court cases challenging Google's ranking of organic results, most notably in the United States. However, these efforts have mostly failed on the basis of the U.S. Constitution's First Amendment considerations.
>
> Although Google (or any search engine) is a technology (i.e., the search engine itself), it is also a legal entity (i.e., the search engine as an incorporated business). As a result, the search engine is afforded (in the United States) certain rights of editorial process (i.e., freedom of speech). Therefore, any legal challenge to the right of a search engine to rank Web pages as it sees fit runs squarely into serious First Amendment considerations [29].

Triggering the sponsored results

In Figure 2.4, within the search box are the two terms that the searcher submitted to the search engine. These terms are collectively known as the query. The query length is the number of terms, which can be from zero (happens all the time) up to some limit imposed by the search engine.

Along with the click on the search button, the query terms are what trigger the results on the SERP to appear. For the sponsored search results (i.e., the advertisements), either one or both of the terms are linked to a keyword (or keywords) selected by the advertiser, which is then linked to one or more advertisements. So, when a searcher submits a query containing a term that is linked in some way to a keyword selected by an advertiser, the corresponding advertisement appears on the SERP.

The linkage between query terms and keywords can come in a variety of flavors, but it generally follows a continuum from precise match to vague match. This level of preciseness is selected by the advertiser.

Composition of the advertisement

If you notice the advertisements in Figure 2.4, they adhere to a general format, composed of three sections, which is detailed in Figure 2.5.

The first section of the advertisement is the headline or title, which is the topmost line of the advertisement. The second section is the snippet or summary, which is the section after the title, typically composed of one or two lines of text. The third

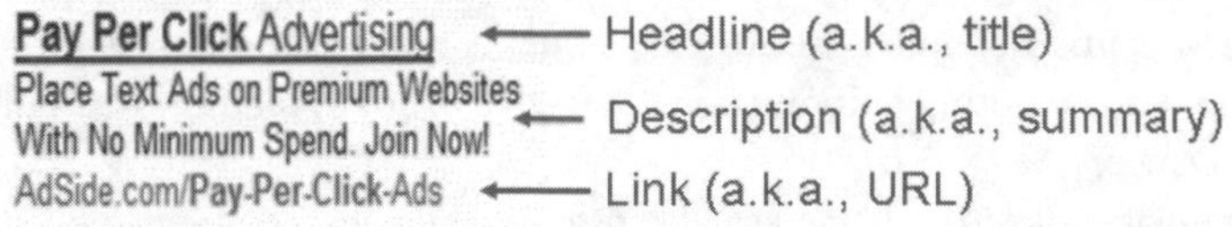

Pay Per Click Advertising ←——— Headline (a.k.a., title)
Place Text Ads on Premium Websites
With No Minimum Spend. Join Now! ←——— Description (a.k.a., summary)
AdSide.com/Pay-Per-Click-Ads ←——— Link (a.k.a., URL)

Figure 2.5. Sample advertisement with highlighted headline, description, and link.

section is the link or URL. This link points to the advertiser's Web site. The link displayed may or may not be the exact URL of the Web page, but it is typically similar. Collectively, the headline, snippet, and link are known as the ad copy.

There may be other components of the advertisement, such as a thumbnail, which is a small image, a geo-location tag, a telephone number, a product review rating, or other metadata.

Potpourri: Metadata is data about data. Metadata can aid a searcher by adding value to a chunk of information, especially for multimedia content.

Rank placement of the advertisement

Note in Figure 2.4 that there are several advertisements on the SERP. Not only are the ads in three different locations (north, east, and south), but the ads are in an ordered listing within each location. The topmost ad in each location is in rank one. The ad below that is rank two, and so on. Ad rank has an effect on several sponsored-search metrics.

Key sponsored-search metrics

When an ad appears on a SERP, this appearance is known as an impression. We can sum up the number of impressions over a given period to calculate the demand or market (based on searchers' queries) for our product or service.

An advertiser wants an ad to appear on a SERP typically to get the searcher to click on the ad's link.

If our ad appears on the SERP, a searcher can (but not necessarily will) click on the ad. These clicks can be recorded for a given time period. We can sum up the clicks to give us an indication of several aspects of our sponsored-search effort, including the effectiveness of our ad and keyword selection.

The ratio of clicks to impressions within the same time period is known as the click-through rate (CTR), which is the basis for a host of sponsored-search metrics. The CTR is a key indicator for the health of our sponsored-search effort. We can establish goals for CTR (and other metrics), which are known as Key Performance Indicators (KPIs).

An advertiser wants a searcher to click on an ad to get the searcher to the advertiser's Web page. An advertiser wants the searcher to go to a given Web page to take some action on that Web page, such as to make a purchase, sign up for a newsletter, or download a paper. This action, whatever it is, is known as a convert or conversion. It is really at the heart of our sponsored-search effort, and it is the goal by which all KPIs should be measured.

These are the core terminology of sponsored search and will serve as the basis for our exploration of the area.

Potpourri: To illustrate the multiple effects that sponsored search can have on a business, consider the process of choosing a product or brand name today. One approach is to get (or design!) a word that is not currently in use but that implies a word that is in use and conveys a positive image to the potential consumer. Why go through this process?

- Search engine technology: Because people use search engines to query the Web, you want a traded term that is not in use for some generic product. In other words, you want it to be unique.
- Trademark: If you develop a term that is unique, then you can legally trademark it and begin building your brand.
- Cognitive aspect of the user: Although you want a term that is unique, you also want a term that cognitively conveys a brand message to the potential searcher or consumer.
- You also do not want any negative implications associated with your term, which your competitors or disgruntled customers can use against you.

So, sponsored search touches on an array of physiological, marketing, legal, and technological processes.

Foundational Takeaways

- We can model sponsored search as a matrix of goals and processes with three actors (i.e., the advertiser, the search engine, and the potential consumer as a searcher).
- Each of these actors has unique goals, but these goals are aligned via an economic incentive.
- The process of each of the actors work in concert to achieve the individual goal of each (i.e., consumer, search engine, and advertiser).
- Given that in sponsored search, the advertiser pays only when a searcher clicks on the advertisements, it is an incentive for the search engine to show only relevant ads. So, the pricing model reinforces the need for only the relevant ads to be shown on SERP. This ensures that both the search engine and advertisers work together to provide a relevant SERP for consumers.

Relating Theory to Practice

In our model of sponsored search, we stripped away the nonessential elements to give us a generic model of the sponsored-search process. However, we can take this approach to another level, by adding elements back into the model that reflect the essential elements of a specific domain, search engine, industry vertical, or potential customer (as Web searcher).

We do this by asking questions, such as:

- What are the particular attributes of the domain?
- What are the unique characteristics of the search engine advertising platform?
- What are the specific goals of advertisers in the industry vertical?
- What are the explicit and implicit goals of potential customers for the domain?

This integrative approach to understanding sponsored search is important, as many specific domains have their own particular attributes that impact the sponsored-search process. For example, managing a sponsored-search campaign for a national health care provider is more different than managing a campaign for a local bakery, although the core elements are identical.

Conclusion

With its rather humble beginnings in 1998, sponsored search rapidly became the primary business model for Web search engines, providing a revenue stream for these gateways to the Web. Running a major Web search engine, with the necessary software, hardware, and people, is a rather costly adventure. Sponsored search provides a monetization of this search traffic, making the search engine economically viable. It is not too much to say that sponsored search has shaped the Web as we know it, financing "free" Web searching that has become indispensable to many of us in our daily lives. As such, especially for those of us that work in the sponsored-search area, it is critical that we understand the process.

The presented model of sponsored search strips the process down to its core elements. We see that there are three major components of the sponsored-search system: the searcher (i.e., potential consumer), the search engine (i.e., advertising platform and market maker), and the advertiser (i.e., content provider). These three components have a shared goal of relevant results in response to a query. The potential consumer wants a relevant ad that addresses the underlying need. The search engine wants to service relevant ads to maximize revenue and prevent searchers from switching to other search services. The advertiser wants only viable consumers to click on its ads in order to manage costs. The search engine provides the technology platform for this process to occur.

As with any process, sponsored search has developed its own jargon, the immersion in which is necessary to understand the practical implementation. Central to this is an understanding of Web search engines.

The SERP is the interface between the advertiser and the searcher. It is generally composed of two types of listings, of which the advertisements can appear in several locations. The ads generally follow a set structure, although the exact format varies with time and search engine.

As for metrics, we are interested primarily in the interaction between the searcher and the advertisement. For this, we track various components of this interaction, including the number of times the ad appears, the number of times searchers click on the ad's link, and the outcome of the searcher visiting the Web site.

However, these metrics tell us what the searchers are doing and not why the searchers are doing what they do. It is the "why" that we explore in the remaining chapters of this book.

The first area of exploration is the area of keyword selection. What are these keywords and what is their purpose? Why do some keywords work and others do not? What is the relationship of these keywords to the consumer? An understanding of the underlying theory of keyword selection will help us address these questions.

References

[1] Sullivan, D. 1998. "The Search Engine Report." Vol. 3 (March)

[2] Pelline, J. 1998. "Pay-for-Placement Gets Another Shot." *CNET News*, vol. 19 (February).

[3] Kaye, B. K. and Medoff, N. J. 2001. *Just a Click Away: Advertising on the Internet*. Needham Heights, MA: Allyn and Bacon.

[4] Sullivan, D. 1998. "GoTo Going Strong." *The Search Engine Land Report* (July 1).

[5] Davis, D. J., Derer, M., Garcia, J., Grecco, L., Kurt, T. E., Kwong, T., Leee, J. C., Lee, K. L., and Skovran, S. 1999. "System and Method for Influencing a Position on a Search Result List Generated by a Computer Network Search Engine." Vol. US 6,269361 B1, U. P. Office, Ed. USA, p. 28.

[6] Fontevecchia, A. 2010. Online Ad Spending Exceeds Print, Hitting $25.8 Billion. (December 20). Retrieved January 4, 2011, from http://blogs.forbes.com/afontevecchia/2010/12/20/online-ad-spending-exceeds-print-hitting-25–8-billion-2/

[7] Johnston, M. 1998. "Web-Design Guru Predicts the Days of the Banner Ad Are Numbered." CNN.com.

[8] Nielsen/Netratings. 1999. "Click Through Rates." In The Nielsen/Netratings Reporter (June 17).

[9] Associated Press. 1996. Procter & Gamble World Wide Web ad strategy raises online ire. April 28.

[10] Couvering, E. V. 2008. "The History of the Internet Search Engine: Navigational Media and the Traffic Commodity." In *Web Search: Multidisciplinary Perspectives*, A. Spink and M. Zimmer, Eds. Berlin: Springer, pp. 177–206.

[11] Voge, K. and McCaffrey, C. 2000. Google Launches Self-Service Advertising Program. (October 23). Retrieved January 6, 2011, from http://www.google.com/press/pressrel/pressrelease39.html

[12] Krane, D. and McCaffrey, C. 2002. Google Introduces New Pricing For Popular Self-Service Online Advertising Program. (February 20). Retrieved January 6, 2011, from http://www.google.com/press/pressrel/select.html

[13] Google. 2010. Google, Corporate Information, Our Philosophy. Retrieved July 13, 2010, from http://www.google.com/corporate/tenthings.html

[14] Saracevic, T. 1975. "Relevance: A Review of and a Framework for the Thinking on the Notion in Information Science." *Journal of the American Society of Information Science*, vol. 26(6), pp. 321–343.

[15] Battelle, J. 2005. *The Search: How Google and Its Rivals Rewrote the Rules of Business and Transformed Our Culture*. New York: Penguin Group.

[16] Fain, D. C. and Pedersen, J. O. 2006. "Sponsored Search: A Brief History." *Bulletin of the American Society for Information Science and Technology*, vol. 32(2), pp. 12–13.

[17] Jansen, B. J. and Mullen, T. 2008. "Sponsored Search: An Overview of the Concept, History, and Technology." *International Journal of Electronic Business*, vol. 6(2), pp. 114–131.

[18] Gallaugher, J. M. 2010. "Google: Search, Online Advertising, and Beyond …" In *Information Systems: A Manager's Guide to Harnessing Technology*. Irvington, NY: Flat World Knowledge.

[19] Jansen, B. 2006. "Paid Search," *IEEE Computer* (July), pp. 88–90.

[20] Geddes, B. 2010. *Advanced Google AdWords*. New York: Wiley.
[21] Libby, B. 2010. *Pay Attention to the Man Behind the Curtain*. (February 24). Retrieved January 19, 2011, from http://www.thesearchagents.com/2010/02/pay-attention-to-the-man-behind-the-curtain/
[22] Google Inside AdWords. 2005. "An AdWords history lesson." In *Inside AdWords*. Mountain View, CA: Google. Retrieved April 4, 2011, from http://adwords.blogspot.com/2005/08/adwords-history-lesson.html
[23] vanRijsbergen, C. J. 1975. *Information Retrieval*, 2 ed. London: Butterworths.
[24] Wilson, T. D. 2000. "Human Information Behavior." *Informing Science*, vol. 3(2), pp. 49–55.
[25] Jansen, B. J. and Resnick, M. 2006. "An Examination of Searchers' Perceptions of Non-Sponsored and Sponsored Links during Ecommerce Web Searching." *Journal of the American Society for Information Science and Technology*, vol. 57(14), pp. 1949–1961.
[26] Jansen, B. J. and Molina, P. 2006. "The Effectiveness of Web Search Engines for Retrieving Relevant Ecommerce Links." *Information Processing & Management*, vol. 42(4), pp. 1075–1098.
[27] Ruskin, G. 2001. Commercial Alert Files Complaint against Search Engines for Deceptive Ads. (July 16). Retrieved November 6, 2010, from http://www.commercialalert.org/issues/culture/search-engines/commercial-alert-files-complaint-against-search-engines-for-deceptive-ads
[28] Jansen, B. J. and Spink, A. 2009. "Investigating Customer Click Through Behaviour with Integrated Sponsored and Nonsponsored Results." *International Journal of Internet Marketing and Advertising*, vol. 5(1/2), pp. 74–94.
[29] Goldman, E. 2010. "Texas AG Investigation." Retrieved April 4, 2011, from http://blog.eric-goldman.org/archives/2010/09/texas_ag_invest.htm

Word cloud generated by Wordle

3

Understanding Customer Intent for Keyphrase Selection

The Database of Intentions is simply this: The aggregate results of every search ever entered, every result list ever tendered, and every path taken as a result. This information represents, in aggregate form, a place holder for the intentions of humankind – a massive database of desires, needs, wants, and likes that can be discovered, subpoenaed, archived, tracked, and exploited to all sorts of ends.

John Battelle,
The Search: How Google and Its Rivals Rewrote the Rules of Business and Transformed Our Culture [1].

When online consumers search for a frame shop, they input a query containing keywords into a search engine. It is these query terms, representing the desires and intentions of the searcher that form the basis of the sponsored-search effort.

In setting up sponsored-search campaigns for our framing business, a critical element is selecting appropriate keyphrases. Triggering our ads, these keyphrases are the links between the potential consumers and the products or services that that we want to sell to them. As such, keyphrases are a critical aspect of any sponsored-search effort. Our keyphrases link to keywords that compose the searcher's query.

If selection of keyphrases is done poorly, nothing else matters – not the ads, not the bids, not the metrics, not even the products we are selling. The searcher will not see the ads if the keyphrases do not show the ads.

At a strictly mechanical level, the keyphrases that we select must in some way match the terms in the query that the potential customer submits to the search engine.

So, referring to our picture-framing shop's sponsored-search effort, if we had to promote our frames, we could select *picture frame* as a keyphrase for a given ad within a geographically targeted area near our brick-and-mortar store. When the searcher enters *picture frame* (or some derivation of this) as a query, the linkage between the query and the ad is made, and our ad appears on the search engine results page (SERP).

However, beyond this straightforward mechanical level, there is a much deeper cognitive, situational, and affective linkage that must occur. Namely, the keyphrases must capture accurately what the searcher is looking for (a search for *frame* could be *picture*, *eyeglass*, or *house*, among many other possible intents), and why the searcher is looking (is it a cheap frame for a knickknack or a special frame for a gift?). Keywords, as Battelle states [1], contain far deeper meanings, with significant implications for e-commerce, online advertising, and Web marketing.

The communication process in which the searcher and the advertiser engage is central to productive keyphrase selection, and the critical element of this process centers on the meaning of information. This information must have an *impact* on the searcher, and the impact that information can have can be very different for different searchers based on the cognitive, situational, and affective linkages that occur in each individual.

- The cognitive aspect is the rational component of information processing during a search.
- The situational aspect is the setting in which the search is occurring.
- The affective aspect is the emotional component affecting the searcher's reaction to information.

Therefore, the keyphrases we select as advertisers must connect not only to the query (in some mechanical sense), but also link to the searcher's underlying intent (in some contextual sense). What is causing the person to search in the first place?

The keyphrases that make this connection to the searcher's intent are successful in achieving the goals of our sponsored-search efforts. Making the appropriate connection is the key underpinning of keyword selection and is the reason certain keyphrases work well and others do not.

It is primarily this connection that we explore in this chapter. Formally, the context in which this linkage occurs is known as a search market, which is any situation where the buyer and the seller do not immediately find each other. In these situations, and especially for sponsored search, words are important.

Potpourri: Words can take on special meaning, well beyond any linguistic aspects, which can really confound keyword advertising efforts.

There is probably no better example than *the seven words you cannot say on television*.

The seven dirty words (i.e., filthy words) are seven English words that the American comedian George Carlin used in a 1972 monologue, "Seven Words You Can't Say on Television."

The seven words became symbolic of both the U.S. government regulation of the national airwaves and efforts to limit lurid content during family television-viewing time, illustrating the impact and varied meaning that these terms can have.

http://en.wikipedia.org/wiki/Seven_dirty_words

A quick note on terminology: A keyphrase is a set of one or more keywords that an advertiser selects to trigger an ad. The ad is triggered when a searcher enters a query that matches the keyphrase. A query is a set of one or more terms (a.k.a., key-terms) submitted by a searcher to a search engine.

So, we are talking about the same concept, except from different perspectives, as shown Table 3.1.

Table 3.1. *Relationship between searcher's query terms and advertiser's keywords*

Advertiser	Searcher (as a potential customer)
Keyphrase	Query
Keyword 1	Term 1
Keyword 2	Term 2
Keyword 3	Term 3
...	...
Keyword n	Term n

Depending on how we structure the matching options, there may be a one-to-one correlation (i.e., the order of the keyword is linked to the order of the query terms). Other times, the order is unimportant. In these cases, a keyword can link to any of the terms in the query.

From both the searcher and the advertiser's perspective, however, we are dealing with words, be it keyphrases or terms. Words are what the searcher and the advertiser use to communicate with each other. To communicate with each other effectively, the searcher and the advertiser must use the same language, which implies each must have a common vocabulary of a sufficient number of words to which each subscribe the same or nearly the same meaning.

One way to look at this communication exchange is that the searcher is using a word submitted to the search engine to represent some meaning. The advertiser is trying to derive the meaning behind the word that the searcher submits in order to convince the searcher that their product or service is the solution the searcher is looking for. This exchange of words through the intermediary of the search engine is the basis for communication between the searcher and the advertiser.

So, if the searcher enters the term *framing*, there are several advertisers that might want their ads to appear on the search engine in response to this query. These advertisers could include picture framers, such as our shop, or could include construction companies interested in framing a house, along with many others. At this point, our communication is unclear, as the intent of the searcher is not known. However, with some additional information, such as a second query or a longer query, the searcher's intent may be more focused.

We illustrate this communication process and attempt to infer intent in Figure 3.1.

To understand why some keywords are successful and others are not, we must focus on this situation at two levels: the individual level (i.e., the searcher as a potential customer) and the aggregate level (i.e., the markct segment of potential consumers for our product). Naturally, the aggregate is composed of a collection of individuals. However, our understanding at the two levels differs greatly. Although we do have some theories to describe the behavior of the individual searcher, these are really little more than heuristics when taken to the practical level, as the multitude of variables intrinsically inherent to the person and extrinsically to the context make hard-and-fast predictions of individual behavior difficult.

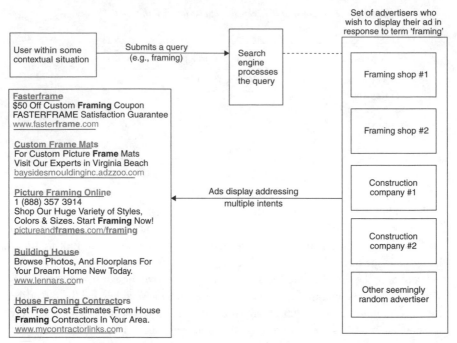

Figure 3.1. Example of query and the ads in response with unsure intent in the linkage between keyterms and keywords.

However, predicting behaviors at the aggregate level is more certain. With enough historical data from enough individuals, we can do much more than describe behavior with heuristics. At the aggregate level, we can make some inferences and predictions of behaviors.

However, an understanding of the individual is important, critically so. We begin by examining the theoretical foundations of information processing at the individual level, relating this to the function of keyword selection in sponsored search. We then move to the aggregate level.

Human Information Behavior at the Individual Level

A fundamental flaw with many sponsored-search efforts – perhaps a holdover from mass media advertising – is that the advertiser views their potential customers or market segment in a mass (i.e., a collective, a group). This viewpoint leads to a blurred focus in keyphrase selection. Instead, it is essential for effective keyphrase development to connect to the individual that wants to buy what the business wants to sell. Picture all the dimensional aspects that compose a typical man or woman who is likely to buy your product. Target your keyphrases for this person.

Chances are that there is another typical type of man or woman that is likely to buy your product and select other keyphrases. Target another set of your keyphrases for this person. There could be many other such individuals.

So, this visualization process of the *individual* involves developing several personas of the typical customer.

At the individual level, we make the assumption that the individual is in some state of information acquisition, either actively or passively gathering information. This assumption is based on the theoretical premise that having more information is more advantageous than not having information. Based on this premise, people whose behavior is guided or controlled by information are more likely to succeed than those people whose behaviors are not guided [2]. This concept is adhered to in several academic fields, including information science [3], finance [4], and natural sciences [5]. Some researchers have even argued that access to information is a vital human function [6], and increased information can contribute to fairness and less bias in decisions [7].

Potpourri: Although most researchers generally adhere to the notion that some information is of benefit, there is a wide range of research that suggests some people actively seek to avoid information (i.e., business owners who may not want to know the true state of their business or terminally ill patients who do not want to know their true condition), or that too much information actually *decreases* the effectiveness of decision making.

Of course, anyone who has managed a project of any complexity will also tell you that at some point the cost of gathering information begins to exceed the benefit of that information.

So, our theoretical assumption is more of a guideline than a hard-and-fast rule.

Our assumption is that information is good and that the searcher wants at least a certain amount of it. But how do people go about gathering information?

People acquire information about the external world by exteroceptors (i.e., a sense organ or a receptor organ that responds to external stimuli), namely vision, audition, olfaction, tactile, and taste. In everyday terms, these are the five senses: eyes, ears, nose, hands (as a representative of touch), and mouths. Sometimes, we are actively seeking information. Other times, we are passively receiving information, and yet other times, we are actively seeking one type of information but receiving another type. Regardless, the brain is continually sifting this stream of information for relevant clues or signals and filtering out the irrelevant signals (i.e., noise). Depending on the circumstances, today's noise may be tomorrow's relevant signal.

Human information processing is how people receive, store, integrate, retrieve, and use the information gathered by their senses, with a focus on the cognitive aspects of information use [8].

In sponsored search, we are concerned with words. Long ago, people recognized individual words (in natural languages like English; not true in all languages) by the way they *sounded* [9]. Later, rules of grammar, spelling, and syntax were devised to permit words to be written, and thus we have the text and written text. Therefore, rather than recognizing a word by sound, one could recognize a word by the way it looked. A person could then receive information via the visual instead of auditory input, although one can say that we still "hear" the word in our minds even when it is written.

For sponsored search, we are primarily interested in this visual input, in that we want the potential customer to see our ads. These ads appear due to the searcher entering a query into the search engine. So, instead of saying a word, the searcher types it into a search engine or speaks and a machine translates the word into text. As such, we are more interested in the actual behaviors of the searchers, especially in their development of the query and the terms they select for the query. This is not to say the cognitive processes are not important (they certainly are) but by necessity we focus on the effect that these cognitive processes have on actual behavior. For keyword selection, we are interested in the query that the searcher formulates.

Where does the searcher get these query terms? The answer to this question illuminates the keyword-selection process.

In the broadest sense, query terms can come from internal or external sources. However, formulating the query is grounded in human information behavior and processing.

• *Human information behavior* is the totality of human behavior in relation to sources and channels of information, including both active and passive information seeking and information use [10].
• *Human information processing* is the method of acquiring, interpreting, manipulating, storing, retrieving, and classifying recorded information [11, 10].

There are a number of personal factors that influence information processing in an individual, including economic class, culture, education, knowledge, and gender [12].

Human information behavior is linked to human information processing, in a feedback cycle (i.e., information behavior → information processing → follow-up behavior). So, whereas human information behavior is concerned with external and exhibited behaviors of the searcher, human information processing is concerned with the internal aspect of the searcher as they assimilate information. Figure 3.2 illustrates the process.

The final aspect of human information behavior is information use behavior, which consists of the physical and mental acts involved in incorporating the information found in the searcher's existing knowledge base. Therefore, it may involve physical acts such as annotating sections on a Web page to note their importance or significance, as well as mental acts that involve, for example, comparison of new information with existing knowledge [10].

Placing this *Behavior → Processing → Use* sequence (see Figure 3.2) within the context of sponsored search, there is a searcher that desires information and, via the query, is taking the first step in a communication process. The advertiser, via the ads linked to these keyterms by keywords, is communicating with the searcher by providing information. The searcher may read the ad, click on the ad, and read the content on the landing page. The searcher then processes in some manner this new information. The searcher decides what to do with this information and whether or not they intend to use it.

With each of these steps, there is cognitive activity. Sometimes this cognitive activity occurs immediately. Other times, cognitive activity occurs (or continues)

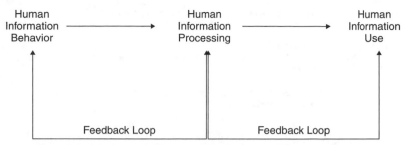

Figure 3.2. The human information behavior – processing – use sequence.

after the communication has been completed, as the searcher reflects further on the information received and integrates it with existing information, beliefs, thoughts, concerns, feelings, and so on.

This helps explain the common phenomenon that occurs in sponsored search, where the searcher may view what appears to be a very relevant ad and do nothing. The searcher may perhaps return to the same ad several times before eventually making a purchase. It is all part of information-processing behavior.

The potential customer as searcher

Human information behavior can be subdivided into more focused sets of behavior, as shown in Figure 3.3.

From Figure 3.3, human information behavior is the broadest area, addressing all aspects of human information interactions. A subset of this is information-seeking behavior, which encompasses the range of information seeking employed in discovering and accessing information resources (both humans and systems) in response to goals and intentions. Information-searching behavior is a subset of information seeking, referring to the actions involved in interacting with an information search system [13]. Information searching is the manifestation where human information behavior and sponsored search meet.

At the highest level, humans access various information objects, and diverse information systems support human information behavior.

At the middle level, humans seek information and eventually use the information gained from information-seeking systems. Either human resources or information from other resources provide affordances to support particular human information-seeking behavior.

At the micro level, primary actions taken by humans during the process of interacting with information-retrieval systems are searching and browsing [13].

It is this subset of information searching that we are most interested in for sponsored search.

Information searching refers to people's interaction with information-retrieval systems, ranging from adopting a search strategy to judging the relevance of information retrieved [10]. The information part of *information searching* is an overloaded term, as the searcher may be looking for something other than information. For this book, we are specifically examining Web searching, which simply is information searching on the Web.

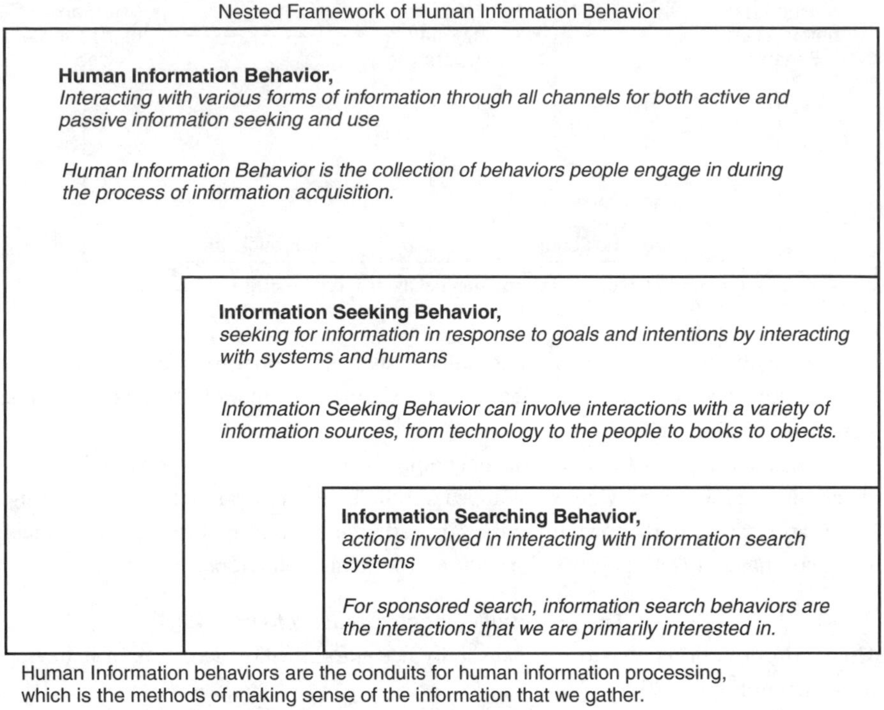

Nested Framework of Human Information Behavior

Human Information Behavior,
Interacting with various forms of information through all channels for both active and passive information seeking and use

Human Information Behavior is the collection of behaviors people engage in during the process of information acquisition.

> **Information Seeking Behavior,**
> *seeking for information in response to goals and intentions by interacting with systems and humans*
>
> *Information Seeking Behavior can involve interactions with a variety of information sources, from technology to the people to books to objects.*
>
>> **Information Searching Behavior,**
>> *actions involved in interacting with information search systems*
>>
>> *For sponsored search, information search behaviors are the interactions that we are primarily interested in.*

Human Information behaviors are the conduits for human information processing, which is the methods of making sense of the information that we gather.

Figure 3.3. Framework of human information behavior, information-seeking behavior, and information-searching behavior.

Potpourri: Interestingly, the first academic studies of Web information searching using query logs from search engines (Excite, Infoseek, and AltaVista) all came out within a few months of each other (late 1998 and early 1999) and in the same outlet (SIGIR Forum).

The three journal articles are:

Jansen, B.J., Spink, A., Bateman, J., & Saracevic, T. (1998). Real life information retrieval: A study of user queries on the Web. *SIGIR Forum, 32*(1), 5–17.

Kirsch, S. (1998). Infoseek's experiences searching the Internet. *SIGIR Forum, 32*(2), 3–7.

Silverstein, C., Henzinger, M., Marais, H., & Moricz, M. (1999). Analysis of a very large Web search engine query log. *SIGIR Forum, 33*(1), 6–12.

In mechanical concepts, the term *search* denotes the specific behaviors of people engaged in locating information [14, p. 5]. In sponsored search, we focus on the economic perspective of search theory, which is the study of an individual's best strategy when choosing from a series of potential opportunities of varying quality. Within the confines of sponsored search, these opportunities are the ad, as surrogates for the products or services we are trying to sell.

In search theory, we are primarily interested in whether or not the searcher searches again, thereby delaying the purchase decision and incurring some delay cost, or stops searching, coming to a decision on whether or not to buy. From search theory, we can develop search models for various contexts illustrating the balancing of the cost of delay against the value of searching again.

Associating keyphrases and queries

When engaging in information searching, the searcher is utilizing the search engine to locate some type of content. For now, we consider content to be anything accessible via a search engine. We consider this content to be multimedia, composed of one or more media types, such as text, images, video, or audio content.

Fundamental to sponsored search is the linkage between the keyphrase that the advertisers bid for and the keyterms that the searchers use in their queries. For both the advertiser and the searcher, these keyphrases and terms represent the underlying product, service, or offerings from the advertiser that the searcher, as a potential customer, is looking for.

This integration of *search* and *advertising* is a salient attribute of the sponsored-search business model [15] and is the critical linking for keyword selection.

Figure 3.4 illustrates this linkage between keyphrases and keyterms.

Establishing the links among searcher need, query terms, and advertiser keyphrase: Search, experience, and credence products and services

Focusing first on searcher needs, we are faced with the question, "how can we classify needs?"

For sponsored search, we make the assumption that the searcher is looking for a product or service, including information about the product or service.

Nelson [16] classifies products (we include the concept of services) into three general types: *search*, *experience*, and *credence* (SEC) goods. This product classification is especially useful, as it captures the underlying uncertainty that consumers face in purchasing these products, and why the consumer is communicating via the search engine to get additional information.

According to the SEC framework, attributes of goods can be analyzed in terms of three properties: search, experience, and credence [16]. "These properties are used to categorize the point in the purchase process when, if ever, consumers can accurately assess whether a good possesses the level of an attribute claimed in advertising" [17, p. 433].

- *Search goods* have attributes that are identifiable through inspection and are accessible to the consumer prior to purchase (e.g., music downloads, pay-for-view movies, books, clothes, etc.)
- *Experience goods* have attributes that are revealed only through consumption by the consumer (e.g., brokerage service, vacation packages, and healthcare)
- *Credence goods* have attributes where the consumer can never be certain of the long-term quality and/or value, even from observations and use (e.g., psychics, tax services, medical treatment, and counseling services)

Now, certainly, the boundaries between these categories can be fuzzy. It is best to consider these classifications to represent regions in a continuum, with significant overlap, as shown in Figure 3.5.

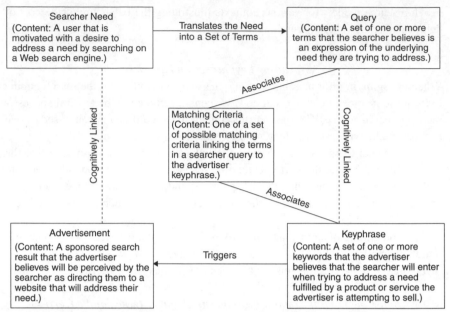

Figure 3.4. Relationship of the searcher, query, keyphrase, and advertisement.

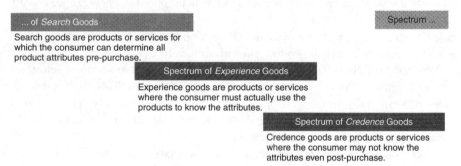

Figure 3.5. Spectrum of SEC goods illustrating an overlap among classifications.

The important factor to consider for sponsored-search efforts is that the defining characteristic underlying this segmentation of goods, namely the prepurchase quality uncertainty of the product/service to the searcher, increases from search to experience to credence goods as quality becomes more difficult to judge [15, 18]. This level of uncertainty has a significant impact on the keyphrase and query term selection by advertiser and searcher, respectively.

Thus, the searcher's underlying motivation for information searching is *uncertainty reduction*. When a searcher is lacking in knowledge of a product, service, or the expected outcome of consumption, the searcher is more likely to engage in uncertainty-reduction processes to minimize the risk and to maximize the consumption value [19]. Naturally, this process of uncertainty reduction is moderated by cost (i.e., if the product or service is inexpensive, the consumer may just purchase it rather than expend the time and effort searching).

Table 3.2. *SEC goods with impact on advertiser and searcher*

Type of product or service	Impact of query selection (searcher)	Effect on keyphrase selection (advertiser)
Search	Searching for specific product or service attributes	Select keyphrases in line with product attributes
Experience	Searching for locations to see, touch, smell, etc. the product or service	Select keyphrases to guide searcher to off-line store
Credence	Searching for reviews, blogs, commentary on product or service	Select keyphrases to guide searcher to social media aligning with marketing goals

We also have to be careful here, as there may be several motivations for searching along with reducing uncertainty, including entertainment or risk reduction. Sponsored-search efforts have to address this range of motivations.

However, uncertainty reduction is undoubtedly a major component of e-commerce searching, and the SEC goods framework can help explain significant portions of the consumer searching behavior, as shown in Table 3.2.

The SEC goods provide a framework that explains much consumer searching. For example, I have a friend who owns a high-end calendar business, with exquisite photos for niche markets, such as kittens, airplanes, and fishing. Most of these customers are repeat customers, many of whom bought a calendar of his at some big-box reseller.

Why the majority of repeat business?

High-end calendars are primarily an experience product. Customers want to see the pictures and feel the quality of the paper. So, my friend advertises in his sponsored-search campaigns mainly on branded terms (name, URL) to jump ahead of the big-box calendar sellers because he makes more money selling directly. However, he participates with the in-store resellers to provide the experience to his potentially future direct customers.

So, from this SEC framework, advertisers can focus on search terms that best fit their product. This is still a difficult task, as years of empirical research has shown that the length of queries is typically very short [20] or very long, which is likely the result of searcher's cut-and-pasting in selections of text.

The reason for this stability of query length during a period when technology has rapidly increased is that the cognitive aspects of the searcher have not changed. In other words, the ability of technology to provide information has increased exponentially (i.e., Moore's Law), but the ability of humans to process it has remained stable.

Potpourri: Why are most query terms short? Some of it may have to do with simple information needs. It may have to do with the cognitive limits of our memory (i.e., the human processing and storage power).

(Continued)

Based on Claude Shannon and Norbert Weiner's information theory research [21], Harvard psychologist George A. Miller [22] proposed the theoretical construct, known as the Magical Number Seven, Plus or Minus Two.

The gist of the construct is that the typical human can process about seven chunks of similar information at any instant in time (sometimes a couple more, sometimes a couple fewer). The concept of chunking is now a foundational element in many theories of memory.

Miller's work included the concept of chunking information in larger and larger groupings while still keeping the concept of seven chucks of similar types.

The impact of this construct on sponsored search is that it helps explain the shortness of queries.

Words in ads probably need to be presented in chunks that the searcher can remember or recognize, and that the searcher has a limit to the amount of information he is able to use at any given time.

What do we know about the actions of the individual searcher?

Considering this conceptualization of Web search for consumer products or services during information searching in a period of uncertainty reduction, what can we say about the searcher's specific behaviors?

A body of empirical work supports the theoretical constructs of the *principle of least effort*, *the uncertainty principle*, and *information obtainability*.

Principle of least effort. The principle of least effort states that when solving problems, a person tends "to minimize the probable average rate of his or her work-expenditure (over time), meaning use the least amount of effort" [23, p. 1]. This proposition that an organism generally seeks a method involving the minimum expenditure of energy in striving for a goal is one of the most enduring tenets in Web searching.

The principle of least effort is related to the psychology principle of satisficing [24]. Satisficing takes the view that people have evolved to make decisions quickly. In order to make these quicker decisions, people choose from a subset of options instead of considering all possible options before acting. By applying some general rules, statistically, the best option in that subset should be close to the best option in the whole set of options, which has been borne out in empirical research on Web search. We see similar rational in the concept of framing [25], which has implications for sponsored search [26].

The principle of least effort is embedded in theories such as information foraging [27] as well. With the information-foraging paradigm, humans forage for information looking for answers according to this searching theory, just like animals foraging for food with time and energy constraints. Given the abundance of information and the increasing growth rate of new information on the Web, information foraging states that humans adopt adaptive strategies to optimize their intake of useful information per unit cost. The information-foraging theory illustrates the application of the principle of least effort as people take actions that get the information they want or think they need with the expenditure of the least cost.

We also see the application of the principle of least effort in sponsored search in the searching attributes of potential customers. Queries are extremely short [28]. There is limited viewing of results or result pages [29, 30]. There is limited viewing of results below the fold [31]. Session duration is very limited [32]. Time on a Web site is restricted [29]. All of these behaviors point to the same thing: Searchers will expend the least amount of effort possible to get satisfactory results.

The uncertainty principle. The uncertainty principle [33] states that the earlier stages of information searching are initiated by a lack of understanding or a limited knowledge, and this cognitive state is uncertainty. The affective symptoms of uncertainty are associated with being vague and unclear about a search topic. The level of uncertainty is connected to information desired and search tactics [34]. Certainly, this makes intuitive sense, but it is important to be clear about what is the motivation for a person to search. A focus on the uncertainty helps in this regard.

Generally, uncertainty deals with a state of limited knowledge by a user in a given context. This uncertainty may be how to express a need, what that need means, or the changing of previously held beliefs.

As the information search progresses, the searcher develops a clearer focus of the topic and a shift occurs from feelings of uncertainty, confusion, and frustration to feelings of increased confidence. The uncertainty principle is closely related to sense-making's concept of a gap or discontinuity [35] that the individual conceptualizes in a certain situation. This situation does not permit the individual to move forward without obtaining new knowledge and constructing a changed sense. Based on new information obtained, the individual can move to bridge the gap and proceed after crossing the gap. The uncertainty principle is also inherent in the Anomalous States of Knowledge (ASK) model [36] of information seeking.

In sponsored search, as with most concepts of consumer search, there is an assumption of the reduction of uncertainty concerning a product choice.

Information obtainability. A construct that has clear impact on sponsored search is the notion of information obtainability. That is, the more accessible the information, the more likely it is that people will use that information. Stated explicitly, "The more difficult and time consuming it is for a customer to use an information system, the less likely it is that he [sic] will use that information system" [37, p. 46]. Phrased more succinctly, *information will be used in direct proportion to how easy it is to obtain* [38]. In fact, the entire concept of Web search has been concerned with making it easier for the searcher to access online information.

What do we know about the intent of the individual searcher?
In addition to the theoretical constructs of the principle of least effort, the uncertainty principle, and information obtainability, we can also determine with increased accuracy the topic (i.e., what is the subject of the searcher's query) and the intent (i.e., what type of content the person is searching for).

The topic of a term is related to the use of the word, an inherent aspect of language and communication. Like most words in the English language, key phrases can be categorized as nouns, verbs, adverbs, adjectives, prepositions, or pronouns. Research has shown that most, although not all, queries are composed of primarily nouns [39] on stop words (a.k.a., skip words).

The user intent [40, 41, 42] is somewhat unique to Web searching. So, given the importance and application of intent, we cover it here.

What can we learn from the underlying intent of a searcher's key terms?

Naturally, different queries often have different underlying needs, and these underlying needs often induce different types of searcher behavior, from click-through behavior to browsing behavior. For example, empirical studies have noted that broad informational queries (e.g., *digital camera*) require more browsing by searchers relative to more focused queries (e.g., *find a Nokia camera*) [43].

The research into user intent in Web search begins with Broder [40], who proposed three broad user-intent classifications for Web queries: *navigational, informational,* and *transactional.* This framework was based on empirical observation, and it has been supported by a string of empirical research in the area of Web searching. For example, Spink and Jansen [44] report that e-commerce-related queries varied from approximately 12 percent to 24 percent using various Web search engine transaction logs. Jansen, Spink, and Pedersen [45] stated that there was a significant use of search engines as a navigation appliance. The researchers report that the top fifteen queries from a 2002 AltaVista search log (e.g., *google, yahoo, ebay, yahoo.com, hotmail, hotmail.com, thumbzilla, www.yahoo.com, babelfish, mapquest, nfl.com, nfl, weather, www.hotmail.com,* and *google.com*) were all likely expressions of a navigational intent. It is apparent that the hypermedia environment of the Web provides a unique capability of using search as a specialized form of browsing. Expanding on Broder's classifications, Rose and Levinson [42] classified search queries using the categories of *informational, navigational,* and *resource,* with hierarchical subcategories of each.

What is user intent?

User intent is *the resource specified by the affective, cognitive, or situational goal expressed in an interaction with a Web search engine.* Referring to Belkin's states of a searching episode [46], intent is akin to goal, and expression akin to method of interaction. Unlike goal, however, intent is concerned with how the goal is expressed because the expression determines what type of resource the user desires to address his or her overall goal. Pirolli [27, p. 65] makes a similar delineation between task (i.e., something external) and need (i.e., the concept that drives the information-foraging behavior). Saracevic's stratified model [47, 48] proposes that user expressions to an information-searching system are based on affective, cognitive, or situational strata.

Certainly, the query is a key component of this expression of intent. The importance of the query is obvious by the considerable amount of research examining various aspects of query formulation, reformulation, and processing [49, 50, 51, 52]. Pirolli [27, p. 65] refers to the query also as an external representation of the need. Note that the query is often an inexact representation of the underlying intent [53, 54, 55, 56].

Derived from research [40, 42], user intent within each category is defined as one of the following:

- *Informational searching*: The intent of informational searching is to locate content concerning a particular topic to address an information need of the searcher. The content can be in a variety of forms, including data, text, documents, and multimedia. The need can be along a spectrum from very precise to very vague.
- *Navigational searching*: The intent of navigational searching is to find a particular Web location. The Web location can be that of a person or organization. It can be a particular Web page, site, or hub site. The searcher may have a particular Web site in mind, or the searcher may just "think" a particular Web site exists.
- *Transactional searching*: The intent of transactional searching is to locate a Web site with the goal of obtaining some other product or service on that Web site. Examples include purchasing a product, executing an online application, or downloading multimedia.

In less academic language, we can define the intent of these three broad categories as:

- Informational – finding
- Navigational – traversing
- Transactional – getting

Each of these three major categories can be further subdivided [41].

Table 3.3 presents a three-level hierarchical taxonomy, with the topmost level being Informational, Navigational, and Transactional. Each of these level-one categories has several level-two classifications. Some classifications also can involve a third-level classification. Table 3.3 also presents definitions of each of the classifications in the user-intent taxonomy.

Graphically, Figure 3.6 presents a hierarchal overview of the user-intent taxonomy, along with potential impact on sponsored search efforts.

With these concepts of human information processing, constructs of individual searching behavior, and advances in determining the intent of the searcher, we can project these behaviors from the individual to the aggregate level.

Human Information Behavior at the Aggregate Level

We now know some things about the individual searcher. Conceptually, we market toward the individual [57].

However, by necessity, we must deal with market segments, which is a subset of the total market of potential customers. This market segment of potential customers is an aggregate set of potential consumers (typically people, but can also be other businesses) who possess similar sets of attributes resulting in the wanting of similar products and/or services.

Using market segmentation, the advertiser can describe and perhaps predict what the potential consumer will do. This ability to predict can help in determining what keyphrases should be selected for sponsored-search effects. This segmentation is concerned with human information behavior at the aggregate level.

Table 3.3. *Definitions of classifications of Web queries*

Levels	Examples of queries
Level One	
(I) *Informational*: queries meant to obtain data or information in order to address an information need, desire, or curiosity.	Child labor law
(N) *Navigational*: queries looking for a specific URL.	Capital one
(T) *Transactional*: queries looking for resources that require another step to be useful.	Buy table clocks
Level Two	
(I, D) *Directed*: specific question	Registering domain name
(I, U) *Undirected*: tell me everything about a topic	Singers in the 1980s
(I, L) *List*: list of candidates	Things to do in Hollywood ca
(I, F) *Find*: locate where some real world service or product can be obtained	PVC suit for overweight men
(I, A) *Advice*: advice, ideas, suggestions, instructions	What to serve with roast pork tenderloin
(N, T) *Navigation to transactional*: the URL the user wants is a transactional site	Match.com
(N, I) *Navigation to informational*: the URL the user wants is an informational site	Yahoo.com
(T, O) *Obtain*: obtain a specific resource or object	Music lyrics
(T, D) *Download*: find a file to download	Mp3 downloads
(T, R) *Results Page*: obtain a resource that one can print, save, or read from the search engine results page	(The user enters a query with the expectation that 'answer' will be on the search engine results page and not require browsing to another Web site.)
(T, I) *Interact*: interact with program/resource on another Web site	Buy table clock
Level Three	
(I, D, C) Closed: deals with one topic; question with one, unambiguous answer	Nine supreme court justices
(I, D, O) *Open*: deals with two or more topics	The excretory system of arachnids
(T, O, O) *Online*: the resource will be obtained online	airline seat map
(T, O, F) *Off-line*: the resource will be obtained off-line and may require additional actions by the user	full metal alchemist wallpapers
(T, D, F) *Free*: the downloadable file is free	Free online games
(T, D, N) *Not Free*: the downloadable file is not necessarily free	"Family Guy" episode download
(T, R, L) *Links*: the resources appears in the title, summary, or URL of one or more of the results on the search engine results page	(As an example, a user enters the title of a conference paper to locate the page numbers, which usually appear in one or more of the results.)
(T, R, O) *Other*: the resources does not appear one of the results but somewhere else on the search engine results page	(As an example, a user enters a query term to check for spelling with no interest in the results listing. I do that!)

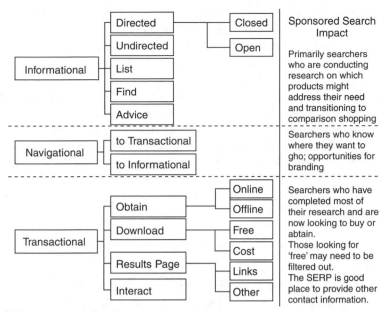

Figure 3.6. Hierarchy of user-intent classification with impact on sponsored search.

To investigate aggregate information behavior, let us once again begin with the concept of search, but instead of search as a set of individual actions, let us consider search as an economic concept.

When we do this, we find that, unlike at the individual level where we had little more than guidelines, we can not only develop rules at the aggregate level but also make some fairly accurate predictions on this information behavior.

Potpourri: In his seminal science fiction series, *The Foundation Trilogy*, Isaac Asimov introduced the concept of *psychohistory*, an inferential scientific discipline based on the premise that, with enough data, one could predict what a set of people would do, even if one could not predict what an individual person would do.

For many years, this was just science fiction.

Not any longer.

The massive amount of data collectable on the Web is providing insights into advertising, customer behavior, language translation, financial markets, disease outbreaks, election outcomes, and many other situations.

So, Asimov might have been on to something. The data is just now catching up.

Let us briefly discuss consumer searching; we will address consumer searching in more detail in Chapter 5. However, we need some background on it to make sense of our discussion on keyterm selection. We anchor our discussion in that of consumer search research [58].

One can theoretically model consumer search as a process where the searcher is in a state of deciding to seek out additional information (i.e., searching again) or not seek additional information (i.e., stop searching). This decision process is a function of the expected benefit of any additional information [59], with the benefit of searching being a reduction in uncertainty.

As the searcher gathers additional information from additional searches, the searcher's expected benefit of seeking new information decreases (i.e., their uncertainty is reduced), and this increased confidence results in a lower probability of the searcher soliciting new information (i.e., doing an additional search).

Now, one can model this consumer search process by developing a model of the search process as the probability that individual i searches an xth time (i.e., submits an addition query xth) as a decrement of the probability of visiting the $(x_i - 1)$st site [based on the work of 17, 36]:

$$\Pr[X_i = x_i] = \frac{(x_i - 1)\theta_i}{x_i} \Pr[X_i = x_i - 1], \quad x_i = 2, 3, ...,$$

Equation 3.1. Probability model of consumer search.

The model presented in Equation 3.1 is simply a rephrasing of the search behavior described earlier, except it is now presented in mathematical symbols rather than words.

The model is recursive. Any series of states in the searching process is just composed of a set of individual search states. Therefore, we can present this recursive model as a logarithmic distribution.

The revised model is presented in Equation 3.2, where $a_i = -[\ln(1-\theta_i)]^{-1}$ and $0 < \theta_i < 1$.

$$\Pr[X_i = x_i] = \frac{a_i \theta_i^{x_i}}{x_i}, \quad x_i = 1, 2, ...,$$

Equation 3.2. Logarithmic probability model on consumer search.

To illustrate the model of consumer search (and how this model is valuable at the aggregate level), Figure 3.7 plots the shape of the consumer search model for a variety of probabilities. To explain Figure 3.7, with a θ of 0.2, there is a 90 percent probability that the searcher will click on only one result. With a θ of 0.5, there is a 71 percent probability that the searcher will click on only one result. At three site visits, we address only 10 percent of searchers with a θ of 0.08. We could do a similar graph (and model) for query length, session length, and landing pages visited. They all would plot similarly.

We could also plot the logarithmic distribution of our model. In these cases, the lines would be straight and of different slopes, but we could derive the same percentages and site numbers. More on this later.

What does this mean?

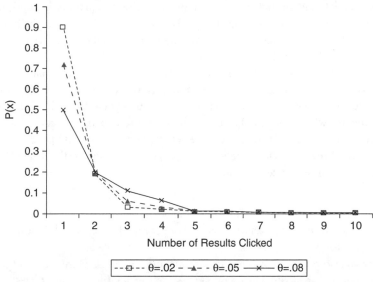

Figure 3.7. Relationship of searcher, query, keyphrase, and result

Searchers as potential consumers typically do not craft long queries, do not submit a lot of queries, and do not click on a lot of results. Therefore, they typically do not visit a lot of sites that are the landing pages of advertisements.

Interestingly, economists at one time found this behavior extremely puzzling, as by common sense and empirical evaluation, the Web lowers search costs. Therefore, searching should increase as theoretically, there are no physical search or transportation costs for online searchers.

However, online searchers are not exhibiting the lengthy search that economic theory would predict given the low physical costs of information search on the Web [60]. Now, we know that searchers are often driven by uncertainty but will expend the least amount of effort to get a reasonable solution, and they will access information that is easiest to get to. We see this in the searching behavior mentioned, such as query length, session length, click-through rates, and sites visited among the aggregate set of searchers.

All this leads us to what we are most interested in – the power law distribution.

The powerful impact of power laws

Most searchers' keyterm behavior, and therefore keyphrases, can be modeled using power law distributions.

Why are these aggregate behaviors explainable by power laws?

It is an outgrowth of the aggregate of the individual behavior resulting from the principle of least effort and information obtainability constructs.

First though, what is a power law?

The graph shown in Figure 3.5 is a power law. A power law is a special kind of mathematical relationship between two quantities. When the frequency of something (i.e., number of occurrences of object or event) varies as a power (a.k.a., exponent, a mathematical notation indicating the number of times a quantity is multiplied by itself) of some attribute of that object (e.g., its size, its rank, its height), the frequency is said to follow a power law. Like the more standard normal or bell curve, the power law is a probability distribution.

There are many phenomena that follow a power law distribution. Many aspects of sponsored search follow power laws, including frequencies of terms used in queries, the frequency of visits to Web sites, and the frequency of clicks on SERP links. This is specifically why some keyphrases are much more expensive than others in the same vertical. A lot more people use these selected phrases or these phrases generate much more of revenue. These high-volume keywords are called the head. The low-volume keywords are called the tail.

Potpourri: Powers laws are related to a business concept known as the law of diminishing marginal returns that, when graphed, often display power laws distributions.

For sponsored search, the law of diminishing marginal returns [61] is that the first dollar of advertising spent will generate more revenue in sales than the next dollar. That second dollar will generate more revenue than the next dollar, and so on. Eventually, we reach a point where it will cost more than a dollar of advertising to generate a dollar of revenue.

The phenomena of the power law also help explain why sponsored search has lowered the cost of advertising relative to its return on investment. With mass media approaches, such as print and television, one has to canvas all the people who are the audience of that outlet to target the relatively small set of potential customers. However, with sponsored search, advertisers can specifically target individual consumers.

What does the power law tell us?

The power law describes phenomena where large events are rare, but small events are quite common. For example, there are a few very large earthquakes, but there are many small earthquakes. There are a few megacities, but there are many small towns. Within the English language, there are a few words (e.g., *a, as, and, the*) that occur very frequently, but there are many words that rarely occur (e.g. *obdormition, tanquam*).

A power law is much different than the normal distribution, which many people are used to dealing with in statistics. A comparison of a normal and power law distribution is shown in Figure 3.8.

In a normal distribution, there is a mean or average, which is a typical value around which other measurements are centered. This distribution describes several phenomena in the world, such as average test scores of a random population, distribution of people's height, or distribution of people's weight. However, not all measurements peak around a typical value. Instead, some things, objects, or events vary over an enormous range, sometimes with many orders of magnitude. A classic example is wealth. The richest person in the world has many times more wealth than the poorest person.

Such variance in magnitude makes fairly common measures, such as average, meaningless. For example, say there is a party of thirty people in the room. As a party

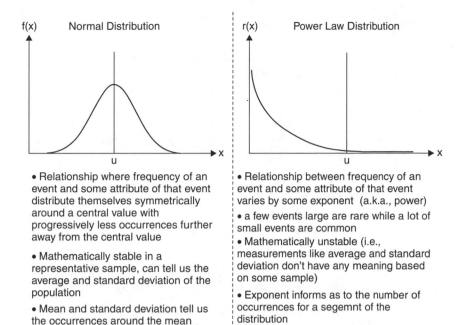

Figure 3.8. Comparison of normal and power law distribution.

game, you decide to calculate the average weight in room. Then, the heaviest person in the world arrives at the party. Regardless of who is at the party, the average weight will go up, but not by much.

Now, let us say instead of weight, you decide to do another party game and calculate the average net worth of your party-goers. Then, the wealthiest person in the world arrives at the party. Regardless of who is at the party, the average wealth of the room will skyrocket.

Weight follows a normal distribution, whereas wealth follows a power law distribution. With distribution of weight, average has meaning. With distribution of wealth, average has little meaning.

Potpourri: This distribution of wealth was one of the first observations of the power law distribution, known now as the Pareto principle.

The Italian economist Vilfredo Pareto observed in 1906 that 80 percent of the land in Italy was owned by 20 percent of the population.

This was the basis for the 80–20 rule, which has cropped up in a variety of disciplines, including real estate (80 percent of the houses are sold by 20 percent of the realtors), quality control (80 percent of the problems are a result of 20 percent of the causes), sales (80 percent of the revenue is generated by 20 percent of the employees), and information retrieval (80 percent precision means 20 percent recall).

(Continued)

> Although 80 percent is not exact mathematically, it appears to be a good ball-park percentage for a lot of systems.
>
> Mathematically, we can empirically calculate the exact percentage. In any system with some resource shared among a large number of participants, there must be a number *p* between 50 and 100 such that "*p* % is taken by (100 − *p*) % of the participants."
>
> The number *p* may vary from 50 (which is the case of equal distribution, in which 100 percent of the population have equal shares of the resource) to nearly 100 (where a few participants have almost all of the resources).

How do we model power laws?

Mathematically, a quantity **x** obeys a power law if it is drawn from a probability distribution where α is a constant parameter of the distribution known as the exponent or scaling parameter.

$$P(x) = Cx^{-\alpha}$$

Equation 3.3. Mathematical model of a power law

Many times, we see power law distributions display a logarithmic chart. For the power law, the distribution when plotted in this fashion follows a straight line quite closely. The **C** represents the percentage of data from a single category. **Alpha (α)** represents the steepness of the slope. Both will have an effect on the percentage of data points that fall within a given range. The higher the **C** value, the greater the percentage of single values at the low end of the curve will be, regardless of the alpha value. From a logarithmic transformation perspective, **C** affects the height of the line.

A logarithmic chart is helpful when examining data from power laws. A logarithmic chart for some given scale is skewed so that a given distance between two rational points on the distribution always represents the same percentage change in that scale rather than the same absolute change, which is the case for a linear chart. In other words, the distance from 1 to 10 is the same as the distance from 10 to 100 on a logarithmic chart, but the latter distance is ten times greater on a linear chart.

Each power law within a given domain has its own exponent, as shown in Table 3.4.

As we can see from Table 3.4, power laws in different domains have different exponents.

The power law distribution (i.e., the exponent) that we are most concerned with in sponsored search, especially for keyphrase selection, is known as Zipf's Law.

Zipf's law

Zipf's Law takes its name from the linguist George Kingsley Zipf who proposed and popularized it [62], although the relationship between words and their frequency of use had been noticed before. Mathematically, it is represented by the Equation 3.3, while *P* is the frequency of a word ranked x and the exponent α is almost about 1.

Table 3.4. *Standard exponents of power laws [63]*

Quantity	Exponent
Number of citations to papers	3.04
Number of hits on Web sites	2.40
Copies of books sold in the United States	3.51
Telephone calls received	2.22
Magnitude of earthquakes	3.04
Diameter of moon craters	3.14
Intensity of solar flares	1.83
Intensity of wars	1.80
Net worth of Americans	2.09
Frequency of family names	1.94
Population of U.S. cities	2.30

This means that the second item occurs approximately half as often as the first, and the third item one-third as often as the first, and so on [62].

In a nutshell, Zipf's Law states there are only a few words used very often; many or most are used rarely. More academically, in some given corpus of natural language utterances (i.e., words), the frequency of any given word is inversely proportional to the rank of that word in a frequency table. So, the most frequently occurring word will happen approximately twice as often as the second most frequent word, three times as often as the third most frequent word, and so forth.

Why does word selection follow Zipf's Law?

One explanation is that Zipf's Law arises from features of natural language and is based theoretically on the principle of least effort. Because neither speakers nor hearers using a given language want to work any harder than necessary to reach understanding, the process that results in approximately equal distribution of effort leads to the observed Zipf distribution.

Why are power laws important for keyphrase selection?

Zipf's Law explains why some of our keyphrases generate a lot of traffic and others generate very little. First, there is certainly a set of keywords that are the hits (i.e., these are at the head of the power law distribution, with a lot of searchers using related keyterms). These are the keyphrases that generate most of the traffic and, maybe, most of the revenue (see Chapter 4). Certainly, we want to target these keyterms.

However, power laws not only highlight the concentrated portion, but they also illuminate the tail. In the tail, one can find small, stable, and lucrative areas of operations.

This is because the Zipf distribution, like all power law distributions, is fractal (i.e., within any segment of the distribution, we find another power law distribution), as shown in Figure 3.9.

So, from Figure 3.9, we see that the volume decreases within each fractal, but the general shape of the plot is similar. So, within each segment, we can locate some high-volume keyphrases. We see this quite often in sponsored-search campaigns, where one may start with a rather large set of keywords and slowly break this large set into smaller and smaller sets.

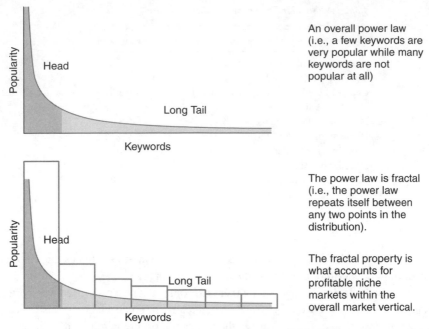

Figure 3.9. Scalar property of power law distribution.

Foundational Takeaways

- The selection of query terms by searchers is a component of human information behavior and is related to human information processing. Therefore, you must view your selection of keywords from a human information-processing perspective.
- At the individual level, we have some guiding heuristics for potential customers as they engage in an information-searching process (e.g., principle of least effort, principle of uncertainty, and principle of information access).
- Using a combination of searcher characteristics, namely the terms they use, we can determine to some degree the underlying intent of searchers. The terms in the query represent one or more concepts for which the person is searching. As such, the submission of a query is the start of a communication process.
- At the aggregate level, most searcher actions are defined by power law distributions in that there is a small number of items that occur most frequently or have the biggest impact. Meanwhile a large number of items occur infrequently and individually have a small impact. This is commonly known as the head and the tail of the distribution (see Figure 3.9). The combined percentages of the tail can combine into a significant amount.

Relating Theory to Practice

Selection of keyphrases is the core of the sponsored-search effort. To successfully select high-performing keyphrases, we must simultaneously focus on the individual and the entire market segment.

- Select one of your products or services and develop a persona of an individual customer for that product. Consider our known theoretical constructs (e.g., principle of least effort, principle of uncertainty, and principle of information access). Market to this one person. Do your keyphrases reflect the behaviors of this individual?
- Isolate the market segment for your product in terms of income, age, and other demographics. Consider what we know about searching and keyterm selection (i.e., searching and term select follow a power law distribution). Does your advertising effort leverage each segment of the market distribution?

Conclusion

One can make the case that keyphrase selection is the heart of any sponsored-search campaign and that they are linked between the potential customer and all other efforts. These keyphrases are conceptually linked to the query terms selected by searchers, who are our potential customers. As individuals, these searchers have sets of actions that are collectively known as human information behaviors.

In sponsored search, we are specifically interested in the aspect of information searching, a person using a Web search engine to locate content. In the act of information searching, we know that users are generally expending the least amount of effort, are attempting to reduce uncertainty, accessing the content that is easiest to get to, and trying to rapidly reduce their number of choices. Leveraging some of these actions and their query terms, you can make some assumptions about what content the searcher would like.

At the aggregate level, most search behaviors are described by power law distribution, including the query terms used. We know, therefore, that a few terms will get used a lot and a lot of terms will be used infrequently.

The objective of the advertiser is to find the "sweet spot" of terms that will generate significant volumes of convertible traffic. This set of keywords is advertiser-dependent. This selection can generally be done through concentration on a few keywords in the head, a lot of terms in the tail, or a combination of both.

These keywords are one of the direct links from the advertiser to the searcher.

The other is the advertisement. What is it about your advertisement that attracts the attention of the searcher? Why out of all the bits of information on Web does the searcher read and click on your ad? What is in the ad or about the ad that interests the searcher and why? This is what we examine next.

References

[1] Battelle, J. 2005. *The Search: How Google and Its Rivals Rewrote the Rules of Business and Transformed Our Culture*. New York: Penguin Group.

[2] Israel, D. and Perry, J. 1990. "What Is Information?" In *Information, Language and Cognition*, P. Hanson, Ed. Vancouver: British Columbia Press, pp. 1–19.

[3] Repo, A. J. 1989. "The Value of Information: Approaches in Economics, Accounting, and Management Science." *Journal of the American Society of Information Science*, vol. 40(2), pp. 68–85.

[4] Easley, D. and O'hara, M. 2001. "Information and the Cost of Capital." *The Journal of Finance*, vol. 59(4), pp. 1553–1583.

[5] Stephens, D. W. 1989. "Variance and the Value of Information." *The American Naturalist*, vol. 134(1), pp. 128–140.

[6] Marin, J. and Poulter, A. 2004. "Dissemination of Competitive Intelligence." *Journal of Information Science*, vol. 30(2), pp. 165–180.

[7] Konow, J. 2005. "Blind Spots: The Effects of Information and Stakes on Fairness Bias and Dispersion." *Social Justice Research*, vol. 18(4), pp. 349–390.

[8] Huitt, W. 2003. *The Information Processing Approach to Cognition*. Valdosta, GA: Educational Psychology Interactive.

[9] Coates, G. 2009. *Notes on Communication: A Few Thoughts about the Way We Interact with the People We Meet*. Sydney: Wanterfall.

[10] Wilson, T. D. 2000. "Human Information Behavior." *Informing Science*, vol. 3(2), pp. 49–55.

[11] Putrevu, S. 2002. "Exploring the Origins and Information Processing Differences between Men and Women: Implications for Advertisers." *Academy of Marketing Science Review*, vol. 10(1), Article 1.

[12] Rodgers, S. and Harris, M. A. 2003. "Gender and E-Commerce: An Exploratory Study." *Journal of Advertising Research*, vol. 43(1), pp. 322–329.

[13] Jansen, B. J. and Rieh, S. 2010. "The Seventeen Theoretical Constructs of Information Searching and Information Retrieval." *Journal of the American Society for Information Sciences and Technology*, vol. 61(8), pp. 1517–1534.

[14] Marchionini, G. 1995. *Information Seeking in Electronic Environments*. Cambridge: Cambridge University Press.

[15] Animesh, A., Ramachandran, V., and Viswanathan, S. 2010. "Quality Uncertainty and the Performance of Online Sponsored Search Markets: An Empirical Investigation." *Information Systems Research*, vol. 21(1), pp. 190–201.

[16] Nelson, P. 1970. "Information and Consumer Behavior." *The Journal of* Political *Economy*, vol. 78(2), pp. 311–329.

[17] Ford, G. T., Smith, D. B., and Swasy, J. L. 1988. "An Empirical Test of the Search, Experience and Credence Attributes Framework." In *Advances in Consumer Research Volume*, vol. 15, M. J. Houston, Ed. Provo, UT: Association for Consumer Research, pp. 239–244.

[18] Darby, M. and Karni, E. 1973. "Free Competition and the Optimal Amount of Fraud." *Journal of Law and Economics*, vol. 16(1), pp. 67–86.

[19] Hu, N., Liu, L., and Zhang, J. 2008. "Do Online Reviews Affect Product Sales? The Role of Reviewer Characteristics and Temporal Effects." *Information Technology and Management*, vol. 9(3), pp. 201–214.

[20] Jansen, B. J. and Spink, A. 2005. "How Are We Searching the World Wide Web? A Comparison of Nine Search Engine Transaction Logs." *Information Processing & Management*, vol. 42(1), pp. 248–263.

[21] Shannon, C. E. 1948. "A Mathematical Theory of Communication." *Bell System Technical Journal*, vol. 27(July/October), pp. 379–423, 623–656.

[22] Miller, G. A. 1956. "The Magical Number Seven Plus or Minus Two: Some Limits on Our Capacity for Processing Information." *Psychological Review*, vol. 63(1), pp. 81–97.

[23] Zipf, G. K. 1949. *Human Behavior and the Principle of Least Effort*. Cambridge, MA: Addison-Wesley Press.

[24] Simon, H. 1981. *The Sciences of the Artificial*, 2d ed. Cambridge, MA: MIT Press.

[25] Andreasen, A. R. 2005. *Social Marketing in the 21st Century*. New York: Sage.

[26] Jansen, B. J. and Resnick, M. 2006. "An Examination of Searchers' Perceptions of Non-Sponsored and Sponsored Links during Ecommerce Web Searching." *Journal of the* American *Society for Information Science and Technology*, vol. 57(14), pp. 1949–1961.

[27] Pirolli, P. 2007. *Information Foraging Theory: Adaptive Interaction with Information*. Oxford: Oxford University Press.

[28] Jansen, B. J., Spink, A., and Saracevic, T. 2000. "Real Life, Real Users, and Real Needs: A Study and Analysis of User Queries on the Web." *Information Processing & Management*, vol. 36(2), pp. 207–227.

[29] Jansen, B. J. and Spink, A. 2004. "An Analysis of Documents Viewing Patterns of Web Search Engine Users." In *Web Mining: Applications and Techniques*, A. Scime, Ed., pp. 339–354.

[30] Jansen, B. J. and Spink, A. 2009. "Investigating Customer Click Through Behaviour with Integrated Sponsored and Nonsponsored Results." *International Journal of Internet Marketing and Advertising*, vol. 5(1/2), pp. 74–94.

[31] Jansen, B. J. and McNeese, M. D. 2005. "Evaluating the Effectiveness of and Patterns of Interactions with Automated Searching Assistance." *Journal of the American Society for Information Science and Technology*, vol. 56(14), pp. 1480–1503.

[32] Jansen, B. J., Spink, A., Blakely, C., and Koshman, S. 2007. "Defining a Session on Web Search Engines." *Journal of the American Society for Information Science and Technology*, vol. 58(6), pp. 862–871.

[33] Kuhlthau, C. 1993. "A Principle of Uncertainty for Information Seeking." *Journal of Documentation*, vol. 49, pp. 339–355.

[34] Vakkari, P. 2001. "A Theory of the Task-based Information Retrieval Process." *Journal of Documentation*, vol. 57(1), pp. 44–60.

[35] Dervin, B. 1976. "Strategies for Dealing with Human Information Needs: Information or Communication?" *Journal of Broadcasting*, vol. 20(3), pp. 324–351.

[36] Belkin, N., Oddy, R., and Brooks, H. 1982. "ASK for Information Retrieval, Parts 1 & 2." *Journal of Documentation*, vol. 38(2), pp. 61–71, 145–164.

[37] Pemberton, J. M. 1989. "Telecommunication: Technology and Devices." *Records Management Quarterly*, vol. 23, pp. 46–48.

[38] Summit, R. K. 1993. "The Year 2000: Dreams and Nightmares." *Searcher*, vol. 1, pp. 16–17.

[39] Jansen, B. J., Spink, A., and Pfaff, A. 2000. "Linguistic Aspects of Web Queries." In *Annual Meeting of the American Society of Information Science*, Chicago, IL, pp. 169–176.

[40] Broder, A. 2002. "A Taxonomy of Web Search." *SIGIR Forum*, vol. 36(2), pp. 3–10.

[41] Jansen, B. J., Booth, D., and Spink, A. 2008. "Determining the Informational, Navigational, and Transactional Intent of Web Queries." *Information Processing & Management*, vol. 44(3), pp. 1251–1266.

[42] Rose, D. E. and Levinson, D. 2004. "Understanding User Goals in Web Search." In *World Wide Web Conference (WWW 2004)*, New York, pp. 13–19.

[43] Attenberg, J., Pandey, S., and Suel, T. 2009. "Modeling and Predicting User Behavior in Sponsored Search." In *15th ACM SIGKDD International Conference on Knowledge Discovery and Data Mining*, Paris, France.

[44] Spink, A. and Jansen, B. J. 2004. *Web Search: Public Searching of the Web*. New York: Kluwer.

[45] Jansen, B. J., Spink, A., and Pedersen, J. 2005. "Trend Analysis of AltaVista Web Searching." *Journal of the American Society for Information Science and Technology*, vol. 56(6), pp. 559–570.

[46] Belkin, N. J. 1993. "Interaction with Texts: Information Retrieval as Information-Seeking Behavior." In *Information retrieval '93. Von der Modellierung zur Anwendung*. Konstanz, Germany: Universitaetsverlag Konstanz, pp. 55–66.

[47] Saracevic, T. 1997. "Extension and Application of the Stratified Model of Information Retrieval Interaction." In *the Annual Meeting of the American Society for Information Science*, Washington, DC, pp. 313–327.

[48] Saracevic, T. 1996. "Modeling Interaction in Information Retrieval (IR): A Review and Proposal." In *the 59th American Society for Information Science Annual Meeting*, Baltimore, MD, pp. 3–9.

[49] Belkin, N., Cool, C., Croft, W. B., and Callan, J. 1993. "The Effect of Multiple Query Representations on Information Retrieval Systems." In *16th Annual International ACM SIGIR Conference on Research and Development in Information Retrieval*, pp. 339–346.

[50] Belkin, N., Cool, C., Kelly, D., Lee, H.-J., Muresan, G., Tang, M.-C., and Yuan, X.-J. 2003. "Query Length in Interactive Information Retrieval." In *26th Annual International ACM*

Conference on Research and Development in Information Retrieval, Toronto, Canada, pp. 205–212.

[51] Cronen-Townsend, S., Zhou, Y., and Croft, W. B. 2002. "Predicting Query Performance." In *25th Annual International ACM SIGIR Conference on Research and Development in Information Retrieval*, Tampere, Finland, pp. 299–306.

[52] Efthimiadis, E. N. 2000. "Interactive Query Expansion: A User-Based Evaluation in a Relevance Feedback Environment." *Journal of the American Society of Information Science and Technology*, vol. 51(11), pp. 989–1003.

[53] Belkin, N. J. 1980. "Anomalous States of Knowledge as a Basis for Information Retrieval." *Canadian Journal of Information Science*, vol. 5, pp. 133–143.

[54] Croft, W. B. and Thompson, R. H. 1987. "I3: A New Approach to the Design of Document Retrieval Systems." *Journal of the American Society for Information Science*, vol. 38(6), pp. 389–404.

[55] Ingwersen, P. 1996. "Cognitive Perspectives of Information Retrieval Interaction: Elements of a Cognitive IR Theory." *Journal of Documentation*, vol. 52(1), pp. 3–50.

[56] Taylor, R. S. 1968. "Question Negotiation and Information Seeking in Libraries." *College & Research Libraries*, vol. 28, pp. 178–194.

[57] Locke, C., Levine, R., Searls, D., and Weinberger, D. 2000. *The Cluetrain Manifesto: The End of Business as Usual*. New York: Perseus.

[58] Johnson, E. J., Moe, W. W., Fader, P. S., Bellman, S., and Lohse, G. L. 2004. "Depth and Dynamics of Online Search Behavior." *Management Science*, vol. 50(3), pp. 299–308.

[59] Diamond, P. A. 1989. "Search theory." In *The New Palgrave: Allocation, Information, and Markets*, J. Eatwell, M. Milgate, and P. Newman, Eds. New York: Norton, pp. 271–286.

[60] Bakos, J. Y. 1997. "Reducing Buyer Search Costs: Implications for Electronic Marketplaces." *Management Science*, vol. 43(12), pp. 1676–1692.

[61] Wessels, W. J. 1997. *Microeconomics the Easy Way*. Hauppauge, NY: Barron.

[62] Zipf, G. K. 1932. *Selected Studies of the Principle of Relative Frequency in Language*. Cambridge, MA: Harvard University Press.

[63] Newman, M. 2006. Power laws, Pareto distributions and Zipf's law. Retrieved November 16, 2010, from http://www-personal.umich.edu/~mejn/courses/2006/cmplxsys899/powerlaws.pdf

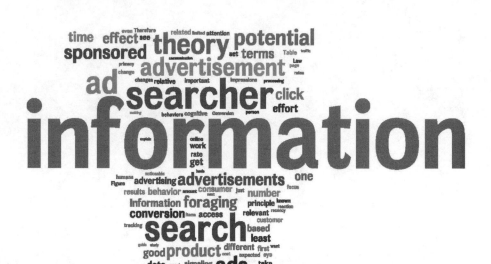

Word cloud generated by Wordle

4

Sending Signals to the Customer with Ads

Just be sure your advertising is saying something with substance, something that will inform and serve the consumer, and be sure you're saying it like it's never been said before.
Bill Bernbach,
cofounder of Doyle Dane Bernbach (DDB),
a worldwide creative advertising agency [1]

Bernbach [1] was a pioneer in the modern advertising field, and as the quote in the epigraph states, advertising is about informing the customer with relevant information that addresses a need and is presented in an attention-getting manner. These are the factors critical for any advertising endeavor.

Referring back to our framing business, our potential customers will be entering queries into search engines that contain terms that link to keyphrases we select. Our ads will appear on the search engine result pages (SERPs) of these search engines in response to these queries. It is these ads that will (or will not) capture the attention of the searcher.

The issue of what our ads should say is of vital significance, as it determines whether or not the searcher becomes a potential customer.

Crafting the advertisement is a mixture of creative art and rigorous science.

The ad is not the product or service that we are offering (i.e., our ad does not directly solve the consumer's problem). In fact, it is not even something that can get the consumer the product or service they need. The ad will only take the customer to the landing page. Once there, our customers might be able to finally address their issue.

Additionally, there is a mandatory synergy between landing page and advertisement. Your landing page must be an extension of your ad copy. Your ad must convey to the searcher that the answer they seek is on the landing page. The primary action that you desire of your customer (i.e., the convert) should generally be above the fold of the landing page.

You can see in this, once again, the principle of least effort. If the landing page is not in synch with the ads, the customer will just depart. If the convert is not easily accessible, the customer will just go to a Web page where it is easy to execute the convert.

Therefore, the ad must be a gateway, a guidepost, a sign, or an enticement for the searchers that directs them to your Web page, which is where the searchers get the product or service that actually addresses their need. Therefore, crafting the advertisement is of critical importance, and you must understand why certain techniques for ad development work and others do not. What are the elements in the ad that catch the searcher's eye and motivate them to take action?

Getting the potential consumer to notice and take action is critical. As with systems in the physical world, a body at rest will remain at rest until acted on by some outside force. In the world of sponsored search, this force is the ad.

For the ad to resonate with a consumer, the ad must have some cognitive or emotional fit with the person. The consumer must readily accept the ad into their learning, problem-solving, or decision-making process in order for the ad to succeed.

In this chapter, we will establish the key underpinnings of developing advertising copy for sponsored search and why certain ads work well and others do not. We will focus at first on the individual level and then the aggregate level.

Searcher Reaction to Advertisements at the Individual Level

One must advertise to a single person. This has long been the hallmark of successful advertising. But who is this individual? With the billions of people who could be potential customers, certainly there must be some heuristics that will make this targeting easier? Luckily, there are, and the application of these heuristics focuses the targeting of the advertisement.

However, for a winning advertisement, it is informative to not think of your potential customers as a mass. Although we may aggregate certain features for efficiency's sake, in the beginning we want to focus clearly on the individual. Thinking in the mass mentality "… gives you a blurred view. Think of a typical individual, man or woman, who is likely to want what you sell." [2].

Concerning advertisements and searchers, we are again centered on the concept of human information behaviors, just like we were with keyword selection (see Chapter 3). However, with keywords, much of our interest was in the cognitive aspects of communication and human information processing, which is still an area in which research is, at best, sketchy and rule-based.

On the advertisement side of things, things are not so bleak. Because reactions to external stimuli (i.e., the ads) are behaviors (i.e., response time to click or not click), reactions to ads are something that we can measure. Because these behaviors are measurable, we have a lot more observed data to work with and therefore have theories, models, principles, and heuristics that can guide us in the development and crafting of advertisements.

In fact, from a purely empirical point of view, the advertisement is the best-known aspect of sponsored-search advertising. You can test every word, every image, and every aspect of display. This is much different than the customer side of things, where the myriad of cognitive, contextual, and affective attributes are nearly endless.

In sum, we know a lot about ads.

So, what do we know about advertisements?

Like when we examined keywords, we are once again concerned with information acquisition and our five exteroceptors [3] or senses (e.g., vision, audition, olfaction, tactile, taste), which is how people acquire information from the external world. Our brain is constantly sifting through the streams of information coming in via the five senses for relevant cues (i.e., signals) rather than irrelevant cues (i.e., noise). Signals and noise are contextual judgments, as today's noise can become tomorrow's signal.

The brain must sift this constant information stream for relevant cues (signals) rather than irrelevant cues (noise). There is a link between information and behavior with information load (i.e., the amount of information attended to at one time) having a functional effect on human performance. Additionally, information load noticeably affects the speed and accuracy of a searcher's response. So, information helps – up to a point. Then, more information may be detrimental.

This is to be expected. Picture everything that must happen between information being received and some measured reaction in a person. The speed of the reaction to information depends on the time required to activate the sensory receptor, transmit nerve impulses from the sense organ to the brain, process nerve impulses in the brain, transmit nerve impulses to muscles, energize and activate muscles, and execute movement. All this must happen between when a searcher sees your ad and decides to click (or not click) on it. This is known as response time, which is the time between the searchers receiving the ad's signal and deciding on a behavior. This response time is measured in seconds [4].

Potpourri: Simple Reaction Time (SRT) is the time it takes to react to stimuli.

Visual SRT is typically range between 150 and 200 milliseconds (0.15 and 0.20 seconds).

Given this typical SRT, the short decision times for reviewing whether or not a landing page is relevant is not surprising. Approximately 20 percent of users take less than one minute [4].

At the individual level, how does one distinguish between signal and noise?

Our answer lies with the signaling theory and, when focusing specifically on search engine results, a concept known as information foraging theory.

Signaling theory

Research into consumer searching on the Web characteristically has an inherent assumption of information asymmetry. In other words, we are making the assumption that consumers search to even out an information imbalance. Otherwise, why would someone search (other than for entertainment) if not to correct an information imbalance?

Information asymmetry is a characteristic in decision-making situations and transactions where one of the participants has more and/or better information than others engaged in the transaction. This information inequality creates an imbalance of power. Therefore, the participant with less information wants to move to a condition of information symmetry to gain more control.

Hence, people search.

Addressing this information imbalance is an underlying motivation for searching, especially in the early stages of a search process. During this searching process, the searcher often uses clues in the decision-making process that guide perceptions of cost, benefits, rewards, and risks associated with choices [5].

In sponsored search, the searcher looks for signals in the advertisements, or information clues that address their lack of information in a trustworthy manner. The process of this occurrence is collectively referred to as signaling theory.

Potpourri: Repetition of signals also seems to play a part, which is the basis for The Three Hit Theory in advertising.

The Three Hit Theory posits that the optimum number of exposures (e.g., hits) to an advertisement to induce learning is three.

The first exposure is to gain consumers' awareness. The second exposure is to show the relevance of the product. The third exposure is to show the benefits of the product.

This is also related to wear-in and wear-out aspects of advertisements.

Signaling theory states that in situations where there is information asymmetry, a signal credibly relays information about a product or service to the consumer. The basis of signaling theory comes from biology and economics, but it also can be applied to understand human communication. The more difficult it is for consumers to assess aspects of a product prior to purchase, the more likely they are to rely on more costly signals to form expectations about the suitability of a product [5].

Signaling theory also addresses why certain signals are more reliable than others in terms of the *costs* to produce the signals [6]. The concept is that during face-to-face communication, people rely on observable features and actions such as facial expressions and ways of speaking to infer implicit informational qualities [7]. In online communications, such as sponsored search, people try to pick up signals from the advertisements to provide clues to the informational qualities of the Web site. Signals that are easy (i.e., less costly) to fake are generally deemed less trustworthy.

So, we have this interesting situation that has probably contributed more to the success of sponsored search than any other factor. The searcher is looking for good signals to address the searching need. The advertiser is, therefore, interested in providing good signals. However, it is not only the advertiser that is interested in crafting good advertisements. The search engine has a vested interest in advertisements that have good signals to generate clicks and take up valuable screen real estate. Therefore, the search engine, as an advertising platform, works to provide good signals to the searcher, most notably in regards to the rank of the advertisement. So, we have:

- The searcher that wants *good signals* in the *advertisement*
- The advertisers that want the *advertisement* to *have good signals*
- The search engine that rewards *advertisements* with *good signals*

Signaling theory is similar to social-information-processing theory [8], which holds that online communicators employ alternative communication cues to compensate the absence of nonverbal cues used in face-to-face interaction [8]. Social-information-processing theory has been supported in several online settings, and the results imply that people put greater emphasis on text-based cues or use alternative cues provided by the online platform [9].

Potpourri: One interesting aspect of signaling theory is what it takes for someone to notice a signal, a difference between two signals, or one signal among many signals.

This measure is often referred to as the theory of just-noticeable differences.

A just noticeable difference is the smallest detectable difference between an initial level and follow-on level of a given sensory stimulus (i.e., signal), which for sponsored search ads is visual. So, we are interested in the magnitude of the difference between two signals.

In many cases, the just noticeable difference can be expressed as a portion of the initial signal. As an example, when comparing two coins, the second coin would have to be some percentage larger than first coin for an average person to notice a difference by touch.

The theory of just noticeable differences may be why techniques such as unusual wording, capitalization, and strange semantics in advertisements have been successful for some advertisers.

A great area for future work in the sponsored search area would be to operationalize these differences in some quantifiable manner.

Naturally, to pick up a signal, one must detect it. With ads, this is done visually. The searcher has to both see and perceive the advertisement.

The perceptual process [10] is the active cognitive process in which the brain strives to make sense of sensory information and fit this to a known pattern or develop some new pattern to make sense of the information. Perceptions typically involve three aspects:

- *Detection* – determination of whether a signal is present or absent
- *Recognition* – noticeable familiarity without the ability to label the stimulus
- *Identification* – full identification of the stimulus, including awareness and labeling

In a way, especially with the meaning of information, our perceptions create our reality. What one perceives from a signal is a result of interplays between past experiences and the interpretation of the perceived information. In sponsored search, aspects such as branding or opinions can greatly influence the searcher's perception of a signal or advertisement. For example, a URL may be trustworthy to one searcher but viewed with suspicion by another searcher.

Potpourri: Perception is a funny thing.

We can have some stimulus in our environment for quite some time and never attend to it.

Then, due to some seemingly random occurrence or event, that stimulus suddenly has meaning, and we begin perceiving this external information. Typically, we are amazed that all this information on the topic we are interested in is suddenly available.

In fact, it has always been there; we are just attending to it now.

There is a related phenomenon concerning attending to information and seeing patterns in this information. The phenomenon goes something like this: We develop an interest in some topic or subject and begin to really focus on it. Suddenly, we begin to see occurrences of information related to this topic. Perhaps, the related information has always been there, only now it is relevant to us.

Information-foraging theory

Signaling theory is a little broad for our purposes. However, the concept of signaling theory that we see appears in something more closely related to information searching, namely *information-foraging theory* [11], which is the implementation of signaling theory for sponsored search (and Web browsing), especially in the concept of information scent.

Potpourri: What is with all the theories?

Do not get confused with all the theories! Sponsored search is a complex area involving a multitude of human, economic, social, cognitive, and technological factors.

Unfortunately, there is limited communication among disciplines in academia.

Therefore, we see overlapping concepts and theories from different disciplines, with multiple names for essentially the same concept.

We also see some foundational constructs (e.g., the principle of least effort, perception), foundational theories (e.g., signaling theory), and applied theories (e.g., information foraging theory) repeated across disciplines with different names.

Information-foraging theory assumes that people use foraging-like mechanisms when searching for information. The theory seeks to describe and understand how humans search for information online. Information-foraging theory is based on the assumption that humans use "built-in" foraging mechanisms when searching for information. The assumption is that these foraging mechanisms evolved to help our animal ancestors find food. So, the theory goes, we humans use a similar process when looking for information.

Information-foraging theory [11] has been developed as a way of explaining human information-seeking and sense-making behavior. During the search process, the searcher, as an informivore (probably carrying the analogy too far!), is continually

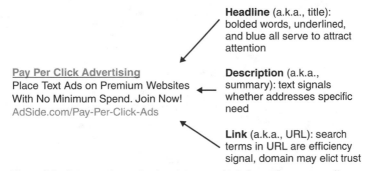

Figure 4.1. Sponsored search advertisement with information scent attributes.

making decisions on what kind of information to look for and whether to look for additional information at the current information source or move to another source. The searcher also decides which path or link to follow to the next information source, and when to stop the search. Information-foraging posits that survival-related traits to respond quickly on partial information and reduce energy expenditures force searchers to optimize their searching behavior and simultaneously minimize the thinking required (i.e., drawing on the principle of least effort).

Whether information foraging is a theory that predicts behavior or a framework to view the searching process, one aspect of information-foraging theory is directly applicable to sponsored-search advertisements: information scent.

Information scent

Information scent is one of the most important concepts in information-foraging theory. Information scent is the subjective sense of both value and cost of accessing information (i.e., viewing a Web page, clicking on a link, reading an ad) based on perceptual cues and the goals of the searcher. It is assumed the information scent is a guide for user behavior during consumer search. We see this all the time in the implementation of sponsored-search advertisements, as shown in Figure 4.1.

Just as animals and early humans relied on scents to help locate food and guide them to promising food locations, searchers rely on various signals in the information environment to get similar answers to locate information. As searchers, people make estimations on the amount of useful information a given choice is likely to provide.

Searchers also evaluate the actual information outcome with their predictions, which is a feedback loop when making future decisions about the information sources. If the information scent is strong, searchers will continue looking in a given information source. When the information scent begins to taper off (i.e., when users no longer expect to find useful additional information), searchers move to a different information source with an increased probability of looking the needed information (Figure 4.2).

Specific information scent in sponsored-search ads is difficult to pin down without empirical testing. However, we know that specific figures give credibility to an ad [12] (i.e., save 10%, lose 9 lbs, etc.).

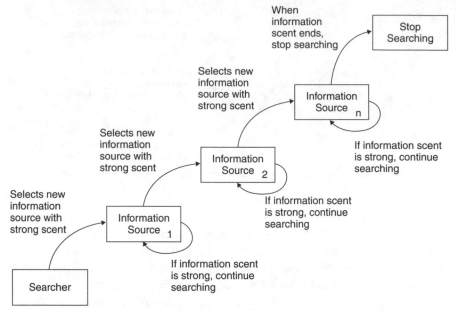

Figure 4.2. Information foraging for searcher, including feedback loops.

Why do people look for signals?

Because there is more information in our environment than we can attend to; therefore, we attempt to channel our attention to the information that matters to us and treat the other information as noise. What matters to us is what we are interested in or what rises above the noise. This is the concept, proposed most succinctly by the political scientist (and economist, and sociologist, and psychologist, and professor!) Simon [13], that a wealth of information creates a poverty of attention. Therefore, people are driven to allocate the attention they do have efficiently.

How do they do this? By looking for signals that show whether or not information is valuable!

This fits well with Schwab's five fundamentals of good advertising [14], which are as follows:

1. Get *attention*
2. Show an *advantage*
3. *Prove* it
4. *Persuade* people of the advantage
5. Ask for *action*

Information overload and attention

Why is the concept of signals so important?

It relates to the concept of information overload [15] and attention. The idea is that an abundance of one item causes a scarcity of some other item [16]. So, in cases of information abundance or even overload, the item that becomes scarce is attention.

Therefore, people develop ways to filter or attend to the information that is important to them at some given time and in some given context, and mentally ignore the other information that is not deemed important.

Signal and scent in sponsored-search advertisements

This leads us, of course, to the question, what is a good signal in a sponsored-search advertisement?

Naturally, this is difficult to answer in all situations, for all searchers, and for all products or services. However, empirical research has highlighted some practical implications of signal and scent.

Branded content

A mountain of empirical research illustrates that a wide variety of searchers consider branded terms in the advertisement a good signal or scent [17, 18]. This is true even if the searcher's query does not contain a branded term. If the advertisement contains a branded term that is related to the industry vertical or product, it statistically increases the probability that the searcher will attend to the advertisement. However, depending on the company, the reaction may be either positive or negative. For more on this, see Chapter 6 on branding.

What is a branded term?

A branded term is a term that refers to a specific company, or product, or service by a company with which the consumer associates an image, concept, feeling, or reputation. So, for our frame shop, it could be the name of the business, *Faster Frames*.

Query content

Perhaps there is no better signal or clue than the actual query term that the searcher submitted to the search engine. This has been shown to dramatically get the searcher to attend to the ad [19, 20].

Search engines have pursued various forms of additionally highlighting and facilitating the use of query terms in the advertisement, such as bolding terms in the advertisement that are also in the query and techniques to dynamically insert the query term or terms into the advertisement.

Action, location, price, and quality terms

Certain product terms seem to be good signals for searchers, although these are somewhat more difficult to implement than brand or query term signals. However, the payoff can be quite good.

These product terms are known collectively as action, location, price and quality (ALPQ) terms:

- *Action* terms that direct the searcher to make the transition from searcher to consumer seem to be good signals. These are typically known as "call to action" terms in the search engine marketing field.
- *Location* terms are those that tie the advertised product or service to a specific geographical location. This is an especially important signal for small- to

medium-size enterprises (SMEs) that typically service a given geographical area (think the perennial pizza place).

- *Price* terms that specifically state a given price, a discount, a markdown, or even "not free" appear to give searchers good signals about whether or not to click on a given advertisement.
- *Quality* terms are words that give the searcher a sense of the value of a product or service. Many branded terms carry quality connotations with them (i.e., referred to as brand image).

How do searchers select a signal in an advertisement?

At the individual level, concerning ad selection, there are three heuristics that address individual human information-processing behavior. The three heuristics are: (1) the principle of least effort, (2) information access, and (3) the Hick-Hyman Law. Two of these (the principle of least effort and information access) are theoretical constructs that also explain searcher selection of query terms (see Chapter 3 keywords).

Principle of least effort. The proposition that an organism generally seeks a method involving the minimum expenditure of energy is one of the enduring tenets in numerous empirical information-searching studies, including Web searching, library studies, and traditional information-retrieval systems [21]. The principle of least effort states that when solving problems, a person tends "to minimize the probable average rate of his or her work-expenditure (over time), meaning use the least amount of effort" [21, p. 1].

The principle of least effort is related to the psychology principle of satisficing by Simon [16]. Simon's view is that people have evolved to make decisions quickly [16]. To make faster decisions, people choose from a subset of options instead of considering all possible options before acting. By applying some general rules, statistically, the best option in that subset should be close to the best option in the whole set of options. This concept has been born out of empirical research [c.f., 22].

The principle of least effort is embedded in information-foraging theory as well [11]. Like animals foraging for food with time and energy constraints, humans forage for information looking for answers according to this searching theory. Given the abundance of information and increasing growth rate of new information, information foraging states that humans adopt adaptive strategies to optimize their intake of useful information per unit cost. The information-foraging theory illustrates the application of the principle of least effort as people take actions that get the information they want or think they need with the expenditure of the least cost.

Information access. Information access is a construct that appears in information-searching and information-retrieval literature. This construct is the notion of information obtainability [23]. That is, the more accessible the information, the more likely it is that people will use that information. As Pemberton explicitly stated, "The more difficult and time consuming it is for a customer to use an information system, the less likely it is that he [sic] will use that information system" [24, p. 46]. Phrased more succinctly, *information will be used in direct proportion to how easy it is to obtain* [23]. Bierbaum sets forth this idea as a "unifying principle" for library and information science [25]. Wilson [26] states that virtually every development in the field of information seeking has been concerned with making it easier for the user to access documents or information.

The lines of research in both fields home in on making information easier to access in terms of interfaces, expression of need or query, contextual help, and information visualization. Although related to the principle of least effort, the construct of information obtainability is focused on technology rather than people. It is especially germane to the field of information retrieval, with its focus on designing and developing system artifacts. Much work in information searching aims at improving the ease of access.

The Hick-Hyman Law. The Hick-Hyman Law is a formula for calculating the time it takes for a person to make a decision faced with a set of possible choices. The Hick-Hyman Law assesses cognitive information capacity in choice reaction experiments. The amount of time taken to process a certain amount of bits in the Hick-Hyman Law is known as the rate of gain of information. Given *n* equally probable choices, the average reaction time T required to choose among them is approximately as follows:

$$\text{Mean CRT} = K \log_2(n+1)$$
$$\text{Where } n = \text{number of choices}$$
$$+1 = \text{has event occured or not}$$
$$K = \text{constant}$$

Equation 4.1. The Hick-Hyman Law for decision making time.

K is a constant that can be determined empirically by fitting a line to measured data. The use of the logarithm in the equation is an expression of depth for a decision hierarchy. Basically, $\log_2$ means that one performs binary search. The +1 addresses the uncertainty about whether to respond or not.

For sponsored search, one can get a rough idea of the processing time for a searcher to assess the ads on the SERP with the Hick-Hyman Law. As the number of ads increases, the searcher will take longer to process the SERP based on the number of ads that they examine in the choice set.

Searcher Reaction to ads at the Aggregate Level

We see the wholesale application of these principles when we investigate searcher behavior at the aggregate level, namely that searchers will expend limited effort in seeking the right advertisement. They will go primarily to ads that are the easiest to get to, and they employ strategies to rapidly narrow their options.

How do these principles explain searcher acts? Let us examine two searcher behaviors: where they look and where they click.

Eye-tracking studies

There seems to be a general trend that searchers keep their eyes focused generally on the portion of the SERP that is nearest the query box. This is understandable. Scanning an entire SERP with multiple sponsored and nonsponsored links takes cognitive effort, and we know that searchers seek to expend the least energy possible and still accomplish their information-seeking task.

Figure 4.3 is an example of a typical heat map for an eye-tracking study of a searcher interfacing with a SERP. A heat map denotes areas of eye focus on the SERP.

One sees from Figure 4.3 that there are four general areas of eye focus. There is a small, concentrated area with the most eye focus; a similar sized but more dispersed area with high eye focus; a larger and very dispersed area of some eye focus; and finally, the largest area with no eye focus.

Notice that most of the attention is focused at the upper left-hand corner of the SERP page, moving about half across the page to the right. There is a focus on the top sponsored-search listing and some brief scans down the both sponsored and non-sponsored listings. Note that there is some recency effect (as cited in [27]), with eye focus on the last result in both sponsored and nonsponsored listings.

This behavior is typically what we would expect from the principle of least effort, principle of information access, and the Hick-Hyman law, namely little expenditure of energy (i.e., trusting of the search engine technology for ranking relevant results), accessing the information that is easiest to get to (i.e., the ones at the top of the list), and a nearly immediate chunking of choices into sets (i.e., those at the top of each list and those not in the top of the list.). These eye-tracking patterns were first observed in the findings of eye-tracking studies conducted by the search engine marketing research firm, Enquiro (now Mediative), which showed this eye-tracking pattern and labeled it "The Google Golden Triangle" [28, 29].

Potpourri: Whenever I see the heat plots from eye-tracking studies, they always remind me of the Golden Ratio and the Golden Triangle.

The Golden Ratio is a mathematical ratio of two parallel lines such that the ratio of the whole to the longest is the same as the longest to the shortest. The Golden Triangle is an isosceles triangle such that the ratio of the hypotenuse to the base is equal to the golden ratio.

The Golden Ratio may explain why slight changes in the location of sponsored results (on the right or east side) affect click-through rates on these ads.

The Golden Triangle may also explain how far down searchers typically scan when first viewing the SERP. It may be affected by the width of the SERP in the browser.

These two questions are open to empirical evaluation.

By now, you can start to see a trend.

People start from the top left and work their way down, jumping back and forth on the page. They also consume information in bits and pieces (i.e., information foraging). They will read a headline. If it is of interest, they will continue to read.

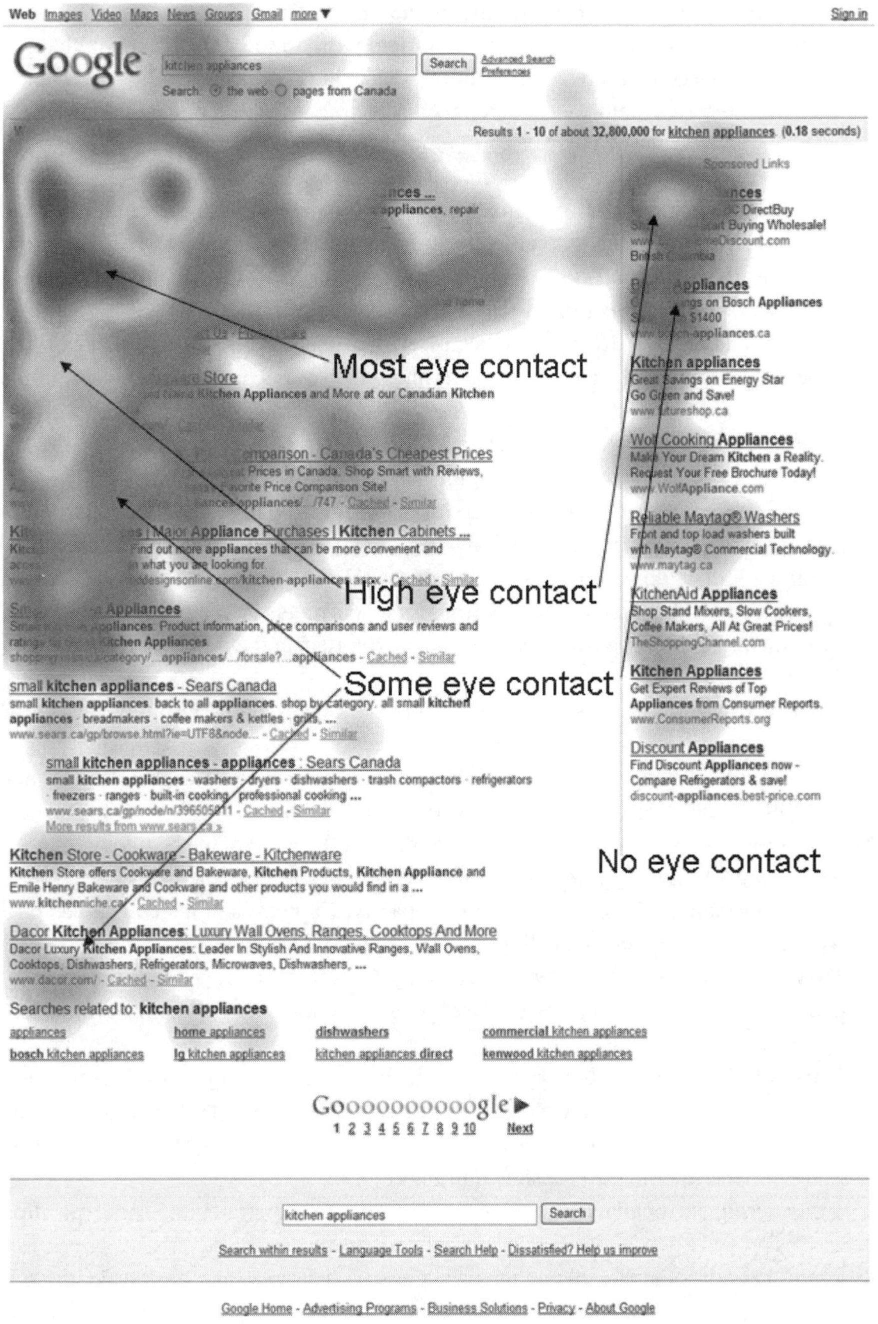

Web Images Video Maps News Groups Gmail more ▼   Sign in

Google   kitchen appliances   Search   Advanced Search
                                                    Preferences
         Search: ⦿ the web ○ pages from Canada

Results 1 - 10 of about 32,800,000 for kitchen appliances. (0.18 seconds)

Sponsored Links

...nces ...
...appliances, repair

...nces
...C DirectBuy
...art Buying Wholesale!
www...neDiscount.com
British Columbia

...Appliances
...gs on Bosch Appliances
...$1400
www.bosch-appliances.ca

Most eye contact

...ware Store
...rame Kitchen Appliances and More at our Canadian Kitchen

Kitchen appliances
Great Savings on Energy Star
Go Green and Save!
www.futureshop.ca

...mparison - Canada's Cheapest Prices
...Prices in Canada. Shop Smart with Reviews,
...orite Price Comparison Site!
...ances/appliances/.../747 - Cached - Similar

Wolf Cooking Appliances
Make Your Dream Kitchen a Reality.
Request Your Free Brochure Today!
www.WolfAppliance.com

Kit...es | Major Appliance Purchases | Kitchen Cabinets ...
Kitch...   Find out more appliances that can be more convenient and
acces...   n what you are looking for
www...   ndesignsonline.com/kitchen-appliances.aspx - Cached - Similar

Reliable Maytag® Washers
Front and top load washers built
with Maytag® Commercial Technology.
www.maytag.ca

High eye contact

Sm...n Appliances
Small...ppliances. Product information, price comparisons and user reviews and
ratin... ...Kitchen Appliances
shopping...category/...appliances/.../forsale?...appliances - Cached - Similar

KitchenAid Appliances
Shop Stand Mixers, Slow Cookers,
Coffee Makers, All At Great Prices!
TheShoppingChannel.com

Some eye contact

small kitchen appliances - Sears Canada
small kitchen appliances. back to all appliances. shop by Category. all small kitchen
appliances - breadmakers - coffee makers & kettles - grills, ...
www.sears.ca/gp/browse.html?ie=UTF8&node... - Cached - Similar

Kitchen Appliances
Get Expert Reviews of Top
Appliances from Consumer Reports.
www.ConsumerReports.org

small kitchen appliances - appliances : Sears Canada
small kitchen appliances - washers - dryers - dishwashers - trash compactors - refrigerators
- freezers - ranges - built-in cooking - professional cooking ...
www.sears.ca/gp/node/n/396505811 - Cached - Similar
More results from www.sears.ca »

Discount Appliances
Find Discount Appliances now -
Compare Refrigerators & save!
discount-appliances.best-price.com

Kitchen Store - Cookware - Bakeware - Kitchenware
Kitchen Store offers Cookware and Bakeware, Kitchen Products, Kitchen Appliance and
Emile Henry Bakeware and Cookware and other products you would find in a ...
www.kitchenniche.ca - Cached - Similar

No eye contact

Dacor Kitchen Appliances: Luxury Wall Ovens, Ranges, Cooktops And More
Dacor Luxury Kitchen Appliances: Leader In Stylish And Innovative Ranges, Wall Ovens,
Cooktops, Dishwashers, Refrigerators, Microwaves, Dishwashers, ...
www.dacor.com/ - Cached - Similar

Searches related to: kitchen appliances

appliances   home appliances   dishwashers   commercial kitchen appliances
bosch kitchen appliances   lg kitchen appliances   kitchen appliances direct   kenwood kitchen appliances

Goooooooooogle ▶
1 2 3 4 5 6 7 8 9 10   Next

kitchen appliances   Search
Search within results - Language Tools - Search Help - Dissatisfied? Help us improve

Google Home - Advertising Programs - Business Solutions - Privacy - About Google

Figure 4.3. Heat map of eye-tracking study for SERP with organic and sponsored results.

Typically, these studies are done only on the first SERP, and not on any of the subsequent ones, so it would be interesting empirical work to see if the behavior changes as the searcher become more engaged in the searching process.

However, the vast majority of searchers never go beyond the first SERP [4, 30].

Rank matters

One of the biggest signals for searchers has nothing to do with the content of the advertisement itself; instead, it has everything to do with where on the SERP listing the advertisement appears.

The aspects of the effect of ad rank on click-through rate (CTR) [31–33, 34, 35] and on conversion rates [36, 37] have been well documented. In fact, the inclination of searchers to trust the rank of advertisements and other results on the SERP is one of the bases for not using click-through data to predict relevance of ads, as there is a positional bias based on the ad's rank (i.e., searchers will click on a result that is near the top).

Why do searchers place so much weight on the rank of the advertisement?

The theoretical founding of this behavior is the position impact on human interaction behaviors. First proposed by Ebbinghaus [38], the serial position effect refers to a position's impact on various human behaviors. Namely, people assign value based on the rank something holds in an ordering. First is always viewed better than second. So, all other aspects being equal, people choose the item at the first rank over the item at the second rank.

There are two subtypes of serial position effects as presented in Ebbinghaus's [38] findings: the primacy effect and the recency effect.

Primacy effect happens due to the limited working memory capacity of human brains [39]. According to Waugh and Norman, initial items in a list tend to attract humans more easily than items positioned at the end, because at the beginning there is far less competition for the limited memory capacity relative to the later stages [39].

Also impacted by the limited memory capacity, Capitani and his colleagues proposed the recency effect, indicating human recall of the most recent items is better given limited short-term memory capacity (as cited in [27]). With the recency effect, humans tend to remember the last few items confronted as compared to those intermediate-ranked items.

This is in line with the U-shaped serial position curve proposed in Ebbinghaus's study. The impact of the primacy or recency effects on sponsored search? Information presented at the two ends demonstrated more obvious recalls than the information presented in the middle [38], as shown in Figure 4.4.

Considering its potential implications on advertising strategies, serial position effect has recently been examined by a number of studies in the advertising area. Prior research on traditional advertising media suggested that on a long time scale, the primacy effect generated a much greater impact on brand advertising campaigns than the recency effect, because the latter can be more easily masked by time [40, 41, 42].

As compared to those aforementioned studies on traditional advertising media, the studies conducted within the online environment become even more complex, considering the additional efforts for recall needed during the system response time.

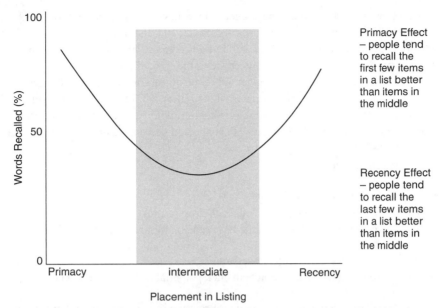

Figure 4.4. Effect of primacy and recency effect on percentage of words recall, resulting in an inverted U-shaped graph.

In their study of serial position effect, for example, Hoque and Lohse [43] examined the serial position effect of an online directory as compared to its impact on the traditional yellow pages. Even with the additional efforts considered, their results still indicate the significant primacy effect on the items recalled. Similar results were also found in other studies indicating the reliable primacy effect on the click-through rate of links placed on a Web page [44, 45]. Extended from their earlier work, Murphy and his colleagues demonstrated both primacy and recency effects on users' online clicking behaviors in their study on Web site click-through rates [46].

What is the overall effect of an advertisement's rank?

Even if signaling theory gets eyes on our ads (which is important), and serial position effect of higher-ranked ads gets us more clicks (important as more traffic means more potential customers), does this all have any effect on conversion rate? Not all ads can be in the top spot, so if an ad is not, we know it will get less traffic. But what is the quality of this traffic?

Let us first go back to the basics. The two foundational factors for determining how many clicks an ad will receive for a given search phrase are

1. *Impressions*
2. *Rank*

An impression is a count of when an ad is served (i.e., displayed) on the SERP. The number of impressions for an ad is based on the number of times the keyphrase(s) linked to this ad is (are) searched and the position of your ad in the rankings for the specified keyphrase(s).

However, even if an ad can be triggered by a keyphrase, the ad will only get an impression if the ad has a position on the SERP that the searcher is viewing. For example, if a search engine displays only five ads on a SERP, ads ranked six or higher will not be displayed unless the searcher views the next SERP.

When we examine CTR for a given ad (controlling for title, description, ad relevance, product, etc.), empirical studies show a drop in CTR by rank. In a series of two articles, Brooks calculated the click potential, defined as the product of relative impressions and relative CTR, to show the expected percentage drop in click volume by rank [31–33].

Brooks reports that:

- *Traffic drops* significantly by rank
- The drop in traffic is *consistent* with each drop in rank
- You can expect a *10x drop* in traffic between ads in rank 1 and rank 10

What is the effect of rank on conversions?
Rank have a significant effect on both click potential and on conversion potential.

- *Click potential*, defined as the product of relative impressions and relative CTR
- *Conversion potential*, defined as the product of conversion rate and click potential

Again, drawing primarily on Brooks, the average conversion rate falls about 20–30 percent between the rank 1 and rank 10 [31–33]. This drop is noticeable, but not dramatically above noise level.

However, the overall impact on conversion potential, defined as the product of conversion rate and click potential, is a 90 percent decrease. This very dramatic decrease is driven by the significant decrease in click potential rather than big differences in conversion rates by rank of the ads.

Brooks provides working factors for calculating changes in clicks by ranks, shown in Table 4.1 [31–33].

Expected Change in Clicks = Relative Impression * Relative CTR
Equation 4.2. Formula for calculating the expected change in conversion resulting from a change in rank.

For example, using the formula in Equation 4.2 and using rank 1 as the baseline, the relative impression is 100 percent and the relative CTR is 100 percent. If this same ad is in rank 2, let us say the data shows that it gets 77 percent of the impressions it did at rank 1 (this is relative impressions) and it gets 77 percent of the CTR it did at rank 1 (this is relative CTR), so the click potential is 60 percent.

Table 4.2 shows the changes in click potential by rank based on data from Brooks [31]. Note that this was based on data from a particular search engine and set of sponsored-search efforts, so click potential for a given sponsored-search effort may vary. However, it provides a trend to leverage against when implementing the technique for your sponsored-search efforts.

Table 4.1. *Factors for changes in clicks by advertisement rank on the SERP*

Factor affecting clicks	Description
Impressions	An impression is counted when your ad is served as part of the search engine results. The number of impressions you get is based on the number of times the keyword you are bidding on is searched and the position of your ad in the rankings for that keyword.
Click-through rate (CTR)	CTR is the metric used to determine what percentage of users click on a given listing. CTR is calculated as clicks divided by impressions. A number of factors influence CTR in addition to rank. These include title, description, ad relevance, and industry. All of these variables should be considered when you work to improve your CTR, even though the drop in CTR by rank was observed consistently in the data for this research, independent of these factors.

Table 4.2. *Changes in click potential by ad rank*

Rank	Relative impressions (%)	Relative CTR (%)	Click potential (%)
1	100.0	100.0	100.0
2	77.2	77.4	59.8
3	71.3	66.6	47.5
4	67.9	57.4	39.0
5	65.8	52.9	34.8
6	62.3	50.2	31.3
7	60.6	39.7	24.0
8	58.3	34.3	20.0
9	58.6	26.0	15.3
10	52.6	26.3	13.9

Leveraging Brooks' work, we can calculate the expected change in conversions from a given rank to rank any other rank: Use the historical data for conversions of an ad in rank A and an ad in rank B, and then multiply it by the following equation:

Expected Change in Conversions = Conversion Potential B / Conversion Potential A

Equation 4.3. Formula for calculating the expected change in conversion resulting from a change in rank.

For example, by moving from rank 2 to rank 4 using the data provided, you can expect the total number of conversions to fall by 51.7 percent (28.2 percent/54.5 percent). The same formula works to calculate the expected change in expected clicks.

Table 4.3 shows the changes in conversion potential by rank based on data from Brooks [32], with the change in conversion potential added. Note that this was based on data from a particular search engine and set of sponsored-search efforts, so click potential for a given sponsored-search effort may vary.

Table 4.3. *Changes in conversion potential by ad rank*

Rank	Click potential (%)	Conversion rate (%)	Conversion potential (%)	Change in conversion potential (%)
1	100.0	100.0	100.0	–
2	59.8	91.1	54.5	−46
3	47.5	75.1	35.7	−34
4	39.0	72.4	28.2	−21
5	34.8	69.3	24.1	−15
6	31.3	71.9	22.5	−7
7	24.0	67.6	16.2	−28
8	20.0	64.9	13.0	−20
9	15.3	72.3	11.1	−15
10	13.9	87.7	12.2	10

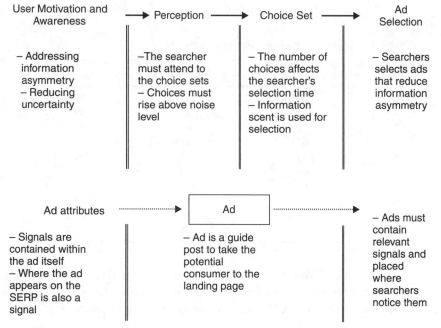

Figure 4.5. Interactive process of searcher/potential customer and advertisement.

Note the slight rise in conversion potential at position 10, due primarily from an increase in the conversion rate in the data. Note in Table 4.3, that there is a double-digit drop in conversion potential for a one position drop in rank for nearly all positions.

Putting this all together to explain searcher interactions with advertisements
So, what is the entire process chain of a searcher interacting with a set of advertisements on a SERP? Figure 4.5 illustrates the process.

As you can see in Figure 4.5, the searcher has some motivation concerning a searching need and therefore is aware of this need. The searchers starts to attend to the environment in relation to this awareness. The perception aspects of the search are alerts that happen after the searcher enters the query. The choice set is the set of results displayed to the searcher in response to the searcher's query. As the searcher begins to scan the advertisement, the searcher is alerted to signals for which ads are relevant [47] and which ones, in chunks, can be discarded. Based on some cognitive analysis, the searcher makes a selection of which ad to click on. At this point, the searcher transitions from the role of searcher to the role of potential customer, given that the ad is a gateway to a location where he or she can access the product or service. The ad, as a gateway, contains certain attributes that the searcher recognizes as signals, including the rank of the ad itself.

Foundational Takeaways

- The basis of advertisement signaling theory, where you want the ad to contain relevant signals or clues for the searcher. Signals are indicators to the searcher that the advertisement is not noise.
- The typical searcher will not expend a lot of energy searching for information, will access the information that is easiest to get, and will take action to limit the number of choices. This is noted in the portion of the SERP that the searcher will examine and in the number of advertisements that the searcher will click on.
- Based on serial positioning theory, rank is a large determinant of the number of clicks that an advertisement will receive, regardless of the signals contained within the ad. Although conversion rates seem to hold pretty steady regardless of rank, the conversion potential drops significantly with each drop in rank down the listing.

Relating Theory to Practice

Your advertisements are signals or clues for the searcher who you want to become a potential customer. This is why we often refer to advertisements as guideposts for searchers, who may be going through different information-processing states and therefore attending to different signals.

- Given your product or service, what are different versions of an ad that you can write that address different information-processing aspects? What keyphrases would you select based on your potential customers? What signals are your advertisements providing?
- You are not the only advertiser bidding on these keyphrases. Using the theory of just-notable differences, what do you have to do to your ads to make them notably different from others?
- Based on data from one of your campaigns, model your search campaigns based on cost, clicks, conversions, and rank. Then, using the conversion potential formula and the data from one of your sponsored-search efforts, calculate the

difference in both cost and in gross revenue if each advertisement in the set of ads were moved up in rank and down in rank. Does this change your bidding strategy?

- Referring to the process of sponsored-search figure, what searcher motivations, signals and ad attributes are relevant for your market?

Conclusion

Our theoretical basis for understanding advertisements in sponsored search is signaling theory and its related information-seeking companion, information foraging theory. Our ads are external stimuli that the searcher needs to pick up as a signal and hopefully use to take action.

There are several principles that can guide us at the individual level. Namely these are that searchers will seek to expend the least amount of effort; that they will access the information that is easiest to obtain, all else being equal; and that the more choices a searcher has, the longer they will take and the more they will chunk information.

What does this mean to the advertiser? Certainly, the attributes of the ad must be novel and relevant. Novel means being different from other ads while still being relevant enough to be a signal for the searcher. Also, rank of the ad is important. It is generally best to be first or last.

It is the advertisements that affect the transition from searcher to potential customer. With transition, the perspective of these people changes, and therefore our models of the people need to transition also.

With our basis of general human information behavior for keyphrases and advertisements, we now explore this person called the consumer who is actually engaging with these keyphrases and advertisements in sponsored search.

What is the process of consumers as they seek to determine whether or not to purchase our product or service? This is what we discuss in the next chapter.

References

[1]   DDB. (unk). Bill Bernbach said …. Retrieved November 3, 2010, from http://www.ddb.com/pdf/bernbach.pdf
[2]   Ogilvy, D. 1983. *Ogilvy on Advertising*. Toronto: John Wiley and Sons.
[3]   Mishra, B. K. 2008. *Psychology: A Study of Human Behaviour*. New Delhi: PHI.
[4]   Jansen, B. J. and Spink, A. 2004. "An Analysis of Documents Viewing Patterns of Web Search Engine Users." In *Web Mining: Applications and Techniques*, A. Scime, Ed., pp. 339–354.
[5]   Gregg, D. G. and Walczak, S. 2010. "The Relationship between Website Quality, Trust and Price Premiums at Online Auctions." *Electronic Commerce Research*, vol. 10(1), pp. 1–25.
[6]   Donath, J. forthcoming "Signals, Truth and Design," Preprint retrieved April 4 2011, at http://smg.media.mit.edu/people/judith/signalsTruthDesign.html
[7]   Donath, J. 2008. "Signals in Social Supernets," *Journal of Computer-Mediated Communication*, vol. 13(1), pp. 231–251.
[8]   Walther, J. B. 1992. "Interpersonal Effects in Computer-Mediated Interaction: A Relational Perspective." *Communication Research*, vol. 19(1), 51–90.
[9]   Walther, J. B. and Parks, M. R. 2002. "Cues Filtered Out, Cues Filtered In." In *Handbook of Interpersonal Communication*, Ed. Knapp, M. L. and Daly, J. A. pp. 529–563.

[10] Harley, T. A. 1995. *The Psychology of Language: From Data to Theory*. East Susex: Erlbaum.

[11] Pirolli, P. 2007. *Information Foraging Theory: Adaptive Interaction with Information*. Oxford: Oxford University Press.

[12] Caples J. (Revised by Fred E. Hahn). 1997. *Tested Advertising Methods*, 5 ed. Upper Saddle River, NJ: Prentice Hall.

[13] Simon, H. A. 1971. "Designing Organizations for an Information-Rich World." In *Computers, Communication, and the Public Interest*, M. Greenberger, Ed. Baltimore, MD: The Johns Hopkins Press, pp. 37–72.

[14] Schwab, V. O. 1962. *How to Write a Good Advertisement: A Short Course in Copywriting*. Chatsworth, CA: Wilshire.

[15] Toffler, A. 1970. *Future Shock*. New York: Random House.

[16] Simon, H. 1981. *The Sciences of the Artificial*, 2d ed. Cambridge, MA: MIT Press.

[17] Ghose, A. and Yang, S. 2008. "Analyzing Search Engine Advertising: Firm Behavior and Cross-Selling in Electronic Markets." In *17th World Wide Web Conference* Beijing, China, pp. 219–225.

[18] Ghose, A. and Yang, S. 2008. "An Empirical Analysis of Sponsored Search Performance in Search Engine Advertising." In *First ACM International Conference on Web Search and Data Mining (WSDM 2008)*, Palo Alto, California, pp. 241–250.

[19] Jansen, B. J., Brown, A., and Resnick, M. 2007. "Factors Relating to the Decision to Click-on a Sponsored Link." *Decision Support Systems*, vol. 44(1), pp. 46–59.

[20] Jansen, B. J. and Resnick, M. 2006. "An Examination of Searchers' Perceptions of Non-Sponsored and Sponsored Links during Ecommerce Web Searching." *Journal of the American Society for Information Science and Technology*, vol. 57(14), pp. 1949–1961.

[21] Zipf, G. K. 1949. *Human Behavior and the Principle of Least Effort*. Cambridge, MA: Addison-Wesley Press.

[22] Berryman, J. M. 2008. "Judgements during Information Seeking: A Naturalistic Approach to Understanding the Assessment of Enough Information." *Journal of Information Science*, vol. 34(2), pp. 196–206.

[23] Summit, R. K. 1993. "The Year 2000: Dreams and Nightmares." *Searcher*, vol. 1, pp. 16–17.

[24] Pemberton, J. M. 1989. "Telecommunication: Technology and Devices." *Records Management Quarterly*, vol. 23, pp. 46–48.

[25] Bierbaum, E. G. 1990. "A Paradigm for the '90s: In Research and Practice, Library and Information Science Needs a Unifying Principle; "Least Effort" Is One Scholar's Suggestion." *American Libraries*, vol. 21, pp. 18–19.

[26] Wilson, T. D. 2008. "The Information User: Past, Present and Future." *Journal of Information Science*, vol. 34(4), pp. 457–464.

[27] Zheng, R. and Zhou, B. 2006. "Recency Effect on Problem Solving in Interactive Multimedia Learning." *Educational Technology and Society*, vol. 9(2), pp. 107–118.

[28] Hotchkiss, G. 2005. Enquiro Eye Tracking Report I: Google. Retrieved July 2005, from http://www.enquiro.com/research.asp

[29] Hotchkiss, G. 2006. "Enquiro Eye Tracking Report II: Google, MSN and Yahoo! Compared." vol. 2006: Enquiro Search Solutions Inc.

[30] Jansen, B. J. and Spink, A. 2003. "An Analysis of Web Information Seeking and Use: Documents Retrieved Versus Documents Viewed." In *4th International Conference on Internet Computing*, Las Vegas, Nevada, pp. 65–69.

[31] Brooks, N. 2004. The Atlas Rank Report I: How Search Engine Rank Impacts Traffic (July). Retrieved August 1, 2004, from http://www.atlasdmt.com/media/pdfs/insights/RankReport.pdf

[32] Brooks, N. 2004. The Atlas Rank Report II: How Search Engine Rank Impacts Conversions (October). Retrieved January 15, 2005, from http://www.atlasonepoint.com/pdf/AtlasRankReportPart2.pdf

[33] Brooks, N. 2006. "Repeat Search Behavior: Implications for Advertisers." *Bulletin of the American Society for Information Science and Technology*, vol. 32(2), pp. 16–17.

[34] Hofacker, C. F. and Murphy, J. 2009. "Consumer Web Page Search, Clicking Behavior and Reaction Time." *Direct Marketing: An International Journal*, vol. 3(2), pp. 88–96.

[35] Pan, B., Hembrooke, H., Joachims, T., Lorigo, L., Gay, G., and Granka, L. 2007. "In Google We Trust: Users' Decisions on Rank, Position, and Relevance." *Journal of Computer-Mediated Communication*, vol. 12(3), Article 3. http://jcmc.indiana.edu/vol12/issue3/pan.html

[36] Varian, H. 2009. "Conversion Rates Don't Vary Much with Ad Position." *Google*, vol. 2010.

[37] Wagner, M. V. 2010. "PPC Mad Scientists Prove Google Right … and Wrong." In *Paid Search*, vol. 2010: Search Engine Land.

[38] Ebbinghaus, H. 1885. *Memory: A Contribution to Experimental Psychology*. New York: Dover.

[39] Waugh, N. and Norman, D. A. 1965. "Primary Memory." *Psychological Review*, vol. 72(2), pp. 89–104.

[40] Newell, S. J. and Wu, B. 2003. "Evaluating the Significance of Placement on Recall of Advertisements during the Super Bowl." *Journal of Current Issues and Research in Advertising*, vol. 25(2), pp. 57–68.

[41] Pieters, R. and Bijmolt, T. 1997. "Consumer Memory for Television Advertising: A Field Study of Duration, Serial Position, and Competition Effects," *Journal of Consumer Research*, vol. 23(4), pp. 263–277.

[42] Terry, S. W. 2005. "Serial Position Effects in Recall of Television Commercials." *Journal of General Psychology*, vol. 132(2), pp. 151–163.

[43] Hoque, A. Y. and Lohse, G. L. 1999. "An Information Search Cost Perspective for Designing Interfaces for Electronic Commerce." *Journal of Marketing Research*, vol. 36(3), pp. 387–394.

[44] Ansari, A. and Mela, C. F. 2003 "E-customization." *Journal of Marketing Research*, vol. 40(2), pp. 131–145.

[45] Drèze, X. and Zufryden, F. 2004. "The Measurement of Online Visibility and Its Impact on Internet Traffic." *Journal of Interactive Marketing*, vol. 18(1), pp. 20–37.

[46] Murphy, J., Hofacker, C., and Mizerski, R. 2006. "Primacy and Recency Effects on Clicking Behavior." *Journal of Computer-Mediated Communication*, vol. 11(2), pp. 522–535.

[47] Brinker, S. 2010. The READY Conversion Optimization Framework. (July 16). Retrieved January 26, 2011, from http://searchengineland.com/the-ready-conversion-optimization-framework-43814

Word cloud generated by Wordle

5

Understanding Consumer Behavior for Sponsored Search

Can advertising foist an inferior product on the consumer? Bitter experience has
taught me that it cannot. On those rare occasions when I have advertised products
which consumer tests have found inferior to other products in the same
field, the results have been disastrous.

David Ogilvy,
Confessions of an Advertising Man [1, p. 156] and *Ogilvy on Advertising* [2].
Credited with revolutionizing modern advertising.

Advertising is perceived by some as a manipulative form of communication. However, successful practitioners in the advertising field have commented that advertising can be amazingly unsuccessful if the product does not resonate with the customer, which the quote from Ogilvy illustrates [1].

Our framing business Web site is up and running and the start of a sponsored-search effort is underway as part of our overall advertising endeavors to attract customers.

What types of customers are most likely to be interested in getting a picture framed? What is their motivation for visiting the Web site of a framing shop? Are they looking to get a picture framed for themselves? Or a picture framed for their mothers? Their spouses? Their friends? Each of these different motivations will influence a customer's behavior, mood, and expectation out of the experience and exchange. These different expectations will influence how we advertise to the customer. The moods will affect what advertisement copy works on them.

Of course, there are the more practical questions of how the potential customer finds the Web site and what strategy the customer employs for both query formulation and selection of a navigation strategy. Does the consumer start at a general-purpose search engine, a social networking site, a niche search engine, or one of several other possibilities? What terms does the searcher select for the query? What price does this potential customer have in mind?

Naturally, these questions have some relationship to our understanding of the linkage between keyphrases, query terms, and the evaluation of individual advertisements. However, you must also focus on the searcher, specifically in regards to consumer strategy and tactics. The consumer strategies and tactics are based on human information behavior and processing, which we have discussed in earlier chapters on keywords (Chapter 3) and advertisements (Chapter 4).

We are now more narrowly focused on the consumer domain, as the domain context will directly influence the potential consumer's behavior.

Perhaps the best way to view the process is by distinguishing between searcher and consumer. Keywords and ads are focused on the person as a searcher. We hope, as the business owner and advertiser, that the person makes the transition at some point from a searcher to a potential consumer. As an advertiser, you are then interested in knowing what, when, how, why, and where people buy or do not buy products and services, and how they make this decision [3].

Consumer behavior is an economic activity. It is focused on contextual, environmental, and situational aspects in which the economic process happens. It is also concerned with decision making and the assumption that this decision making happens under varying conditions of uncertainty.

Note of caution here. Naturally, consumer behavior has many elements beside online consumer behavior; however, for the purposes of our investigations of sponsored search, we confine ourselves to online behaviors, specifically on the Web and Internet. So, wherever you see consumer behavior or any of its subcomponents in this book, mentally insert *online* in front of it.

We will investigate consumer behavior within the confines of sponsored search from two subcomponents, specifically:

- *Consumer searching behavior*: the use of Web or Internet technologies to locate information concerning commercial products or services.
- *Consumer purchasing behavior*: the process that leads to a purchase, or not purchase, of a commercial product or service.

This chapter presents the key underpinnings of consumer searching and consumer purchasing behavior for sponsored search, which are two related and intertwined concepts. We focus first on the consumer searching behavior and then move to the consumer purchasing behavior, specifically by focusing on the buying funnel (as an application of consumer searching behavior) and consumer decision making (as an application of consumer purchasing behavior). We then tie these two concepts together within the overall framework of a communication process that occurs between the searcher/consumer and the advertiser.

Communication theory more adequately explains the entire advertiser-consumer process, but the buying funnel and consumer decision-making components allow us to link the theoretical foundations in communication to what we see day to day in our sponsored-search efforts. Therefore, although flawed and limited, the buying funnel and consumer decision making do add value for day-to-day implementation.

Potpourri: At the heart of consumer searching and decision making is information.

Information has economic value as it permits consumers to make choices that have higher expected payoffs or higher expected utility than they would obtain from choices made in the absence of information.

However, what is information?

The answer to this question is a matter of considerable academic debate. However, information has some interesting qualities that we can define, and these qualities affect sponsored search advertising.

- Information is itself *both a product and a service*. It exists in some physical form, and it exists in the form of the value it provides to customers.
- Consuming information *does not use it up* or change it. So, information has the product attribute of permanence.
- Information is also nonrivalrous, meaning that consuming information *does not exclude someone else from also consuming* it.
- Information can become out of date, so it also has the attribute of obsolescence.
- Information has *near zero marginal cost*, meaning that once the first copy is in existence, making other copies is cheap.
- Information is *nonexclusive*, meaning that if it is known, it is difficult to exclude others from its use.

With these special attributes, information complicates many standard economic theories that apply to other products [4].

The attributes of information also make it a challenging product/service for advertisers to utilize.

We begin with consumer searching on the Internet.

Consumer Searching Behavior

Although there is a large body of research that examines information searching and Web searching in general, we take a more economic, information science view of search instead. This allows us to focus specifically on the searching behavior as that of eventual consumers.

From this perspective, we are interested in the searcher's optimizing strategies when faced with a range of options. Some factors that influence this optimization are:

- *Quality* of the choices in the set of options
- *Cost* of not making a choice (i.e., cost of delay)
- *Environmental factors* such as the rate a good is consumed, price of the product, and wealth of the consumer.

In the area of sponsored search, we are interested in a consumer's search strategy while gathering information concerning a purchase for a product/service to address a need, want, or desire. By strategy, we mean this in the classic game theory sense of a plan of action or series of planned behaviors for some given situation that might arise. You will see game theory once again in Chapter 8 on auctions.

Now, the idea that customers have a search strategy is certainly an assumption. It is possible that sometimes customers may just process information unconsciously.

This is especially apparent when task involvement is quite low or when customers are just information browsing instead of having a specific goal. These customers may not have a clear search strategy at all. In these cases, the consumers may be more likely to adopt heuristic information processing rather than systematic information processing that we normally associate with a strategy.

As such, a consumer search strategy determines that consumer's searching behaviors. As an example, a simple search strategy may be to look for the lowest-priced product down to some amount, then look for the best-quality product in this price range.

Consumer searching online has certainly altered the role of advertising. For many decades, the advertising model was one of mass media used to market to a mass audience. With limited information channels (i.e., information scarcity) for the consumers, this mass model was acceptable as a means of getting commercial information to people.

However, with increased channels for information dissemination and the quantity of information (i.e., information abundance), this mass media business model is not as effective as before, given the new online context. There are many information choices for consumers across many mediums. The individual consumer has access to a much more tailored information environment. Also, with Internet and Web information channels, consumers are in greater control of what advertising information they view, rather than passively accepting whatever is broadcast over some mass medium.

It would be a mistake, however, for advertisers to dismiss mass media approaches as immaterial. Rarely has one communication medium totally replaced another. Instead, the communication media get repurposed to address different needs. For example, mass media advertising can be good at generating demand, which sponsored search is not so effective at achieving.

From the perspective of sponsored search and delivering tailored content, the mass media mode of advertising is not effective. On the Internet, consumers can individually search for information concerning the products and services that they desire to purchase. One can view the process from the perspective of the Internet being a *consumer-driven* information environment. In other words, the potential consumer as a searcher *can* and *must* locate the information among several choices or locations.

This aspect of consumer search, with the consumer both in charge and responsible for information gathering, is a fundamental aspect of sponsored search.

However, what specifically is consumer search (broadly, not just online)?

There are two basic dimensions of consumer information search modes: internal and external [5].

- *Internal information search*: The internal information search construct represents the retrieval of knowledge from memory.
- *External information search*: The external information search construct represents the motivated acquisition of information from the environment.

Certainly, there is interplay between these two, as internal information (a.k.a., tacit knowledge) interacts with information gathered from external searching. However, for our focus on sponsored search, we are interested in the external information searching, specifically on the Internet. External search precedes many consumer decisions [6].

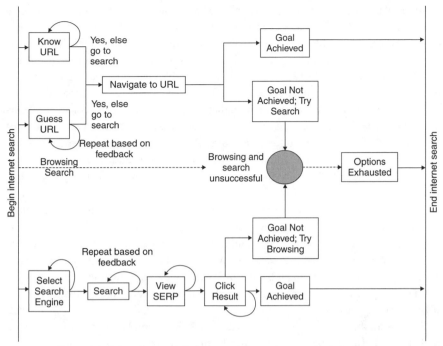

Figure 5.1. Flow diagram of consumer information search on the Internet.

A conceptualization of a consumer search on the Internet is shown in Figure 5.1.

Referring to Figure 5.1, there are a series of parallel but also sequential steps that a consumer engages in when searching on the Internet. When searching for information on the Internet, consumers can (and are required to) manage their strategy and tactics. This includes searching, direct navigation, and browsing on the Internet.

From a consumer behavior viewpoint, the execution of a search activity requires management of the search, performance of the navigational tasks of visiting Web sites, and assimilating collected information. The information-seeking consumer's tasks include [7]:

- *Destination* selection (i.e., information source selection)
- *Movement* to the desired destination (i.e., navigating to the information source, which includes reviewing results snippets)
- *Analysis* of the information available there in the light of the previous information available.

Destination selection and movement to the desired location arc tasks that are inherent to active information search by a task-oriented consumer in any environment, especially one within the sponsored-search domain. Analysis is usually an internal process unique to the individual consumer.

Focusing on sponsored search, at each interaction in the search process, the consumer is in a sequential process of selecting choices from a set of available information choices. The set of choices could be prices in different stores for a given good, the qualities of products or services, a collection of Web sites, or results on a search engine results page (SERP). This leads one to theoretically modeling consumer search as a process where the searcher is in a state of deciding to seek out additional information or not to seek additional information, and hence stop searching. This searcher decision process is a function of the expected benefit of any additional information [8], with the benefit of additional information being measured as a reduction in uncertainty.

The information that the consumer gathers becomes part of the consumer's current state of the decision process and, at each stage of the information-searching process, the need for additional information is reviewed by the searcher, even if at some superficial level. If the search process is abandoned or suspended, then searching is halted. If the searcher deems further information is necessary, then another search is conducted.

Therefore, the consumer search is a process in which the consumer's decision to seek additional information is a function of the expected benefit of that added information [8]. As the consumer obtains more information at each stage of the search process, the expected benefit of seeking new information generally decreases, resulting in a lower probability that the consumer will solicit additional information.

In other words, the longer a person searches, the likelihood that they will continue searching decreases.

To capture this process, as we discussed in Chapter 3 on keywords, we model the probability that individual i searches an xth time as a decrement of the probability of searching the $x_i -1st$ time [8, 15]. This the foundational assumption for our searching equation presented in the keyword chapter, based on the work of Johnson and colleagues [9]. Specifically, one can model consumer searching as the probability that individual i searches an xth time (or submits an addition query xth) as a decrement of the probability of searching $(x_i -1)st$ time [9]:

$$\Pr[X_i = x_i] = \frac{(x_i - 1)\theta_i}{x_i} \Pr[X_i = x_i - 1],$$

$$x_i = 2, 3, \ldots,$$

Equation 5.1. Probability model on consumer search.

The model presented in Equation 5.1 is a mathematical representation of the consumer search process described earlier.

The model is recursive (at any point in the process, it is just composed of a set of individual searches). We can present this recursive model as a logarithmic distribution [9], which has some advantages for presentation. A logarithmic distribution presents segments between any two points in equal percentage rather than the absolute distance. In other words, the distance from 1 to 10 is the same as the distance from 10 to 100 on a logarithmic chart, whereas the latter is ten times as long on a linear chart.

The revised model is presented in Equation 5.2.

$$\Pr[X_i = x_i] = \frac{a_i \theta_i^{x_i}}{x_i}, \qquad x_i = 1, 2, \ldots,$$

Equation 5.2. Logarithmic probability model on consumer search.

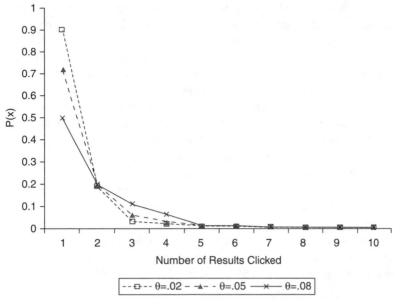

Figure 5.2. Relationship of consumer clicks by rank of ad.

To illustrate the model of consumer search (and how this model is valuable at the aggregate level), Figure 5.2 plots the shape of the probability distribution for visitations of ads by rank. We see that the distribution of clicks by rank follows a fairly standard power law distribution.

What does this mean?

Searchers as potential consumers typically do not spend a lot of time searching and gathering information about their decisions. (Note: There are some exceptions.) We have already seen that consumers do not craft long queries, do not submit a lot of queries, and now we see that they do not click on a lot of results, either organic or sponsored.

Although economic theory dictates that they should search a lot, there are constructs, such as the principle of least effort [10], that explain why consumers do not do so.

Potpourri: One product attribute that consumers search for is price, and price is tied directly to demand.

In fact, the fundamental theorem of demand states that the rate of consumption falls as the price of the good rises.

The cause of this reduced demand (in general inversely correlated with price) is the outcome of the *substitution effect*. As prices rise, consumers will find substitutes for higher-priced goods and services, choosing less costly alternatives.

Conversely, there is a context in which the *substitution effect* does not hold. As the wealth of the individual rises, demand increases, shifting the demand curve higher at all rates of consumption.

This is called the *income effect*. As wealth rises, consumers will move away from less costly, perhaps inferior, goods and services, choosing higher-priced alternatives for a variety of perceived benefits, such as quality or status.

Concerning their perceived lack of searching, consumers have a trade-off between the cost of search, usually measured by time, and the benefit of that search [9]. A strict consumer search model assumes that consumers are likely to search for information as long as they believe that the benefits of acquiring information outweigh the cost of information search as indicated in the economics of information theory [11].

However, a more workable consumer search model should assume that consumers are likely to search for information until they believe they have a reasonable solution, regardless of the cost-benefit ratio. This behavior, again, illustrates the concept of satisficing [12, 13] and the principle of least effort [14].

Additionally, the searcher may actually be doing more searching then it first appears from just looking at their online activities.

Information gathering is a continuous process, even when the purchase is not foreseen or when there are no active actions on the part of the consumer. Therefore, when a purchase decision is to be made, relatively little explicit search may be required [15]. This aspect is known as prepurchase search or ongoing search. By ignoring ongoing search, we can understate the amount of information consumers have at their disposal when making a purchase. [15].

Search determinants, motives, and outcomes

One manner of explaining how much time and effort a consumer actual spends on gathering information for purchase is a factor of determinants, motives, and outcomes [15] of the purchase.

Search determinants. Search determinants are factors that cause or influence the extent of the consumer search.

- In a *prepurchase context*, search determinants include the immediate level of consumer involvement, the market environment, situational factors, and product familiarity.
- For *ongoing consumer search*, search determinants include enduring involvement (i.e., a continuing interest or enthusiasm rather than the temporary product interest resulting from purchase requirements). It also includes market factors such as the availability of product information and time or other situational constraints [15].

Search motives. Search motives are the consumer's underlying reason for actually searching for product information.

- The consumer's primary motive for prepurchase search is typically to *enhance the quality of the purchase* outcome.
- Ongoing consumer search may involve two basic motives.

  - First, the consumer may be motivated to *acquire a reserve of commercial information* that might be potentially useful in the future, for self or others.
  - Second, the consumer may be *motivated by pleasure or recreation*. In these incidents, the consumer is engaging in an ongoing search for intrinsic satisfactions (i.e., search as recreation) [15].

Table 5.1. *Relationship of determinants, motives, and outcome attributes*

Search level (time and effort)	Search determinants	Search motives	Search outcomes
High levels of time and effort	Uncertainty and risk perceptions	Primary motive for prepurchase search is to enhance the quality of the purchase outcome	Better choice decisions, increased product and market expertise, and heightened satisfaction with a purchasing job well done
High levels of time and effort	Market environment, situational factors, and product familiarity	Acquire a bank of product information potentially useful in the future	Increased efficiencies of future purchasing
Low levels of time and effort	Market factors such as the availability of product information and time	Cognitive or informational stimulation, while others seek sensory stimulation in the consumption experience	Increased personal influence and social reputation
Low levels of time and involvement	Buyer's short-term involvement	Have fun or to experience positive affect	Leads to impulse buying

Outcomes of search. Search outcomes are the results of the consumer search process.

- For both prepurchase and ongoing search, outcomes include *better decisions*, increased product and market expertise, and heightened satisfaction with a purchasing job well done [15].
- Outcomes can also be the *ability to share* this product information with others, being recognized for expertise in an area.

Table 5.1 summarizes consumer search determinants, motives, and outcomes.

The buying funnel and consumer decision-making models

Okay, consumers search but they typically do not spent a lot of time doing it. How can we operationalize this to some extent for sponsored search, specifically to assist in keyword selection and advertisement creation?

The Buying Funnel. A common view of consumer searching at the individual level is that of the buying funnel, which is a staged process that a consumer engages in to purchase a product or service [16, 17]. The funnel analogy suggests that consumers systematically narrow the initial-consideration set as they weigh options, make decisions, or buy products.

The buying funnel is the consumer parallel to the organization's sales funnel. The sales funnel frames the customer buying process from the producer's point of view with the aim of funneling the potential customers to a successful transaction [18].

The buying funnel is historically rooted in the writings of E. St. Elmo Lewis, a late-1800s American advertising and sales pioneer. In a material for an advertising course [19], Lewis developed the buying funnel (a.k.a., the AIDA model) as a sales tool based on his personal observations of empirical customer behaviors in the life insurance sales area.

His idea of the buying funnel was not necessarily an explanation of the consumer buying process but rather a funnel model to explain the mechanisms of personal selling.

Note the phrase "personal selling."

In the buying-funnel model, Lewis stated that successful salespeople followed a hierarchical, layered process using the four cognitive phases that buyers follow when accepting a new idea or purchasing a new product. Lewis held that sales personnel should aim for different sales objectives for their prospects and their customers at each level of the buying funnel.

Since its inception – the model was already in wide use by 1925 [19] – the buying funnel, more widely known in scholarly literature as the AIDA model, has served as a framework to study how advertising affects consumers. Additionally, it was the basis for numerous motivation-driven consumer behavior research models. As such, the buying funnel is used in search engine marketing campaigns for conceptually understanding customer behavior.

Foundationally, the buying funnel rests on human information-processing theory, which is at the core of most consumer behavior models [20]. Information-processing theory postulates that consumer decision making involves a five-stage process: (1) problem recognition, (2) information search, (3) alternative evaluation and selection, (4) outlet selection and purchase, and (5) postpurchase processes [21, 22].

Specifically, in practice, the buying funnel is a staged process for describing the way consumers make their buying decisions, from becoming aware of the existence of a need all the way to the final purchase of a product or service that addresses this need or desire. Although there are several variations depending on the source, the buying-funnel model is typically depicted as stages, with each stage relating to the cognitive phase that the consumer is in.

Although there are various labels for each stage, one common labeling system is *Awareness*, *Research*, *Decision*, and *Purchase* (see Figure 5.3), which is the labeling scheme that we use here.

- The first stage is *Awareness*, when a customer realizes that there is a product that can solve his/her problem or need.
- After a consumer realizes that a product can address a problem, he or she finds a specific product line and becomes more knowledgeable about this type of product or service. This stage is called *Research*.
- The third stage is *Decision*, when a consumer is deciding between different brands of a specific product by forming choice set.

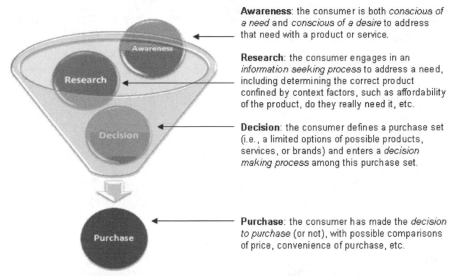

Awareness: the consumer is both *conscious of a need* and *conscious of a desire* to address that need with a product or service.

Research: the consumer engages in an *information seeking process* to address a need, including determining the correct product confined by context factors, such as affordability of the product, do they really need it, etc.

Decision: the consumer defines a purchase set (i.e., a limited options of possible products, services, or brands) and enters a *decision making process* among this purchase set.

Purchase: the consumer has made the *decision to purchase* (or not), with possible comparisons of price, convenience of purchase, etc.

Figure 5.3. The four-stage buying funnel with definitions of each stage.

- The final stage of the buying funnel is *Purchase*. This stage is when a consumer knows what specific product and brand they intend to purchase, and they are typically comparing price, convenience to order, or similar aspects of purchase before buying.

The gist of the buying funnel is that it models how advertisers can reach consumers. This model states that consumers pass through the four cognitive stages as they decide what product or service to purchase.

The buying funnel fits nicely with concepts of decision making [23]. In consumer decision making, the decision maker goes through stages, including intelligence and choice. *Awareness* aligns well with *intelligence*. *Research* and *decision* line up well with *design*, and *purchase* aligns well with *choice*. So, there is psychological foundational support for the buying funnel.

Although not without dissent [24], this model is widely cited and referred to in the practitioner press [c.f., 25, 26, 27] and in marketing literature [c.f., 28, 29, 30]. For example, Nimitz [31] states that the buying funnel is crucial to better understand the customer, giving the advertiser better chances of selling a product or service. Laycock [32] stresses that the Internet makes it so easy for a consumer to research a product before actually making a purchase that the buying funnel is critical to understanding why some keywords perform well and others do not.

So, viewing the buying funnel as a query classification scheme, every keyphrase will fall into one stage of the buying funnel.

Unfortunately, the buying funnel has not stood up to empirical testing, although it may be a worthwhile paradigm for classifying aspects of individual consumer searching behavior at the query level based on empirical searching decisions [9].

Potpourri: There are many well-known concepts that have no basis in either empirical or theoretical research.

For example, the buying funnel was based on St. Lewis's perceptions of financial advertising for commercial and savings banks. There is little rigorous support for the concept; however, it still provides a useful framework to view a complex process.

Maslow's hierarchy of needs is another concept without basis from the psychology domain.[1]

The same goes for Bloom's Taxonomy in the area of learning.[2]

The Three Laws of Robotics is a pure science fiction creation from Isaac Asimov.[3]

In the area of Web searching, there is no theoretical grounding for the informational-navigational-transactional categories [33]. In each of these areas, however, the paradigms caught on and shaped future thought, practice, and research.

[1] http://en.wikipedia.org/wiki/Maslow's_hierarchy_of_needs
[2] http://en.wikipedia.org/wiki/Bloom's_Taxonomy
[3] http://en.wikipedia.org/wiki/Three_Laws_of_Robotics

So, what could account for this widely accepted model not accurately describing actual consumer behavior?

One possible explanation is the principle of least effort [10].

Built on information-processing theory [21, 22], the buying funnel is a rational process that assumes potential consumers act rationally and expend resources to find the optimal solution. This is theoretically grounded in the rational-actor paradigm [34].

However, the principle of least effort takes a slightly different approach, although also rooted in information-processing theory [21, 22]. When presented with a problem or decision, people will take the route that requires expending the least amount of energy for arriving at a satisfactory answer, even if it is not the most optimal. In other words, people (including potential consumers) will engage in satisficing [35]. So, consumers may rationally begin a process akin to the buying funnel, but if they encounter a solution that fits their general expectations of a satisfactory solution, they will stop. We also see this behavioral searching construct in information-foraging theory [36].

So, imagine a potential customer mentally considering a product, say a portable music player, with an expected price that he/she is willing to pay. Let us say this consumer goes to a search engine, enters "portable music player" in the search box, scans the SERP ads, and sees an ad from a trusted source with a sales price below what the potential customer was willing to spend. It would seem reasonable by both the rational-actor theory and principle of least effort that the customer might just convert at this point rather than progressing through any additional information-searching process.

In terms of the buying funnel, the consumer may begin with a general *awareness* query, maybe expecting to research multiple options before arriving at a decision and

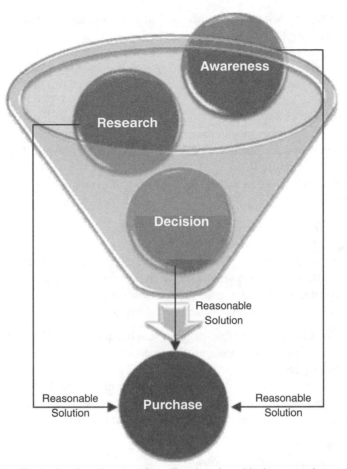

Figure 5.4. The buying-funnel process for online shopping with alternate paths to purchase.

making a purchase. However, if this consumer encounters a possible solution that generally fits the parameters of what they are seeking, they will take the path of least effort and just make the purchase.

As the cost increases, the more effort they are willing to expend in researching the item. With their searching need not well articulated, these searchers might be more open to impulse buying, which leads to increased purchasing.

Therefore, for many products and services, the hierarchical staged buying funnel is not an appropriate model for explaining the entire online purchase process. Although it may be an appropriate process for some products and services, each stage of the buying funnel may lead directly to a convert, based on individual factors of the consumer and product or service (see Figure 5.4).

Multiple paths to purchase from any stage of the buying funnel are an example of the compressing of the buying funnel, known as the hierarchy of effects [37] in this context, due to the Web's enabling capabilities.

Consumer buying behavior. Another well-known concept to explain consumer behavior on the Web is consumer buying behavior.

The outcome of consumer searching is often a purchase or some other type of conversion defined by the advertiser. Although this purchase decision can be considered as a step in the consumer search process, it is such a core part of commerce that consumer buying behavior is a field in its own right.

The consumer buying process is usually presented as a hierarchical staged model consisting of one or more prepurchase, purchase, and postpurchase phases. The prepurchase phase includes need recognition, information search, evaluation of alternatives, and product choice [6].

Concerning the consumer buying process, we will use a six-phased process. The six phases are:

1. *Problem Recognition*: awareness of need or desire
2. *Search*: gathering of information to reduce uncertainty
3. *Evaluation of Alternatives*: evaluating available information and choices
4. *Purchase Decision*: determining whether or not to make the purchase
5. *Purchase*: the act of procuring the product or service
6. *Postpurchase Evaluation*: assessment of the product or service purchase.

Naturally, not all consumer buying decisions lead to a purchase, and not all consumer buying decisions include all six stages. This is determined by the degree of complexity of the buying decision.

One of the most predominant determinants of complexity is the level of impulse buying and the frequency of purchase for the product or service [38]. Impulse buying, in its purest form, is defined as consisting of four components [39]:

- It is *unplanned*.
- It the result of an exposure to *stimulus*.
- It is decided "*on-the-spot*."
- It involves an emotional and/or cognitive *reaction*.

The relationship between frequency and impulse is shown in Figure 5.5.

From Figure 5.5, we see different levels of consumer engagement:

- *Low Frequency–Low Impulse*: high levels of consumer buying engagement
- *Low Frequency–High Impulse*: low levels of consumer buying engagement
- *High Frequency–Low Impulse*: high levels of consumer buying engagement
- *High Frequency–High Impulse*: low levels of consumer buying engagement.

Common elements of buying funnel and consumer buying behavior

In addition to similarities in stages, both the buying funnel and the consumer buying behavior models have the elements of uncertainty and bounded rationality in common.

Uncertainty. One reason consumers search for prepurchase information is to reduce their uncertainty about a decision. The range of possibilities for a consumer during a

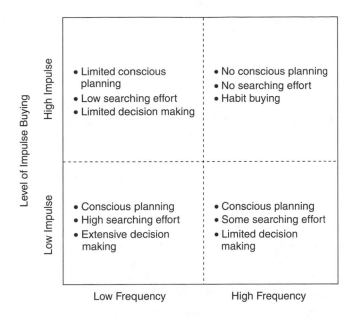

Figure 5.5. Consumer buying behaviors based on type of product.

buying decision is typically framed within a goal of reducing uncertainty. Information search is often seen as a mean to lessen decision-related uncertainty [6]. Therefore, greater uncertainty should lead to more extensive search behavior.

Uncertainty is typically divided into two types:

1. *Knowledge uncertainty* – ambiguity concerning information about the alternatives' attributes
2. *Choice uncertainty* – ambiguity about which alternative to choose

The interplay between these two types of uncertainty leads to different consumer searching behaviors.

Choice uncertainty (CU) increases search behavior whereas knowledge uncertainty (KU) reduces search. High KU is associated with a potentially reduced ability to efficiently use new information, which makes information search more costly, therefore possibly reducing search [6, 40].

There are several variables that explain consumer uncertainty [6], including:

- *Market* environmental variables
- *Situational* variables
- *Product* importance variables
- *Cost* of search variables
- *Demographical* variables
- *Individual* difference variables
- *Knowledge* and *experience* variables

During the consumer buying process, the consumer is attempting to reduce uncertainty as related to one or more of these variables.

Bounded rationality. In any decision-making process, there are boundary conditions, known as bounded rationality. The concept of bounded rationality assumes that people do not follow a rational decision-making process in which people clearly define a problem, generate alternatives, evaluate all alternative solutions, and then select the best approach before implementing it.

Potpourri: Many consumer buying models are based on the assumption that the consumer is a rational actor, resulting in decisions based on the perceived marginal utility of the purchase of a product.

Rational actor does not mean rational person.

To maximize outcomes, a rational actor attempts to maximize value with respect to a set of preferences.

However, there is plenty of empirical evidence to show that people often act irrationally, emotionally, with a lack of information, or even destructively.

For the purposes of consumer buying theory, a rational actor chooses from a set of available alternatives relative to some preferences, context, emotion, situation, and so forth at a given time.

So, take the consumer buying theory as a general guideline of a cognitive process.

Bounded rationality [41] holds that people in general, and consumers in our case, decide rationally only in a limited number of situations. Consumers make choices according to what is often a simplified interpretation of the situation. In these situations, rationality is "bounded." Consumers seldom have access to all relevant information and must rely on a "strategy of satisfying" to make the best decision on limited information. In these situations, consumers choose a reasonable choice that seems satisfactory rather than seek the best solution.

So, again, we see the concept of the principle of least effort. Bounded rationality sees people as information-processing entities wherein uncertainty comes from a lack of information. There are a number of factors at work that limit the bounds of rational decision making, including:

1. *Incomplete*, imperfect, or even misleading *information*
2. *Complex problems*
3. *Limited cognitive* human information processing
4. Practical *limits on time* available for decision making
5. *Conflicting preferences* or goals

We see this aspect of the interplay between rationality and irrationality in the writing of practitioners in the field of advertising, based on their experience and studies of advertising campaigns. For example, Schwab [42, p. 66] writes that you must provide empirical evidence and facts in your advertisement copy in order to provide the customer with a reason and excuse to purchase the product that, emotionally, they already want to purchase.

airline ticket. But they may also be thinking of that picture framed for their spouse, a hotel for the trip, and Junior's upcoming visit to the local college.

What does this matter to the advertiser?

It means that there are usually targets of opportunity or serendipitous events that serve as touch points to reach the consumer.

We see this a lot in the area of cross-selling, where a searcher searches for one item, clicks on a related ad, and then purchases something else.

Potpourri: RFM analysis (recency, frequency, monetary) is a quantitative marketing technique to determine which customers are the best ones for a particular business.

The method relies on three factors related to a particular business:

- *Recency*: how recently has a customer purchased?
- *Frequency*: how often has a customer purchased?
- *Monetary*: how much has a customer spent?

RFM analysis is based on a power law distribution, summarized via the marketing axiom that "80 percent of your business comes from 20 percent of your customers."

The reasoning behind RFM analysis is simple. *Customers who purchased in the past are more likely to purchase in the future*.

Many times in RFM analysis, you assign the customer a ranking number of 1, 2, 3, 4, or 5 (with 5 being highest) for each one of the RFM parameters. The three scores together are referred to as an RFM cell. You then sort the list to determine which customers were the "best customers" in the past, with a cell ranking of "555" being ideal.

RFM analysis can be a useful tool for addressing and leveraging the current customer base. However, the approach does have its limitations. For example, a company must use some other metric not within RFM analysis to ensure it does not oversolicit the customers with the highest rankings.

Also, RFM analysis can cause a business to neglect customers in the low-cell rankings, thereby missing opportunities to grow the business.

Foundational Takeaways

- From the seller's perspective, you want to take potential customers through the stages of the buying funnel:
  - *Awareness*
  - *Research*
  - *Decision*
  - *Purchase*
- From the viewpoint of the consumer, your search should take on the following consumer buying process:
  - *Problem/Need recognition*
  - *Information search*

This integration of rationality and emotion in the consumer is what makes advertising both a science and an art.

Issues with the buying funnel and the consumer decision process buying behavior

Both the buying funnel and the consumer decision process are flawed, although they do provide workable insights into the area of consumer behavior in sponsored search.

In the buying funnel, the seller comes across as being in charge. The advertiser guides the consumers, like sheep, though a series of gates to the final purchase. We do not hear from the consumer at all in this model.

In the consumer buying process, the consumer is in charge. The consumer has taken total control of the purchase process, with the advertiser almost nonexistent.

In actuality, we know that neither of these scenarios is the actual case. The advertiser and the potential consumer are in a communication process. Both the query and the advertisement are the communication messages between the two in sponsored search.

Communication Theory

Given that both the buying funnel and consumer decision making view different actors as in charge, it is more helpful to view the advertiser-consumer exchange as one where neither is in charge.

Instead, sponsored search is a communication process. Figure 5.6 illustrates the fundamentals of any communication process, including that between the advertiser and the consumer in sponsored search.

A communication process conveys a message (i.e., a chunk of information) to someone. There is a sender, a message, a channel of communication, and a receiver. Challenges of communication processes include accurately conveying the message to the receiver, who may or may not provide feedback. There are always constraints. There is also the context, which also affects the communication between any sender and receiver. Certainly, this sender-message-receiver-feedback progression describes the sponsored-search process.

Viewing sponsored search as a communication process has several advantages. Most notably, neither the consumer, as in the buying funnel, nor the advertiser, as in the consumer buying process, is a passive participant. In a communication process, both the consumer and the advertiser are active participants in that they are both engaging in a commercial exchange and their individual and combined actions will affect the outcome of the exchange.

To understand the constructs of the communication process deeper, we look at Watzlawick's five axioms of communication [43]. The five axioms are:

- *Axiom 1: "One cannot not communicate."*

  Every behavior is a kind of communication, and people are constantly communicating with each other. Therefore, any perceivable behavior, including the absence of behavior, can be interpreted by others as having meaning [43].

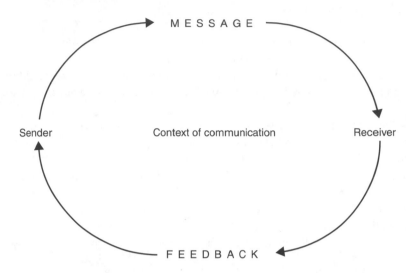

Constraints of communication

Figure 5.6. Fundamentals of communication process with sender, receiver, and feedback within a context and with constraints.

So, when a searcher submits a query and your ad does not appear, that lack of an ad communicates a message to the searcher. It prevents communication between your company and this potential customer. Perhaps this is want you want (e.g., you might not be interested in the searcher who uses the term *free* in the query). So, it could be the exact message you want to convey (i.e., "sorry, our product is not for you").

However, this might not be your intent. We focus exceedingly on the keywords included in our sponsored search efforts and new ones to add. However, an occasional review of the words not included can shed some light on the message we are sending.

At some level, the communication aspect is rather binary. If you decide not to use a particular keyphrase, your advertisement will not be available to those consumers. So, you are effectively preventing communication.

- *Axiom 2: "Every communication has a content and relationship aspect such that the latter classifies the former and is therefore a metacommunication."*

  Each person responds to the content of communication in the context of the relationship between the communicators that is both the sender and the receiver. The context provides metadata about the information exchanged in the communication [43].

  This is notably true in sponsored search, where the consumer is entering the communication process with some established mind-set (i.e., context). Perhaps the consumer is just looking for the cheapest price. Perhaps they are in a hurry and just want to get the product they need ordered. Perhaps the consumer has had past experience with your company, which affects the trust associated with the Web site.

  Your ad needs to fit into the consumer's context. It probably necessitates several ads to suit the various contexts in which a consumer might search for your product or service.

- *Axiom 3: "The nature of a relationship is dependent on the punctuation of the partners' communication procedures."*

Punctuation refers to the process of organizing groups of messages into meanings, like the punctuation of written language. Punctuation by the sender can sometimes alter the meaning considerably [43].

The crafting of advertisements is a perfect example of this axiom in action. The precise phrasing of a headline, the wording choice in the description, or the manner of the display link can all impact, either positively or negatively, the communication process.

- *Axiom 4: "Human communication involves both digital and analogic modalities."*

  In other words, communication contains discrete, defined elements (i.e., digital) that are also different in some respect (i.e., analogic) based on the context and are delivered or transferred in some manner (i.e., modalities) [43].

  In sponsored search, you can control many of the communication factors, such as keyphrases and advertisement copy. You can even, to some extent, control where the advertisement is shown on the SERP.

  However, there are other factors that affect the communication process that are more difficult to control.

  The reputation of the search engine in the marketplace will effect how the searcher perceives your advertisement (see branding section in Chapter 6 BAM! Branding Advertising and Marketing for Sponsored Search). The other advertisements on the SERP will also impact the perception of your advertisement. For example, if the other companies advertising on a given keyphrase have a negative brand image, this negative image may affect how the searcher perceives your business.

- *Axiom 5: "Interhuman communication procedures are either symmetric or complementary, depending on whether the relationship of the partners is based on differences or parity."*

  A symmetric relationship is one in which the parties involved behave as equals from a power perspective. A complementary relationship is a communication relationship of unequals [43].

  In most search markets, the relationship is asymmetrical, in that the advertiser has more information concerning the product that the consumer. This impacts the communication process, making the searcher naturally somewhat wary, perhaps impacting a response to an advertisement.

  In this regard, it supports the advertising principles of informing, providing empirical evidence, and supplying facts to the consumer [42]. Your advertisement must address this information asymmetry in which the consumer views the relationship.

In each of these communication axioms, we can see the elements of the sponsored-search process. By viewing the searcher and the advertiser in a communication process, each sending messages and receiving feedback, keyphrases, advertisements, and consumer behavior assume the more natural roles than one sees in the search process. Within this overall communication framework, we can leverage models like the buying funnel and consumer buying behavior for particular aspects of implementation.

Remember that you are Dealing with a Person, not a Model

All of these models – actually any model, no matter how complex – are simplifications of the real-world process.

As an example, how many times does a person only have one goal? I submit, rarely. A person may be searching with the intent to purchase some product, say an

- *Evaluation of purchases*
- *Purchase decision*
- *Postpurchase evaluation*

- Combining the two, the consumer and the advertiser are in a communication process ruled by five axioms.

  - *Axiom 1: One cannot not communicate.*
  - *Axiom 2: Every communication has a content and relationship aspect such that the latter classifies the former and is therefore a metacommunication.*
  - *Axiom 3: The nature of a relationship depends on the punctuation of the partners' communication procedures.*
  - *Axiom 4: Human communication involves both digital and analogic modalities.*
  - *Axiom 5: Interhuman communication procedures are either symmetric or complementary, depending on whether the relationship of the partners is based on differences or parity.*

Relating Theory to Practice

- For your keywords, develop criteria and classify them into stages of the buying funnel. Then, compare ROI for each of these keywords. At which stage of the buying funnel are you making the most money? Does this make sense for your product/service and market segment?
- For your keywords, develop criteria and classify them into stages of the consumer decision-making process. Then, compare ROI for each of these keywords. At which stage of the consumer decision-making process are you making the most money? Does this make sense for your product/service and market segment?
- Examine your keywords from the perspective of a communication process between you and the potential customer. For the query linked to each keyword, what is the question the consumer is asking? Now, evaluate the advertisements associated with these keywords. Does the advertisement answer the customer's question or point the customer to the answer? What communication message is your advertisement sending?

Conclusion

In this chapter, we examined consumer behavior, coming at it from three perspectives.

First, we discussed the buying funnel, which is a staged process from the advertiser's view of selling a product to a potential customer. Despite having several variations, the buying funnel is a common hierarchical consumer model.

However, there is substantial empirical evidence that the buying funnel does not represent the actual process for all products and services. Typically, there is substantial interplay and impact based on the product or service. For example, a customer may quickly make a decision on purchasing an inexpensive product after some very basic searching research. Also, there are impulse buys, where a consumer makes a purchase after just becoming aware of a product.

These factors, plus the impact of easily making a purchase on the Web, has contributed to a medium that places the consumer with more power in the communication process, relative to mass media types of advertising.

We then discussed the consumer buying process, where the potential customer progresses through an ordered, generally hierarchical, and linear sequence of steps to come to the decision point on whether or not to make the purchase. Much of this process is based on the consumer being a rational actor, which we know by practice the consumer is not. Rationality is bounded by context, situation, environment, and emotion.

Whereas the buying funnel views the process from the viewpoint of the advertiser, the consumer purchasing process takes the consumer's point of view. In both cases, the role and impact of the other major actor is minimized.

We end the consumer behavior discussion by incorporating both the advertiser and the consumer within a communication process. In this communication process, both the advertiser and the consumer are empowered, seeking or providing relevant information and actively pursuing their goals.

With our searcher now becoming a potential customer, we must take a journey into the consumer literature that addresses the exchange and media influences between the consumer and the advertising efforts of the business. In fact, our perspective of the advertiser now changes to one of a business, although in the cases of advertising agencies, the advertiser may be a surrogate for the actual business that the sponsored-search effort represents.

The exchanges and media influences of the business are key concepts in the branding, advertising, and marketing aspects of sponsored search, which we discuss in the next chapter.

References

[1] Ogilvy, D. 1963. *Confessions of an Advertising Man*. London: Atheneu.

[2] Ogilvy, D. 1983. *Ogilvy on Advertising*. Toronto: John Wiley and Sons.

[3] Sandhusen, R. L. 2000. *Marketing*, 3rd ed. Hauppage, NY: Barron's Educational Series.

[4] DeLong, J. B. and Froomkin, A. M. 1999. Speculative Microeconomics for Tomorrow's Economy. (November 22). Retrieved September 18, 2010, from http://personal.law.miami.edu/~froomkin/articles/spec.htm#N_1

[5] Engel, J., Blackwell, R., and Miniard, P. 1995. *Consumer Behavior*, 8th ed. Fort Worth, TX: Dryden.

[6] Lauraeus-Niinivaara, T., Saarinen, T., and Öörni, A. 2007. "Knowledge and Choice Uncertainty Affect Consumer Search and Buying Behavior." In *40th Hawaii International Conference on System Sciences*. Honolulu, HI. p. 82.

[7] Hodinson, C., Kiel, G., and McColl-Kennedy, J. R . 2000. "Consumer Web Search Behaviour: Diagrammatic Illustration of Wayfinding on the Web." *International Journal of Human-Computer Studies*, vol. 52(5), pp. 805–830.

[8] Diamond, P. A. 1989. "Search Theory." In *The New Palgrave: Allocation, Information, and Markets*, J. Eatwell, M. Milgate, and P. Newman, Eds. New York: Norton, pp. 271–286.

[9] Johnson, E. J., Moe, W. W., Fader, P. S., Bellman, S., and Lohse, G. L. 2004. "Depth and Dynamics of Online Search Behavior." *Management Science*, vol. 50(3), pp. 299–308.

[10] Zipf, G. K. 1949. *Human Behavior and the Principle of Least Effort*. Cambridge, MA: Addison-Wesley Press.

[11] Lauraéus-Niinivaara, T. 2010. "Uncertainty Is the Other Side of the Coin of Information Online Search." In *43rd Hawaii International Conference on System Sciences*, Honolulu, HI, pp. 1–10.

[12] Claxton, J. D., Fry, J. N., and Portis, B. 1974. "A Taxonomy of Prepurchase Information Gathering Patterns." *Journal of Consumer Research*, vol. 1(December), pp. 35–42.

[13] PeterSimon, H. B., Sherrell, D. L., and Ridgway, A. N. M. 1986. "Consumer Search: An Extended Framework." *The Journal of Consumer Research*, vol. 13(1), pp. 119–126.

[14] Bloch, P. H., Sherrell, D. L., and Nancy M. Ridgway, 1986. "Consumer Search: An Extended Framework," *The Journal of Consumer Research,* vol. 13(1), pp. 119–126.

[15] Bloch, P. H., Sherrell, D. L., and Ridgway, N. M. 1986. "Consumer Search: An Extended Framework." *The Journal of Consumer Research*, vol. 13(1), pp. 119–126.

[16] Ramos, A. and Cota, S. 2008. *Search Engine Marketing*. New York: McGraw-Hill.

[17] Seda, C. 2004. *Search Engine Advertising: Buying Your Way to the Top to Increase Sales.* Boston: New Riders.

[18] Dubberly, H. and Evenson, S. 2008. "The Experience Cycle." *Interactions*, vol. 15(3) (May–June), pp. 11–15.

[19] Moore, I. 2005. *Does Your Marketing Sell? The Secret of Effective Marketing Communications*. London: Nicholas Brealey Publishing.

[20] Bettman, J. R., Luce, M. F., and Payne, J. W. 1998. "Constructive Consumer Choice Processes." *Journal of Consumer Research*, vol. 25(3), pp. 187–217.

[21] Hawkins, D. I., Best, R. J., and Coney, K. A. 1995. *Consumer Behaviour: Implications for Marketing Strategy*, 6th ed. Homewood, IL: Irwin Publishing.

[22] Sirakaya, E. and Woodside, A. G. 2005. "Building and Testing Theories of Decision Making by Travellers." *Tourism Management*, vol. 26(6), pp. 815–832.

[23] Simon, H. A. 1977. *The New Science of Management Decision*, 3rd ed. Englewood Cliffs, NJ: Prentice-Hall.

[24] Rimm-Kaufman, A. 2006. Click Streams, Complexity, and Contribution: Modeling Searcher Behavior Using Markov Models. (February 27). Retrieved August 6, 2009, from http://www.rimmkaufman.com/content/rkg-ses-ny-feb06-search-behavior.pdf

[25] Ash, T. 2008. Landing Pages and the Decision-Making Process. (October 29). Retrieved August 6, 2009, from http://searchenginewatch.com/3631328

[26] Fou, A. 2009. How to Use Search to Calculate the ROI of Awareness Advertising. (March 12). Retrieved August 6, 2009, from http://www.clickz.com/3633054

[27] Ryan, K. 2009. What's on Your Mind? (July 9). Retrieved August 6, 2009, from http://search-enginewatch.com/3630177

[28] Howard, J. A. and Sheth, N. J. 1969. *Theory of Buyer Behaviour*. New York: Wiley.

[29] Meyerson, M. and Scarborough, M. E. 2007. Mastering Online Marketing: 12 Keys to Transform Your Website into a Sales Powerhouse. Newburgh, NY: Entrepreneur Press.

[30] Young, R. A., Weiss, A. M., and Stewart, D. W. 2006. *Marketing Champions: Practical Strategies for Improving Marketing's Power, Influence, and Business Impact*. New York: Wiley.

[31] Nimetz, J. 2007. B2B Marketing in 2007: The Buying Funnel vs. Selling Process. (March 27). Retrieved August 6, 2009, from http://www.searchengineguide.com/jody-nimetz/b2b-marketing-i-1.php

[32] Laycock, J. 2007. Understanding the Search Buying Cycle. (March 5). Retrieved August 6, 2009, from http://www.searchengineguide.com/jennifer-laycock/understanding-t.php

[33] Broder, A. 2002. "A Taxonomy of Web Search," *SIGIR Forum*, vol. 36(2), pp. 3–10.

[34] Slovic, P., Finucane, M., Peters, E., and MacGregor, D. G. 2002. "Rational Actors or Rational Fools: Implications of the Affect Heuristic for Behavioral Economics." *Journal of Socio-Economics*, vol. 31(4), pp. 329–342.

[35] Simon, H. A. 1957. *Models of Man: Social and Rational*. New York: John Wiley and Sons.

[36] Pirolli, P. 2007. *Information Foraging Theory: Adaptive Interaction with Information*. Oxford: Oxford University Press.

[37] Ray, M. 1974. "Marketing Communication and the Hierarchy-of-Effects." In *New Models for Communication Research*, P. Clarke, Ed. New York: Sage.

[38] Kollat, D. T. and Willett, R. P. 1967. "Customer Impulse Purchasing Behavior." *Journal of Marketing Research*, vol. 4(1), pp. 21–31.

[39] Piron, F. 1991. "Defining Impulse Purchasing." In *Advances in Consumer Research*. vol. 18, R. H. Holman and M. R. Solomon, Eds. Provo, UT: Association for Consumer Research, pp. 509–514.

[40] Urbany, J. E., Dickson, P. R., and Wilkie, W. L. 1989. "Buyer Uncertainty and Information Search." *Journal of Consumer Research: An Interdisciplinary Quarterly*, vol. 16(2), pp. 208–215.

[41] Manzini, P. and Mariotti, M. 2009. "Consumer Choice and Revealed Bounded Rationality." *Economic Theory*, vol. 41(3), pp. 379–392.

[42] Schwab, V. O. 1962. *How to Write a Good Advertisement: A Short Course in Copywriting*. Chatsworth, CA: Wilshire.

[43] Watzlawick, P., Beavin, J. H., and Jackson, M. D. 1967. *Pragmatics of Human Communication: A Study of Interactional Patterns, Pathologies, and Paradoxes*. New York: W. W. Norton.

Word cloud generated by Wordle

6

BAM!: Branding, Advertising, and Marketing for Sponsored Search

We knew it would be impactful when we saw that we could achieve profitability.
When we could see that our ads and some of our syndication deals could
actually cause a shift in business models.
Marissa Mayer,
First Vice President of Search Product and User
Experience at Google, speaking about advertising and search [1]

Our frame shop is not in business to advertise. It is interested in selling products and services to generate revenue. But it must advertise to stay in business. So, it is first a business and then an advertiser. This is an important shift in perspective, one that has continually haunted advertising agencies [see 2, 3, 4]. A good ad, for example, may be different from the viewpoint of the creator (i.e., is this ad creative, funny, catchy, or different?) than the businessperson (i.e., does this ad sell products?).

As such, the businessperson has a different perspective of the sponsored-search process than strictly the searcher or the advertiser. We must examine some business functions that both impact and are impacted by sponsored search. As Mayer points out in the epigraph [1], sponsored search changed the online business model. However, sponsored search is also based on foundational concepts inherent in any business effort.

In this chapter, we will introduce the foundational business elements of branding, advertising, and marketing, showing how each relates to sponsored search. Specifically, we define branding, advertising, and marketing, highlighting the aspects pertinent to sponsored search. Although there are many other facets of business (human resources, accounting, taxes, strategic planning, etc.), the areas of branding, advertising, and marketing are the core business facets that impact sponsored-search efforts. Thus, we cover them here.

Branding

What is a brand?

A brand is a unique attribute, name, term, design, or symbol. Your brand can be synonymous with your company, product lines, and individual products. Like our ads in sponsored search, branding is a communication process between your business and the potential consumers. A communication process facilitates a relationship. People build a relationship, which can be very personal, with your brand but not your company per se. The best brands build an emotional connection with consumers, leading to customer loyalty and repeat sales, which are usually the most profitable for the business and most satisfying for the customers. It is the satisfied customer that returns to buy a product. So, done correctly, it is a win-win situation.

Within this relationship, branding is used for the identification of products and services. The etymological origin of the word comes from the *branding* of cattle and initially referred to the act of naming a product or service. Nowadays, branding is nearly anything that differentiates products or services in such a way that makes them more familiar and desirable than similar products or services [5].

Research has shown that brands have a significant impact on consumers' perception and selection of products. Branding is a top business priority, as a brand is a company's most valuable intangible asset [6].

Branding is an essential element in sponsored search. Branding traits are inherent to the entire process, from the search engine selection, to the search engine results page (SERP), to the individual ad, to the advertiser's Web site. We know that brands affect searchers' relevance judgments of results in a variety of subjective, affective, cognitive, and contextual manners [7, 8]. Searchers also have different perceptions of each search engine's performance and distinct responses to each engine [9].

What is branding?

Branding is making consumers aware of a company's goods or services by seeing the "brand" and presenting an idea of what that image means [10]. From the perspective of the business, branding is a process involving all activities that assign a brand to a product or service. This is an extensive definition that incorporates service branding [11, 12] and corporate branding [13].

- *Service branding* is a process of forming a brand for a product of a service provider.
- *Corporate branding* is the process of building an organizational brand.

For our purposes, we are primarily focusing on service branding, although many of the concepts apply to corporate branding as well. Service branding must be applied with the context of the consumer [14].

Figure 6.1 presents a model of branding across the entire spectrum or process of search, adopted from the work of Esch et al. [15]. We see that the entire branding process is divided into three components:

- *Antecedents*: the precursors and background that establish the setting
- *Interaction*: an exchange between a customer and a product, service, or company
- *Outcomes*: the result or effect of an interaction.

The solid line represents known significant effects. So, brand awareness positively impacts brand image. Brand image impacts both brand satisfaction and brand trust. The combination of brand satisfaction and brand trust impacts brand attachment, which is a measure of the strength of the relationship between the customer

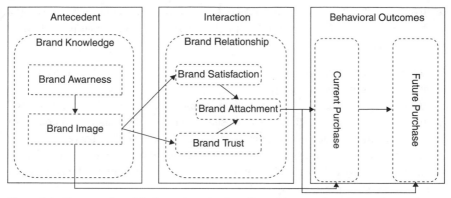

Figure 6.1. Conceptual model of search engine branding with antecedents, interaction, and outcomes.

and the business. Brand attachment influences both current and future purchases. Additionally, future purchases are influenced by current purchases.

We discuss each of these branding concepts further, as each can have a nuanced effect on the branding of a business, product, or service. These concepts can impact the effectiveness of a sponsored-search effort.

Potpourri: Branding matters in Web search and sponsored search, and this has been demonstrated empirically.

Jansen, Zhang, and Schultz [9] investigated the effect of a search engine's brand on people's evaluation of the search results. They measured the effect of search engine brand by switching the branding elements on the search engine results page. So, the results in response to a query were the same. The only thing that changed was what search engine the searcher thought the results came from.

The researchers report that a positive search engine brand image in the mind of the searchers resulted in results being worth about 10–15 percentage points in relevance rating.

In fact, the search engine brand was more influential when evaluating sponsored results relative to organic results.

Brand knowledge

Branding research traditionally focuses on investigation of brand knowledge. This is conceptualized by an associative network memory model of two components: *brand awareness* and *brand image* [16].

Brand awareness is related to the strength of the brand node or trace in memory, as reflected by consumers' ability to identify the brand under different conditions [17]. Brand awareness consists of *brand recognition* and *brand recall*.

- *Brand recognition* is the consumers' ability to confirm prior exposure to the brand when given the brand directly as a cue.

- *Brand recall* relates to consumers' ability to retrieve the brand when given the product category, the needs fulfilled by the category, or some other type of probe as a cue [16].

Therefore, the ultimate outcome is for a brand to be recognized and recalled by customers, aided or unaided.

Brand image (a.k.a. brand perception or brand opinion) is built on consumers' brand associations and attitudes. It has been considered an integral component of brand equity and has been widely employed in various brand equity frameworks [16]. However, there is less agreement on the precise definition of brand image. Keller defined brand image as "perceptions about a brand as reflected by the brand associations held in consumer memory" [16].

In their study using tangible products, Esch et al. [15] found that brand knowledge alone is not sufficient for building strong brands in the long term. Brand relationship factors must be considered as well. Unlike strictly tangible goods, sponsored search is a mix of technology and service (i.e., tangible and intangible). Hence, it is possible that branding effects might differ in this context due to a higher level of uncertainty and risk.

> **Potpourri**: Once a brand image has formed in a person's mind, it is rather difficult to change. This can be a good thing if your brand image is positive, as your company will often get the benefit of the doubt. However, it can be a bad thing if your company falls into a negative brand image.
>
> The theoretical basis for this is framing, a social theory. A frame is schema for interpretation that folks rely on to place meaning and understanding on life events.
>
> Why do folks do this? It is easier than figuring things out from scratch each time, which is another manifestation of the principle of least effort. Usually, framing works fine for us.
>
> There is a social aspect to framing when it takes on a social construction. This helps explain why certain companies can benefit from the bandwagon effect, which is where people often believe or do things just because other people believe or do things.
>
> The bandwagon effect influences Web searching and sponsored search. It their study, Jansen and McNeese [18] asked study participants why they used a certain search engine. One of the most frequent answers was because 'it is popular."

Brand relationship

Direct effects mean a straight relationship between brand knowledge and behaviors. The more brand knowledge consumers have, the higher the possibility that they will make a purchase.

Indirect effects suggest another path between brand knowledge and future behaviors, which has the brand relationship as a mediator. Online businesses pursue various means in developing this relationship, even down to approaches in how to say thank you to a customer [19].

With this path, brand knowledge has a positive effect on brand relationship, and brand relationship has a positive effect on behavior outcomes. Therefore, brand knowledge alone has an indirect effect on behaviors. Without a positive relationship, brand knowledge itself has less power influencing consumers' purchasing behaviors.

Esch et al. [15] found that the indirect effects of brand knowledge via brand relationships on behavioral outcomes are larger than its direct effects, which indicates that brand relationship variables such as brand trust, brand satisfaction, and brand attachment are critical for predicting future behaviors. This implies that a familiar brand with a positive image must build a positive brand relationship with the consumer to secure future sales.

It is important to consider how companies build brand relationships with consumers. Brand relationship research states that brand perceptions affect consumers because of the knowledge systems and the concepts consumers store in memory. Brands are part of a psycho-social-cultural context [15, 20]. Consumers engage in relationships with brands, similar to the personal and intimate relationships consumers form with other people. The brand relationship process can generate cognitive benefits as well as positive effects that result in a bond between the brand and the consumer [20].

Brand relationships include both exchange and communal aspects. These are represented by brand satisfaction and brand trust, and interdependence between the entities, as reflected by brand commitment. These factors can affect a consumer's loyalty to a brand, with several aspects of search engine loyalty [21]. Exchange aspects of brand relationship involve economic factors and offer primarily utilitarian benefits [15], which are represented by brand satisfaction. As an important predictor of consumers' future behavior, brand satisfaction is a significant determinant of repeat sales, positive word of mouth, and consumer loyalty [22]. Traditionally, brand satisfaction research was mostly cognitive in nature. In the mid-1990s, research started to not only criticize the overwhelming dominance of this paradigm [23], but also increasingly to investigate effective antecedents of satisfaction. Rather than treating brand satisfaction as a simple one-dimensional construct, some researchers attempted to study satisfaction at a deeper level, arguing that satisfaction is multidimensional and incorporates cognitive and emotional elements [24, 25]. Naturally, brands want customer satisfaction to be based not only on a cognitive evaluation of product quality but also on an effective response with little or no information processing.

Communal aspects of a relationship involve feelings about other people [15], and trust is the primary positive result of such relationships. Trust can be defined in many ways, including as the generalized expectancy an individual holds that the word of another can be relied on [26]; the extent that a person is confident in and willing to act on based on the words, actions, or decisions of others [27]; and, uniquely in the consumer domain, the willingness of the average consumer to rely on the brand to perform its stated function [28]. In relationship marketing literature, trust is defined as the perception of confidence in the exchange partner's future actions [29]. Trust is the basic mechanism used to build and maintain a relationship and fosters a long-term orientation in marketing relationships [29]. Because the conduct of e-commerce across jurisdictional boundaries involves risk, the issue of trust is arguably of greater importance for online exchanges compared to traditional exchanges [30, 31].

The essence of a relationship is some kind of interdependence between the entities involved [15]. We adopt commitment as a reflection of interdependence over time. Morgan and Hunt [29] argued that commitment is central to relationship marketing. Relationships are built on the foundation of mutual commitment [32]. Commitment is "an enduring desire to maintain a valued relationship" [33]. Commitment in its various forms fosters stability by implicating the self in relationship outcomes and by encouraging derogation of alternatives in the environment [34]. It is believed to be associated with motivation and involvement [35], positive effect and loyalty [36], and performance and obedience to organizational policies [37].

Table 6.1 summarizes the various components of a brand and provides a short definition of each component.

Branding is well researched in general marketing literature. However, the effect of branding in the search engine area has received scant attention [38, 39], although the effect has received some acknowledgement. For example, Jansen, Zhang and Schultz [40] investigated the effect of brand awareness, and Bailey, Thomas, and Hawking [41] examined how brand name influences users' preference. Brand trust and loyalty are also significant constructs in Internet marketing literature [42]. Brand attitude [43] and brand familiarity [44] have also received some attention in Internet marketing literature.

Branding in sponsored search

Branding focuses on business itself and the customers of that business. How does this manifest itself during the act of a searcher interacting with a search engine?

Drawing primarily on a series of studies conducted by the author and coresearchers, along with prior published work [c.f., 45, 46, 18, 8], there appears to be a multifaceted branding effect in the Web search process that affects keyword advertising, as illustrated in Figure 6.2. The effect is a four-stage process involving search engine, SERP, ad, and landing page.

- **Stage 1 – Choice of search engine**: The first element of branding in sponsored search is the user's selection of a particular search engine. This choice is based on the user's perception of the marketplace, including the perceived performance of the particular search engine relative to other known search engines. The impact of this first element of branding is that it directs traffic to specific search engines and away from other search engines. With market buzz, habit, familiarity, and word of mouth, certain search engines can develop a sizeable market share relative to others. Also, built in applications such as search toolbars into the browsers is another technique used to increase market share and usage of the search engine.
- **Stage 2 – Evaluation of search engine results page**: The second element of branding is the user's perception of the particular search engine's aggregate SERP. This is determined by the user's view of that particular search engine, of its strengths and shortcomings. This stage of branding affects the number of clicks that the user will make on that search engine for a given query.
- **Stage 3 – Selection of individual link**: The third element is the evaluation of the individual links on the SERP of a particular search engine for a given query. This

Table 6.1. *Table summary of important branding constructs*

Branding Component	Definition
Brand knowledge	An associative network memory model of two components: brand awareness and brand image [16].
Brand awareness	Related to the strength of the brand node or trace in memory, as reflected by consumers' ability to identify the brand under different conditions [17].
	Types of brand awareness:
	Brand recognition – consumers' ability to confirm prior exposure to the brand when given the brand directly as a cue [16].
	Brand recall – consumers' ability to retrieve the brand when given the product category, the needs fulfilled by the category, or some other type of probe as a cue [16].
Brand image	"Perceptions about a brand as reflected by the brand associations held in consumer memory" [16].
Brand relationship	Consumers tend to engage in certain types of relationships with brands, which are similar to the personal and intimate relationships consumers form with other people.
Brand satisfaction	Exchange aspects of a relationship involve economic factors and offer utilitarian benefits [15]. Brand satisfaction is the primary positive result of exchange relationships.
Brand trust	Communal aspects of a relationship involve feelings about other people; they transcend self-interest [15]. Trust is the primary positive result of such relationships. Trust is defined as the perception of confidence in the exchange partner's future actions [29].
Brand commitment	"An enduring desire to maintain a valued relationship" [33, p. 316].

is based on both the user's perception of the particular search engine and the user's perception of the aspects of that particular link (i.e., rank, title, summary, URL). This influences the evaluation of a given link as relevant or not relevant. There is also an element of trust in terms of whether the link is sponsored or not, as shown by research [8]. Koufaris and Hampton-Sosa perceived company reputation and the willingness to customize products and services can significantly affect initial trust [47].

- **Stage 4 – Perception of landing page**: The fourth element of branding concerns the land page itself. While stages one, two, and three depend on the overall view of a search engine, this fourth stage of branding appears to depend solely on the Web site itself in terms of content, trust, professional appearance, ease of use, and brand knowledge. There appears to be very little carryover of any search engine brand on the evaluation of the Web sites once the user departs from the search engine. The impact is that once the search engine – any search engine – gets the user to the Web site, the branding of the search engine has little effect on bringing value (i.e., achieving the Web site's goals for visitors, such as executing a transaction) to the Web site itself.

The implication for advertisers is clear – branding on the Web is a multistage issue. The brand of the major search engine that the advertiser advertises on carries certain

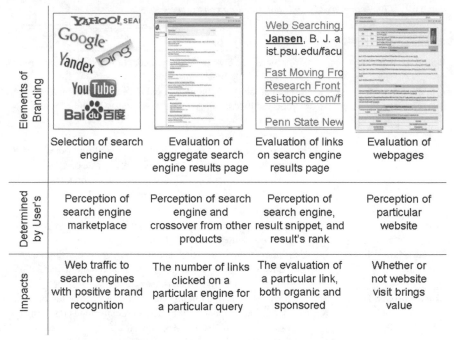

Elements of Branding			
Selection of search engine	Evaluation of aggregate search engine results page	Evaluation of links on search engine results page	Evaluation of webpages
Determined by User's			
Perception of search engine marketplace	Perception of search engine and crossover from other products	Perception of search engine, result snippet, and result's rank	Perception of particular website
Impacts			
Web traffic to search engines with positive brand recognition	The number of links clicked on a particular engine for a particular query	The evaluation of a particular link, both organic and sponsored	Whether or not website visit brings value

Figure 6.2. Four elements of branding during the Web-searching process.

worth in terms of performance evaluation. This affects the decision of the user to visit a particular search engine and the evaluation of the search engine's overall effectiveness as measured by the clicks that a user will execute before leaving the SERP.

The brand of a search engine also affects how the user evaluates individual links. However, this is somewhat moderated by the link snippet itself. The title, the summary, and the URL all affect how users view a particular link. This appears to conform to prior work examining aspects of the link snippet. Jansen and Resnick have shown that the title is a determinant of relevance, whereas the combined title-description of the ad is a determinantof nonrelevance for a given link [8]. We have seen this before in other, non-Internet forms of advertising, where the headline is the most-read item of any advertisement [2].

Hotchkiss has noted that slight variations in how individual links are displayed on the SERP can affect user evaluation [48]. Therefore, whereas the brand of a search engine may help or hinder, the manner in which the content provider titles the page, presents the URL, and summarizes the landing page also influences user evaluation. In addition, the rank of the link has a major effect. Several studies have shown that the rank at which the search engine chooses to present the link has a major effect on user evaluation of that link [49, 50]. This bias of trusting the search engine is apparent even when the ordering of links has been altered to place possibly less useful links higher in the results listing [51].

Finally, it does not matter which search engine sends traffic to a site. Once the user leaves the search engine, the branding aspects of the Web site take over. The relevance of the content to the user's query or information need, the user's perceived professionalism of the page, the user's trust in the site, along with other factors such as load time, all affect the user's positive or negative view of the Web site and brand. Therefore, once the user is at the Web site, the onus is on the content providers to convert the visit into actionable results. Now certainly, there must be a cognitive link between the advertisement and the content on the landing page.

Branded keyphrases

There is always the question of whether or not to bid on branded keyphrases [52]. Branded keyphrases are those that refer to your company name, including official, informal, and variations of spelling or misspellings. In general, branded keyphrases (e.g., Google, Apple) do not refer to specific product names (i.e., Buzz, iPod), unless the product name contains the name of the company or business (e.g., Google Maps, Apple iPad).

Branded keyphrases typically are of one of the following four general types [53]:

- *Brand-pure keyphrases*: include the brand word or words themselves, misspellings, and deviations. Brand-pure keyphrases are the most narrow and focused set of branded keyphrases. These are generally isolated into a separate ad group or campaign.
- *Navigational brand keyphrases*: include "brand Web site," "brand homepage," "brand company," "brand city-name," and even the "www.brand.com" (as empirical tests have shown that people search on URLs [54]), plus many others. Navigational brand keyphrases are the set of keyphrases where the searcher is trying to find your company's Web site.
- *Brand-related keyphrases*: include things like executive names along with other terms and phrases that may be connected with the brand. A lot of these will be developed as you perform analysis on the results you get from your initial broad match (i.e., a matching option that incorporates variations of the keyphrase) to brand-pure keywords.
- *Brand-plus keyphrases*: your brand plus category, product, or other keywords. These are often mixed in with other nonbrand keywords.

The arguments for not bidding on branded keyphrases are generally along the lines of the branded keyphrases already ranking well organically. Why should I now pay for something that I will be getting for free?

This question, of course, can and should be empirically tested for a particular advertiser, as each context is somewhat different. When this has been empirically tested, the results are generally that overall click-through rate (with both organic and sponsored combined) is higher than either individually. However, there is limited reported evidence on whether or not the overall conversion rate has also increased. It would seem that the conversion rate would be unaffected, although the overall percentage of conversions would increase in correlation to the increased number of clicks.

So, from an empirical perspective, it generally makes sense to bid on branded keyphrases, although the pricing and evaluation of these keyphrases need to be separate from nonbranded ones.

From a conceptual perspective, it also makes sense to bid on branded keyphrases. The theoretical basis that supports this heuristic is the concept of customer choice sets.

Customer choice sets. The customer choice set is the foundation for bidding on branded keyphrases, with consumer choice being a very nuanced area [55]. The idea is that there is only so much screen real estate. If you do not take the sponsored ad slot, some other advertiser will. This increases the customer choice set in a way that is detrimental to you because it gives your competitors an opportunity to introduce their brand and products to your potential customers.

This is the conceptual basis for an advertising blockage, where at a particular point in time or place, one advertiser has bought all available outlets.

One can also derive the concepts of customer market segmentation and customer brand image from the underlying customer choice set construct [56]. Namely:

- *Customer market segmentation*: In some searching situations, consumers focus exclusively on the sponsored listings, so your advertisement needs to be there in order to market to this market segment.
- *Customer brand image*: Customers may have an expectation of seeing your branded ad in the sponsored-search listings. When it does not appear, it may create a negative brand image.

So, from both an empirical and theoretical basis, it generally makes sense to bid on branded keyphrases. However, as always true in advertising, "test, measure, and adjust." But bidding on branded keyphrases is a good starting point.

With this basis in branding, let us now examine another foundational element of sponsored search: advertising.

Advertising in Sponsored Search

We continually refer to our efforts as keyword advertising. The keyword portion is fairly obvious. But what is advertising?

Starch, one of the developers of many modern advertising techniques, said that "*advertising is selling in print*" [57, p. 5]. Schwab says that advertising's purpose is simply to make a people buy a product or a service [58].

Advertising did not spring up in conjunction with sponsored-search platforms. Modern advertising developed with the rise of mass production in the late nineteenth and early twentieth centuries. Many of the same conceptualizations and principles of early advertising are inherent to and, in many cases, have been rediscovered with sponsored search, as is well documented in decades of practitioner and academic research [2, 59, 3, 4].

In a very mechanical sense, we can link advertising to eyeballs, with the catchy phrase "Eyeballs are golden!" We want to get their advertising message in a place where people can see it, and the more people who can see it, generally the better [5]. Any advertising effort must, at some level, address the Three Ws of Advertising [2, p. 5]

- *Where* to advertise
- *When* to advertise
- *What* to say in advertisements.

Advertising elements defined

Advertising typically contains some mentions of a product or service, or maybe an organization. The advertising message includes how that product or service can benefit the consumer. In others, the needs, desires, or wants that the product or service addresses for the consumer are included.

The goal of advertising is to persuade a consumer to purchase a particular product, either now or in the future. The goal of advertising is to get people to act [60], so advertising is the actions of calling something to the attention of the public via a sponsored message. As such, advertising is closely synchronized with branding, especially brand knowledge, image, and recall.

Advertising is generally paid for and is usually identified as being sponsored or bought by some organization. By including a clear and conspicuous statement that labels an ad as "paid" in some form, it reduces the appearance of being deceptive.

More formally, advertising is "any paid form of non-personal communication about an organization, product, service, or idea by an identified sponsor" [61, p. 9]. This communication is delivered through selected media outlets that typically require payment for message placement [62].

Note that in this definition, we leave out some marketing aspects, such as word-of-mouth and viral marketing, which have some similarities to advertising. We acknowledge the overlap and just point out that the boundaries between concepts are seldom as clear as we would like.

Regardless, we can extend this general definition of advertising to the Internet:

> Online advertising is when a company pays or makes some sort of financial arrangement to post on someone else's Internet space, advertising information with the intent of achieving the advertiser's goal, such as generating sales or brand recognition [5].

We can then narrow this definition to sponsored search:

> Advertising in the sponsored-search domain is a message displayed by a sponsored-search platform, on a search engine's results page, Web site, or other online page on the Internet, as the result of a commercial arrangement between a search engine and an advertiser.

As in other forms of advertising, the goal of sponsored-search advertising is to persuade potential customers to purchase or take some action related to the advertiser's products, services, or business. Although different in form, sponsored search is still at its core a form of persuasive communications.

Who are these Sponsored Search Advertisers?

Advertisers are those who pay for the advertisements. They are generally companies or organizations that purchase the time or space to accomplish a marketing or corporate objective [5].

Advertisers pay for ads to communicate with consumers, which is true with sponsored-search advertising. Sponsored-search advertising is contingent on at least three factors:

- *Size of market*: What is the demand for a particular product or service?
- *Size of audience*: How many potential customers are there for this product or service?
- *Size of advertising budget*: How much can one afford to spend?

Depending on the advertising goals, the communication between the advertiser and consumer can take different forms.

Although certainly true at the very basic level, eyes do not directly translate to accomplishing business goals. Instead, we need to get at the core of advertising.

At its heart, advertising is a commercial form of persuasive communication! Markets are conversations [63], and the Internet is a conversation [63]. So, with sponsored search, you have a lot of opportunities for communication!

Persuasive communication is the process of guiding people toward the adoption of an idea, attitude, or action by rational and emotional means. Persuasion is a form of social influence.

Persuasive communication is a problem-solving strategy that relies on *appeals*. This is what advertising is attempting to do. An ad's goal is to appeal to potential customers to get them to buy your product or service, either now or in the future.

> **Potpourri**: A Frenchman, Théophraste Renaudot, placed the first advertisements in the newspaper, *La Gazette de France*, in the 1630s [64].
>
> *La Gazette de France* appears to have been the first commercial publication to include paid advertising in its pages, allowing the newspaper to lower its price, extend its readership, and increase its profitability.
>
> Nearly all commercial newspapers soon copied the advertising formula.
>
> The phrase "advertising agency" originated in 1842 when Volney B. Palmer opened his business providing advertising service in Philadelphia, Pennsylvania. This event is widely accepted as the birth of modern advertising. It marks the beginning of a creative industry that has radically transformed the practice of business [64].

As such, advertising as persuasive communication addresses several needs, including:

- *Customer awareness* (i.e., alerting a potential consumer that a certain product or service is available)
- *Customer reminder* (i.e., reminding a potential customer that they may need a particular product or service)
- *Obtaining more customers* (i.e., growing a market for a particular product)
- *Improving business* (i.e., expanding a range of products or services).

As with other advertising channels, we view sponsored search as a pure advertising medium. The objectives are to encourage information search by potential consumers, to prompt direct action from these searchers, to relate searcher needs to our advertisements and our products, to encourage recall of past product or service satisfaction from prior customers (i.e., promote good brand recall), and to modify attitudes or reinforce attitudes among prior customers (i.e., promote good brand recall).

Due to this persuasive communication construct, we see a list of keyterms in ads that result in getting attention, generating emotion, or a strong call-to-action. These terms have proven themselves as being persuasive. Some examples of these terms include:

- Free
- New

- Cheap
- Sale
- Special offer
- Time limited offer
- Tricks
- Tips
- Enhance
- Discover
- Fact
- Learn
- At last
- Free shipping

Potpourri: See and Say has been one of the most effective rules of thumb in advertising, supported by empirical evidence in mass media advertising, especially television advertising.

In a nutshell, See and Say is:
– being able to *SEE* the product
– and *SAY* the words about the product at the same time.

Although based on mass media, the concept carries over well to sponsored search. Images of the product are shown in conjunction with the product's name. Searchers then see the product while they are reading the accompanying text.

Strong call-to-action phrases are also based on persuasive communication construct, such as:

- Buy Today
- Save 50%
- Download Free Trial Now
- Sale Ends Tomorrow

Potpourri: There is an interesting tenet in advertising, known as the third-person effect.

Basically, the third-person effect is the tendency of people viewing advertising, as well as other domains, to assume that OTHER people will be influenced by an advertisement but they themselves remain unaffected, see through it, and so on. However, empirical evidence shows that we ourselves are typically just as influenced as other people.

So, there is a tendency for individuals to assume that communications exert a stronger influence on others than on the self.

However, the third-person effect does not emerge in all contexts or circumstances for all people. The effect appears to be particularly prevalent when the ad contains recommendations that are not perceived to be personally beneficial, when the issue is personally important, or when there is a lack of trust of the source [65].

Advertising techniques

Advertising techniques are tools that an advertiser can implement to persuade potential customers by attracting attention, engaging effectively, triggering emotions, or changing minds, all in the effort to achieve the advertising goal.

> **Potpourri**: Typically, one hears that it is best to appear in both the nonsponsored and sponsored listings, as there will be a click-through lift by appearing in both.
>
> As discussed earlier, the construct of consumer choice sets is a foundational support for this practice.
>
> The practical advertising support for such a suggestion may be in the concept of an advertising blockade, where one controls all the media channels for a given group of consumers.
>
> Because some searchers only look at organic or sponsored listings, being in both on a given SERP will probably result in click-through lift.
>
> The most famous advertising blockade in history was for the Ford Mustang in 1964. The advertising firm of J. Walter Thompson, the lead agency for the Ford advertising effort, purchased ALL available television time in the United States from 9:30 PM to 10:00 PM on the day of the launch.
>
> Seventy-five (75) percent of all Americans tuned in that night to watch the commercial [66].

There is a great deal of advertising research that focuses on the structures of advertisement, specifically identifying and classifying characteristics of the message.

Fowles and Fowles [67] identified fifteen classic advertising appeals using television ads that aimed at the needs, desires, or wants of potential consumers:

- *Need for sex* – despite getting a lot of attention when it did occur, the explicit use of sex in advertising is surprisingly low, although it depends on how you define sex. Examples are the beautiful men and women used in many car advertisements.
- *Need for affiliation* – by far the largest number of ads use this approach, as many people seem to have an internal desire to belong to something larger. Examples are advertisements showing the family around the breakfast table.
- *Need to nurture* – the appeal to paternal or maternal instincts, which again appears to be an intrinsic trait of many. Examples are advertisements with mothers and babies.
- *Need for guidance* – can appeal to your desire for someone to care for you, so you will not have to worry. This also relates to the want of solving your problems quickly. Examples are advertisements to correct tax bills or lose weight.
- *Need to aggress* – basic tendency to get even or get back at. Examples are ads that involve neighbors or that "other" group of kids at school.
- *Need to achieve* – most people want to be successful and that usually means achieving something. The ability for the person to accomplish something that seems difficult identifies the product with winning. Many times, sports figures as spokespersons project this image.

- *Need to dominate* – again, this is related to a problem or perceived shortcoming that limits acquiring power. Examples are slogans such as "master the possibilities."
- *Need for prominence* – people generally want to be admired, respected, or have high social status. Examples are people who own tasteful china, classic diamonds, and fine clothes.
- *Need for attention* – we want people to notice us, or we want to be looked at in a positive way. Cosmetics are an example of this advertising approach.
- *Need for autonomy* – within a crowded environment, we want to be singled out or be an individual. This approach can also be used negatively: You may be left out if you do not use a particular product. Examples are advertisements with emphasizing a person within a crowd based on some item of clothing.
- *Need to escape* – the desire for flight and escape is very appealing and pleasurable; you can imagine adventures you cannot have. Examples are advertisements for faraway resorts.
- *Need to feel safe* – to be free from threats and to be secure. Examples are the appeal of many insurance and bank ads.
- *Need for aesthetic sensations* – beauty attracts us, and classic art or dance makes us feel creative, enhanced. Examples are advertisements with classic works of art or performance.
- *Need to satisfy curiosity* – facts support our belief that information is quantifiable and numbers and diagrams make our choices seem scientific. Examples are use of precise discounts in advertisements or specific improvement that result from the use of a product.
- *Psychological needs* – people have certain needs, such as to sleep, eat, and drink in this category. So, we see advertisements for food, drink, sleep aids, medicine, and so forth that address these psychological desires.

Potpourri: In the book, *CA$HVERTISING*, Drew Eric Whitman [60] outlines eight Life Forces that are human's *biologically programmed desires*.

1. *Survival* enjoyment of life … life extension
2. *Enjoyment* of food and beverages
3. *Freedom* from fear, pain, and danger
4. *Sexual* companionship
5. *Comfortable* living conditions
6. *To be superior* … winning … keeping up with the Joneses
7. *Care and protection* of loved ones
8. *Social approval*

Whitman [60] also outlines nine Secondary Wants, which are as follows:

1. To be *informed*
2. *Curiosity*
3. *Cleanliness* of body and surroundings
4. *Efficiency*

5. *Convenience*
6. *Dependability*/Quality
7. *Expression* of beauty and style
8. *Economy*/Profit
9. *Bargains*

These seem reasonable desires and wants at which to target advertising efforts and are in line with research in fundamental and basic human needs [68].

Advertising types

One can classify advertising into three broad categories: brand advertising, direct response, and positioning advertising.

Brand advertising. With brand advertising, the aim is to build a successful and positive connection between the brand and the consumer. With a successful connection, the business and associated products and services are known quantities to customers. This connection has an element of comfort, trust, and attention, which are core elements of the relationship we try to establish via persuasive communications.

Potpourri: One of the most successful branding advertising efforts was conducted by P&G. Owing to its immense advertising budget and lengthy list of retail products, P&G has had a great influence on advertising practice in the United States and hence, throughout the world.

P&G sponsored and produced a radio program in the 1930s and television programs in the 1950s designed with no other purpose than to reach the audiences most likely to buy its products, namely stay-at-home housewives.

Hence, the term "soap opera," as the advertisements during these shows typically were for household items like soap.

We see a similar journey on the Internet as businesses work to attract new consumers, meaning venturing out beyond just the pull aspect of sponsored search.

Effective marketing at this point requires a shift from buying advertising space to developing online locations that attract consumers, including digital assets such as Web sites about products, programs to foster word of mouth, applications that customize advertising based on the context and the consumer, and pages on social networking sites.

Although this shift can be difficult and seem risky, given the lack of metrics for this type of branding, businesses can gain great exposure online (just like P&G did on radio and television).

With this exposure, businesses can influence online word of mouth, utilize tools that track and monitor online conversations about brands [69], and then react or be proactive with the conversation.

Direct response advertising. With direct-response advertising, one is advertising to directly sell (without a middleman) a product or service to the consumer, which can either be an individual or another business. Direct-response advertising is where most advertising dollars are spent; it is the engine of advertising, as the goal of most advertising messages are to clearly promote a specific product to a targeted audience of consumers [70]. Direct advertising is really at the heart of sponsored search.

Potpourri: Here is the headline of the direct-response advertisement that made history:

They Laughed When I Sat Down
At the Piano
But When I Started To Play!~

This was the headline for an advertisement for mail-order piano lessons crafted by John Caples, who is considered by many to be one of the greatest copywriters of all time.

He was a copywriter for forty-nine years, producing (in addition to numerous advertisements) several articles and books on the subject of crafting advertisements, including the classic, *Tested Advertising Methods* [2].

His headline and accompanying advertisement copy for piano lessons is created with launching a new school of advertising based on empirical data and testing [71].

This was years before sponsored search provided online methods of tracking advertisements. Caples did it using coupons, codes, and phone numbers!

Position advertising. The purpose of position advertising is to instil a single sentence, slogan, or image into the marketplace that a brand, as either a business or product, can be known for. Position advertising is used to reach targeted customers in a crowded marketplace for the sole purpose of increasing awareness.

Position advertising is needed because consumers are bombarded with a continuous stream of advertising messages. The consumer reacts to this high volume of advertising by accepting only what is consistent with prior knowledge or experience or what they perceive as relevant within a given context.

One can position a product in several ways, such as:

- By product *differences*
- By product *attributes* or benefits
- By *price*/quality
- By product *users*
- By product *usage* or application
- against a particular *competitor*
- against an entire *product category*
- By *association*
- By *problem*

Potpourri: Good wine needs no bush.

This saying proverbially means that products that are made well do not need to be advertised, as these high-quality products sell themselves via their own product attributes. *(Continued)*

The literal origin of this saying dates from the middle ages, before most people could read. Therefore, shops and stores had signs hanging outside with pictures of their wares, so that potential patrons could know what products the shops sold.

In this context, shops that sold wine had a picture of a bush with grapes on it hanging outside their establishments so that thirsty drinkers would know that *vino* was available inside.

However, the saying "Good wine needs no bush" developed for the shops that sold very good wine. Everyone would soon hear about it and come flocking, regardless of the sign outside.

Naturally, we don't hear this exact saying anymore.

However, we do hear its modern equivalents, with sayings such as "Quality sells itself."

Advertising is a key process in communicating aspects of the product or service to consumers. However, a business must also be concerned with several other aspects that are bundled together in a concept known as marketing.

Marketing in Sponsored Search

Separate from both branding and advertising (although with a lot of overlap and synergy) is the philosophy of marketing, which is based on the premise that businesses must analyze the needs of their potential consumers and then make business decisions to address these needs. To be successful, businesses must meet their customers' needs better than the competition can.

As such, the key drivers of marketing become:

- Customer *wants*
- *Possibilities* of addressing this want
- Customers *satisfaction*.

The outcome of these drivers is the *marketing concept* that centers on:

- Focusing on potential customer *needs* before developing the product
- Aligning *functions* of the company to focus on those needs
- Realizing a *profit* by successfully satisfying customer needs over the long term.

Achieving these outcomes is called marketing. Marketing is all about connecting with customers. In the 1960s, the economist Philip Kotler changed the perception of marketing from a collection of specific tasks to an integrated progression [72]. Kotler saw marketing as a social process in which individuals obtained what they needed or wanted by exchanging products [72].

Specifically, marketing is the activity, set of institutions, and processes for creating, communicating, delivering, and exchanging offerings that have value for customers, clients, partners, and society at large [5]. There are several types of markets, including business to consumer, business to business, consumer to consumer, consumer to business, and reseller, so who the customer is can vary.

More specifically, marketing consists of strategies and tactics used to identify, create, and maintain relationships with customers that result in value for both the customer and the marketer [73]. As with advertising, the concept of communication is inherent to marketing. As such, marketing has several elements that work in conjunction with and conceptually encompassing both brandingand advertising.

Similar to advertising, marketing requires an understanding of how the consumer makes decisions. Once this is determined, marketing then focuses business strategies (which might include aspects of branding and advertising) and resources on the most influential consumer touch points.

These touch points are typically viewed in the metaphor of the buying funnel (see Chapter 5). Consumers start with several potential brands in mind (a.k.a., the wide end of the funnel), and marketing is then directed at them as they methodically reduce that number and move through the funnel. At the end, they emerge with one brand they chose to purchase. As discussed in the chapter on consumer behavior, the buying funnel is a business-oriented paradigm [74].

How does one move a consumer through the buying funnel?

The answer to this question is at the heart of marketing. To answer this question, we must consider the marketing activities, principles, and product levels.

Potpourri: Many books and documents point to the Internet and Web as technologies that have transformed marketing.

However, possibly none has made an impact like The Cluetrain Manifesto, which has both gained a legitimate standing and a cult-like following.

At the heart of the The Cluetrain Manifesto are ninety-five theses organized as a call to action for businesses in the online marketplace.

Rick Levine, Christopher Locke, and David Weinberger wrote The Cluetrain Manifesto in 1999, and a book elaborating on the ninety-five theses [22] was published in 2000, by the same authors, along with Doc Seals.

Although there are several major points presented, the heart of the manifesto is that the Internet enables a previously unattainable level of business-to-consumer and consumer-to-business communication.

The manifesto also presents a call to action for businesses to respond to this new marketplace environment.

The entire book is available on the Web.

Marketing activities

There are four general types of marketing activities that can help marketers address consumers at these touch points [75].

- *Prioritizing* objectives and spending
- *Tailoring* the messaging
- *Investing* in consumer-driven marketing
- *Winning* the in-store (or online) battle

Let us address each of these marketing activities in more detail.

Prioritizing objectives and spending. Although it is most common to focus on the ends of the buying funnel by either building awareness or generating loyalty among current customers ready to buy, there are many other possible touch points in the buying funnel [76]. One can influence the buying decision at the research and decision stages by presenting the potential customer with the correct targeted information. To do this, marketing efforts for a product may need to shift from a focus on brand position to a more targeted emphasis on price or convenience for the customer to make a purchase.

Tailoring the messaging. The marketing message must change to win the customer in whatever part of the buying funnel may be needed in order to reach that particular customer. Therefore, a general message cutting across all stages may not be effective and may need to be replaced by a message addressing a specific point in the buying funnel, such as initial consideration or active evaluation of a choice set.

Investing in consumer-driven marketing. Awareness queries are often lucrative points in the buying funnel [76]. These are good places to attract new customers and attract potential purchasers before they ever get to any formal buying phase of searching. Therefore, it can be worthwhile for businesses to invest in these active evaluation phases of searching as consumers seek information, reviews, and recommendations, shown in research reported in Jansen and Simone [76].

Winning the in-store (online) battle. Even with all the affordances of online shopping, many consumers hold off on purchasing until they are in a store. As such, the combination and integration of online and offline marketing has to be synchronized to be effective. Online images of merchandising and packaging that are in line with what is in the store can be a very important selling factor. Also, consumers want to look at and examine products in action. Some of this can be done online with links to videos, images, and consumer reviews. In-store and online integration has become essential to marketing and selling.

Integrating all customer-facing activities. The different aspects of a business that customers see, such as Web sites, press, loyalty programs, social media, and sponsored-search efforts, have to be coordinated and in synch with each other to send a coherent marketing message to the customer.

Marketing principles

One of the aims of marketing is to gain knowledge of the customers, competitors, the industry vertical, and other aspects of the business. For a marketing effort to succeed, both the customer and the marketer must feel they are receiving something worthwhile in return for their efforts. Without a strong perception of value, it is unlikely a strong relationship can be built.

But how does one implement these activities and the related strategies and tactics? The classic set of marketing activities is summarized by the four P's: Product, Price, Placement, and Promotion [77, 78]. The four P's trace their roots to the early 1950s, when Neil H. Borden redefined the role of the marketing manager by introducing the marketing mix as an integrated set of tactics to realize organizational objectives and create a closer, higher-value relationship with customers [77]. The term "marketing mix" became popularized after Borden published his 1964 article, *The Concept of the Marketing Mix*. Borden began using the term in his teaching in the late 1940s, although he credits another professor, James Culliton, for actually being the first to describe the marketing manager as a "mixer of ingredients" [77].

The ingredients in Borden's marketing mix included product planning, pricing, branding, distribution, personal selling, advertising, promotions, packaging, display, servicing, physical handling, fact finding, and analysis.

In the late 1950s, McCarthy [78] condensed the number of variables in the marketing mix into four principal categories that today are known as the four P's of marketing:

- *Product*: select the tangible and intangible benefits of the product.
- *Price*: determine an appropriate product pricing structure.
- *Promotion*: create awareness of the product among the target audience.
- *Place*: make the product available to the customer.

The overlay of the four P's, within a given context, provides a business with their target audience, as shown in Figure 6.3, with the targeted market and potential markets.

Where all four P's overlap is the target market, as these are the consumers who are interested in your product, have the means to purchase the product, are in the right location, and who respond to the promotion.

There are also potential markets where some but not all of the four P's fit a consumer's criteria. For these consumers, they may represent potential buyers at given times, such as discounts, sales, or alternate products.

Finally, the four P's operate with constraints inherent in the marketplace, such as economic conditions, competitive factors, societal trends, technology, and political regulations.

Since McCarthy [78], additional P's have been added to the marketing mix, along with some C's. We focus on a set of seven P's (product, price, promotion, place, packaging, positioning, and people) and three C's (customers, competition, and company). As products, markets, customers, and needs change rapidly, businesses must continually revisit these seven P's and three C's to make sure they are on track and achieving the maximum results possible.

The seven P's and three C's are as follows.

Product. Product is a tangible object, an intangible service, or intangible digital content that is produced or manufactured. Tangible products are something that you can touch and feel, such as a book or computer. Intangible services include booking a vacation or reserving a hotel room. Intangible content is digital media (i.e., think bits instead of atoms) like ringtones or songs or software. So, we use the term *product* in a broad sense to include both products and services, both tangible and intangible. Generally, products are subject to a life cycle involving a growth phase followed by an eventual period of declining growth and eventual stabilization as the

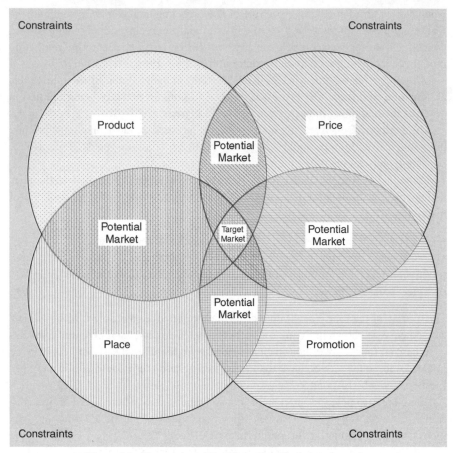

Figure 6.3. The overlap of the 4Ps to identify the target market

product approaches market saturation. However, growth does not equal profitability, and many stable products are still revenue generators for companies.

For a business to retain its competitiveness in the market, product differentiation is required. Product differentiation is the process or means that separates your product from others in the marketplace. It can range from new features to special packaging. Related to this differentiation are the levels (or benefits) of the product to the consumer, which we discuss in depth later.

For sponsored search, advertisers must isolate their products' features, attributes, or offerings to relate the product to the target audience.

Price. Price is the amount of currency for which a business will sell its product. There are several pricing schemes, ranging from a set price paid in full at the time of purchase to an installment with interest over time. The price is one of the key elements tied to a product, and it is symbolic of several product characteristics in the mind of the customer. These characteristics can include status, quality, and value. As such, businesses should continually examine the price set for their products and services to ensure the price is appropriate for the target market segment.

For sponsored search, price is one key product attribute for which a consumer close to the purchase phase will search online. There are many attention-getting key-phrases related to price, including *discount*, *sale*, and *free*.

Potpourri: Pricing a product or service can get really tricky. Two examples to illustrate this are *prestige pricing* and *fractional pricing*.

Prestige price is the practice of charging higher prices for goods or services to give the impression to the consumer that there is added value for the cost. Prestige pricing capitalizes on people's notions that correlate price with quality. So, a high-priced product is viewed superior in quality to a similar product priced for significantly less.

Fractional pricing is the practice of costing products in odd prices or a little less than a higher round number (e.g., $9.99, $19.99, $7.97, etc.). Fractional pricing is based on the psychological pricing theory that consumers ignore the last digit and do not properly round up.

Promotion. Promotion includes all the channels and media used by a business to communicate to customers about its products or services. Promotion is how a business markets and sells products or services. Naturally, a business must balance communicating effectively while also being cost efficient.

Promotion is tied significantly with sponsored search, as ad copywriters can often increase the response rate from sponsored search ads by simply changing the headline on an advertisement [2]. This improvement comes from continual testing. A rule of thumb is that whatever copy or promotion is working today will eventually not work, as consumer tastes change, competitors copy the essence of the message, or the product changes. Therefore, new promotion techniques, approaches, offerings, and strategies are continually needed.

Although there is certainly crossover, promotion is typically viewed as having six distinct elements:

* *Traditional advertising* – (a.k.a., "above the line advertising" [79]) any paid communications included in print, broadcast, and support media.
* *Public relations* – concerned with maintaining a public image for a business, and typically encompasses official but unpaid communications, such as press releases, exhibitions, conferences, seminars or trade fairs, and events.
* *Personal selling* –primarily word of mouth but can be any informal product-related communication by consumers, satisfied customers, or people specifically engaged to create word-of-mouth momentum (i.e., not apparently paid).
* *Sales promotion* – specific efforts by the sales staff, usually most notable by word of mouth, demonstrations, coupons, and deals.
* *Direct marketing* – marketing that reaches customers by communications directly addressed to the customer.
* *Internet/interactive marketing* – marketing of products or services over the Internet, including that of sponsored search.

Whereas advertising is most closely linked to sponsored search, these other efforts can be synchronized in an integrated marketing communication (IMC) effort that provides a lift to sponsored-search campaigns.

Potpourri: One of the most successful promotions ever executed, and a wonderful example of how small things can make a big difference, is the Hotmail example of viral promotion and use of its current customers' social network to grow the customer base.

Sabeer Bhatia and Jack Smith founded Hotmail on July 4, 1996, and it was the first Web-based e-mail service that was free to most Internet users. The name Hotmail is a mesh of the words HTML, on which the application was based, and mail.

Within five months of launch, Hotmail had more than 8 million subscribers, and it had grown to 12 million by the end of the first year.

How did Hotmail generate such a large user base so fast?

Certainly, as the first company to provide free e-mail to the general Internet population, Hotmail generated a lot of free press on television, in newspapers, and through other mass media channels. In other words, they were newsworthy on their own. This media attention certainty generated some customers.

However, what added to their growth was a simple tactic that leveraged the social connections of exiting Hotmail customers.

Hotmail placed a small signature below all outgoing mails that recommended and provided a link for recipients of the e-mail messages to sign up for Hotmail (i.e., "Get your free Web-based mail at hotmail.com").

This very simple promotional tactic was extremely successful, and it resulted in an unbelievable growth rate. Within two years, Hotmail had more than 30 million subscribers, all without any Internet banner advertising or television commercials. It was nearly all from this viral marketing technique.

Hotmail's simple act of placing a promotion at the end of an e-mail message is a classic example of leveraging an existing audience, all while being fairly nonintrusive.

Place.   Place is where a product or service is actually sold in the marketplace. It is the location where the customer can purchase the product. A business can sell a product in many different places, and sometimes a small change can have a dramatically positive effect on sales.

There are a variety of such places in the marketplace, including both physical and virtual. Some businesses sell directly via a salesperson. Others sell via telemarketing efforts. Some companies are primarily brick-and-mortar stores or sell in the retailer establishments of other businesses. Others are primarily catalogs or mail-order operations, whereas others sell at trade shows. Some sell in joint ventures with other similar products or services. Some companies use manufacturers' representatives or distributors. Or course, many businesses sell via the Internet. Often companies use a combination of one or more of these methods and are characterized as being multi-channel marketers.

Deciding where the best place – or places – is for the customer to receive the critical buying information at the point of purchase is a key marketing decision.

Regardless of the type or number of places, a sponsored-search effort has to be aware of each available place of purchase and direct the customer to appropriate one.

Packaging. Packaging is how your product or service appears to consumers. Naturally, packaging refers to the material surrounding your actual product. However, packaging also refers to the employees of the business and the appearance they project. Packaging refers to the business space, such as salesroom, offices, Web site, and social media pages. It refers to company brochures, press releases, and other visual elements of your company. Everything either helps or hurts the packaging of your product and service. It all affects your customer's confidence in the quality and reputation of the product.

Sponsored-search advertisements, in all their aspects, are part of this packaging – from how the headlines read, to which rank the advertisements appear, to what key-term triggers the ad, to what image appears with the text of the ad, to the URL that is displayed.

Positioning. Positioning is how your product, service, or company is thought of in the marketplace by consumers. How do people think and talk about you when you are not present? How do people think and talk about your company? What positioning do you have in your market, in terms of the specific words people use when they describe you and your offerings to others? Position advertising is a direct method of achieving position in the market place.

How customers view a business can be a critical determinant of success in a competitive marketplace [80]. Many times a customer's view of a business may be a single attribute, either positive or negative. For example: "the service of this airline sucks," "this store always has cool stuff!" or "the chef in this restaurant always makes great desserts!"

For sponsored search, the keyphrases and advertisement copy must be in line with what the customers think of the business. Or, if the advertisement is branding-related, the advertisement copy should be structured so as to change the business's position in the marketplace.

People. People refer to the individuals, both inside and outside of the business, who are responsible for each element of sales and marketing, including strategy and activities. This includes getting the right people involved in the process and then getting the right people to the right part of the process. On the flip side, people can also mean people outside the business or related business, such as those in the supply chain.

Although many of these people are far removed from the mechanics of sponsored-search efforts, it is important that they understand the goal of the advertising effort that may affect the business's marketing processes.

Customer. Customer is one who uses the products or services that your business provides. Markets consist of human beings, not demographic sectors [63]. Sometimes customers pay for the products or services or use of these products. Other times they may just use (i.e., consume) the product without payment, such as businesses that work on a *freemium* model. Regardless, a better understanding of the needs and usage patterns of customers can assist in many marketing aspects, including sponsored search. Isolating who are the customers means proper market segmentation and demographics. Who are the potential consumers? What are their motivations? How much money are they willing to spend on your product or service?

Most businesses find that customer impact follows a power law distribution such as the 80–20 rule. In other words, a relatively small set of customers (e.g., 20 percent) provides most of the business revenue (e.g., 80 percent).

However, a customer is not necessarily someone who is currently purchasing or about to purchase a product. Instead, one can classify customers into three groupings from the larger group of consumers:

- *Existing customers* – those individuals who have purchased or used a business' products or services, usually within some designated time period set by the company. Existing customers are by far the most important of the customer groups because these people have a current relationship with the business. Additionally, existing customers often represent the best opportunity market for future sales, assuming they are satisfied with their present relationship with the business. Getting these existing customers to purchase more of a product or cross-selling other products to them is generally cheaper and faster than finding new customers. Existing customers are also usually easier to reach with promotional appeals.
- *Former customers* –those people who have formerly purchased or used the business's product but no longer do so because they are now using a competitor's product. The value of this customer group generally depends on the previous business-customer relationship.
- *Potential customers* – those who have yet to purchase but who may eventually become existing customers. Therefore, potential customers must have a need for a product, possess the resources to purchase the product, and have the desire or means to buy the product. Potential customers are important for a business because they can replace existing customers that become former customers. Attracting new customers allows the business to grow by increasing the existing customer base.

Sponsored-search efforts, notably in terms of continual testing and analytics, can have a major effect on correct and effective demographic targeting.

Competition. Competition includes the other companies that are competing with your business to gain the same customers. The competition can be the businesses with products or services that are similar to yours, or can be represented by companies that offer substitute products or services.

Usually, the goal of marketing is to establish some differential in one or more of the business areas to gain some competitive advantage [81].

One well-known framework for analyzing the competitive landscape is the five forces [82], which posits that there are five important forces that determine competitive power in any business situation. These are:

1. *Supplier Power*: The fewer the supplier choices you have, the more powerful your suppliers are and the weaker your competitive position.
2. *Buyer Power*: If you have a few, powerful buyers, then these buyers are better able to dictate pricing and other terms to you.
3. *Competitive Rivalry*: If you have many competitors with equally attractive products or services, then you will likely have little power in the market, as suppliers and buyers will go elsewhere if they do not get a good deal from you.
4. *Threat of Substitution*: If substitution for your product or service is easy and substitution is viable, then this substitution weakens your competitive situation.
5. *Threat of New Entry*: If you have strong and durable barriers to entry in your market, then you can preserve a favorable position and leverage it.

Competition can affect sponsored-search efforts in many ways, including higher bids on keyphrases, competition over ad position, and increased efforts for advertisements to stand out on the SERP.

The key aspect for keyword advertising is that there are usually competitors in the marketplace, so businesses will rarely have location or space all to themselves.

Company. Company is the actual organization created to conduct business, typically by providing a product or service to consumers. A business makes certain strategic decisions, especially in the area of maximizing corporation strengths, that affect how the company develops. These decisions can include whether to make a product in-house versus outsource it, corporate focus on a particular feature in its area, and how cost-effective the company is in making the product.

The company will influence what type and model of sponsored-search efforts are undertaken, as the keyword advertising effort must be in line with the strategy aspects of the company.

Continual evaluation

It is important to the seven P's and three C's that they be regularly reviewed to take into account changes in customer needs and other external influences. Marketing managers need to adapt their set of controllable variables to face new conditions. Promotion and price can be adjusted in the short term, whereas the product itself or its distribution channels cannot.

Decisions involving the marketing mix reinforce one another and strengthen the overall product's position if they are internally consistent and pursued over a longer period of time.

The following two metrics express this process:

- *Mix coherency* – refers to how well the components of the mix blend together. For example, a strategy of selling expensive luxury products at discount stores creates a poor coherency between distribution and product offering.
- *Mix dynamics* – refers to how the mix must be adapted to a changing business environment, to changes in the organization's resources, and to changes in the product life cycle.

Marketing level of products

Certainly, at the center of marketing is the product, as it is the reason that a business is in business. Simply, a product (or service) is what the business is offering for sale to potential customers.

A continual review of the product focuses on whether or not the product is appropriate and suitable for the potential consumer in the market that the business is targeting.

Kotler [83] distinguished three components for a potential market segment (i.e., a set of potential consumers):

- *Need*: a lack of a basic requirement.
- *Want*: a specific requirement for products or services to match a need.
- *Demand*: a set of wants plus the desire and ability to pay for the exchange.

Customers will choose a product based on their perceived value of it. Satisfaction is the degree to which the actual use of a product matches its perceived value at the time of purchase. A customer is satisfied only if the actual value is the same or exceeds the perceived value.

You can assess your product's value via a series of questions. Is your product or service superior in some significant way to another product available from your competitors? If so, what is the attribute of superiority? If not, could you develop an area of superiority for the product? If there is not a superior attribute, should you be offering this product or service at all in the current marketplace?

Kotler [83] defined five levels to a product:

- *Core benefit* – the fundamental need or want that consumers satisfy by consuming the product or service.
- *Generic product* – a version of the product containing only those attributes or characteristics absolutely necessary for it to function.
- *Expected product* – the set of attributes or characteristics that buyers normally expect and agree to when they purchase a product.
- *Augmented product* – inclusion of additional features, benefits, attributes, or related services that serve to differentiate the product from its competitors.
- *Potential product* – all the augmentations and transformations a product might undergo in the future.

The attributes of a product have a direct bearing on how you craft the ad copy, as an ad can discuss the feature of a product or the benefits of a product, for example.

Kotler noted that much competition takes place at the Augmented Product level rather than at the Core Benefit level [72], or as Levitt put it: "New competition is not between what companies produce in their factories, but between what they add to their factory output in the form of packaging, services, advertising, customer advice, financing, delivery arrangements, warehousing, and other things that people value" [84].

Kotler's [83] model of product attributes provides a tool to assess how the organization and their customers view their relationship and which aspects create value.

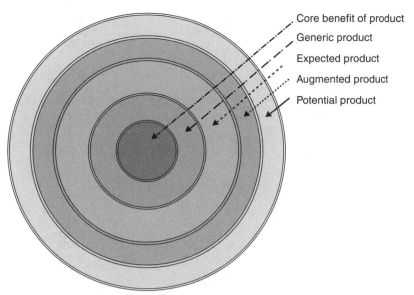

Core benefit of product
Generic product
Expected product
Augmented product
Potential product

Figure 6.4. Five attributes of a product: core, generic, expected, augmented, and potential.

Potpourri: There is a continual concern over the ethics of marketing, because one can take these goals and aims (all very legitimate) one step too far and become a questionable practitioner.

We see this practice a lot in the SEO area of online marketing, with questionable reporting practices to clients and very questionable techniques to optimize search engine rankings.

The American Marketing Association has committed itself to promoting high standards of acceptable conduct in the marketing process, publishing guidelines on ethics in marketing, including:

Ethical Values

- *Honesty* – to be forthright in dealings with customers and stakeholders.
- *Responsibility* – to accept the consequences of our marketing decisions and strategies.
- *Fairness* – to balance justly the needs of the buyer with the interests of the seller.
- *Respect* – to acknowledge the basic human dignity of all stakeholders.
- *Transparency* – to create a spirit of openness in marketing operations.
- *Citizenship* – to fulfill the economic, legal, philanthropic, and societal responsibilities that serve stakeholders.

See http://www.marketingpower.com/AboutAMA/Pages/Statement%20of%20Ethics. aspx for the complete ethics guidelines.

	Concepts of			BAM Impact on ...
	Branding	Advertising	Marketing	Sponsored Search
Tactical	**Web search** selection of engine evaluation SERP link evaluation page evaluation	**Advertising types** brand direct response positional	**Product attributes** core benefit generic product expected product augmented product potential product	**Tactics** keywords ad copy ad testing ad scheduling
Strategic	**Constructs** brand awareness brand image brand satisfaction brand trust brand attachment	**Advertising factors** size of market size of audience size of budget	**7Ps and 3Cs** product price promotion place packaging positioning people customers competition company	**Strategy** bidding budget allocation campaigns goals and aims expected ROI

Figure 6.5. BAM framework of branding, advertising, and marketing concepts and the effect these concepts have on the tactics and strategies of sponsored search.

BAM Framework

We integrate some of the key concepts of branding, advertising, and marketing into a combined BAM framework, shown in Figure 6.5.

In Figure 6.5, the top row is the tactical focus and the bottom row is the strategic focus of sponsored-search efforts. We see that brand, advertising, and marketing concepts impact both strategy and tactical aspects of sponsored search. The elements within each row's cell are the specific branding, advertising, and marketing components that impact sponsored search.

The strategy level of sponsored search (i.e., bidding strategy, budget allocation, account structure, effort goals and aims, and expected ROI) is impacted by branding constructs, advertising factors, and the seven P's and three C's of marketing.

Strategically, the elements of branding (i.e., awareness, image, satisfaction, trust, and attachment) are key drivers that set the parameters of the keyword advertising effort, both enabling and constraining. The advertising aspects of market, audience, and budgets are additional enablers and constraints. Finally, the seven Ps and three Cs define the marketing process for the sponsored-search effort, impacting bidding, budget, campaigns, goals, aims, and ultimately the ROI.

At the tactical level, branding concepts of Web search, advertising types, and product attributes impact sponsored-search tactics such as keyphrase selection, ad copy, ad testing aspects, and ad scheduling.

There is a continual branding element in all phases of Web search, from selection of the search engine, to evaluation of SERP, to evaluation of individual results, to evaluation of the landing page.

The advertising goal, whether branding, direct response, or position, will certainly impact nearly all elements of the sponsored-search effort.

Finally, the five categories of products attributes serve both as the inspiration for and the imposed constraints for sponsored-search efforts.

Foundational Takeaways

- *Branding* is a process involving all activities to assign a brand to a product or service. Branding for search on the Web is a multistage process of search engine selection, evaluation of the SERP, selection of an individual link, and then evaluation of the landing page. A *brand* is a unique attribute, name, term design, or symbol.
- *Advertising* is a commercial promotion of some product or service intended to persuade a potential consumer to take some action.
- *Marketing* is a social process where individuals obtain what they need or want by exchanging products, commonly defined as the seven P's and three C's.

Relating Theory to Practice

Branding, advertising, and marketing are the foundation of our sponsored-search effort. We have dealt with them in very broad concepts in this chapter to get to their core meanings.

Now, we must take the foundational elements and apply them directly to our sponsored search efforts by examining the particular market segment that we operate in.

We focus on key questions, such as:

- What brand image do consumers have of our product or company?
- What is the brand relationship we are trying to develop with our advertising?
- What brand knowledge does our advertising convey to consumers?
- Which of the seven P's and three C's is our sponsored-search effort focusing on?
- Which branded keyphrases are beneficial to bid on?
- What brand message do our advertisements convey? (e.g., cheapest price, luxury, reliability, etc.)
- What is our overall marketing objective in terms of consumer engagement?
- What product attributes do we want to inform the customer of?

From a marketing perspective, there are several questions that we can ask before we even begin our sponsored-search efforts, including:

- Do you know your market, such as size, spread, and needs?
- Who is your best prospect? In terms of age, income, gender, or geography?
- Who is your competition?
- What is the sales potential?
- What price point is needed to break even?
- When do you make a profit?
- What is the sales potential?
- Is your product subject to seasonality?
- What price will the market respond to and call?

These types of questions should be worked into one's overall marketing effort. They take the foundational concepts of branding, advertising, and marketing and translate them into actionable objectives for sponsored search.

Conclusion

Branding, advertising, and marketing are the foundational elements of any sponsored-search effort. These three elements are woven through nearly every element of sponsored search.

The concept of the brand is really at the heart of everything we do. The image of the product in the mind of the consumer can be an extreme positive, making selling easier, or severely negative, making no amount of advertising beneficial to a product. Our advertising and marketing efforts must also be focused on improving the brand relationship that our potential customers have with our products or services.

To the business, advertising means generating sales. However, a sale can either be now or at some point in the future. So, advertising can focus on branding, or some other component of the marketing effort, with the goal being a future sale rather than an immediate one.

Although our goal is to generate sales, the customer wants information. Perhaps they are looking for the price of a given product. Maybe this information is something about the product's features. Or it could be how the product will make the customer feel at an emotional level. Regardless, the advertising must communicate the desired information to the consumer.

Sponsored-search efforts are part of the marketing process. As such, we must integrate the key components of marketing into our sponsored-search campaigns. Of the many aspects that the marketing process addresses, the key aspect has to be the levels of our product. These levels (core, generic, expected, augmented, and potential) articulate what our advertisements can convey to the consumer and our branding message should be.

However, how do we know if we are applying these branding, advertising, and marketing principles effectively or efficiently? These are concepts that do not lend themselves directly to mathematical formulas or calculations. There are nearly endless possibilities for attitude and selection when it comes to sponsored-search advertisements. How do we measure success?

For this, we turn to sponsored-search analytics, which we address in the following chapter.

References

[1]   Hardy, Q. 2009. "The Big Deal: Google's Marissa Mayer." *Forbes*. Retrieved April 4, 2011, from http://www.forbes.com/2009/07/30/marissa-mayer-google-intelligent-technology-mayer.html

[2]   Caples J. (Revised by Fred E. Hahn). 1997. *Tested Advertising Methods*, 5th ed. Upper Saddle River, NJ: Prentice Hall.

[3]   Ogilvy, D. 1963. *Confessions of an Advertising Man*. London: Atheneu.

[4]   Ogilvy, D. 1983. *Ogilvy on Advertising*. Toronto: John Wiley and Sons.

[5] Kaye, B. K. and Medoff, N. J. 2001. *Just a Click Away: Advertising on the Internet.* Needham Heights, MA: Allyn and Bacon.

[6] Keller, K. L. and Lehmann, D. R. 2006. "Brands and Branding: Research Findings and Future Priorities." *Marketing Science*, vol. 25(6), pp. 740–759.

[7] Jansen, B. J., Brown, A., and Resnick, M. 2007. "Factors Relating to the Decision to Click-on a Sponsored Link." *Decision Support Systems*, vol. 44(1), pp. 46–59.

[8] Jansen, B. J. and Resnick, M. 2006. "An Examination of Searchers' Perceptions of Non-Sponsored and Sponsored Links during Ecommerce Web Searching," *Journal of the American Society for Information Science and Technology*, vol. 57(14), pp. 1949–1961.

[9] Jansen, B. J., Zhang, M., and Schultz, C. 2009. "Search Engine Brand and the Effect on User Perception of Searching Performance." *Journal of the American Society for Information Sciences and Technology*, vol. 60(8), pp. 1572–1595.

[10] SEMPO (2009). Search Engine Optimization & Marketing Glossary. Retrieved April 11, 2009, from http://www.sempo.org/learning_center/sem_glossary#b

[11] Berry, L. L. 2000. "Cultivating Service Brand Equity." *Journal of the Academy of Marketing Science*, vol. 28(1), pp. 128–137.

[12] deChernatony, L., Drury, S., and Segal-Horn, S. 2003. "Building a Services Brand: Stages, People and Orientations." *The Service Industries Journal*, vol. 23(3), pp. 1–21.

[13] Keller, K. L. and Richey, K. 2006. "The Importance of Corporate Brand Personality Traits to a Successful 21st Century Business." *Journal of Brand Management*, vol. 14(1/2), pp. 74–81.

[14] Brinker, S. (2010). 4 Principles of Conversion Content Marketing. (August 11). Retrieved January 26, 2011, from http://searchengineland.com/4-principles-of-conversion-content-marketing-48115

[15] Esch, F.-R., Langner, T., and Bernd H.Schnmitt, G. 2006. "Are Brands Forever? How Brand Knowledge and Relationships Affect Current and Future Purchases." *Journal of Product and Brand Management*, vol. 15(2), pp. 98–105.

[16] Keller, K. L. 1993. "Conceptualizing, Measuring, and Managing Customer-Based Brand Equity." *Journal of Marketing*, vol. 51(1), pp. 1–22.

[17] Percy, L. and Rossiter, J. R. 1992. "A Model of Brand Awareness and Brand Attitude Adverting Strategies." *Psychology and Marketing (1996–1998)*, vol. 9(4), pp. 263–274.

[18] Jansen, B. J. and McNeese, M. D. 2005. "Evaluating the Effectiveness of and Patterns of Interactions with Automated Searching Assistance." *Journal of the American Society for Information Science and Technology*, vol. 56(14), pp. 1480–1503.

[19] Niehaus, S. 2010. Conversion-Optimized Touch Points: The Thank You Page. (July 23). Retrieved January 26, 2011, from http://searchengineland.com/conversion-optimized-touch-points-the-thank-you-page-44704

[20] Fournier, S. 1998. "Consumer and Their Brands: Developing Relationship Theory in Consumer Research." *Journal of Consumer Research*, vol. 24(4), pp. 343–353.

[21] Garnier, M. 2009. "Search Engine Loyalty: Considering the Commitment-Loyalty Link from a Hedonic Versus Utilitarian Perspective." *International Journal of Internet Marketing and Advertising*, vol. 5(1/2), pp. 43–73.

[22] Bearden, W. O. and Teel, J. E. 1983. "Selected Determinants of Consumer Satisfaction and Complaint Reports." *Journal of Marketing Research*, vol. 20(1), pp. 21–28.

[23] Hunt, S. D. 1993. "Objectivity in Marketing Theory and Research." *Journal of Marketing*, vol. 57(2), pp. 76–91.

[24] Liljander, V. and Strandvik, T. 1997. "Emotions in Service Satisfaction." *International Journal of Service Industry Management*, vol. 8(2), pp. 148–169.

[25] Strauss, B. and Neuhaus, P. 1997. "The Qualitative Satisfaction Model." *International of Service Industry Management*, vol. 8(3), pp. 236–249.

[26] Rotter, J. B. 1967. "A New Scale for the Measurement of Interpersonal Trust." *Journal of Personality*, vol. 35, pp. 651–665.

[27] McAllister, D. J. 1995. "Affect- and Cognition-Based Trust as Foundations for Interpersonal Cooperation in Organizations." *Academy of Management Journal*, vol. 38, p. 25.

[28] Chaudhuri, A. and Holbrook, M. B. 2001. "The Chain of Effects from Brand Trust and Brand Affect to Brand Performance: The Role of Brand Loyalty." *Journal of Marketing*, vol. 65(2), pp. 81–93.

[29] Morgan, R. M. and Hunt, S. D. 1994. "The Commitment-Trust Theory Of Relationship Marketing." *Journal of Marketing*, vol. 58(3), pp. 20–38.

[30] Ratnasingham, P. 1998. "The Importance of Trust in Electronic Commerce." *Internet Research*, vol. 8(4), p. 313.

[31] Walther, J. B. 1995. "Relational Aspects of Computer-Mediated Communication: Experimental Observations Over Time." *Organization Science*, vol. 6(2), pp. 186–203.

[32] Berry, L. L. and Parasuraman, A. 1991. *Marketing Services*. New York: The Free Press.

[33] Moorman, C., Zaltman, G., and Deshpande, R. 1992. "Relationships between Providers and Users of Marketing Research: The Dynamics of Trust within and between Organizations." *Journal of Vocational Behavior*, vol. 14, pp. 224–247.

[34] Johnson, D. J. and Rusbult, C. E. 1989. "Resisting Temptation: Devaluation of Alternative Partners as a Means of Maintaining Commitment in Close Relationships." *Journal of Personality and Social Psychology*, vol. 57, pp. 967–980.

[35] Mowday, R. T., Steers, R. M., and Porter, L. W. 1979. "The Measurement Of Organizational Commitment." *Journal of Vocational Behavior*, vol. 14, pp. 224–247.

[36] Kanter, R. M. 1968. "Commitment and Social Organisation: A Study of Commitment Mechanisms in Utopian Communities." *American Sociological Review*, vol. 33, pp. 499–517.

[37] Angle, H. L. and Perry, J. L. 1981. "An Empirical Assessment of Organizational Commitment and Organizational Effectiveness." *Administrative Science Quarterly*, vol. 26(March), pp. 1–13.

[38] Ha, H.-Y. and Perks, H. 2005. "Effects of Consumer Perceptions of Brand Experience on the Web: Brand Familiarity, Satisfaction and Brand Trust." *Journal of Consumer Behaviour*, vol. 4(6), pp. 438–452.

[39] Sicilia, M., Ruiz, S., and Reynolds, N. 2006. "Attitude Formation Online: How the Consumer's Need for Cognition Affects the Relationship between Attitude towards the Website and Attitude towards the Brand." *International Journal of Market Research*, vol. 48(2), pp. 139–154.

[40] Jansen, B. J., Zhang, M., and Schultz, C. D. 2009. "Search Engine Brand and the Effect on User Perception of Searching Performance." *Journal of the American Society for Information Science and Technology*, 60(8), 1572–1595.

[41] Bailey, P., Thomas, P., and Hawking, D. 2007. "Does Brand Name Influence Perceived Search Result Quality? Yahoo!, Google, and WebKumara." In *Proceedings of the 12th Australasian Document Computing Symposium*, Melbourne, Australia.

[42] Falk, L. K., Sockel, H., and Warren, H. 2007. "A Holistic View of Internet Marketing." *Competition Forum*, vol. 5(1), pp. 9–14.

[43] Balabanis, G. and Reynolds, N. L. . 2001. "Consumer Attitudes towards Multi-Channel Retailers' Web Sites: The Role of Involvement, Brand Attitude, Internet Knowledge and Visit Duration." *Journal of Business Strategies*, vol. 18(2), pp. 105–131.

[44] Park, J. and Stoel, L. 2005. "Effect of Brand Familiarity, Experience and Information on Online Apparel Purchase." *International Journal of Retail and Distribution Management*, vol. 33(2/3), pp. 148–160.

[45] Hotchkiss, G. 2005. "Enquiro Eye Tracking Report II: Google, MSN and Yahoo! Compared." Vol. 2006: Enquiro Search Solutions.

[46] Jansen, B. J. 2007. "The Comparative Effectiveness of Sponsored and Non-sponsored Results for Web Ecommerce Queries." *ACM Transactions on the Web*, vol. 1(1), p. Article 3.

[47] Koufaris, M. and Hampton-Sosa, W. 2004. "The Development of Initial Trust in an Online Company by New Customers." *Information & Management*, vol. 41(3), pp. 377–397.

[48] Hotchkiss, G. 2006. "Enquiro Eye Tracking Report II: Google, MSN and Yahoo! Compared." Vol. 2006: Enquiro Search Solutions.

[49] Brooks, N. (2004). The Atlas Rank Report I: How Search Engine Rank Impacts Traffic. (July). Retrieved August 1, 2004, from http://www.atlasdmt.com/media/pdfs/insights/Rank Report.pdf

[50] Brooks, N. 2004. The Atlas Rank Report II: How Search Engine Rank Impacts Conversions. (October). Retrieved January 15, 2005, from http://www.atlasonepoint.com/pdf/AtlasRankReportPart2.pdf

[51] Pan, B., Hembrooke, H., Joachims, T., Lorigo, L., Gay, G., and Granka, L. 2007. "In Google We Trust: Users' Decisions on Rank, Position, and Relevance." *Journal of Computer-Mediated Communication*, vol. 12(3), Article 3. http://jcmc.indiana.edu/vol12/issue3/pan.html

[52] Jansen, B. J., Sobel, K., and Zhang, M., forthcoming "Understanding the Effect of Branded Terms in Phrases and Ads for Sponsored Search," *International Journal of Electronic Commerce*.

[53] Danuloff, C. 2010. "21 Secret Truths of High-Resolution PPC." Click Equations, Philadelphia.

[54] Jansen, B. J., Spink, A., and Pedersen, J. 2005. "Trend Analysis of AltaVista Web Searching." *Journal of the American Society for Information Science and Technology*, vol. 56(6), pp. 559–570.

[55] Iyengar, S. 2010. *The Art of Choosing*. New York: Hackette.

[56] Bosley, S. 2007. "9 Tips for Effective Political Paid Search Advertising." Vol. 2010. Charlottesville, VA: RKG.

[57] Starch, D. 1923. *Principles of Advertising*. Chicago: Shaw Company.

[58] Schwab, V. O. 1962. *How to Write a Good Advertisement: A Short Course in Copywriting*. Chatsworth, CA: Wilshire.

[59] Hopkins, C. 1924. *Scientific Advertising*. New York: Cosimo Classics.

[60] Whitman, D. E. 2009. *CA$HVERTISING: How to Use More Than 100 Secrets of Ad-Agency Psychology to Make Big Money Selling Anything to Anyone*. Franklin Lakes, NJ: The Career Press.

[61] Alexander, R. S. 1963. *Marketing Definitions: A Glossary of Marketing Terms*. Chicago: American Marketing Association.

[62] Lavidge, R. and Steiner, G. 1961. "A Model for Predictive Measurements of Advertising Effectiveness." *The Journal of Marketing*, vol. 25(October), pp. 59–62.

[63] Locke, C., Levine, R., Searls, D., and Weinberger, D. 2000. *The Cluetrain Manifesto: The End of Business as Usual*. New York: Perseus.

[64] Pincas, S. and Loiseau, M. 2008. *A History of Advertising*. Cologne, Germany: Taschen.

[65] Perloff, R. M. 1993. "Third-Person Effect Research 1983–1992: A Review and Synthesis." *International Journal of Public Opinion Research*, vol. 5(2), pp. 167–184.

[66] Hughes, M. 2006. *Buzzmarketing: Get People to Talk About Your Stuff*. New York: Penguin Group.

[67] Fowles, J. and Fowles, R. B. 1976. *Mass Advertising as Social Forecast: A Method for Future Research*. Westport, CT: Greenwood Press.

[68] Doyal, L. and Gough, I. 1991. *A theory of Human Need*. London: Macmillian.

[69] Jansen, B. J., Zhang, M., Sobel, K., and Chowdury, A. 2009. "Twitter Power: Tweets as Electronic Word of Mouth." *Journal of the American Society for Information Sciences and Technology*, vol. 60(11), pp. 2169–2188.

[70] MacInnis, D. and Jaworski, B. 1989. "Information Processing from Advertisements: Toward an Integrative Framework." *The Journal of Marketing*, vol. 53(4), pp. 1–23.

[71] White, G. 1997. "The Story behind the Man behind History's Most Famous Ad." In *Tested Advertising Methods*, 5th ed., Caples J. (Revised by Fred E. Hahn), Ed. Upper Saddle River, NJ: Prentice Hall. pp. ix–xii.

[72] Kotler, P. 2002. *Marketing Management*, 11th ed. New York: Prentice Hall.

[73] Boone, L. E. and Kurtz, D. L. 2008. *Contemporary Marketing*, 13th ed. Mason, OH: Thomas High Education.

[74] Hotchkiss, G. 2009. *The BuyerSphere Project: How Businesses Buy from Businesses in the Digital Marketplace*. Kelowna, Canada: Enquiro.

[75] Court, D., Elzinga, D., Mulder, S., and Vetvik, O. J. (2010). The consumer decision journey. *Business Today* (October 23). Retrieved April 4, 2011, from http://www.mckinseyquarterly.com/The_consumer_decision_journey_2373

[76] Jansen, B. J. and Simone, S., 2011 "Bidding on the Buying Funnel for Sponsored Search Campaigns," *Journal of Electronic Commerce Research*, 12(1), 1–18.

[77] Borden, N. H. 1964. "The Concept of the Marketing Mix." *Journal of Advertising Research*, vol. 4(1), pp. 2–7.

[78] McCarthy, J. E. 1960. *Basic Marketing – A Managerial Approach*. Homewood, IL: Richard D. Irwin.

[79] Belch, G. and Belch, M. 2003. *Advertising and Promotion: An Integrated Marketing Communications Perspective*. New York: McGraw-Hill.

[80] Ries, A. and Trout, J. 2001. *Positioning: The Battle for Your Mind*. New York: McGraw Hill.

[81] Porter, M. E. 1998. *Competitive Advantage: Creating and Sustaining Superior Performance*. New York: Free Press.

[82] Porter, M. E. 1998. *Competitive Strategy: Techniques for Analyzing Industries and Competitors*. New York: Free Press.

[83] Kotler, P. and Keller, K. L. 2006. *Marketing Management*. New York: Prentice Hall.

[84] Levitt, T. 1969. *The Marketing Mode: Pathways to Corporate Growth*. New York: McGraw-Hill.

Word cloud generated by Wordle

7

Sponsored-Search Analytics

Half the money I spend on advertising is wasted; the trouble is, I don't know which half.
John Wanamaker,
American retailer, credited with creating the modern department
store and modern concept of advertising (attributed)

For our frame shop's keyword advertising campaigns, we are now set and running, with an understanding of our customers as reflected in keyphrases and advertising copy. We have an understanding of the branding, marketing, and advertising aspects of our campaigns and how these campaigns relate to our business. We know who our customers are and how they behave. So, we are set.

Or are we?

As Wanamaker supposedly point out with advertising in general, how do you know that your advertising dollars are making a difference?

Now that our campaign is running, how do we know if it is effective? How do we tell if we are using our advertising dollars efficiently? Are we accomplishing our goals and are we reaching them in the best possible way? Are we targeting the correct customers? Are there opportunities that we are missing?

To address these questions, we need to evaluate our sponsored-search effort.

To do this, we must measure the performance of our campaigns, including both the costs and returns. This effort is known as sponsored-search analytics, which falls in the realm of marketing research and, more specifically, Web analytics [1, 2]. Evaluation is an integral part of advertising, and there is increasing sophistication in measurement techniques. Advertisers are demanding quantified results and more scientific approaches to understanding the effectiveness advertising [3].

So, despite what we thought we knew, we are now faced with some questions. How is the account performing? How do we even measure how the campaigns are performing? What data do we collect? What analysis do we perform? What do the results mean? Measurement implies goals. What goals are we concerned with?

These questions and related ones are addressed via sponsored-search analytics.

In this chapter, we review the foundational element of sponsored-search analytics, beginning with an introduction to marketing research and Web analytics. We then add the theoretical foundation of sponsored-search analytics. Following this, we discuss the research concepts of validity, creditability, and reliability. We end with an introduction to privacy issues and click fraud with online analytics.

Potpourri: In any analysis, there are obviously things we know and things we do not know.

However, there is another element to puzzle.

In fact, there is a 2x2 of *known-unknown* and *aware-unaware*. This 2x2 is a common framework in any aspect of risk mitigation or use of data analysis for forecasting.

Basically, the idea is as follows:

- There are things that you know about (i.e., the known).
- There are things you do not know about (i.e., the unknown).
- Naturally, if you know something, you are aware of it by definition.
- However, the unknown falls into two categories.
- There are the unknowns that you are aware of (e.g., missing data).
- There are the unknowns that you are unaware of (e.g., massive and unpredictable change in the business environment).

Some refer to the unaware unknowns as the unknown unknowns!

These unknown unknowns are where the companies that are nimble and can quickly adjust gain the upper hand.

Sponsored-Search Analytics

Sponsored-search analytics (SSA) is collecting, measuring, analyzing, and reporting keyword advertising data for purposes of monitoring, understanding, and optimizing keyword advertising marketing.

As evident from the definition, SSA has several subcomponents that may contain several subtasks as well. So, SSA can get complex fairly quickly. It is easy to get lost in the details, tactics, and mechanics and lose sight of the overall purpose implied with SSA.

The goal of SSA is to establish a process that facilitates measurement of a keyword advertising effort relative to a set of quantifiable objectives set by business goals. As such, SSA means research, specifically marketing research.

With this key aspect in mind, effective SSA becomes significantly more difficult to ensure. How do we know if we are collecting, measuring, analyzing, reporting, monitoring, understanding, and optimizing in a manner that accomplishes our objectives and the underlying business goals? Proper analysis requires an understanding of the theoretical and methodological foundations of SSA, which we address in this chapter.

When conducting SSA concerning users and information systems, there is a variety of methods at one's disposal, including qualitative, quantitative, or a mix of both. The selection of an appropriate method is critically important if the analyst is to have effective outcomes and be efficient in execution. The method of data collection also involves a choice of methods [4].

Log analysis is a method for data collection and a research method for both system performance and user behavior analysis. It has been used since 1967 [5] and in peer-reviewed research since 1975 [4].

Potpourri: Meister and Sullivan [5], in 1967, appears to be the earliest documented log analysis and analytics reporting.

The analysis was on a working system from NASA and focused primarily on system performance aspects and measures rather than user behavior.

Penniman [4] established many of the basic log analysis techniques that are still in use today, as documented in one of the first academic and peer-reviewed publications in the area.

Penniman's work not only incorporated system aspects, but a healthy analysis of user behavior, including the first use of Markov modeling of user states to predict user behavior.

Many of his techniques and concepts are the basis for transaction log and Web analytics today.

Therefore, SSA assists us in managing our sponsored-search efforts as a science, not as an art. SSA helps us understand and see causes and effects and identify the correct procedure to measure what we want. Thus, our sponsored-search efforts become more efficient and effective. SSA assists us in mitigating risk.

A note on efficiency: There are many things in sponsored search that we might like to try; however, we must realize that some things are just too costly in terms of time or money to attempt, measure, and analyze. However, the advantage of sponsored-search analytics is that it allows us to evaluate each campaign and advertising efforts by a known scale of cost (e.g., cost of advertising) and result (e.g., return on investment). In other words, an understanding of SSA can prevent us from taking some costly avenues until we develop some more effective means for doing so. In the end, SSA helps us improve our efficiency.

Potpourri: There are many times when the effectiveness and efficiency pair are in conflict.

Effectiveness is a measure of how well a system is accomplishing what it is supposed to accomplish.

Efficiency is a measure of how a system utilizes its resources to accomplish its goal.

The two principles are simultaneously in sync with each other and in a state of tension.

Ideally, we want both – efficiency without sacrificing effectiveness.

Taken too far, efficiency can drive out opportunity, and our system no longer grows, becoming less effective over time.

In the end, we want effectiveness over efficiency.

The two can also be mutually supporting. For example, by focusing on effectiveness in sponsored-search campaigns via tracking and executing campaigns that truly get the most ROI, one can then secure more resources in terms of time or money to become more efficient.

Sponsored-search analytics provide evidence on whether our advertising is producing or not, and is therefore an aspect of marketing research.

Marketing Research

When engaging in SSA, we are engaging in research. Research is the process of investigating something in a systematic and scientific manner with the goal of increased knowledge about that phenomenon. Specifically, we are engaging in marketing research, which the American Marketing Association defines as:

> "[T]he function that links the consumer, customer, and public to the marketer through information – information used to identify and define marketing opportunities and problems; generate, refine, and evaluate marketing actions; monitor marketing performance; and improve understanding of marketing as a process. Marketing research specifies the information required to address these issues, designs the methods for collecting information, manages and implements the data-collection process, analyzes, and communicates the findings and their implications [6]."

In marketing research, gathering and analyzing information on the markets where we conduct sponsored search is a fundamental step in making good marketing, advertising, and business decisions. Very often the most valuable information that we are most interested in for sponsored search addresses customers' interests and buying behaviors. This data tells us about the many factors that will influence how customers or potential customers make purchasing decisions.

As online marketers, we perform analytics on our keyword advertising efforts to make better decisions in the future. Marketing research supports this by providing information about our customers, marketing efforts, and products. From these, we get options or courses of action for our sponsored-search campaigns.

Potpourri: Consumer marketing research as a statistical science was pioneered by Arthur Nielsen, founder the AC Nielsen Company in 1923 [7].

The Nielsen Company was one of the first companies to provide reliable and objective information on marketing, advertising, and sales programs for businesses.

The company is probably best known for the Nielsen ratings, which measure television, radio, and newspaper reach.

However, Nielsen//NetRatings also measure Internet and digital media audiences, and Nielsen BuzzMetrics measures consumer-generated media.

The concept of an Internet and Web consumer marketing research company launched other companies, such as comScore, which also provide consumer marketing research for the Internet.

However, for collecting the necessary data for SSA, we must use some form of a logging system that records the user-systems interactions for analysis. This data-collection method is known as transaction logging.

Metrics

What do we test?

To address this question, you must determine your metrics, which is concerned with building standards and measuring against them. Metrics, therefore, reflect goals and the practical application of them being measured to see change in efforts toward those goals.

We evaluate every aspect of our sponsored-search effort, including every keyphrase, every ad, every term in an ad, every image, and every display URL, to make them better. And our focus is quantitative. You, as the owner or advertising professional, may not like the terms or pictures. You may find the wording odd or juvenile. You make find the images unattractive or rude. However, it does not matter because the goal is to develop a campaign that accomplishes the efforts goals. We want the ads and keyphrases and images that pay.

Why are we concerned about metrics?

Well, conversions have to come from somewhere, and it is advantageous for you to know where they come from. Metrics inform you of this. In SSA, you compare the cost and the results of all expenditures on each keyphrase. Therefore, we must understand some definitions in the measurement area.

Measurement is the assignment of numbers to objects, events, or situations in accord with some rule (i.e., a *measurement function* [8]).

The property of the objects that determines the assignment according to that rule is called *magnitude* [8].

The measurable attribute, the number assigned to a particular object is called its *measure*, the amount or degree of its magnitude [8]. It is to be noted that the rule defines both the magnitude and the measure [8].

The metrics of reach and frequency as measurements of sponsored search effects and analysis have been used in advertising for at least twenty-five years. What should be reported, however, is effective reach. That is, to be meaningful, media reach and frequency measurements must be related to advertising communication goals.

Potpourri: "Correlation does not imply causation" is a common catchphrase in empirical analysis.

Its meaning is that just because two variables are correlated does not mean that one causes the other.

Typically, correlation is a necessary but not sufficient condition for causation.

Most advertising has an objective to capture attention and maintain awareness. Advertising analysts for this reason have measured the effect of frequency based on communication goals. Thus, if we accept communication measurements, there is available research now in the public domain that could allow planners to judgmentally set frequency goals to provide better direction in media planning.

In sponsored search, conversions (both offline and online) originate from search engine traffic. Sometimes this traffic comes from keyphrases that are directly related to our products and services. However, other times, conversions are generated by keyphrases that are seemingly unrelated to the products that the consumer eventually purchases.

Metrics, specifically as applied to keyphrase management, help us recognize these relationships, and therefore automatically allocate spending among those terms that convert at the target profit goal.

Potpourri: The McNamara fallacy refers to Robert McNamara, the United States Secretary of Defense from 1961 to 1968, and his belief as to what led the U.S. military to defeat in the Vietnam War.

McNamara quantified success in the war in terms of enemy body count while ignoring other variables of success and failure.

The McNamara fallacy has been outlined as a four-step trap.

The first step measures whatever can be easily measured. Within reason, this is fine, as long as one is aware of its shortcomings.

The second step disregards that which cannot be easily measured or gives it an arbitrary quantitative value. Unfortunately, this leads to artificial empirical findings that can be misleading if the assumptions are incorrect.

The third step presumes that what cannot be measured easily is not really important. This is typically always incorrect and leads to important areas of a process being ignored.

The fourth step carries the third step to its logical conclusion by saying what cannot be easily measured does not really exist or impact the system's overall success. This is rarely true and results in ineffective decision [9].

There are many basic and intervening measures and metrics. These, however, are but surrogates for the ultimate measure, which is our cost per customer or cost per dollar of sale or return on sales. The ultimate metric is cost per customer, which is the only way to gauge sponsored-search advertising.

Transaction Logging for Data Collection

A transaction log is an electronic record of interactions that have occurred between a system and users of that system. In sponsored search, these log files can come from the actual sponsored-search platform, a SEM agency platform, or your own server logs – basically any application that can record user-system-information interactions. Basically, it is a file that stores interaction data. Figure 7.1 shows a sample of a transaction log from a sponsored-search effort.

SSA is the methodological approach to studying online systems and users of these systems, and is rooted in transaction log analysis, although there are other Web analytics methods for data tracking (i.e., page tagging).

Peters defines transaction log analysis as the study of electronically recorded interactions between online information-retrieval systems and the people who search

Day	Ad	Sales	Engine	Cost	Impressions	Position	Clicks	Orders	Items
20xx-10-20	4637617	0	2	0	0	0	0	0	0
20xx-10-21	4637617	0	2	429	195	1	19	1	6
20xx-10-22	4637617	0	2	2152	956	1	61	1	2
20xx-10-23	4637617	0	2	1090	911	1	34	1	3
20xx-10-24	4637617	0	2	27773	41431	1	600	1	3
20xx-10-25	4637617	0	2	37369	75473	1	803	1	3
20xx-10-26	4637617	0	2	34946	81902	1	759	2	3
20xx-10-27	4637617	0	2	43407	99275	1	918	2	4
20xx-10-28	4637617	0	2	31668	66039	1	689	2	1
20xx-10-29	4637617	0	2	31528	41546	1	685	2	1
20xx-10-30	4637617	0	2	29629	46357	1	648	3	3
20xx-10-31	4637617	0	2	33817	45485	1	742	4	2

Figure 7.1. Sponsored-search transaction logs with click and conversion data.

for information found in those systems [10]. Since the advent of the Internet, we have modified Peter's (1993) definition, expanding it to include systems other than information-retrieval systems.

Transaction log analysis is a broad collection of methods that include several sub-categorizations, including Web log analysis (i.e., analysis of Web client and server logs), blog analysis, and search log analysis (i.e., analysis of search engine logs [11]). Transaction log analysis enables macroanalysis of aggregate use data and patterns and microanalysis of individual search patterns. The results from the analyzed data develop systems and services based on user behavior or system performance.

Transaction log analysis has been incorporated into the overall field of Web analytics, which includes transaction log analysis with the incorporation of goals and awareness beyond the system to the organization to the business goals.

From the user behavior side, SSA is a class of empirical, unobtrusive methods (a.k.a., nonreactive or low-constraint). Unobtrusive methods allow data collection without directly asking participants. Research literature specifically describes unobtrusive approaches as those that do not require a response from participants [c.f 12, 13, 14]. This data can be observational or come from existing data. Another example is that of TV ratings that are based on what people actually watch (i.e., TiVo logs) versus what people say they watch (i.e., a survey).

Unobtrusive methods are in contrast to obtrusive or reactive approaches such as questionnaires, tests, laboratory studies, and surveys [15]. A laboratory experiment is an example of an extreme obtrusive method. Certainly, the line between unobtrusive and obtrusive methods is sometimes blurred. For example, conducting a survey to gauge the reaction of users to information systems is an obtrusive method. However, using the posted results from the survey is an unobtrusive method.

The use of logs for the evaluation of sponsored-search efforts falls conceptually within the confines of the behaviorism paradigm of research and analysis. Therefore, the behaviorism approach is the conceptual basis for the SSA approach.

Behaviorism

Behaviorism is an analysis approach that emphasizes the outward behavioral aspects of thought. Strictly speaking, behaviorism dismisses the inward experiential and procedural aspects [16, 17]. It has come under critical fire for this narrow viewpoint.

However, for SSA, we will take a more accepting view of behaviorism. In this more open viewpoint, behaviorism emphasizes the observed behaviors without discounting the inner aspects that may accompany these outward behaviors. This more accommodating outlook of behaviorism supports the viewpoint that one can gain much from studying expressions (i.e., behaviors) of users when interacting with advertising campaigns. These expressed behaviors may reflect either aspects of the searcher's inner cognitive factors or contextual aspects of the environment in which the behavior occurs, or both.

The underlying proposition of behaviorism is that all things that people do are behaviors. These behaviors include actions, thoughts, and feelings. With this underlying proposition, the behaviorism position is that all theories and models concerning people have observational correlations. The behaviors and any proposed theoretical constructs must be mutually complementary. Strict behaviorism would further state that there are no differences between the publicly observable behavioral processes (i.e., actions) and privately observable behavioral processes (i.e., thinking and feeling).

For SSA, we also take the position that due to contextual, situational, or environmental factors, there may be times when there is disconnection between the cognitive and affective behaviors. Therefore, there are sources of behavior that are both internal (i.e., cognitive, affective, expertise) and external (i.e., environmental and situational). Regardless, behaviorism focuses primarily on only what an observer can see or manipulate, and it is behaviors that we are primarily interested in for SSA.

We see the effects of behaviorism in many studies, especially in SSA. Behaviorism is where the observable evidence is critical to the research questions or methods in an analysis. Within such a perspective, there is no knowable difference between two states unless there is a demonstrable difference in the behavior associated with each state. This is especially true in any experimental research where the manipulation of variables is required. A behaviorism approach at its core seeks to understand events in terms of behavioral criteria [18, p. 22]. The behaviorist study demands behavioral evidence.

Analysis grounded in behaviorism always involves *somebody* doing *something* in a *situation*. Therefore, all derived research questions focus on *who* (actors), *what* (behaviors), *when* (temporal), *where* (contexts), and *why* (cognitive). The actors in a behaviorism paradigm are people whose behavior is studied at a certain level of aggregation (e.g., individuals, groups, organizations, communities, nationalities, societies, etc.). Such analysis must focus on all aspects of what the actors do. These behaviors have a temporal element, when and how long these behaviors occur. The behaviors occur within some context, and thus are embedded in environmental and situational features. The cognitive aspect to these behaviors is the rational and affective processes internal to the actors executing the behaviors.

From this perspective, each of these components – actor, behaviors, temporal, context, and cognitive – are behaviorist constructs. However, for SSA, we are primarily concerned with behaviors.

Behaviors

Like all human activities, sponsored search is ultimately based on individual behavior, which is the essential variable in an SSA-based study.

A variable in analysis or empirical research is an entity representing a set of events where each event may have a different value. In SSA, time on page or number of clicks may be variables for a given study. The particular variables that an analysis is interested in are derived from the research questions driving the study.

One can define variables by their use in a study (e.g., independent, dependent, extraneous, controlled, constant, and confounding) and by their nature. Defined by their nature, there are three types of variables: environmental (i.e., situation, environment, or contextual events), subject (i.e., events or aspects of the subject being studied), and behavioral (i.e., observable events by the subject of interest).

For SSA, a behavior is the essential construct of the behaviorism paradigm. At its most basic, a behavior is an observable activity of a person, animal, team, organization, or system. Like many basic constructs, behavior is an overloaded term, as it also refers to the aggregate set of responses to both internal and external stimuli. Therefore, behaviors address a spectrum of actions. Because of the many associations with the term, it is difficult to characterize a term like behavior without specifying a context to provide meaning.

However, one can generally classify behaviors into four general categories, which are as follows:

- Something that one can *detect* and therefore record.
- An *action* or a specific goal-driven event that represents a purpose other than the specific action that is observable (e.g., it is not just a click, it is a purchase).
- Some *skill* or skill set.
- A reactive *response* to environmental stimuli.

In some manner, the analyst must observe these behaviors. By observation, we mean studying and gathering information on a behavior concerning what the searcher does. Classically, observation is visual, where the analyst uses his or her own eyes. However, recording devices, such as cameras, can assist in making observations. We extend the concept of observation to include other recording devices, notably logging software. Transaction log analysis focuses on descriptive observation and logging the behaviors as they would occur.

Table 7.1. *An example of an ethogram for sponsored search*

Behavior	Description
Impression	An appearance of an advertisement in response to a searcher's query that is linked to a keyphrase
Click	A searcher clicking on the URL of an advertisement and going to the resulting landing page
Click on Order Button	A searcher demonstrating an intent to actual order by clicking on the order button
Order	A placement of a purchase by a customer as the result of a click on an advertisement
Items Ordered	The number of products that a customer places within an order

When studying behavioral patterns during SSA and other similar approaches, analysts use ethograms. An ethogram is an index of the behavioral patterns of a unit. An ethogram details the different forms of behavior that an actor displays. In most cases, it is desirable to create an ethogram in which the categories of behavior are objective, discrete, and do no overlap with one another. The definitions of each behavior should be clear, detailed, and distinguishable. Ethograms can be as specific or general as the study or field warrants. We generally want our behaviors to adhere to the MECE principle [19], with each behavior being mutually exclusive and collectively exhaustive. Basically, you want no omission and no duplication.

There are a variety of examples of ethograms in relation to Web searching. Spink and Jansen [20] and Jansen and Pooch [21] outline some of the key behaviors for search log analysis, a specific form of SSA. Hargittai [22] and Jansen and McNeese [23] present examples of detailed classifications of behaviors during Web searching. As an example, Table 7.1 presents an ethogram of searcher behaviors during a searching session that involves sponsored results.

There are many ways to observe behaviors. In SSA, we are primarily concerned with observing and recording these behaviors in file. As such, one can view the recorded fields in the log as trace data.

Trace Data

The analyst has several options for collecting data for analysis, but there is no one single best method for collection. The decision about which approach or approaches to use depends on what needs to be investigated, how one needs to record the data, what resources are available, what the timeframe available for data collection is, how complex the data is, what the frequency of data collection will be, and how the data is to be analyzed.

For sponsored-search data collection, we are generally concerned with observations of behavior. The general objective of observation is to record the behavior in a naturalistic setting. When investigating user behaviors, the analyst must make a record of these behaviors to have access to this data for future analysis. The searcher, the analyst, or a third party can make the record of behaviors.

However, transaction logging is an indirect method of recording data about behaviors and the searchers themselves. With the help of logging software, transaction logging makes these data records on behavior via traces. Thus, transaction log records are a source of trace data.

What is trace data?

The processes by which people conduct the activities of their daily lives create things, create marks, or reduce some existing material. Within the confines of research, these things, marks, and wears become data. Classically, trace data is the physical remains of interaction [14, p. 35–52]. This creation can be intentional (i.e., notes in a diary) or accidental (i.e., footprints in the mud). However, trace data can also be found through third-party logging applications. In transaction log analysis, we are primarily interested in data from third-party logging. We refer to data recorded in logs as trace data.

Potpourri: Beware of the streetlight effect in SSA, which is the tendency to measure what we can rather than what is actually important or what we are really interested in.

In much published literature on sponsored search (and Web searching), there is considerable focus on impressions and clicks, using these as surrogates for the effectiveness of a search session or the effectiveness of an advertisement. Researchers (and others) do this because getting actual conversion data is difficult, just as getting actual searcher-relevant judgments on documents is difficult. Therefore, one measures using the data one has, which is typically impressions and clicks.

These are the metrics that one can most easily get or see; hence, the name "streetlight effect." In essence, we only investigate what we can see.

Analysts use physical or, as in the case SSA, virtual traces as indicators of behavior. These behaviors are the facts or data that researchers describe or use to make inferences about events concerning the actors.

By convention, trace data is classified into two general types [14]. These two general types of trace measures are erosion and accretion. Erosion is the wearing away of material, leaving a trace. Accretion is the buildup of material, making a trace. Both erosion and accretion have several subcategories. In SSA, we are primarily concerned with accretion trace data.

Trace data offers a sharp contrast to directly collected data. The greatest strength of trace data is that it is unobtrusive. The collection of the data does not interfere with the natural flow of behavior and events in the given context. Because the data is not directly collected, there is no observer present in the situation where the behaviors occur to affect the actors' actions. The unobtrusive and nonreactive nature of trace data makes it a very valuable research course. In the past, trace data was often time-consuming to gather and process, making such data costly. With the advent of transaction-logging software, trace data for the studying of the behaviors of users and systems has become affordable, convenient, and thus, very prevalent.

Interestingly, in the physical world, erosion data is what typically reveals usage patterns (i.e., trails worn in the woods, footprints in the snow, wear on a book cover). However, with SSA, logged data provides us the usage patterns (i.e., access to a Web site, typing of queries, addresses of Web pages viewed). Specifically, transaction logs are a form of controlled-accretion data, where the analyst alters the environment to create the accretion data [14, p. 35–52]. With a variety of tracking applications, the Web is a natural environment for controlled-accretion data collection.

Like all data-collection methods, trace data for studying sponsored search interactions has strengths and limitations. Trace data is valuable for understanding behavior (i.e., trace actions) in naturalistic environments, offering insights into human activity obtainable in no other way. For example, data from transaction logs is on a scale available in few other places. However, one must interpret trace data carefully and with a fair amount of caution, as trace data can be misleading.

For example, with the data in transaction logs, the analyst can say a given number of searchers only looked at the first result page. However, using trace data alone, the analyst could not conclude whether the searcher left because they found their information and were satisfied or because they could not find it and were frustrated. This is a common problem with unobtrusive methods.

Unobtrusive Method

Unobtrusive methods are analytical practices that do not require the analyst to intrude in the context of the actors. Additionally, unobtrusive methods do not involve direct elicitation of data from the actors.

This approach is in contrast to obtrusive methods like laboratory experiments and surveys that require the researchers to interject themselves physically into the environment being studied. This intrusion can lead the searchers to alter their behavior to look good in the eyes of the analysts, or for other reasons. For example, a questionnaire is an interruption in the natural stream of behavior. Respondents can get tired of filling out a survey or resentful of the questions being asked.

Why is it important for analysts not to intrude on the environment? Well, there are at least three justifications. First is the uncertainty principle (i.e., Heisenberg's uncertainty principle). Heisenberg's uncertainty principle is from the field of quantum physics. In quantum physics, the outcome of a measurement of some system is not deterministic or perfect. Instead, a measurement is characterized by a probability distribution. The larger the associated standard deviation is for this distribution, the more "uncertain" the characteristic measured for the system. Heisenberg's uncertainty principle is commonly stated as, "One cannot accurately and simultaneously measure both the position and momentum of a mass." Position and momentum are measurements that are intrinsically linked but also in tension with one another by definition. Both measurements cannot be taken simultaneously.

When analysts are interjected into an environment, they become part of the system. Therefore, their just being present affects measurement. A common example in information technology is the interjection of a recording device into an existing information technology system. This interjection may slow the response time of the system that it is trying to measure.

The second justification is the observer effect. The observer effect refers to the difference in a person's behavior or activity by being observed. People may not behave in their usual manner if they are being interviewed while carrying out an activity or they know that they are being watched. In analysis, the observer effect specifically refers to changes that the act of observing makes on the phenomenon being observed. In information technology, the observer effect is the potential impact that observation can have on a process output while the process is running. A good example of the observer effect in transaction log analysis is pornographic searching behavior. Participants rarely search for porn in a laboratory study; however, trace data shows it is a common search topic [24].

The third justification for unobtrusive methods is observer bias. Observer bias is error that the researcher introduces into measurement when observers overemphasize behavior they expect to find and fail to notice behavior they do not expect. Many fields have common procedures to address this, although those are seldom used in information and computer science. For example, medical trials are normally double-blind (i.e., both the researcher and the participants do not know which treatment is received) rather than single-blind (i.e., the participants do not know which treatment is received) to avoid observer bias. Observer bias is introduced when researchers see a behavior and interpret it according to what it means to them, whereas it may mean something else to the person showing the behavior. Trace data helps in overcoming observer bias in the data collection. However, as with other methods, it has no effect on the observer bias in interpretation of the results from data analysis.

Unobtrusive measurement reduces the biases that result from the intrusion of the researcher or measurement instrument. However, unobtrusive measures reduce the degree of control that the researcher has over the type of data collected. For some constructs, there simply may not be any available unobtrusive measures.

We discuss three types of unobtrusive measurement applicable to SSA, which are indirect analysis, context analysis, and secondary analysis. Transaction log analysis is often an indirect analysis method [c.f 25, 26, 27, 28]. The analyst is able to collect the data without introducing any formal measurement procedure. In this regard, transaction log analysis typically focuses on the interaction behaviors occurring among the users, system, and information.

Content analysis is the analysis of text documents. The analysis can be quantitative, qualitative, or a mixed-methods approach. Typically, the major purpose of content analysis is to identify patterns in text. Content analysis has the advantage of being unobtrusive and, depending on whether automated methods exist, can be a relatively rapid method for analyzing large amounts of text. In transaction log analysis, content analysis typically focuses on search queries or analysis of retrieved results [c.f 29, 30, 31, 32, 33].

Secondary data analysis, like content analysis, makes use of already existing sources of data. However, secondary analysis typically refers to the re-analysis of quantitative data rather than text. Secondary data analysis is the analysis of preexisting data in a different way to address different research questions than originally intended during data collection. Secondary data analysis utilizes the data that was collected by someone else. Transaction log data is commonly collected by Web sites for system performance analysis. However, analysts can also use this data to address other questions [34, 35, 36, 37, 38, 39, 40, 41].

As a secondary-analysis method, SSA has several advantages. It efficiently uses data collected by a Web site application. This gives the researcher access to a potentially large sample of users over a significant duration, often allowing the researcher to extend the scope of the study considerably [42]. Because the data is already collected, the cost of existing transaction log data is cheaper than collecting primary data.

However, the use of secondary analysis is not without difficulties. Secondary data is frequently not trivial to prepare, clean, and analyze, especially large transaction logs. Analysts must often make assumptions about how the data was collected, as the logging applications were developed by third parties. Additionally, there are the ethical concerns of using transaction logs as secondary data. By definition, the analyst is using the data in a manner that may violate the privacy of the system users. In fact, some point out a growing distaste for unobtrusive methods due to increased sensitivity toward the ethics involved in such analysis [13].

Sponsored-Search Analytics as an Unobtrusive Method

Sponsored-search analytics have significant advantages as a methodology approach for the study and investigation of behaviors. These advantages include:

- *Scale*: Transaction log applications can collect data to a degree that overcomes the critical limiting factor in laboratory user studies. User studies in laboratories are typically restricted in terms of sample size, location, scope, and duration.
- *Power*: The sample size of transaction log data can be quite large, so inference testing can highlight statistically significant relationships. Interestingly, the amount of data in transaction logs from the Web is sometimes so large that nearly every relationship is significantly correlated due to the large power.
- *Scope*: Because transaction log data is collected in a natural context, the researchers can investigate the entire range of user-system interactions or system functionality in a multivariable context.
- *Location*: Transaction log data can be collected in naturalistic, distributed environments. Therefore, the users do not have to be an artificial laboratory setting.
- *Duration*: Because there is no need for specific participants to be recruited for a user study, transaction log data can be collected over an extended period.

All methods of data collection have both strengths not available with other methods and inherent limitations. Sponsored-search logs have several shortcomings. First, transaction log data is not nearly as versatile relative to primary data, as the data may not have been collected to answer the same research questions. Second, sponsored-search data is not as rich as some other data-collection methods are and, therefore, not available for investigating the range of concepts some researcher may want to study. Third, the fields that the sponsored-search application records are often only loosely linked to the concepts they are alleged to measure (e.g., a click is often used as a surrogate for relevance of a result to a query). Fourth, with sponsored-search logs, the users may be aware that they are being recorded and may alter their actions. Therefore, the user behaviors may not be altogether natural.

SSA also suffers from shortcoming deriving from the characteristics of the data collection. Hilbert and Redmiles [43] maintain that all research methods suffer from some combination of abstraction, selection, reduction, context, and evolution problems that limit scalability and quality of results. SSA suffers from these five shortcomings:

- *Abstraction problem* – how does low-level data relate to higher-level concepts?
- *Selection problem* – how does one separate the necessary data from the unnecessary data prior to reporting and analysis?
- *Reduction problem* – how does one reduce the complexity and size of the data set prior to reporting and analysis?
- *Context problem* – how does one interpret the significance of events or states within state chains?
- *Evolution problem* – how can one alter data-collection applications without impacting application deployment or use?

Potpourri: Many aspects of Web analytics can be difficult with many caveats and potential pitfalls. One classic example is known as "the hotel problem," named by and credited to Rufus Evison [44].

The hotel problem is used as an example to show the effect that the date range has on Web analytics results, and that comparing results between different data ranges can cause seemingly nonsensical measurements.

The hotel analogy is a simple way to illustrate this point, by showing that the unique visitors for each day in a week might not add up to the same total as the unique visitors for that week. (Note: It could be day to week, week to month, month to year, or whatever.)

The hotel problem basically goes like this.

A hotel has two rooms. Each room has a guest each day during the week. Therefore, the unique visitors per day are two.

One might think that to get the unique visitors for the week, you just add them up for the seven days, which would be fourteen, assuming the hotel is full each day.

However, this methodology is flawed. Why?

What if one guest stayed in the hotel for seven days? This guest would be counted as a unique visitor each individual day but only once when counting unique visitors for the entire week.

So, assuming one guest stayed in a room the entire seven days, and the other room had a new guest each day, our unique visitors for each day would be two.

Our unique visitors for all seven days would be eight.

Because each method has its own combination of abstraction, selection, reduction, context, and evolution problems, there is a need for complementary methods of data collection and analysis.

This is similar to the conflict inherent in any analyst approach. Each analysis method for data collection tries to maximize three desirable criteria:

- *Generalizability* – the degree to which the data applies to an overall population.
- *Precision* – the degree of granularity of the measurement.
- *Realism* – the relation between the context in which evidence is gathered and the contexts to which the evidence is to be applied.

Although the analyst always wants to maximize all three of these criteria simultaneously, it cannot be done. This is one fundamental dilemma of the analysis process. The very things that increase one of these three features will reduce one or both of the others.

Credibility, Validity, and Reliability

The elementary steps of the scientific method are:

- Construct a *hypothesis*
- *Test* the hypothesis
- Analysis the *data*
- Report the *findings*.

You basically follow the same steps in SSA.

Trace data from sponsored-search logs should be examined during analysis with the same criteria used for all research data. These criteria are credibility, validity, and reliability. In short, these concepts mean that analysis performed poorly will not yield relevant results. Although there can be many issues, issues with credibility, validity, and reliability often relate to how the data is collected.

Credibility refers to how trustworthy or believable the data-collection method is. The researcher must make the case that the data-collection methodology records the data needed to address the underlying research questions.

Validity describes if the measurement actually measures what it is supposed to measure. There are three kinds of validity:

- Face or *internal validity* addresses the extent to which the contents of the test or procedure look like what the researcher is trying to measure.
- Content or *construct validity* addresses the extent to which the content of the test or procedure is adequately representative of the contextual attributes of the situation.
- *External validity* is the extent to which one can generalize the research results across populations, situations, environments, and contexts.

In inferential or predictive analysis, one must also be concerned with statistical validity, which is the strength of the independent and dependent variable relationships. This is most notable in analysis such as A/B testing and multivariable testing [45, 46], where sample size is important. Basically, you want enough data or samples to ensure you have statistical significance.

Potpourri: A/B testing can certainly trace its origins in advertising back to the days of the mail-order business [47, 48, 49].

However, it can be traced back even further to Sir Francs Bacon [50] in 1620, who is considered the father of empirical research and the first known proponent of the what is now considered scientific variable testing.

There are multiple formulas for sample size depending on the type of sample on uses. However a general formula for sample size is:

$$n = \left[\frac{Z_{\frac{\alpha}{2}}\sigma}{E} \right]^2$$

Equation 7.1. Sample size calculation

Where n = sample size, E is the desired margin of error, σ is the population standard deviation, and $z_{\alpha/2}$ is the critical value. α represents the confidence level required (for a 95 percent confidence level, one would choose α of 0.05). E represents the margin of error as chosen by the analyst; the exact value of this will depend to the research being done. $z_{\alpha/2}$ is obtained by looking at a z-table.

As an example of the calculation if $\alpha = 0.05$, E = 5, $\sigma = 15$, then $z_{\alpha/2} = 1.960$ and n = 34.5744, which is rounded up to 35. Thus, one would need a sample size of 35. Typically for any quantitative analysis, one needs 35 to 40 subjects as a rule of thumb.

Potpourri: Much of quantitative statistical analysis is based on analysis of variances (ANOVA), which is based on normal distributions, means, and standard deviations.

This type of quantitative statistical analysis was developed by Sir Ronal A. Fisher, whose work laid nearly the entire foundation of modern statistical science [51].

You must be aware in any statistical analysis what the probability is of being wrong. As Schwab [52] points out, the law of probability can lead to large errors if the sample size is too small.

Potpourri: The law of probability is really interesting, as it is a more precise description of our actions as we strive for success.

Basically, the law of probability is about the chances of something occurring. So, when we select a sample size that gives of a certain confidence interval, it is a probability of being correct (or valid or successful) and a probability of being incorrect (or invalid or unsuccessful).

There is rarely any guarantee of 100 percent either way.

Reliability is a term used to describe the stability of the measurement. Will the measurement measure the same thing in the same way in repeated tests? Or phrased another way, can the research results be applied to a wider group than just those from whom the data is collected? Reliability is chiefly concerned with making sure the method of data gathering leads to consistent results.

Potpourri: The Texas sharpshooter notion is a logical fallacy in which information that has no relationship is interpreted or manipulated until it appears to have meaning.

The name comes from a joke about a Texan who fires some shots at the side of a barn, then paints a target centered on the biggest cluster of hits and claims to be a sharpshooter.

The fallacy applies to those situations where one does not have an ex ante or prior expectation of the particular data relationship in question.

The fallacy comes from the tendency of people to see patterns where no real pattern exists or where there is no basis to believe a pattern exists. It is related to the clustering illusion, which refers to the tendency in human cognition to interpret patterns in randomness where none actually exist.

Therefore, in building theory from empirical data (known as grounded theory), we can examine data and possibly determine that some pattern or relationship exists.

To avoid the Texas sharpshooter fallacy, we would then explore other datasets to see if the same pattern exists or test the correlation in a control experiment.

Note that we would need to use NEW data gathered under independent conditions. If we use the same data in which we originally detected the pattern for hypotheses testing, we would be committing the Texas sharpshooter fallacy.

(Note: Nothing against Texas. Lived there for two years and loved it!)

How do we address the issues of credibility, validity, and reliability? Based on previous research [53], we know there are six questions that we must address in every analysis project using trace data from sponsored-search logs.

- *Which data is analyzed?* The analyst must clearly articulate in a precise manner and format what trace data was recorded. With transaction log software, this is much easier than in other forms of trace data, as logging applications can be reverse-engineered to clearly articulate exactly what behavioral data is recorded.
- *How is this data defined?* The analyst must clearly define each trace measure in a manner that permits replication of the research on other systems and with other users. As transaction log analysis has proliferated in a variety of venues, more precise definitions of measures are developing [54, 32, 33].
- *What is the population from which the analyst has drawn the data?* The analyst must be cognizant of the actors, both people and systems, who created the trace data. With transaction logs on the Web, this is sometimes a difficult issue to address directly, unless the system requires some type of log-on from which profiles are then available. In the absence of these profiles, the analyst must rely on demographic surveys, studies of the system's user population, or general Web demographics.
- *What is the context in which the analyst analyzed the data?* It is important for the researcher to clearly articulate the environmental, situational, and contextual

factors under which the trace data was recorded. With transaction log data, researchers should provide complete information about the temporal factors of the data collection (i.e., the time the data was recorded) and the make-up of the system at the time of the data recording, as system features undergo continual change. Transaction logs have the significant advantage of time sampling of trace data. In time sampling, the analyst can make observations at predefined points of time (e.g., every five minutes), and then record the action that is taking place, using the classification of action defined in the ethogram.

- *What are the boundaries of the analysis?* Analysis using trace data from transaction logs is tricky, and the analyst must be careful not to overreach with the research questions and findings. The implications of the analysis are confined by the data and the method of the data collected. For example, with transaction log data, one can clearly state whether or not a searcher clicked on a link. However, transaction log trace data itself will not inform the analyst as to why the user clicked on a link.
- *What is the target of the inferences?* The analyst must clearly articulate whether the relationship among the separate measures in the trace data is to inform descriptively or make inferences. Trace data can be used for both descriptive analyses. These descriptions and inferences can be at any level of granularity (i.e., individual, collection of individuals, organization, etc.). However, Hilber and Redmiles point out that transaction log data is best used for aggregate level analysis, in their experiences [55].

Transaction logs are an excellent way to collect trace data on users of Web and other information systems. The use of trace data to understand behaviors makes the use of sponsored-search logs and SSA an unobtrusive research method.

Click Fraud

Metrics and measurements can also help us address one of the negative aspects of sponsored search.

Click fraud is a problem with keyword advertising and other forms of online advertising, according to online marketing firm iProspect (http://www.iprospect.com/). Click fraud involves the intentional clicking on sponsored links with the purpose of gaining undue monetary returns or harming a particular content provider. Click fraud can take various forms, but the result is usually the same. Advertisers pay for unproductive traffic generated by perpetrators who repeatedly click on a sponsored link with no intention of giving value to that provider. It may seem self-evident that click fraud is unethical, but it is more difficult to explain exactly why this is the case, although researchers have made the attempt using moral concepts such as the *Golden Rule*, the *light-of-day test*, *free-riding*, and the *morality of the marketplace* [56].

To operationalize click fraud, one must first define *value*, which is at the heart of the click fraud issue, and then provide more formal definitions of a *click*, *sponsored link*, and *sponsored result*.

- *Value* is the use of information, employment of a service, purchase of a product, or a transaction by a visitor to a Web site that is consistent with the content provider's goal.

- *Sponsored result* is a set of title, text, and other material associated with a particular sponsored link.
- *Sponsored link* is a uniform resource locator (URL) serviced by a search engine in response to a query in a SERP or in a contextual manner on relevant Web sites or in e-mail.
- *Click* is the act of initiating a visit to a Web site via a sponsored link.

From these terms, we can formally define:

1. *Valid click*: an intentional click on a sponsored link by a visitor where there is a realistic probability of generating value once the visitor arrives at the Web site.
2. *Invalid click*: a click on a sponsored link that has no probability of generating value.

   a. *Fraudulent click*: an intentional click by a perpetrator on a sponsored link with no intention of generating value (a.k.a. click fraud).

      i. *Identifiable click fraud* is a pattern of fraudulent clicks by a perpetrator that one can distinguish from valid clicks.
      ii. *Unidentifiable click fraud* is a fraudulent click or a pattern of fraudulent clicks by a perpetrator that one cannot distinguish from valid clicks.

   b. *void click*: an invalid click that is not a fraudulent click (e.g., a double-click on a sponsored link, a click on a sponsored link when the Web site is down)

      iii. *Identifiable void click* is a void click that one can distinguish from the set of valid clicks.
      iv. *Unidentifiable void click* is a void click that one cannot distinguish from the set of valid clicks.

   c. *Slip-through rate*: a set of invalid clicks that the search engine detection mechanisms do not identify.

We see from these definitions that click fraud is a multilevel issue. From the entire body of visits to a search engine, some of these visits result in one or more clicks on sponsored links, reportedly about 20 to 30 percent [57]. Most of these clicks are valid in that they have the potential of bringing value to the content provider. Some of these clicks, however, are invalid, having no possibility of generating value to the provider. These invalid clicks can be intentional and malicious. We define the malicious ones as fraudulent clicks. Other invalid clicks are just not valid for other reasons. For instance, the user could have double-clicked on a sponsored link. We refer to these clicks as void clicks. Void clicks are reasonably easy to identify because they are typically analyzed at the aggregate level. There are patterns of behavior for valid clicks and when patterns deviate from these norms, it is a good indication that the clicks could be void. Examples of such patterns are time between clicks by a user on the same sponsored link and time on the visited page. Therefore, many, if not most, void clicks are reasonably identifiable.

Click fraud is a more difficult area to address. In these cases, perpetrators are attempting to make their fraudulent clicks look like valid clicks. Therefore, identifying fraudulent clicks is much more difficult because the level of analysis needs to be both at the

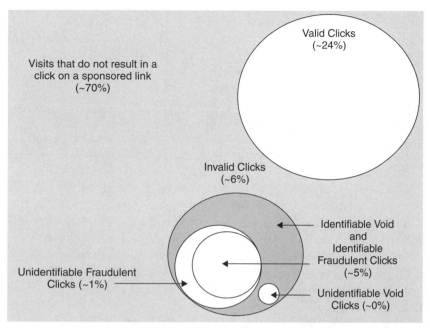

Figure 7.2. The click space when discussing click fraud.

aggregate level and the individual level. Figure 7.2 illustrates the relationship among *valid clicks*, *invalid clicks*, and *overall visits*, based on previously reported data.

If we view the entire space of visits to the search engine (i.e., the click space) as 100 percent, we know that at least 70 percent of these visits do not result in a click on a sponsored link. This figure is based on a number of user studies and popular press reports. Therefore, valid and invalid clicks on sponsored links make up about 30 percent of all visits. A variety of popular press reports [58] had reported that search engines are screening about 15 percent of invalid clicks (both void and fraudulent clicks) or approximately 5 percent of all clicks.

The accuracy of search engines in filtering these invalid clicks is not precisely known; however, we can reasonably estimate that it is 80 percent or higher. Taking the conservative end with 80 percent accuracy, this leads to the conclusion that invalid clicks make up 6 percent (i.e., 20 percent of 30 percent) of all clicks on sponsored links. Assuming that the unidentified void clicks are nearly zero, this means that slightly more than 1 percent of fraudulent clicks go undetected (i.e., the slip-through rate). Although a low percentage, this can translate into real cash when one considers that the search engines are earning billions of dollars per year (e.g., if a search engine earns $8 billion, one percent translates into $80 million).

These percentages are only for sponsored links off the SERP. There are no comparable numbers for sponsored links from contextual sites (i.e., where search engines display sponsored links on specific Web sites). However, one suspects that these incidents of click fraud are much higher. Complaints of invalid clicks and poor traffic from content providers seem to substantiate this higher rate of fraudulent clicks on these contextual ads [59]

Potpourri: Click fraud has been around from almost the beginning of sponsored search. See this entry from the **alt.religion.scientology> GoTo.com search engine** Usenet newsgroup dated December 31, 1998

Check that date again: 1998 – the year that sponsored search started!

Subject: Re: GoTo.com search engine

Date: 1998/12/31

—BEGIN PGP SIGNED MESSAGE—

In article <36geb4e5.36201 … @news.xs4all.nl>, a … @xs2all.nl says …

Hmmm… now if one could only automate the click-through process, we could run up quite a bill :)

Wow, goto.com seems to be quite suseptible (sic) to abuse, give that they generate links that look like:

http://www.goto.com/d/search-redirect?url=http%3A%2F%2Fwww.oursites.
org%2Flydiabeckham%2F&searchID=12975B5951364A44&bid=50&rID=2265
469788077037071&aID=36061eOd17ed&rank=l&rawq=scientology

of course all as one long string. Note that the bid amount is encoded in the URL (in tenths of a penny). If goto.com uses the bid amount from the URL that you feed them, you could submit something like

http://www.goto.com/d/search-redirect?url=http%3A%2F%2Fwww.oursites.
org%2Flydiabeckham%2F&searchID=12975B5951364A44&bid=5000&rID=22
65469788077037071&aID=3606IeOdI7ed&rank=l&rawq=scientology

to have Lydia charged $5.00 per hit. Also, goto.com either suppresses multiple hits from the same IP address, or they don't. If they do suppress them, then folks accessing goto.com via a proxy server won't cost the advertisers as much as folks acessing (sic) them directly. However, if they DON'T suppress multiple hits from the same IP address, then you simply write a script to fetch that URL above multiple times, say once every 3 minutes and let it run in the background for a few days. Lydia might get a surprising bill!

Of course, goto.com feeds you a http redirect (302) in reply to the above URL, and most browsers just automatically pick up the real site from that. However, an abuse script as described above will simply ignore the response from goto.com anyway.

So, there were people trying to game the system almost at the beginning.

Foundational Takeaways

- Sponsored-search analytics (SSA) is the collecting, measuring, analyzing, and reporting of keyword advertising data for purposes of monitoring, understanding, and optimizing search engine marketing.
- SSA is the basis for which we judge the effectiveness and efficiency of our sponsored-search efforts.
- SSA is based on behaviorism, in that a behavior has meaning associated with it.
- The units of measurement used in SSA are trace data, collected via some logging software.

- Measurement in SSA is goal-directed and withstands reliability, credibility, and validity tests.
- Measurements will differ based on the different view that we have of our sponsored search effort.

Relating Theory to Practice

SSA provides insights into keyword advertising efforts, both to discover the new and to optimize the current. With SSA, we can track, test, and examine reports. From this analysis, we can refine our campaigns, including keyphrases and ads.

However, we can also apply SSA for effective analysis by focusing on higher order metrics and measures by asking ourselves some key questions.

- Do your measures have validity (i.e., are they really measuring the overall goals of your advertising effort, including things like customer lifetime value, attribution, and cross channel sales)?
- Do your measures have credibility (i.e., are they measuring what they ought to be measuring, including catching all sales and intermarketing communication)?
- Do your measures have reliability (i.e., they measuring all they should be, including things like returns, cancels, and call center spillover)?

Conclusion

In this chapter, we defined sponsored-search analytics, showing how it relates to market research. We discussed how it is grounded in the methodology of transaction log analysis and the concept of behaviorism. We also discussed the core concepts of behaviors, trace data, and the unobtrusive method, highlighting the inherent elements of sponsored search analytics. Finally, we discussed the critical research concepts of credibility, validity, and reliability, providing questions that one can propose in any analysis project and key concepts of metrics and measures. We also touched on the issue of click fraud in sponsored search, defining some key elements.

However, as we have gone through our sponsored-search effort, we have primarily focused on the externals, the aspects that the customer sees in some fashion. We have discussed the keywords, the ads, the searching, and the methods of measuring these aspects.

As such, we have skipped a discussion of a very important aspect, namely how advertisers "get" these keywords that link our ads to the searcher queries, from which we track the success or failure of our branding, advertising, and marketing efforts. Certainly, the search engine does not provide these for free. And there must be other advertisers also interested in these keywords. How much do these keywords cost us?

The answer to these questions lies in the area of game theory, which is the underpinning of the online keyword auction where we secure the use of certain keywords. So, in this respect, we remove our advertising hat and replace it with the hat of the consumer.

References

[1] Kaushik, A. 2007. *Web Analytics: An Hour a Day*. Indianapolis, IN: Wiley.

[2] Peterson, E. 2004. Web Analytics Demystified: A Marketer's Guide to Understanding How Your Web Site Affects Your Business. New York: Celilo Group Media.

[3] Pedrick, J. H. and Zufryden, F. S. 1991. "Evaluating the Impact of Advertising Media Plans: A Model of Consumer Purchase Dynamics Using Single Source Data." *Marketing Science*, vol. 10(2), pp. 111–130.

[4] Penniman, W. D. 1975. "A Stochastic Process Analysis of Online User Behavior." In *The Annual Meeting of the American Society for Information Science*, Washington, DC, pp. 147–148.

[5] Meister, D. and Sullivan, D. 1967. "Evaluation of User Reactions to a Prototype On-Line Information Retrieval System: Report to NASA by the Bunker-Ramo Corporation. Report Number NASA CR-918." Bunker-Ramo Corporation, Oak Brook, IL.

[6] Directors, A. M. A. B. O. 2004. Definition of Marketing. Retrieved December 14, 2010, from http://www.marketingpower.com/aboutama/pages/definitionofmarketing.aspx

[7] Schultz, D. E., Barnes, B. E., Schultz, H. F., and Azzaro, M. 2009. *Building Customer-Brand Relationships*. London: M.E.Sharpe.

[8] Boyce, B. R., Meadow, C. T., and Kraft, D. H. 1994. *Measurement in Information Science*. Orlando, FL: Academic Press.

[9] Handy, C. 1994. *The Empty Raincoat*. London: Random House Business.

[10] Peters, T. 1993. "The History and Development of Transaction Log Analysis." *Library Hi Tech*, vol. 42(11), pp. 41–66.

[11] Jansen, B. J. 2006. "Search Log Analysis: What Is It; What's Been Done; How to Do It." *Library and Information Science Research*, vol. 28(3), pp. 407–432.

[12] McGrath, J. E. 1994. "Methodology Matters: Doing Research in the Behavioral and Social Sciences." In *Readings in Human-Computer Interaction: An Interdisciplinary Approach*, 2nd ed, R. Baecker and W. A. S. Buxton, Eds. San Mateo, CA: Morgan Kaufman Publishers, pp. 152–169.

[13] Page, S. 2000. "Community Research: The Lost Art of Unobtrusive Methods." *Journal of Applied Social Psychology*, vol. 30(10), pp. 2126–2136.

[14] Webb, E. J., Campbell, D. T., Schwarz, R. D., and Sechrest, L. 2000. Unobtrusive Measures (Revised Edition). Thousand Oaks, CA: Sage.

[15] Webb, E. J., Campbell, D. T., Schwartz, R. D. D., Sechrest, L., and Grove, J. B. 1981. *Nonreactive Measures in the Social Sciences*, 2nd ed. ed. Boston, MA: Houghton Mifflin.

[16] Skinner, B. F. 1953. *Science and Human Behavior*. New York: Free Press.

[17] Watson, J. B. 1913. "Psychology as the Behaviorist Views It." *Psychological Review*, vol. 20, pp. 158–177.

[18] Sellars, W. 1963. "Philosophy and the Scientific Image of Man." In *Science, Perception, and Reality*. New York: Ridgeview Publishing Company, pp. 1–40.

[19] Rasiel, E . and Friga, P. N. 2002. *The McKinsey Mind: Understanding and Implementing the Problem-Solving Tools and Management Techniques of the World's Top Strategic Consulting Firm*. New York: McGraw-Hill.

[20] Spink, A. and Jansen, B. J. 2004. *Web Search: Public Searching of the Web*. New York: Kluwer.

[21] Jansen, B. J. and Pooch, U. 2001. "Web User Studies: A Review and ramework for Future Work." *Journal of the American Society of Information Science and Technology*, vol. 52(3), pp. 235–246.

[22] Hargittai, E. 2004. "Classifying and Coding Online Actions." *Social Science Computer Review*, vol. 22(2), pp. 210–227.

[23] Jansen, B. J. and McNeese, M. D. 2005. "Evaluating the Effectiveness of and Patterns of Interactions with Automated Searching Assistance." *Journal of the American Society for Information Science and Technology*, vol. 56(14), pp. 1480–1503.

[24] Jansen, B. J. and Spink, A. 2005. "How Are We Searching the World Wide Web? A Comparison of Nine Search Engine Transaction Logs." *Information Processing & Management*, vol. 42(1), pp. 248–263.

[25] Abdulla, G., Liu, B., and Fox, E. 1998. "Searching the World-Wide Web: Implications from Studying Different User Behavior." In *the World Conference of the World Wide Web, Internet, and Intranet*, Orlando, FL, pp. 1–8.

[26] Beitzel, S. M., Jensen, E. C., Chowdhury, A., Grossman, D., and Frieder, O. 2004. "Hourly Analysis of a Very Large Topically Categorized Web Query Log." In *The 27th Annual International Conference on Research and Development in Information Retrieval*, Sheffield, UK, pp. 321–328.

[27] Cothey, V. 2002. "A Longitudinal Study of World Wide Web Users' Information Searching Behavior." *Journal of the American Society for Information Science and Technology*, vol. 53(2), pp. 67–78.

[28] Hölscher, C. and Strube, G. 2000. "Web Search Behavior of Internet Experts and Newbies." *International Journal of Computer and Telecommunications Networking*, vol. 33(1–6), pp. 337–346.

[29] Baeza-Yates, R., Caldefon-Benavides, L., and Gonźalez, C. 2006. "The Intention Behind Web Queries." In String Processing and Information Retrieval (SPIRE 2006), Glasgow, Scotland, pp. 98–109.

[30] Beitzel, S. M., Jensen, E. C., Lewis, D. D., Chowdhury, A., and Frieder, O. 2007. "Automatic Classification of Web Queries Using Very Large Unlabeled Query Logs." *ACM Transactions on Information Systems*, vol. 25(2), p. Article No. 9.

[31] Hargittai, E. 2002. "Beyond Logs and Surveys: In-Depth Measures of People's Web Use Skills." *Journal of the American Society for Information Science and Technology*, vol. 53(14), pp. 1239–1244.

[32] Wang, P., Berry, M., and Yang, Y. 2003. "Mining Longitudinal Web Queries: Trends and Patterns." *Journal of the American Society for Information Science and Technology*, vol. 54(8), pp. 743–758.

[33] Wolfram, D. 1999. "Term Co-occurrence in Internet Search Engine Queries: An Analysis of the Excite Data Set." *Canadian Journal of Information and Library Science*, vol. 24(2/3), pp. 12–33.

[34] Brooks, N. 2004. The Atlas Rank Report I: How Search Engine Rank Impacts Traffic. (July). Retrieved August 1, 2004, from http://www.atlassolutions.com/uploadedFiles/Atlas/Atlas_Institute/Published_Content/RankReport.pdf

[35] Brooks, N. 2004. The Atlas Rank Report II: How Search Engine Rank Impacts Conversions. (October). Retrieved January 15, 2005, from http://www.atlassolutions.com/pdf/RankReportPart2.pdf

[36] Choo, C., Detlor, B., and Turnbull, D. 1998. "A Behavioral Model of Information Seeking on the Web: Preliminary Results of a Study of How Managers and IT Specialists Use the Web." In 61st Annual Meeting of the American Society for Information Science, Pittsburgh, PA, pp. 290–302.

[37] Chowdhury, A. and Soboroff, I. 2002. "Automatic Evaluation of World Wide Web Search Services." In 25th Annual International ACM SIGIR Conference on Research and Development in Information Retrieval, Tampere, Finland, pp. 421–422.

[38] Croft, W. B., Cook, R., and Wilder, D. 1995. "Providing Government Information on the Internet: Experiences with THOMAS." In Digital Libraries Conference, Austin, TX, pp. 19–24.

[39] Joachims, T., Granka, L., Pan, B., Hembrooke, H., and Gay, G. 2005. "Accurately Interpreting Clickthrough Data as Implicit Feedback." In 28th Annual International ACM SIGIR Conference on Research and Development in Information Retrieval, Salvador, Brazil, pp. 154–161.

[40] Montgomery, A. and Faloutsos, C. 2001. "Identifying Web Browsing Trends and Patterns." *IEEE Computer*, vol. 34(7), pp. 94–95.

[41] Rose, D. E. and Levinson, D. 2004. "Understanding User Goals in Web Search." In *World Wide Web Conference* (WWW 2004), New York, pp. 13–19.

[42] Kay, J. and Thomas, R. C. 1995. "Studying Long-Term System Use." *Communications of the ACM*, vol. 38(7), pp. 61–69.

[43] Hilbert, D. M. and Redmiles, D. F. 2000. "Extracting Usability Information from User Interface Events." *ACM Computing Surveys*, vol. 32(4), pp. 384–421.

[44] Evison, R. 2010. "Hotel Problem." Personal Communication with Jim Jansen.

[45] Brinker, S. 2010. 4 out of 5 Conversion Experts Prefer A/B Testing. (May 19). Retrieved January 26, 2011, from http://searchengineland.com/4-out-of-5-conversion-experts-prefer-ab-testing-41791

[46] Eisenberg, B. and Quarto-vonTivadar, J. 2008. *Always Be Testing: The Complete Guide to Google Website Optimizer*. Indianapolis, IN: Wiley.

[47] Caples J. (Revised by Fred E. Hahn). 1997. *Tested Advertising Methods*, 5th ed. Upper Saddle River, NJ: Prentice Hall.

[48] Hopkins, C. 1924. *Scientific Advertising*. New York: Cosimo Classics.

[49] Ogilvy, D. 1963. *Confessions of an Advertising Man*. London: Atheneu.

[50] Gaukroger, S. 2001. *Francis Bacon and the Transformation of Early-Modern Philosophy*. Cambridge: Cambridge University Press.

[51] Box, J. F. 1978. *R. A. Fisher: The Life of a Scientist*. New York: Wiley.

[52] Schwab, V. O. 1962. *How to Write a Good Advertisement: A Short Course in Copywriting*. Chatsworth, CA: Wilshire.

[53] Holst, O. R. 1969. *Content Analysis for the Social Sciences and Humanities*. Reading, MA: Perseus Publishing.

[54] Park, S., Bae, H., and Lee, J. 2005. "End User Searching: A Web Log Analysis of NAVER, a Korean Web Search Engine." *Library & Information Science Research*, vol. 27(2), pp. 203–221.

[55] Hilbert, D. and Redmiles, D. 1998. "Agents for Collecting Application Usage Data Over the Internet." In Second International Conference on Autonomous Agents (Agents '98), Minneapolis/St. Paul, MN, pp. 149–156.

[56] Fisher, J. and Pappu, R. 2006. "Cyber-Rigging Click-Through Rates: Exploring the Ethical Dimensions." *International Journal of Internet Marketing and Advertising*, vol. 3(1), pp. 48–59.

[57] Kerner, S. M. 2005. Google's "Golden Triangle." (May 4). Retrieved January 6, 2011, from http://www.internetnews.com/xSP/article.php/3502611

[58] Grow, B., Elgin, B., and Herbst, M. 2006. Click Fraud: The Dark Side of Online Advertising. Retrieved January 6, 2011, from http://www.businessweek.com/magazine/content/06_40/b4003001.htm

[59] Helm, B. 2006. Click Fraud Gets Smarter. Retrieved January 6, 2011, from http://www.businessweek.com/technology/content/feb2006/tc20060227_930506.htm

auction search advertisers sponsored bid advertiser keyphrase bids score keyphrases ad price value engine auctions position quality bidding advertising bidders slot SERP perfect combination page CTR Effective different valuation equilibrium information pay just score actually really game use may still space online Second selling product many also effect see much good high one i.e. click based process determine best relevant top example bid Therefore highest given market stability point Google Bidder advertisement known true Figure strategy get advertiser's

8

The Serious Game of Bidding on Keywords

All of a sudden, we realized we were in the auction business.
Eric Schmidt,
Google's second CEO [1]

As Schmidt notes in the epigraph [1], major sponsored-search platforms are partly major auction houses. How does this auction affect our frame shop business?

In the course of developing the advertising for our frame shop, we have performed an analysis of our customers to target our efforts to those most likely to buy our products. We have performed market research, understanding how we will evaluate our advertising's return on investment. We have also reviewed the concepts of branding, advertising, and marketing to provide direction to our overall endeavor. Finally, we have designed our ads to appeal to potential customers and selected the keyphrases that we want to trigger our ads.

However, we must alert the search engine that we want our ads to appear with these keywords, and we must also pay the search engine for showing our ads. How do we do tell the search engine to display certain ads when the searcher's query contains certain words? How do we pay the search engine? More importantly for the advertiser, how much do we pay the search engine? What is a fair price to pay? How do we relate this price per keyphrase to what our business makes from the advertising?

We do these things via a bidding process. In this bidding process, we tell the search engine how much we would be willing to pay if it shows a particular advertisement in response to a query that we link to a particular keyphrase. The search engine also sets a floor price.

Where does this keyphrase price come from?

It comes from the workings of an online auction, which is a marketing mechanism for letting advertisers, as bidders, price the value of keyphrases. The keyphrases are the triggers for ads on a sponsored-search platform. In this context, the auction is an economic mechanism in a formal sense, with allocation processes and payment rules.

Like us, other advertisers want their ads to show with their keyphrases, and these advertisers want their ads to appear in the "best" position on the search engine results page (SERP), just like we do for our framing shop.

Therefore, the auction allows for a floating price (i.e., a valuation, which is an appraisal of the value of something) for each keyphrase for a ranking of advertisements, from highest to lowest, depending on the demand for that keyphrase. So, an online auction allows for a floating price for each keyphrase-advertisement-position combination on a SERP.

Why can everyone not just pay a set price?

There are three main reasons:

- *Different keywords have different values.* The keyphrases for our frame shop might be very moderately priced, as most framing is not a high-margin business relative to some other businesses. Keyphrases related to high-priced luxury goods, potential class action lawsuits, and other high-priced services are worth much more. Because no one really has this knowledge in advance to determine this value, search engines let the market decide via the auction. So, one can view an auction as a *price discovery mechanism*, which is needed in sponsored search because the search engine cannot possibly know how to price the different keyphrases a priori (i.e., in advance). In general, the keyphrase values depend on the profit margin of the products sold and the likelihood of conversion for a given keyphrase.
- *The SERP has limited screen real estate.* There can only be so many ads, and in many keyphrase markets there are far more advertisers than there are spaces for their ads. So, the search engines again let the market decide who gets the space based on price. Those who bid the highest obviously want the limited real estate more than those who bid less.
- The effect of *ad rank*. We have discussed the effect that ad rank has on click-through rate (CTR) and conversions (see Chapter 4 on advertisements). Advertisers generally want their ads to be at the top of the results listing on the SERP. The online auction is the mechanism for determining which advertiser gets their ad in the various positions. Again, those who bid the highest obviously want it more than those who bid less.

On the surface, our sponsored-search auction is fairly simple. There is an advertiser who selects a set of one or more keyphrases related to a product or service. There is typically more than one advertiser for any set of keyphrases. Therefore, each advertiser interested in a keyphrase states a bid, which is the maximum amount that the advertiser is willing to pay per click for a given keyphrase. This, in essence, is the sponsored-search auction.

However, beyond this simple explanation, there are a lot of unanswered questions. How does the advertiser decide what to bid? When does the payment from the advertiser to the search engine take place? What triggers this payment? How does the search engine decide where to place an ad on the SERP listing?

Our simple explanation actually skips over a lot of complexity.

Let's Talk Auctions!

What is an auction?

At its core, an auction is an allocation mechanism. The term "auction" is from the Latin root "auctus," meaning "to increase."

Potpourri: Although there is no evidence of when the first auction occurred, there are records of auctions as far back as 500 BC in Greece. At that time, women were auctioned off as wives, with auctions being the only "official" method for a father to sell a daughter.

In Roman times, the buyer in the auction was known as the emptor, leading to the phrase many know, caveat emptor, or *buyer beware*.

The first online auction business appears to be the Japanese company Aucnet, which sold automobiles online. Aucnet was closely followed by Onsale in May 1995 and eBay in September 1995 [2].

GoTo.com – later Overture – opened their sponsored-search auction in 1998, with Google opening their version in 2000. Microsoft entered the sponsored-search auction business in 2006 [3]. Yahoo!, which had purchased Overture in 2003, introduced a revamped sponsored-search auction in 2007. Baidu modeled both the Google auction and presentation in 2009.

The auction process or platform, typically called a market, takes some set of resources and allocates these resources to those participating in the auction based on a pricing mechanism known as a bid. Therefore, an auction is simply a market with an explicit set of rules to determine resource allocation. The prices of these resources are based on bids from the participants in that market [4].

For sponsored search, the search engines are the *market* as the keyphrase bidding platform where advertisers (virtually) gather. The resource is the *ad positions*, which is the SERP real estate for ad placement. The participants are the *advertisers*. The prices of SERP real estate and placement are determined by the *bids* on keyphrases that link searcher queries to the advertisements.

In principle, online auctions are not much different than the auctions that one may see at a county fair in the United States, an estate sale, or at some high-priced auction house, such as Sotheby's or Christie's. These are usually standard auctions, where the resource goes to the participant that placed the highest bid.

Potpourri: Most auction research is based on game theory, which attempts to mathematically model player situations, actions, and strategies in games. In most games, one's success often depends on the acts of others.

Game theory research is often based on having perfect information.

In a game with perfect information, all players know all actions that have taken place (e.g., chess, checkers).

Other types of games have imperfect information (e.g., most card games).

The assumption of perfect or imperfect information, although a simple concept, has a great effect on any analysis of a game, market, or auction.

Although some auction academics use perfect information (it makes analysis earlier), for practical cases, it is best to assume an auction where information is imperfect [5]. That is, the bidders do not know all the actions of the other bidders.

(Continued)

Therefore, the best *available* indicator of near-perfect information in auctions like those of sponsored search is the price of a product. For example, the average bid of a keyphrase in a vertical with many advertisers reflects the best information available, given that there is no perfect information [6].

To me, at least, this process has a lot in common with the *wisdom of the crowd* [7], in which a set of independent decisions by separate individuals collectively is often right. In the case of sponsored-search auctions, the crowd's wisdom appropriates perfect information in the auction.

In the earliest form of sponsored search [8], from GotTo.com, the keyphrase auction was standard in that the highest bidder was always the winner. However, most sponsored-search auctions are now nonstandard auctions, where the *winner* of the auction is not always the bidder with the highest bid. More on that later.

Most sponsored-search auctions are also sealed-bid auctions, where the amount of the bids of one participant is not known to the other market participants. This is different from an open auction (e.g., a cattle auction or an auction at Sotheby's), where everyone participating knows all the bids. The original sponsored-search auction was an open auction (see Chapter 2 overview of sponsored search).

So, although there are some similarities to standard auctions, as you can see, there are also some noticeable differences with sponsored-search auctions.

Moreover, keyword bidding and the allocation implementation can get rather complex rather quickly, especially given the scale of major sponsored-search auctions. In sponsored search, millions of both bid and price adjustments occur in near–real time, depending on the traffic to the sponsored-search platform.

The complexities of online auctions have lead to their academic study and research, in a discipline known as auction theory, which is an offshoot and an applied branch of game theory.

Auction theory focuses on how people act in an auction, viewing the auction as a game. Auction theorists typically focus on issues such as the efficiency of a given auction design (i.e., how well the auction achieves the goals of all parties in the auction, including the auctioneer), optimal and equilibrium bidding strategies, and effectiveness of the auction in terms of revenue generation. Equilibrium strategies are optimal with respect to opponents' bids held fixed. When a game hits equilibrium, each player in the game is implementing a strategy that is unlikely to change. In classic auction theory, the participants are interested in maximizing their own situation without considering others [9].

Auction theory research has lead to the development of several auction formats or types of auction markets. The format that we are most interested in is the Generalized Second Price auction and its poster-child auction, the Vickrey auction, as well as the generalized form, the Vickrey-Clarke-Groves auction.

Potpourri: Google AdWords was the first sponsored-search platform that utilized the format now known as Generalized Second Price auction.

The Generalized Second Price auction quickly became the standard for keyword auctions, with an amazingly broad impact on the Web and e-commerce.

Although Hal Varian, the first Google chief economist, is best known as the face of Google AdWords, the credit for developing the Google AdWords system goes to Salar Kamangar, the ninth employee at Google, and Eric Veach, another early Google employee and Distinguished Engineer.

These two Googlers (Kamangar was a biological sciences major and Veach was an engineer) implemented Page and Brin's vision that ads should be useful and welcoming into the search process, not annoying intrusions.

Kamangar and Veach apparently recreated the concept of a Generalized Second Price auction but with some unique implementations, with Kamangar handling the business side and Veach the mathematics. En route, they discovered second-price auctions existed in other forms in the past, including being used in Treasury auctions.

Google soon scrapped its direct marketing of search engine results ad space via a sales force [1], moving to rely near totally on the Google AdWords platform.

We will discuss these in more detail later in this chapter. However, it is beneficial, for the nonauction theorist, to get a conceptual understanding of the sponsored-search auction before looking at these formal models. So, let us first review the implementation aspects of sponsored-search auction mechanics. Then we can discuss its theoretical underpinnings.

Overview of the Sponsored-Search Auction

Every time a searcher submits a query to a search engine that has a sponsored-search platform or serves sponsored ads, an online keyword auction takes place. Triggered by one or more query terms, these online auctions are for keyphrases that advertisers bid on.

The sponsored-search auction has the same goal as most of other auctions: bring buyers and sellers together and determine how resources should be traded or allocated. In the case of the sponsored-search auction, the search engine is selling ranked ad space and the advertisers are buying this space. The search engine is both the market maker (i.e., it sets the rules of the auction) and the seller (i.e., it controls the resource).

However, the sponsored-search auction has a unique twist. The advertisers bid on keyphrases rather than on the ranked ad space itself. So, the link from the bid to the actual auction product is not direct. Also, there may be several keyphrases that are triggered by a term in a search query, so there may be several auctions selling ranked ad space occurring simultaneously. The search engine picks which of an advertiser's qualifying ads to serve in response to a query, and it then ranks the chosen ad against the chosen ads from other advertisers. A common example of this is a broad-matched keyphrase that may have multiple keyphrases and associated ads from which the search engine must select the handful to display to the searcher. The search engine is the final arbiter of who wins the auctions and how SERP space is allocated.

Oh, and this is done in a period measured in milliseconds.

Now, one may ask: "Why let advertisers bid just on keyphrases? Why not let advertisers bid on specific positions on keyphrases?" Or, why bid at all? Just let the advertisers pay some set amount for an ad display in a given position on the SERP.

There are several factors that prevent this straightforward type of approach. First, the search engine does not know at any given time what a keyphrases is worth. Second, most advertisers will prefer the top position or slot to the second slot, the second slot to the third slot, and so on. So, there needs to be some allocation mechanism, which is what an auction is. Third, as a seller of ad space, the search engine is in the business to make a profit. So, to rank advertisers efficiently, the search engine needs to know the advertiser's willingness to pay. The search engine uses this willingness to pay as an implicit ranking of the slots.

So, having advertisers bid on keyphrases is a reasonable approach.

In addition to the bid, advertisers must also determine how much the keyphrase is actually worth to them. This valuation will influence how much they are willing to bid.

Once there is some data, advertisers can determine this value with some calculations. Otherwise, an advertiser must use heuristics or data provided by the search engine based on the data from other advertisers. The advertiser's valuation of the keyphrase and the advertiser's bid are typically different, albeit generally closely related, assuming a rational advertiser.

The valuation is the amount of return on investment (ROI) or return on advertising (ROA) that the advertiser expects to receive based on a potential customer clicking on the ad associated with a keyphrase and purchasing something. The advertiser must also factor in the clicks where the potential customer does not buy anything, as these clicks still cost. This valuation generally becomes the upper boundary for the advertiser's bid.

Auction theory [10, 11] has generally shown that there is no advantage to bidding higher than one's willingness to pay, as it is a weakly dominated strategy (i.e., it does not get the bidder any advantage relative to any other bidder). From common sense, this approach does not seem like a good long-term strategy either.

Therefore, we can generally assume that the advertiser's true bid is motivated by minimizing cost, and therefore risk, by bidding the lowest possible price between the reserve bid (i.e., the minimum bid that the search engine will allow) and the valuation of the click (i.e., the upper bound of the advertiser's bid). So, these typical advertisers use sponsored search to maximize the difference between total margin dollars driven (i.e., the number of units of the product sold in a given period multiplied by the dollar unit margin) and the advertising spend (i.e., get the most profit possible from products sold via sponsored search), which is the base assumption of more academic sponsored-search auction models.

However, there are certainly exceptions. For example, some advertisers may aim to maximize order volume at a break-even point for their sponsored-search efforts. These businesses may expect profit from repeat purchases in brick-and-mortar stores instead of on the initial sale online.

In its actual implementation, even with simplifying assumptions, the sponsored-search auction is a really nuanced, layered systems. Each layer is an abstraction of the actual process. So, let us look at the sponsored-search auction progressively, layer by layer.

Figure 8.1. Simplified view of the sponsored-search auction.

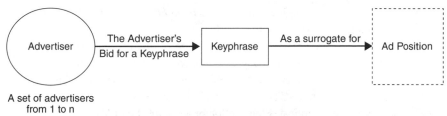

Figure 8.2. Better view of the sponsored-search auction.

An overly simple view of the sponsored-search auction is shown in Figure 8.1.

Advertisers place bids on keyphrases, which is the resource that the auction bidding process is organized around. However, keyphrases are not what the search engines are selling. Instead, the search engines are selling ad space and ranking of ad space on the SERP.

This aspect of selling ad space versus selling keyphrases has implications for the auction, and for issues like trademark infringement [12]. In trademark lawsuits in the United States, the courts have generally upheld the right of advertisers to show ads triggered by the branded keyphrases of other companies, even competitors, the legal rationale being that the search engine was actually selling the ad space [13]. However, most sponsored-search platforms prohibit the use of trademarked terms within ad copy by those not owning the trademarked term or not resellers of the trademarked product. Even here, there are some exceptions with fair use.

So, the concept of the auction as advertisers bidding on keyphrases and the search engine selling ad space is illustrated in Figure 8.2.

The sponsored-search auction selling advertisement space is a critical aspect to remember, as it makes sponsored-search auctions different from many other auctions. Although advertisers are bidding on keyphrases, the search engines are selling ad space. This ad space is also ranked, where the ranks at the top of the list are more valuable than ranks lower on the list [14, 15]. Most advertisers want to be at the top of the list. The reason by now should be obvious: These top-ranked ad positions bring in the most search traffic, because potential consumers click on these ads more often than those further down the listing (see Chapter 4 on advertisements).

Therefore, these keyphrases that advertisers are bidding on in the auction are really surrogates for an ad position in a results listing, which is really a surrogate for

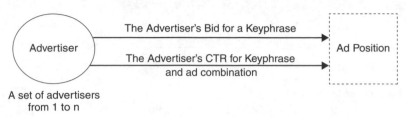

Figure 8.3. Even better view of the sponsored-search auction.

a percentage of the search engine's traffic. This percentage of traffic has some correlation to the ranked ad position on the SERP.

Most sponsored-search platforms use some type of quality score (i.e., an assessment of the relevance of the ad copy and related content relative to a searcher's query) for a keyphrase-advertisement combination, typically based on historical or estimated click-through rate (CTR), as shown in Figure 8.3.

This quality score complicates the auction process for the bidders.

Generally, the search engine does not disclose the bids of the other advertisers (i.e., it is a closed auction). However, if the sponsored-search auction used just the bid, with enough empirical data gathered by adjusting bids and seeing the resulting change in ad placement, an advertiser could approach perfect information (i.e., determine the bids of the other advertisers), assuming that aspects such as dayparting and personalization were not part of the picture (which they are – and these further complicate the auction). However, the introduction of the quality score nearly prevents this, as the advertiser does not know the effect of the quality score on the ad's position.

The quality score algorithm is yet another aspect of the auction that only the search engine knows.

If the quality score is held constant, then the advertisers could still approach the kind of perfect information needed to bid optimally, even if the actual quality scores are never learned. However, in competitive verticals, acquiring perfect information to bid optimally, as defined by auction theorists [10, 6], is difficult, as the quality scores can continually change.

So, look at all the factors that are unknown in competitive market verticals.

The bids of the other advertisers may be changing from one auction to the next. The quality score of the keyphrase-advertisement-landing page combination may be changing as CTRs, ad copy, and landing pages change. New advertisers are continually entering or leaving the auction. Advertisers are constantly changing their dayparting and geo-targeting options. Ads associated with a keyphrase via broad matching options must be considered. There are just a lot of possible unknowns to say with any certainty that an individual advertiser has perfect information.

However, these unknowns, in practice, are not much of a hindrance, as an advertiser can get a reasonable bid based on reasonable information [6]. Moreover, the number of unknowns makes it more difficult to game or spam the auction with vindictive bidding [10]. So, generally, advertisers can get reasonable, albeit not perfect, information.

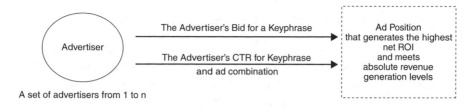

Search Engine (who runs the auction)

Figure 8.4. An even more accurate view of the sponsored-search auction.

So, the view of the auction in Figure 8.3 is closer to what is actually occurring in a sponsored-search auction. However, even this is not exactly true.

The ad position is really a surrogate for what most advertisers are really after – a keyphrase-advertisement-position that results in the highest possible ROI permitted by the advertiser's volume of sales or possible budget constraints over a given period.

This aspect of revenue generation is an additional complicating factor in sponsored-search auctions. The bid is a cost to an advertiser; however, if that bid generates revenue (actually generates profit is more accurate), then the advertiser can keep bidding in the keyphrase auctions with, theoretically, no budget constraints, because the benefits of participating in the auctions outweigh the costs.

This view of the sponsored search with the focus of the advertiser on ROI is shown in Figure 8.4.

The advertiser will bid for a keyphrase that gets the advertisement the position that generates the most profit. Now, we are getting a more accurate view of a sponsored-search auction.

However, there is still one aspect that this view does not address. A difference in the sponsored-search auction from a typical auction is that the item being bid on, the keyphrase, is not unique. There are possibly dozens of equally good keyphrases that will get advertisers the ad position they desire. In fact, the method of matching on the selected keyphrase can allow the advertiser to sidestep the specific keyphrase auction, from the auction perceptive, but still allow the advertiser to play in the showing of their ads for the given keyphrase from the advertiser's perspective [16].

This mechanism of selling ad space by auction ensures that both the search engine and the advertiser have the opportunity for the highest return for displaying advertisements. The bidding process also helps ensure that advertisers receive the most prominent and relevant displays, via algorithms, for the advertisements they can afford. Because most sponsored-search auctions factor in aspects other than price, more relevant ads tend to be in the most prominent positions, as shown in Figure 8.4, which is beneficial to the searcher.

Potpourri: Google AdWords became a phenomenon in the advertising world as one of the most successful and profitable advertising platforms ever developed.

Another famous advertising medium is the series of Super Bowl ads in the United States.

The Super Bowl is the National Football League's championship game, and the TV advertisements during these games have taken on a life of their own.

The first Super Bowl ad sold for $42,000 in 1967 [17], which is $277,938 in 2010 dollars. In 2010, a half-minute Super Bowl ad sold for nearly $3 million [18].

There are certainly many differences between television ads and sponsored-search ads. TV ads are a push form of advertising, used to create demand. Sponsored-search ads are a pull form of advertising, designed as responses to existing demand. However, there are some interesting conceptual similarities between sponsored-search and Super Bowl advertisements.

Whereas many consumers view television ads as an annoyance, many consumers look forward to the Super Bowl ads. Many folks tune in just to watch the ads.

This same concept – of ads not being an annoyance – is one of the underpinnings of sponsored-search systems. Make the ads relevant or (even better!) make them so good that people cannot wait to see them!

In fact, the 2010 Super Bowl ad, *Parisian Love*, by the search engine, Google, was a major advertising hit (http://www.youtube.com/watch?v=nnsSUqgkDwU). So, an interesting mix of a pull advertising company using push advertising.

In our analysis, note that we are making several simplified assumptions that are also often made in formal analysis of sponsored-search auctions.

- We are assuming a *closed auction* where new bidders are not entering and old bidders are not leaving. (Some verticals are quite fluid, and many advertisers use dayparting techniques.)
- We are assuming that there is just *one keyphrase* that will work. (This is rarely the case. Even with branded terms, there are misspellings and abbreviations.)
- We are *ignoring matching options*, which will affect how much an advertiser will bid on a given keyphrase. Matching options restrict which ads will compete in which auctions. (A change in matching options will affect the ROI calculations for an advertiser.)
- We are assuming there is *only one auction*, where the advertiser cannot just go to another search engine or similar auction to advertise. (For many sponsored-search efforts, there are many keyphrase auctions that will work for a given product or service.)
- We are *ignoring any product or budget constraints*. If a sponsored-search effort is generating profit, we can, theoretically, increase our advertising to generate even more revenue. However, at some point, the cost of an additional advertising dollar exceeds the revenue generated. Conversely, there is friction in the system, so our profits are delayed, impacting when the advertising can spend the revenue. (Bottom line, most advertisers have some type of constraint that limits their advertising spending.)
- We are assuming that one can actually *determine the true value of a click*. With searchers sometimes visiting a landing page multiple times and with both online and offline purchasing option that are not directly from a click on an advertisement, the calculation of the valuation of a click is not straightforward.

- We are assuming that a sponsored-search auction is the only way, strategically, for a business to advertise and will therefore affect the advertiser's decisions in the auction. (Most advertisers also focus on SEO tactics or have *intermarketing communication* (IMC) advertising efforts that might include television, radio, or print advertising channels.)

These are all critical assumptions of which one must be aware within the context of the sponsored-search auction. However, for the purposes of explanation, these assumptions make the presentation clearer. We keep the assumptions with the clarification that they represent the auction at a particular moment in time and that the conditions can rapidly change.

Additionally, all models are simplifications of the real-world process that is going on, so we should not be surprised that it happens with sponsored search. The assumptions listed earlier are limitations to keep in mind when applying these auction models to real-world efforts.

Sponsored-Search Auction Bid Scenarios

Walking through a sponsored-search auction under different conditions helps see how the process of bidding and pricing plays out under varying market conditions and assumptions. For a good review of the bidding process on both branded and nonbranded keyphrases, see various works by Shah [19–21].

We first examine the issue of being truthful, which is auction talk for placing a bid that reflects the actual value you have determined for the resource.

Example – Each Advertiser Bids Truthfully

There is a given keyphrase that three advertisers, A, B, and C, wish to link to one or more of their ads. The search engine has based a minor minimum floor on bids, and the valuation from the three advertisers is more than this minimum.

Each advertiser places a bid.

- Bidder A bids $1.00
- Bidder B bids $1.10
- Bidder C bids $1.20

In this scenario, C wins the bid but pays only $1.11, because in the sponsored-search auction, advertisers do not pay their actual bid; instead, they pay the second-highest bid plus a small delta (i.e., a small change, think of it as one cent). This is the basis for the Generalized Second Price auction, which is one of the sponsored search's most famous auction implementations.

Recall that the search engine is the auctioneer, and the advertisers are also paying the search engine, as the search engine is also the seller of the resource (i.e., keyphrases).

So, why would a search engine use the Generalized Second Price approach? It would seem in the Generalized Second Price auction that the search engine is getting less revenue because it is not getting the best price per keyword. Certainly the search engines would like to receive the highest price possible, just as the advertisers would like to pay the lowest price possible.

However, the Generalized Second Price auction offers some advantages to both the search engine and the advertisers, which make it an attractive model for an auction. Most notable among these advantages is reasonable stability. A Generalized Second Price auction achieves this stability by encouraging advertisers to not bid too high as an adversarial technique (i.e., there is no use in bidding extremely high to try and force a competitor to bid higher, to really "win" the top space, etc.). From an overall auction perspective, this has the advantage of keeping the auction stable, with few wide or wild price swings once the auction reaches a point of stability. This is especially true relative to a first-price auction [22] (i.e., you pay what you bid). The first-price auction has no point of equilibrium or stability, so the bids can constantly be in flux.

However, stability is a range, not an exact point, and there can be situations in a sponsored-search auction where it may be advantageous to bid somewhat higher than optimal to hurt a competitor [c.f., 23]. However, this strategy has limitations and beyond a certain bid point it becomes counterproductive, returning the auction to equilibrium. So, the Generalized Second Price auction is still considered stable within a small range of bids.

Why do you care about a stable auction?

Stability is an important element in continuous auctions such as sponsored search, as it permits advertisers to develop rational and predictable bidder strategies.

Let us explore some sample scenarios with advertisers and different bidding strategies to see the stability effect in action. Specifically, let us examine examples of how bidding high is not a good strategy over time with the Generalized Second Price auction.

Example – one advertiser bids high. Let us say the general valuation for a click in this industry vertical is $1.00.

What if one advertiser tried to drive up the keyphrase price? (Note: The motivation could be anything from trying to use up the advertising budget of the other advertisers to just waking up on the wrong side of the bed.) Let us take a look at this possible scenario.

Once again, we have three bidders.

- Bidder A bids $1.00
- Bidder B bids $3.00
- Bidder C bids $1.20

Notice that the bid for advertiser B is way out of whack with the other advertisers. Advertiser B wins the bid, but in the sponsored-search auction, advertiser B pays $1.21 for any clicks, which is the second-highest bid plus a small delta.

Why would advertiser B place such a high bid? Maybe advertiser B believes that such a high bid would guarantee a top slot because other advertisers would be bidding much lower. In this case, advertiser B achieved the objective and did not hurt the other advertisers in the market.

However, this is a dangerous tactic, because one can quickly overvalue the keyphrases for a particular industry vertical. Therefore, advertiser B probably overbid the price point. In other words, if the advertiser was forced to actually pay the bid price, the advertiser would probably start to lose money and, therefore, be forced to lower the bid to a true valuation in time. This would return the auction to stability.

However, in this case of overbidding, it really did no harm. Every advertiser got a slot at a reasonable price.

Let us now alter the scenario.

Example – more than one advertiser bids high. Again, let us say the general valuation for a click in this industry vertical is $1.00.

We again have our three bidders, but in this case, both advertisers B and C adopt a high-bid strategy.

- A bids $1.00
- B bids $3.00
- C bids $2.90

With more than one advertiser adopting this high-bid strategy, advertiser B again wins the auction but has to pay $2.91 and therefore loses $1.91 on each click. Advertiser C pays $1.01, losing but a cent. Advertiser A pays the true value, assuming the floor for this auction was $0.99.

With the reasonable assumption that advertisers have access to the same information, namely the valuation of a click, this example shows that it can be a dangerous strategy for an advertiser to bid more than a click is worth.

This assumption, however, goes back to the issue of perfect information. The value of a click for a given keyphrase may be very different among companies. Each company has its own price points, different product selections, and different promotions, which all impact the value of the sponsored-search traffic for each business. Assuming rational behavior and perfect information, you could hypothesize that the bid landscape for the keyphrase accurately reflects the different value of traffic for each advertiser. However, many advertisers neither can nor do measure the value of traffic, especially in the low- to mid-volume traffic keyphrases, where the data is sparse. So, assuming perfect information is probably overly optimistic. However, assuming equal expertise, products, and information among advertisers, overbidding is not a good strategy. It is easy to get burned.

So, with the sponsored-search auction, although there may be an occasional spike with advertisers testing out new strategies and new advertisers entering the market, the auction generally is stable and punishes advertisers for overbidding. Although this is a trait in other types of auctions, the characteristics of the sponsored-search auction have a point of stability and, therefore, avoid constant updates in bids [22].

Also, recall that search engines service multiple ads on a given SERP. In many instances, the CTR for two adjacent positions may not be that different. This is another incentive not to overbid. Your ad in position two may be just as valuable as being in position one, once the price of the bid is factored in.

Naturally, there are situations where some advertisers will bid very high for very legitimate reasons, such as branding (i.e., always want their ad to appear in the premium positions on the SERP, typically the north position above the organic results listing) or bragging rights (i.e., always want to be the top position). However, in these cases, the advertiser is applying nonmonetary value to the evaluation of the keyphrase's ROI. Typically, in these cases, the other advertisers just let them go at it.

What about Auction Factors Other than Price?

As stated previously (see Figure 8.4), although the auction bids are on keyphrases, the advertiser is actually bidding on the expected ROI from an ad position on the SERP. How an advertiser's ad performs over time affects the auction, specifically the price that the advertiser has to pay to get the desired volume of traffic within their advertising requirements.

In the preceding examples of our three advertisers, we focused strictly on money. In practice, however, the search engine actually determines which ad position a particular advertiser gets for a particular keyphrase based on the past performance of that keyphrase-ad combination. The search engine sets the starting performance at some value to reflect neutrality, setting this initial value (i.e., quality score) based a priori (i.e., before empirical evidence).

Although varying across advertisers and a proprietary algorithm for the search engines, the initial quality score is most probably based on the relationship between keyphrase and advertisement, the quality of the landing page, relative performance of other ads in an ad grouping, historical performance of the advertiser's account, and other similar factors. From personal experience, the initial quality score is typically a medium value (e.g., a 5 on 10-point scale).

Think of this practice as a restaurant that always saves the best tables in the house for the local, repeat customers. These repeat customers do not get a discount or pay less for the meal, but they get added value for their money. That is, they get the best seat. The restaurant does this because these are their best customers and are most likely to return.

If you are not one of these regular customers, you have to work a little harder (i.e., tip the hostesses) to get one of the premium tables. If you frequent the restaurant often enough, you become one of the repeat customers, and the premium you need to pay goes away.

Search engines use a similar concept. In the auction, everyone is treated equally in that all advertisers have an opportunity to bid on the keyphrases, and the entry price of the keyphrases is the same to the advertisers (although technically, a search engine can have bidder-specific reserve prices [24]). If all advertisers are new (actually if their accounts and/or ads are new) then the bid price nearly correlates directly with ad position. The highest bidder gets the best position, the next highest bidder gets the next-best position, and so on.

However, the direct correlation between bid and position diminishes as other factors, such as CTR, begin to influence position. This may happen very quickly as the sponsored-search systems have become extremely accurate at CTR estimation with little amounts of data.

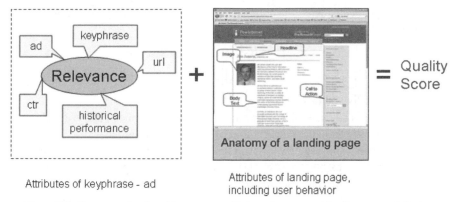

Attributes of keyphrase - ad

Attributes of landing page,
including user behavior

Figure 8.5. Components of quality score combining relevance and landing-page attributes.

As the ads, triggered by particular query terms, begin to diverge in CTR (i.e., the marketplace culls the good ads from the bad ads), the search engine will start factoring relative CTR into the assignment of ad position.

An ad's combined bid and quality score directly determines the ad's ultimate position in the results listing. The quality score – a phrase first used by Google, and the concept adopted by many other search engines – factors in aspects such as CTR at a given ad position and relevant of the landing page.

Ads with higher quality scores are rewarded by the search engine with a higher position in the ad listing and lower cost per click (CPC). Ads with a low quality score are pushed down the ad listing, forcing advertisers to bid higher to maintain their ranking. However, if a keyphrase-ad combination's quality score falls too low, there is a risk that the ad will not appear at all because the search engine considers the ad irrelevant to the keyphrase. Conversely, the more relevant ads appear higher in the listing on the SERPs, earn high quality scores, and thus cost less to the advertisers.

For the advertiser, a high quality score means more clicks for less money. To the search engine, it means servicing more relevant content to the searcher. To the searcher, it means more relevant content in the SERP in response to a query (Figure 8.5).

This process has an interesting effect on auction performance.

- It *mitigates poor bidding practices* such as bid jamming (i.e., bidding just below a competitor to exhaust that competitors advertising revenue) and other adversarial tactics because it makes the implantation of these tactics much more difficult. To be precise, bid jamming can still occur, but the effect will be mitigated over time as the quality score will begin to trump the bid or continually drive up the bid.
- It helps *improve the searching experience* for the search engine user. The use of the quality score has the effect of improving the quality of the advertising stream by serving relevant ads to the searcher.
- It *rewards advertisers* with relevant ads. Advertisers with a high quality score for a keyphrase-advertisement-landing page combination will get more bang for their advertising buck, with better ad placement on the SERP.

Ad rank is specifically determined for each and every search (i.e., every time a query is submitted) using the formula:

Ad Rank = max CPC x quality score

Equation 8.1. Equation for calculating the rank of the ad.

Let us take a look at this equation in practice.

An advertiser's ad placement is determined by the bid on the keyphrase multiplied by the advertiser's ad quality score for that keyphrase. So, a simple way to view this is that the advertiser's bidding power is a multiple of the associated ad's quality score. If the quality score is double that of competing ads, the bidding power is also doubled.

The formula for this is shown in Equation 8.2:

Effective Bid = advertiser bid X quality score

Equation 8.2. Effect of quality score on the advertiser's bid.

So, Equation 8.1 shows the effect of quality score on the ad position. Equation 8.2 shows the effect of quality score on the advertiser's cost.

If the quality score is good, the advertiser's keyphrase-advertisement-landing page combination is rewarded by a good ad position at a cheaper bid. If the quality score is bad, the advertiser's keyphrase-advertisement-landing page combination is penalized by requiring a higher bid for a given ad position.

Let us look at some sample scenarios to see the effect, looking at examples with the same bids and quality score, different bids and same quality score, same bids and different quality score, and finally different bids and different quality score.

Example – identical advertiser bids and quality scores

Bidder A bids $1.00
Keyphrase-ad-landing page combination quality score is: 1

Effective bid: = $1.00

Bidder B bids $1.00
Keyphrase-ad-landing page combination quality score is: 1

Effective bid: = $1.00

Bidder C bids $1.00
Keyphrase-ad-landing page combination quality score is: 1

Effective bid: = $1.00

In this example, with all advertisers being equal, the quality score has no effect.

The effective bid for all advertisers is the same. All advertisers are bidding the same and the ads are performing equally. In this case, the search engine would determine who gets what ad position based on some proprietary algorithm.

Example – different bids and identical quality scores

Bidder A bids $1.00
Keyphrase-ad-landing page combination quality score is: 1

Effective bid: = $1.00

Bidder B bids $1.10
Keyphrase-ad-landing page combination quality score is: 1

Effective bid: = $1.10

Bidder C bids $1.20
Keyphrase-ad-landing page combination quality score is: 1

Effective bid: = $1.20

In this example, with all ads performing equally, the assignment of ad position is determined by the advertiser's bid. The quality score has no effect. The effective bids for all advertisers are correlated to their bids. Advertiser C would get the top slot. Advertiser B would get the second slot. Advertiser A would get the third slot.

Example – same bids and different quality scores

Bidder A bids $1.00
Keyphrase-ad-landing page combination quality score is: 1

Effective bid: = $1.00

Bidder B bids $1.00
Keyphrase-ad-landing page combination quality score is: 2

Effective bid: = $2.00

Bidder C bids $1.00
Keyphrase-ad-landing page combination quality score is: 3

Effective bid: = $3.00

In this example, with all advertisers having equal bids, the ads' positions are determined by the ads' performance. So, the quality score is the major determinate. The effective bids for the advertisers with the best quality score are rewarded. Advertiser C would get the top slot. Advertiser B would get the second slot. Advertiser A would get the third slot.

Example – different bids and different quality scores

Bidder A bids $1.00
Keyphrase-ad-landing page combination quality score is: 1

Effective Bid: = $1.00

Bidder B bids $1.10
Keyphrase-ad-landing page combination quality score is: 2

Effective Bid: = $2.20

Bidder C bids $1.15
Keyphrase-ad-landing page combination quality score is: 3

Effective Bid: = $3.45

In this example, all advertisers have different bids and different quality scores. Both the bid and the quality score determine ad position to varying degrees. Because the difference in bids is very slight in this particular example, the quality score is the major determining factor. This is common in many competitive sponsored-search verticals. Advertiser C would get the top slot. Advertiser B would get the second slot. Advertiser A would get the third slot.

So, all things being equal, it pays to have the best-performing ad for a given keyphrase market. It permits you to bid less and get a better slot for your ad in the results listing.

Now that we know how the sponsored-search auction works, let us examine the theoretical underpinning of such auctions.

The theoretical basis for the sponsored-search auction is the Generalized Second Priced (GSP) auction. The Vickrey auction is the ideal form of GSP auction, so we start here with a brief discussion of the ideal form.

A Vickrey auction

A Vickrey auction is a type of sealed-bid auction where bidders submit bids without knowing the bid of the other people in the auction. The highest bidder wins, but the bidder pays the amount of the second-highest bid.

Very similar to the Standard English auction that one might see at a livestock sale, where all bids are public and known by all, the Vickrey auction gives bidders an incentive to bid their true value. Naturally, this view of the value can be false, incorrect, or misguided. This possibility aside, however, each advertiser believes their valuation is correct. The concept of each buyer bidding the true value of the resource, known as incentive compatibility, is important in auctions, in that it drives the auction toward some point of stability.

Why do we care about stability?

Stability helps both the seller and the bidders plan better if there are repeat auctions. More importantly, stability in an auction helps avoid the winner's curse, which is an occurrence where different bidders have different values for the resources and the bids of the other buyers are unknown.

The winner's curse usually arises in common-value auctions with imperfect information. Assuming that it is a single-item auction (Note: This is not a sponsored-search auction, but there are still some good takeaways), the winner in that situation tends to overpay and actually ends up in a worse overall situation than the buyers who did not win the auction (hence the name, winner's curse). In sponsored-search auctions, you can also avoid the winner's curse by leveraging empirical data from your account or data from similar accounts.

However, if the auction is in equilibrium, there is no winner's curse because the bidders account for this effect in their own bids and adjust accordingly. Therefore, each bid represents the true valuation of the resources by the buyer.

The pure Vickrey auction deals with auctions where a single good is being sold (i.e., a *second-price sealed-bid auction*). When multiple identical resources are for sale, things get more complex, and one can apply the same payment principal (i.e., have all winning bidders pay the amount of the highest nonwinning bid). This is known as a *uniform price auction*. Unfortunately, this situation does not result in bidders bidding their true valuations in most situations, and the auction does not reach stability.

Vickrey-Clarke-Groves (VCG) mechanism

A generalization of the Vickrey auction that maintains the incentive to bid truthfully is known as the Vickrey-Clarke-Groves (VCG) mechanism. The idea in VCG is that each player in the auction pays the opportunity cost (i.e., the cost of the next-best choice available) that their presence in the auction introduces to the other players. The auction system assigns the items in a socially optimal manner, ensuring each bidder receives at most one item. This system charges each individual the harm they cause to other bidders.

For example, suppose there are two ad slots, position 1 and position 2, that are being auctioned between two advertisers. The advertisers can bid on each position. (Note: This is a little different than our standard sponsored-search auction, but we'll just go through this example to see the effect of the VCG auction. As far as I know, no sponsored-search auction uses this form.)

- Bidder A bids $10 for position 1 and bids $5 for position 2.
- Bidder B bids $5 for position 1 and bids $3 for position 2.

The outcome of the auction is determined by maximizing bids. We see that both A and B would prefer position 1; however, the socially optimal assignment (i.e., best for all bidders) is to give position 1 to A (the achieved value to A is 10) and position 2 to B (the achieved value to B is 3). So, the total achieved value of the auction is 13. Achieved value is how much value a buyer or set of buyers actually achieves during an auction. In this example, an achieved value of 13 is the best that the auction can do.

Next, to decide payments, the opportunity cost each bidder imposed on the rest of the bidders is considered. If B had not been in the auction, A would still be assigned position 1, so no harm was done to A by B participating in the auction.

If A were not in the auction, B would have gotten position 1 with a valuation of 5. Thus, A caused $2 worth of harm to B because B ended up paying $2 less for position 2 than he would have for position 1. Thus, A is charged $2.

Not surprisingly, after reading the mechanisms of the auction, the VCG auctions are a great academic exercise but are almost nonexistent in practice [25]. In addition to being impractical (e.g., exponential effort to prepare bids, disclosure of confidential information, opportunities for cheating, can be money-losing, etc.) [26], face it – the VCG auction just does not pass the "back of napkin" test for the nonauction theorists.

Potpourri: "Back of napkin" calculations (a.k.a., "back of envelope" for the non-foodies) are not guesses and are not oversimplifications. Although not reaching the standards of a scientific or mathematical proof, a good "back of napkin" calculation captures the essence of a concept, process, or idea in clear and straightforward language.

"Back of napkin" calculations transcend many fields including investing ("Don't invest in anything that can't be explained on the back of a napkin."), business ("Don't start a business that can't be explained in thirty seconds."), and job hunting ("Have your job pitch no longer than an elevator ride.")

If neither the Vickrey nor the VCG auctions are used for sponsored search, what is?

A generalized second price auction

Although the VCG auction is not employed for keyword advertising, there is a generalized variant of a Vickrey auction, named Generalized Second Price (GSP) auction, which is different from the VCG mechanism but still a generalization of the second-price auction for a single item.

The GSP is the theoretical basis for most sponsored-search auctions. Given the number of transactions and the impact that it has had on the Internet and businesses, the GSP auction may be the most successful auction implementation ever in existence, with millions of GSP occurring daily.

Viewed from a pure auction theory viewpoint, the GSP auction is not entirely truthful, meaning that there are situations that can arise where advertisers are better off not bidding their true value per click. Therefore, the advertisers may bid in a way that does not lead the auction to equilibrium. Without equilibrium in a GSP [27], auction instability and bidding wars can occur [28], although most of these points of instability are based on static game theory structure (i.e., set number of players, playing a pure strategy, and not changing) [10, 29, 6].

Although the GSP auction can theoretically reach a point of instability, in practice this is not typically a major problem, owing to several factors [16]:

- Advertisers are continually *entering and leaving* the market. This flux makes it difficult for a single advertiser to pursue a vindictive or destabilizing strategy for an extended period of time.
- There are *multiple keyphrase auctions* that will typically accommodate the needs of a given advertiser. Given these options, if a single auction does become too unstable, an advertiser can just move to a different but similar auction and achieve similar results.
- The *effect of different matching options* on keyphrases introduces flux in an auction that makes it difficult for any one advertiser to manipulate. With most sponsored-search systems offering matching options, from exact to very broad, a wide and varying range of advertisers can participate in any given auction.
- The *effect of quality score* over the long run tends to drive the auction to stability. With quality score rewarding advertisers with relevant content and penalizing those with irrelevant content, it tends to make it cost-prohibitive to destabilize an auction for an extended period.
- The *search engine as both market maker and seller* has a stabilizing impact on the auction. The search engine establishes the structure for the auction and has an incentive to offer the searcher a worthwhile experience. Therefore, via actions such as quality score and minimum bids, the search engine acts to keep auctions stable.

One of best-known points of stability is the Nash equilibrium, which is a set of bids so that, given these bids, no advertiser has an incentive to change their bidding behavior. There is always at least one Nash equilibrium set of bids for a GSP auction, and among the equilibrium, there is always one that maximizes total advertiser valuation (i.e., all advertisers get the most from their bids). In other words, the GSP auction always has an efficient Nash equilibrium.

Potpourri: The Nash Equilibrium [30, 31] is a concept in game theory strategy. It refers to a point where all players in the game have nothing to gain by changing their strategy. Hence, the game is in equilibrium and, therefore, stable. Stability is a key component for online auctions, such as those associated with sponsored search.

A key component of the Nash Equilibrium is that all players must know the strategies of the other players. Although not really possible in a sponsored-search auction, advertisers can get a close approximation of the other advertiser's strategies, which is good enough.

The Nash Equilibrium entered pop culture with the 2001 American movie, *A Beautiful Mind*, directed by Ron Howard and starring Russell Crowe, Ed Harris, and Jennifer Connelly.

A full-information (i.e., perfect information) Nash equilibrium is often used for modeling sponsored-search auctions, even though the sponsored-search auction does not operate under conditions of perfect information. The argument for the assumption of a full-information Nash equilibrium is that even if the bidders do not know exactly what the other advertisers are bidding, there is the possibility of updating bids until the auction gets to the best level, meaning that the resulting Nash equilibrium is about the same as if there had been full information in the first place [6]. The advantage of the GSP auction is that it has a pure-strategy Nash equilibrium and avoids a pattern of constant updates in bids [22].

The following mathematical model captures the essential features of sponsored-search auctions, based on integration from multiple sources [10, 28, 32, 33, 29].

A generic sponsored-search auction is defined by the following:

- A set of k advertising slots with CTR $\emptyset_1 > ::: > \emptyset_k$, where $\emptyset_i$ is the probability that the user clicks on the advertisement in slot I (i.e., the CTR of $1 > i$).
- Assume that higher slots get the best CTR and that CTR will generally fall geometrically. That is, CTR decreases by position and follows some algorithm sequence.
- A set of n advertisers participating in the auction, each with a private valuation v_i for a click, $v_1 > ::: > v_n$ (i.e., a set of advertisers who each set their own bid on a click for an ad-keyphrase combination).
- Assume that $k > n$ (i.e., there are always more ad slots than advertisers).
- With knowledge of the mechanism and of their own private valuations, each advertiser submits a bid to the auction. We denote player i's bid by b_i.
- The mechanism:
  - computes an allocation χ of the k slots to k different players;
  - χ_s is the identity of the player that is allocated to slot s (i.e., the search engine assigns some ad slot to some advertiser's ad);
  - charges a price ps to the player χ_s for each click on his advertisement with $p_s <= b_i$ (i.e., charge the advertiser some price that is no higher than the bid);
  - if player i is allocated slot s at price ps, player i's expected utility is $\emptyset_s (v_1 - p_s)$ (i.e., the advertiser gets the net value from a click that is their valuation minus the price paid).

The GSP auction has some general allocation and payment guidelines, including:

- *Slots correspond to bids*: Advertisers are allocated slots in decreasing order of bids, adjusted for some quality score
- *Bids are a just a bit more than the bid below*: For each slot **s**, the payment p_s of player χ_s is one increment more than p_{s-1} from player χ_{s-1}
- *Payment is based on serving an ad*: Advertisers who do not win a slot make no payment and gain no utility.

When modeled as a static game of complete information, GSP has a continuum of Nash equilibrium. Exactly one of these equilibriums [6] results in advertiser payments identical to those that would be made if the mechanism employed was a VCG auction. This equilibrium is also the cheapest envy-free equilibrium from the advertisers' point of view. In that equilibrium, bids follow a recursive formula:

The highest-value bidder's bid, b_1, is unidentified because any bid $b_1 > b_2$ will suffice to obtain the highest position.

$$
b_i = \begin{cases}
> b_2 & \text{for } i = 1, \\
v_i - \dfrac{\theta_i}{\theta_i - 1}(v_i - b_i + 1) & \text{for } 2 \leq i \leq k, \\
v_i & \text{for } k < i \leq n.
\end{cases}
$$

Equation 8.3. Effect of quality score on advertiser bid.

This is Nash equilibrium of the GSP for which there is no incentive for any advertiser to dramatically change their bidding strategy.

Foundational Takeaways

- Sponsored-search auctions are online auctions where the bidder pays a small delta more than the second-highest bid.
- There are three players in the auction that you need to be aware of: you as advertiser, the other advertisers, and the search engine.
- In general, although there are incentives for each bidder in the GSP auction to bid the actual value of the keyphrase, this is not true in all scenarios. The GSP is not a pure truthful auction in the sense that advertisers can, and occasionally do, enter bids that do not represent their true value.
- As auction and market maker, there is incentive in the auction for the search engine to maximize revenue and to drive the auction to stability by offering a worthwhile searching experience to the searcher.
- Although the auction is for keyphrases, the ultimate item of value is the ad position on the SERP, which is correlated to customer traffic.
- The bid price for the keyphrase does not directly determine the ad position, but the general principles of the GSP auction still hold.
- The auction is not closed (i.e., bidders can enter and bidders can leave).

- There are always budget constraints, cash-flow issues, or volume constraints for some, if not all, of the advertisers, which limits the amount of keyword advertising spend available.
- There are always other keyphrase options.
- There is a variety of keyphrase matching options that affect the valuation of a click, and therefore the bid, of a keyphrase.
- There are other advertising options beside sponsored search, which affects the bid price at a given moment in time.

Relating Theory to Practice

- Using various combinations of *expected clicks per bid* and *CPC per bid*, determine your optimal bid (i.e., the bid that optimize profit). Bidding above the optimal bid will reduce overall profits. Bidding under the optimal bid will leave profitable clicks on the table.
- There are multiple reasons beside profit for bidding on a keyphrase, including aspects such as branding. For example, there are also advantages in occupying screen real estate on the SERP if the cost imposed on your competitors is more than the cost you pay for occupying the ad position. Identify keyphrases where you would bid slightly above your optimal bid to impose added cost on your competitors (i.e., your absolute decrease in profits is less than the competitor's absolute increase in CPC).
- Rarely is any product tied to just one keyphrase. More often, there are several keyphrases and match types impacting a product, requiring a portfolio perspective (i.e., examining the entire collection of keyphrases for a product). As you monitor keyphrase bids, note the possible impacts that these changes are having on ROA for other keyphrases. Sometimes, increasing the performance of one keyphrase may actually reduce overall returns for the entire keyphrase collection.

Conclusion

In this chapter, we discussed the auction mechanism that underlies sponsored search. It is the economic engine of sponsored search, which is the economic engine of the Web.

The auction portion is a keyword-allocation process, where advertisers bid on keyphrases. However, these keyphrases are surrogates for the real item of value – ad positions. The keyphrases are really limitless, but the ad positions are a scare commodity limited to the SERP screen real estate. Because the space for ads is limited, there is a ranking of positions from best to worst.

The keyword auction is rather straightforward. The advertisers, acting as bidders, state bid prices for keyphrases. Using a mechanism known as the GSP auction, the search engine accesses the bids and charges the top bidder the price of the second-highest bid plus a small delta. The second-highest bidder pays the price of the third-highest bidder plus a small delta, and so forth. This occurs for all bidders. Based on this ranking of bidders, one can easily develop a ranking of ads from these advertisers.

However, in the overall sponsored-search auction, additional elements come into play. First, the CTR of the keyphrase-ad-landing page combination affects the ad's placement. This is referred to as quality score. If an ad has gotten good CTR rates in the past, then that ad may be ranked ahead of an ad with a higher bid but lower CTR. Although the allotment mechanisms vary, comparing quality scores lead to an online auction model where the general principles of the GSP still hold.

The sponsored-search auction model has had some criticism, most notably that the keyword auction is not theoretically stable, although many of these analyses are based on some nonrealistic assumptions. Additionally, there have been criticisms that the search engine, as market maker, has a built-in incentive to maximize profit for itself at the expense of the bidders in the auction. This is true, although advertisers could just take their advertising dollars elsewhere, given that the marketplace is open.

The overall effect of economic assignment of value by the advertisers and marketplace determination by consumers has led to an effective online advertising process where the search engine, advertisers, and consumers are served and rewarded.

Let us now review, in an integrated fashion, all the disparate components of sponsored search.

References

[1] Levy, S. 2009. "Secret of Googlenomics: Data-Fueled Recipe Brews Profitability." *Wired Magazine*, Retrieved April 4, 2011, from http://www.wired.com/culture/culturereviews/magazine/17–06/nep_googlenomics

[2] Doyle, R. A. and Baska, S. 2002. "History of Auctions: From Ancient Rome to Today's High-Tech Auctions." Retrieved April 4, 2011, from http://www.absoluteauctionrealty.com/history_detail.php?id=5094

[3] Peterson, K. 2006. Microsoft's adCenter Is Google, Yahoo! Rival. (May 4). The Seattle Times, http://seattletimes.nwsource.com/html/businesstechnology/2002970721_microsoft04.html.

[4] McAeee, R. P. and McMillan, J. 1987. "Auctions and Bidding." *Journal of Economic Literature*, vol. 25(2), pp. 699–738.

[5] Krishna, V. 2002. *Auction Theory*. San Diego, CA: Academic Press.

[6] Varian, H. R. 2007. "Position Auctions." *International Journal of Industrial Organization*, vol. 25(6), pp. 1163–1178.

[7] Surowiecki, J. 2004. *The Wisdom of Crowds: Why the Many Are Smarter Than the Few and How Collective Wisdom Shapes Business, Economies, Societies and Nations*. New York: Random House.

[8] Jansen, B. J. and Mullen, T. 2008. "Sponsored Search: An Overview of the Concept, History, and Technology." *International Journal of Electronic Business*, vol. 6(2), pp. 114–131.

[9] Zhou, Y. and Lukose, R. 2006. "Vindictive Bidding in Keyword Auctions." In *Second Workshop on Sponsored Search Auctions, Conference on Electronic Commerce (EC'05)*, Ann Arbor, MI.

[10] Edelman, B. and Ostrovsky, M. 2007. "Internet Advertising and the Generalized Second Price Auction: Selling Billions of Dollars Worth of Keywords." *American Economic Review*, vol. 9(1), pp. 242–259.

[11] Urbany, J. E., Dickson, P. R., and Wilkie, W. L. 1989. "Buyer Uncertainty and Information Search." *Journal of Consumer Research: An Interdisciplinary Quarterly*, vol. 16(2), pp. 208–215.

[12] Rosso, M. A. and Jansen, B. J. 2010. "Brand Names as Keywords in Sponsored Search Advertising." *Communications of the Association for Information Systems*, vol. 27(1), Article 6.

[13] Goldman, E. 2010. Google Gets Complete Win in Rosetta Stone Case. (August 4). Retrieved February 2, 2011, from http://blog.ericgoldman.org/archives/2010/08/google_gets_com.htm

[14] Brooks, N. 2004. The Atlas Rank Report I: How Search Engine Rank Impacts Traffic. (July). Retrieved August 1, 2004, from http://www.atlassolutions.com/uploadedFiles/Atlas/Atlas_Institute/Published_Content/RankReport.pdf

[15] Brooks, N. 2004. The Atlas Rank Report II: How Search Engine Rank Impacts Conversions. (October). Retrieved January 15, 2005, from http://www.atlassolutions.com/pdf/RankReportPart2.pdf

[16] Athey, S. and Nekipelov, D. 2010. A Structural Model of Sponsored Search Advertising Auctions (working paper). (May). Retrieved February 2, 2011, from http://www.stanford.edu/group/SITE/SITE_2010/segment_3/segment_3_papers/nekipelov.pdf

[17] Advertising Age 2005. "38 Years of Super Bowl Ad Stats." In *Advertising Age*: Advertising Age.

[18] Associated Press. 2010. "Super Bowl Ad Prices Dip, but Still Pricey." In *CBS News Sports*.

[19] Shah, S. 2010. Analyze This: The Subtle Science of Bidding, Part 1: The Real Story. (June 18). Retrieved January 19, 2011, from http://searchengineland.com/the-subtle-science-of-bidding-part-2-brand-keyword-management-45387

[20] Shah, S. 2010. Analyze This: The Subtle Science of Bidding, Part 2: Brand Keyword Management. (July 16). Retrieved January 19, 2011, from http://searchengineland.com/the-subtle-science-of-bidding-part-2-brand-keyword-management-45387

[21] Shah, S. 2010. Analyze This: The Subtle Science of Bidding, Part 3: Second Order Effects. (August 13). Retrieved January 19, 2011, from http://searchengineland.com/the-subtle-science-of-bidding-part-3-second-order-effects-46983

[22] Lahaie, S. 2006. "An Analysis of Alternative Slot Auction Designs for Sponsored Search." In *7th ACM Conference on Electronic Commerce*, Ann Arbor, MI, pp. 218–227.

[23] Libby, B. (2010). Search Marketing Advice from Machiavelli. Retrieved January 19, 2011, from http://www.thesearchagents.com/2010/07/search-marketing-advice-from-machiavelli/

[24] Ostrovsky, M. and Schwarz, M. 2009. Reserve Prices in Internet Advertising Auctions: A Field Experiment (Research Paper No. 2054). (December 24). Retrieved February 2, 2011, from http://ssrn.com/abstract=1573947

[25] Ausubel, L. M. and Milgrom, P. 2006. "The Lovely but Lonely Vickrey Auction." In *Combinatorial Auction*, P. Cramton, Y. Shoham, and R. Steinberg, Eds. Cambridge, MA: MIT Press, pp. 17–40.

[26] Rothkopf, M. H. 2007. "Thirteen Reasons Why the Vickrey-Clarke-Groves Process Is Not Practical." *Operations Research*, vol. 55(2), pp. 191–197.

[27] Aggarwal, G., Goel, A., and Motwani, R. 2006. "Truthful Auctions For Pricing Search Keywords." In *7th ACM Conference on Electronic Commerce*, Ann Arbor, MI.

[28] Cary, M., Das, A., Edelman, B., Giotis, I., Heimerl, K., and Karlin, A. R. 2007. "Greedy Bidding Strategies for Keyword Auctions." In *8th ACM Conference on Electronic Commerce (EC'07)*, San Diego, CA, pp. 262–271.

[29] Lahaie, S., Pennock, D., Saberi, A., and Vohra, R. 2007. "Sponsored Search Markets." In *Algorithmic Game Theory*, R. Nisan and V. Tardos, Eds. Cambridge: Cambridge University Press, pp. 4–25.

[30] Nash, J. 1950. "Equilibrium Points in N-Person Games." *Proceedings of the National Academy of Sciences*, vol. 36(1), pp. 48–49.

[31] Nash, J. 1951. "Non-Cooperative Games." *The Annals of Mathematics*, vol. 54(2), pp. 286–295.

[32] Easley, D. and Kleinberg, J. 2010. *Networks, Crowds, and Markets: Reasoning About a Highly Connected World*. Cambridge: Cambridge University Press.

[33] Feng, J., Bhargava, H., and Pennock, D. M. 2007. "Implementing Sponsored Search in Web Search Engines: Computational Evaluation of Alternative Mechanisms." *Informs Journal on Computing*, vol. 19(1), pp. 137–148.

Word cloud generated by Wordle

9

Bringing It All Together in a Framework of Sponsored Search

Whenever a theory appears to you as the only possible one, take this as a sign
that you have neither understood the theory nor the problem which it
was intended to solve.
Karl Popper,
considered one of the most influential philosophers
of science in the twentieth century [1].

While implementing a sponsored-search effort for our framing business, we must
address many aspects that consume our attention, including keyphrase selection, ad
creation, market research, insight into the consumer as both a searcher and a customer, elements of branding for our product, advertising and marketing concepts,
and bidding strategies.

These aspects may seem like a list of separate components that you somehow
make fit into this thing called "sponsored search." But although we discuss them
separately, the separation is artificial. Each of these elements is totally integrated into
the complete picture of a sponsored-search effort. The separation is an artifact of the
discussion, as a method of simplification.

In real life and practice, one cannot select keyphrases without understanding the
market and the potential consumer. One cannot design an advertisement without an
understanding of cognitive, affective, and situational aspects of the customer. One
cannot begin marketing without understanding the product attributes. One cannot
develop advertisements that get results without understanding the customer and the
bidding process. One cannot bid effectively without understanding measurement and
metrics and competition.

It is a lot to deal with and become an expert in! Moreover, it is all related.

Potpourri: People have a tendency to overestimate what they know. More accurately, people put more faith in the concept of what they know than they really
should. This is related to the caution stated by Popper in the epigraph [1].

We do this individually and also in groups and in society. So, we should expect
it with our views of the foundational elements of sponsored search and even the
implementation aspects.

(Continued)

The one thing that we mostly know about scientific theories and models is that they are eventually proven incorrect.

This is not just true for "science back in the old days." It is happening now with our current theories and paradigms.

One of the most interesting examples to illustrate this is known as Schrödinger's cat paradox, which is a thought experiment to expose the bizarreness of, and perhaps incorrectness of, quantum mechanics.

Basically, a cat is put in a box where there is poison in a flask, a radioactive source, and a Geiger counter that releases the poison if radiation is detected.

The paradox is this. Mathematically, there becomes a stable period (i.e., more than a moment, an enduring and stable time) where, according to quantum mechanics, the cat is both dead and alive [2].

Quantum mechanics may be correct. Still, you should approach all theories and models with a skeptical eye.

All the disparate components are related and form an integrated whole that is sponsored search.

Where in previous chapters we dealt with each component separately, let us now bring it all together and look at the entire sponsored-search system.

We first looked at the theoretical basis for this totality view, which is general systems theory. Then, we examine the sponsored-search system, focusing on the interactions inherent within.

General Systems Theory

Much of science is focused on dissecting a complex system into its fundamental components, which is what we've done with our review of sponsored search so far.

A system, such as sponsored search, can be divided into its individual components so that each component can be analyzed as an independent entity. One can also add the components in a linear fashion to describe the totality of the system. Both are *reductionist* approaches that look internally and examine the subsystems within the system. These classic reductionist view of science permits focused analysis of foundational concepts.

However, there is an alternate view that focuses on the whole system, known as general systems theory [3]. According to general systems theory, conceptions of reduction are incorrect, at least at times. Instead, in general systems theory, a system is characterized by the interactions of its components and the nonlinearity of those interactions. In other words, we take the totality and the complexity of interactions into account simultaneously.

Potpourri: General systems theory has a lot in common with chaos theory and complexity theory.

Chaos theory addresses the study of complex dynamical systems (i.e., systems that follow a fixed rule over time), where the system is highly dependent on initial conditions. This means that very slight fluctuations in the initial conditions can radically affect the end state of the system. So, a ball balancing on a hilltop (using the classic example) may fall in many directions depending on very slightly changing atmospheric conditions.

Known commonly as the butterfly effect, these small changes in initial conditions make long-term prediction impossible.

However, a chaotic system is not random. These systems are dynamical so their future state is determined by the initial state. These systems only appear to be random because slight changes are amplified so much over time.

So, how do we address chaotic systems?

We continually sample data and measure the system to do short-term predictions. For example, we might not be able to predict what the weather will be two months from now, but we can predict with good accuracy what the weather will be in two hours.

According to this view of systems, knowing one part of a system enables us to know something about another part. In general systems theory, rather than a linear approach, we analyze systems using two approaches:

- *Cross-sectional* approach deals with the interaction within a system.
- *Developmental* approach deals with the changes in a system over time.

Specifically for us, we are concerned with elements and patterns within the sponsored-search effort, the foundational components of sponsored search, and the interdependence within the sponsored-search system. We are interested in the temporal aspects of sponsored search, such as the auction process. So, we are both concerned with sponsored search in a cross-sectional perspective and a developmental perspective.

What follows are more precise definitions of critical terms in general systems theory:

- *Element* – any identifiable entity within a system
- *Pattern* – any relationship of two or more elements
- *System* – any pattern whose elements are related in a sufficiently regular way to justify attention
- *Component* – any interacting element in an acting system
- *Interaction* – a situation where a change in one component induces a change in another component
- *Interdependent* – a situation where a change in an element induces a change in another element.

We will use these terms as we take an integrated view of sponsored search.

General Systems View of Sponsored Search

Figure 9.1 illustrates the general framework of the sponsored-search system. The sponsored-search system is composed of foundational and structural components. Cutting across these structural and foundational components are inherent constructs,

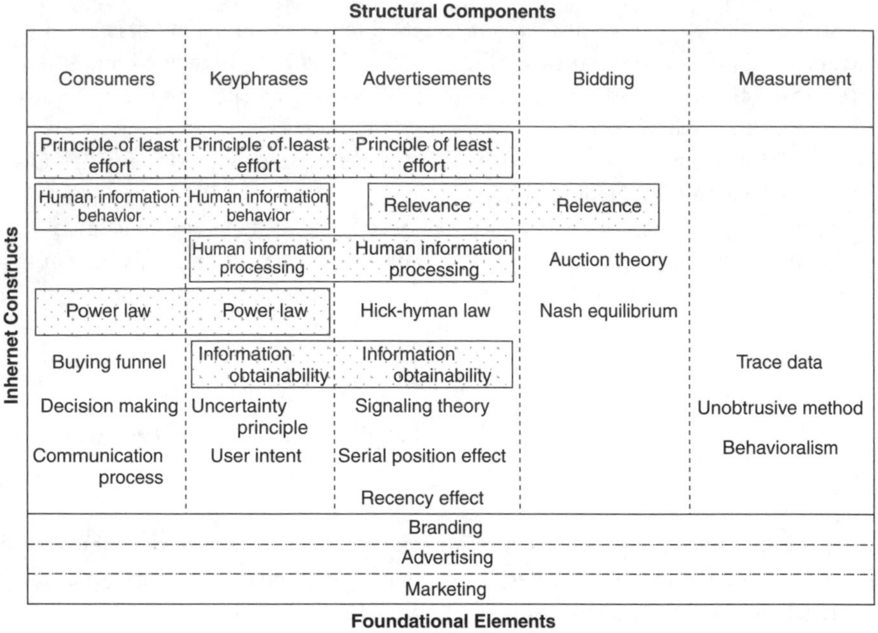

Structural Components

	Consumers	Keyphrases	Advertisements	Bidding	Measurement
	Principle of least effort	Principle of least effort	Principle of least effort		
	Human information behavior	Human information behavior	Relevance	Relevance	
		Human information processing	Human information processing	Auction theory	
	Power law	Power law	Hick-hyman law	Nash equilibrium	
	Buying funnel	Information obtainability	Information obtainability		Trace data
	Decision making	Uncertainty principle	Signaling theory		Unobtrusive method
	Communication process	User intent	Serial position effect		Behavioralism
			Recency effect		

Inhernet Constructs (left vertical label)

Branding
Advertising
Marketing

Foundational Elements

Figure 9.1. Framework of the general systems view of sponsored search with foundational elements, structural elements, and inherent constructs.

which is the third component. Each of these components is composed of elements that interact with one another in complex patterns. There elements are interdependent, as shown in the cross-section view of Figure 9.1.

Let us review sponsored search from this integrated framework.

Potpourri: In the book *The 100: A Ranking of the Most Influential Persons in History*, Michael H. Hart ranks one hundred most influential people in human history, along with some honorable mentions [4].

Hart does a statistical analysis using attributes of the people on the list, noting that there is a clustering by location and time. Hart credits this clustering to particular societies' ability to communicate more effectively. This increased ability to communicate has a positive effect on the society's ability to innovate.

With this viewpoint, sponsored search (as the economy engine of the Web) is a significant social enhancer.

Given that Google was the search platform that really took the sponsored-search concept and made it the economic engine of the Web, Sergey Brin and Larry Page really deserve credit for shaping the Web and Internet as we know it. Their efforts were most influential.

By the way, there were two other interesting correlations that Hart discovered with the people on his list: There were high occurrences of gout and no living descendents. Nothing to do with sponsored search, but I found it interesting.

Foundational components are those components that provide the base concepts and elements for sponsored search as an e-commerce endeavor, specifically branding, advertising, and marketing. They impact all structural components.

Structural components are those elements that form the building blocks of the sponsored-search process, including the consumers, the keyphrases that link advertisements to the query terms, the online auction bids, the advertisements, and the analytics that provide the measurement of the overall process. They are all impacted on by the foundational components and are defined, in terms of interaction patterns, by the inherent constructs.

Inherent constructs are those concepts that collectively form a theoretical view of sponsored search. They set the groundwork for modeling sponsored search or any of its subsystems.

Let us examine each of these components further, beginning with branding, advertising, and marketing.

Foundational components

The elements of branding, advertising, and marketing are the basis of the sponsored-search system as it relates to the business or organization for which the sponsored-search effort exists.

Branding. A brand is the identity of a specific product, service, or business. A brand can take many forms, including name, sign, symbol, color combination, or slogan. A legally protected brand name is called a trademark. The larger concept of a brand can encompass identity, as the brand affects the perceived personality of a company, product, or service. The act of branding usually involves the repetition of an image, slogan, or product name within a message to get consumers to associate related qualities with the brand.

Branding is a key element of the sponsored-search system in that sponsored-search efforts, especially advertisements, are continually reinforcing the business's brand in the mind of the searcher.

Advertising. Advertising is a form of commercial communication with the intent to persuade a targeted audience (i.e., consumers or potential customers) to purchase or take some action regarding products or services. These products or services are related to a brand, and the specific communication is encapsulated in a message known as an advertisement.

Advertising is commercial because the communication is usually paid for or identified through one or more message sponsors (i.e., advertisers). The consumer views the advertisement via some media where they know or at least are alerted to the fact that the message is paid for by an advertiser. Through the communication process of advertising, advertisers typically seek to generate increased consumption of a product or service.

Advertising is a key element of the sponsored-search system in that the principles of advertising are directly applicable to sponsored-search advertisements in terms of crafting ad copy and appealing to potential customers.

Marketing. Marketing is the process by which a company attempts to create customer interest in its products or services. It generates the strategy that underlies sales techniques (i.e., advertising), business communication (i.e., branding), and business development (i.e., new products and services). Therefore, marketing is an integrated process through which a company builds positive consumer relationships and creates value for both the consumers and the business.

Marketing identifies potential customers, satisfies the existing customers, and works to generate repeat customers. With the customer as the focus of its activities, marketing is one of the major components of any business. The main goal of a marketing strategy is to keep the business profitable.

Marketing is a key element of the sponsored-search system in that sponsored search is a direct form of communication with the consumer and potential marketing segments.

Structural components

The structural components provide the compartmentalized aspects of sponsored search, including the consumer, keyphrases, advertisements, bidding, and measurements.

Consumer. A consumer is any person that may potentially use a product or service from a business, although the concept occurs in different contexts and domains, so the nuanced usage of the term may vary. Businesses may be concerned with several target demographics. These concerns typically focus on variables aimed toward a buy/not-buy decision of the consumer. Therefore, the aspect of consumer decision making-process is inherently a key element of sponsored search.

Consumers are key elements of the sponsored-search system. Consumers have varying levels of prior knowledge of a business's products and services, including product attributes such as price. Therefore, the search engine is an intermediary between the business and consumers. Advertisers choose which keyphrases they want to target, and consumers enter keywords into search engines to search through the links that appear on the SERP.

The goal for the advertiser is to target consumers in the least expensive, most effective manner. Consumers want to minimize the search costs involved with finding an acceptable product or service. If advertisers choose their keyphrases well, the consumer receives relevant advertisements. Thereby, the costs for both are reduced.

Keyphrases. From a linguistic perspective, a keyword is a term or set of terms that occurs in a collection of texts more often than we would expect by chance alone. One calculates a keyterm using a statistical test, typically log linear, by comparing the word frequencies in a text against their expected frequencies derived in a much larger corpus, which acts as a reference for general language use.

Keywords are those in a collection of queries that relate queries to keyphrases selected by advertisers to trigger sponsored-search ads.

Keyphrases are critical elements of the sponsored-search system in that they tie the advertisement to the searcher and hopefully convert this searcher into a potential customer. Therefore, the keyphrase has to trigger a relevant advertisement that transitions the searcher into the customer phases of the online interaction.

Bidding. Bidding is the making of an offer, typically within the confines of a competitive auction. A price offer is called a bid, the term generally used in sponsored-search auctions.

In sponsored-search systems, given the amount of online content and searches, automated bidding systems typically handle the bids from advertisers. The minimum bid or needed bid is typically done via a cost-per-click (CPC) bidding model, although other methods can be used, such as cost per impression, cost per mille (thousand) (CPM), or cost per action (CPA). However, the CPC option seems like the most balanced option. The CPM option is biased toward the publisher, and the CPA option is biased toward the advertiser. One can expect that a certain mix of these models will coexist within automated bidding systems, depending on the practical consideration of both sides.

We also see these bidding auctions moving toward cost/value economic equilibrium overall and for advertisers specifically. With the maturing and adoption of the Internet as an advertising platform by most advertisers in the world, more and more online advertising segments are reaching economic equilibrium. In other words, the price tag of click/impression/action is approaching the mean value of the click/impression/action to advertisers. This lowers the opportunities for click arbitrage and very cheap client acquisition, which is a characteristic of a mature market.

Bidding is a key element of the sponsored-search system in that it directly links the sponsored-search effort to the bottom line, revenue, and profit.

Advertisements. An advertisement is a paid announcement, typically for some type of product or service, but it can also be for a business or organization. The goal of an advertisement is generally to increase consumption of a product or use of a service, even if indirectly, via branding communication. Advertisements communicate some information to consumers. This information usually includes the name of a product or service and how that product or service benefits the consumer.

Advertisements are key elements of the sponsored-search system in that these are the messages that transition the person from role of searcher to role of consumer.

Measurements. Sponsored-search analytics are about measurements.

Measuring is the process of determining the magnitude of a quantity, such as length or mass, relative to a unit of measure. Measurement is the specific result obtained from the measuring process. For example, Web analytics is the measurement, collection, analysis, and reporting of Internet data for purposes of understanding and optimizing Web usage. Sponsored-search analytics is a process for measuring keyword advertising traffic for business and market research. Typically, this measurement is directly in sponsored-search efforts.

Sponsored-search analytics applications can also assist businesses in measuring the results of integrated marketing campaigns, such as print advertising campaigns, by estimating how traffic changed after the launch of a new advertising campaign. Sponsored-search analytics provide data on the number of keyphrase searches, number of ad impressions, number of clicks, return on investments, and so on. Sponsored-search analytics can also be leveraged to find popularity trends of keyphrases for market research purposes.

Measurement is a key element of the sponsored-search system in that it allows for analysis, reflection, evaluation, and improvement in the next round of planning and implementation.

Inherent constructs

Inherent constructs are the building blocks that explain aspects of sponsored search as a system. These theoretical building blocks collectively form a theoretical view of sponsored search and set the groundwork for modeling sponsored search or any of its subsystems. As shown in Figure 9.1, some of these constructs apply primarily and directly to more than one structural components, and all are related to foundational components.

The inherent cross-cutting constructs of sponsored search are:

- *Auction theory*: how people act in an auction, viewing the auction as a game. Auction theorists typically focus on issues such as the efficiency of a given auction design (i.e., how well the auction achieves the goals of all parties in the auction, including the auctioneer), optimal and equilibrium bidding strategies, and effectiveness of the auction in terms of revenue generation. In classical auction theory, participants are interested in maximizing their own situation without considering others. Auction theory, specifically the General Second Price auction, is the background for most sponsored-search auctions. (Element of Bidding component.)

- *Behaviorism*: an analytical approach that emphasizes the outward behavioral aspects of thought. Behaviorism, as defined for sponsored search, emphasizes the observed behaviors without discounting the inner aspects that may accompany these outward behaviors. This more accommodating outlook of behaviorism supports the viewpoint that one can gain much from studying expressions (i.e., behaviors) of users when interacting with advertising campaigns. These expressed behaviors may reflect aspects of the searcher's inner cognitive factors but also contextual aspects of the environment within which the behavior occurs. In sponsored-search analytics, we are concerned with behaviors. (Element of Measurement component.)

- *Buying funnel*: a staged process for describing the way consumers make their buying decisions, from becoming aware of a need all the way to the final purchase of a product or service that addresses the need. There are various labels for each stage; one common labeling system is *Awareness*, *Research*, *Decision*, and *Purchase*. The buying funnel helps explain consumer searching behavior. (Element of Consumer component.)

- *Communication process*: conveys a message (i.e., information) to someone. A sender, a message, a channel of communication, and a receiver are involved. Challenges of communication processes include accurately conveying the message to the receiver. The communication process provides the explanation for the exchange between the searcher and the advertiser. (Element of Consumer component.)

- *Consumer decision making*: usually presented as a hierarchical staged model consisting of one or more prepurchase, purchase, and postpurchase phases. The prepurchase phases include need recognition, information search, evaluation of alternatives, and product choice. Consumer decision making assists in explaining the consumer purchasing process. (Element of Consumer component.)

- *Hick-Hyman Law*: a formula for calculating the time it takes for a person faced with a set of choices to make a decision. The Hick-Hyman Law is impactful on advertisements. (Element of Advertisements component.)

- *Human information behavior*: the totality of human behavior in relation to sources and channels of information, including both active and passive information seeking and information use [5]. Human information processing primarily affects consumers and keyphrases. (Element of Consumer and Keyphrase components.)

- *Human information processing*: the method of acquiring, interpreting, manipulating, storing, retrieving, and classifying recorded information [6, 5]. (Element of Keyphrase and Advertisements components.)

- *Information foraging theory*: an application of signaling theory in Web search. Information foraging states that humans adopt adaptive strategies to optimize their intake of useful information per unit cost. Related to signaling theory that explains advertisement development. (Element of Advertisements component.)

- *Information searching*: refers to people's interactions with information-retrieval-systems, ranging from adopting search strategy to judging the relevance of information retrieved [5]. Human information processing primarily affects keyphrases and advertisements. (Element of Consumer, Keyphrases, and Advertisements components.)

- *Nash equilibrium*: a concept in game theory strategy. It refers to a "point" in the "game" where all players in the game have nothing to gain by changing their strategy. Hence, the game is in equilibrium and, therefore, stable. Stability is a key component for online auctions, such as those associated with sponsored search, and allows advertisers to develop rational advertising plans. (Element of Bidding component.)

- *Power law*: a special kind of mathematical relationship between two quantities. When the frequency of an event varies as a power of some attribute of that object, the frequency is said to follow a power law. A power is an exponent: a mathematical notation indicating the number of times a quantity is multiplied by itself. An attribute of an object can be, for example, its size, its rank, or its height. Like the standard bell curve, the power law is a probability distribution. Power laws can explain consumer behaviors and keyphrase selection where there are few elements that occur very frequently (i.e., the head) and a whole bunch of elements that occur very infrequently (i.e., the tail). (Element of Consumer and Keyphrases components.)

- *Principle of information obtainability*: the more accessible the information, the more likely it is that people will use that information. The construct of information obtainability impacts keyphrases and advertisements. (Element of Keyphrases, and Advertisements components.)

- *Principle of least effort*: an organism generally seeks a method involving the minimum expenditure of energy [7]. The principle of least effort impacts consumers, keyphrases, and advertisements. (Element of Consumers, Keyphrases, and Advertisements components.)

- *Principle of uncertainty*: earlier stages of information searching are initiated by a lack of understanding or limited knowledge [8]. The uncertainty principle impacts keyphrases. (Element of Consumer, Keyphrases, and Advertisements components.)
- *Recency effect*: humans tend to remember the last few items they see as compared to those intermediately ranked items. The recency effect addresses why the advertisement at the end of the list get high numbers of clicks. (Element of Advertisements component.)
- *Relevance*: how pertinent, connected, or applicable something is to a given matter. Relevance impacts advertisements and bidding, although it is also tied to keywords and consumers. (Element of Advertisements and Bidding components directly, but also subsumed within human information behavior and human information processing.)
- *Serial position effect*: a position's impact on various human behaviors. Serial position effect helps explains the effect of rank on advertisements, with the advertisements in the first position on the list getting most of the clicks. (Element of Advertisements component.)
- *Signaling theory*: searchers often use clues in the decision-making process that guide perceptions of cost, benefits, rewards, and risks associated with choices [9]. (Element of Advertisements component.)
- *Trace data*: the traces, remains, or wear produced by processes in which people conduct the activities of their daily lives. These processes often create things or marks, or reduce some existing material. Within the confines of research, these things, marks, and wear become data. The trace data from logging software is the interactions between searcher, search engines, and Web sites. This trace data then becomes the data for sponsored-search analytics. (Element of Measurement component.)
- *Unobtrusive method*: analytical practices that do not require the analyst to intrude in the context of the actors. Unobtrusive methods do not involve direct elicitation of data from those being observed. Sponsored-search analytics leverage the unobtrusive method of data collection. (Element of Measurement component.)

Foundational Takeaways

- Sponsored search is an integrated system with structural, foundational, and inherent components.
- These components are composed of several elements that are key constructs of sponsored search.
- To understand the details of sponsored search, we take a reductionist approach by examining individual components and elements.
- To understand the big picture of sponsored search, we take a general systems approach and examine the system from a cross-sectional and developmental perspective.

Relating Theory to Practice

Figure 9.1 is a generalized concept of the entire sponsored-search system. However, we can take this general framework and apply it at a particular level, focusing in on more practical details. Take the sponsored-search system framework in Figure 9.1 and apply it to your account.

- What are the unique and particular elements within the overarching structural and foundational components?
- How are you implementing the inherent constructs for your vertical?
- What specific patterns can you detect in your sponsored-search efforts, especially in the areas of bidding, keyphrases, and advertisements?

Conclusion

A general systems view of the sponsored-search system integrates structural and foundational components.

We examine elements of the inherent cross-cutting component of sponsored search, including human information behavior, human processing theory, information searching, relevance, principle of least effort, principle of uncertainty, principle of information obtainability, Hick-Hyman Law, Power law, signal theory, information foraging theory, serial position effect, recency effect, buying funnel, consumer decision making, communication process, behaviorism, auction theory, and the Nash equilibrium.

Foundational components include the elements of branding, advertising, and marketing.

Structural components include the elements of consumer, keyphrase, bidding, advertisement, and measurement.

Web search engines are indispensable tools for interacting on the Web. In addition to addressing information requests, modern Web search engines are navigational tools that take people to specific Web sites or aid in browsing. People also employ search engines as applications to carry out e-commerce transactions. People continue to employ search engines in new and increasingly diverse ways, and search engines are constantly trying to improve the retrieval aspects of their services. One novel innovation for improving Web retrieval has been sponsored search. With sponsored search, major Web search engines such as Yahoo!, Microsoft Bing Google, and Ask have significantly altered online commerce. Battelle provides an overview of the factors that have led to the development of these sponsored Web search platforms [10].

Within the confines of this Web environment, sponsored search has made an enormous impact on the accessibility of information and services on the Web. Sponsored search has played a critical role in supporting access to the many free services provided by search engines (i.e., spell-checking, currency conversion, flight times, desktop searching applications, etc.) that have rapidly become essential to so many Web users. Without the workable business model of sponsored search, it is doubtful if the major Web search engines could finance anything close to their current infrastructures. These infrastructures provide the capability to crawl billions of Web pages; index several billion documents including text, images, videos, newspapers, blogs, and audio files; accept millions of Web queries per day; and present billions of links per week.

Sponsored search has also provided a workable business model for metasearch engines, which are beneficial for searchers needing high recall and requiring a thorough coverage of a topic.

Sponsored search additionally provides an effective method for overcoming the inherent biases in the technical implementation of particular Web search engines [11], as well as allowing content providers to move their links to the first SERP at a relatively low cost.

In doing so, sponsored search is an essential tool vital to the success of many businesses. It is fair to say that without sponsored search, the Web search engine market – and the Web! – would look far different than it does today.

However, it appears that nothing remains the same on the Web. So, we can expect sponsored search to evolve in the future. In the next chapter, we look at possible changes to sponsored search and the drivers of these changes.

References

[1] Popper, K. 1972. *Objective Knowledge: An Evolutionary Approach*. Oxford: Oxford University Press.

[2] ErwinSchrödinger (Translated by John D. Trimmer). 1980. "The Present Situation in Quantum Mechanics: A Translation of Schrödinger 'Cat Paradox Paper'." *Proceedings of the American Philosophical Society*, vol. 124(1), pp. 323–338.

[3] vonBertalanffy, L. 1976 [1956]. *General System Theory: Foundations, Development, Applications*. New York: Braziller.

[4] Hart, M. H. 1992. *The 100: A Ranking of the Most Influential Persons in History*. New York: Citadel Press.

[5] Wilson, T. D. 2000. "Human Information Behavior." *Informing Science*, vol. 3(2), pp. 49–55.

[6] Putrevu, S. 2002. "Exploring the Origins and Information Processing Differences between Men and Women: Implications for Advertisers." *Academy of Marketing Science Review*, vol. 10(1), Article 1.

[7] Zipf, G. K. 1949. *Human Behavior and the Principle of Least Effort*. Cambridge, MA: Addison-Wesley Press.

[8] Kuhlthau, C. 1993. "A Principle of Uncertainty for Information Seeking." *Journal of Documentation*, vol. 49, pp. 339–355.

[9] Gregg, D. G. and Walczak, S. 2010. "The Relationship between Website Quality, Trust and Price Premiums at Online Auctions." *Electronic Commerce Research*, vol. 10(1), pp. 1–25.

[10] Battelle, J. 2005. *The Search: How Google and Its Rivals Rewrote the Rules of Business and Transformed Our Culture*. New York: Penguin Group.

[11] Introna, L. and Nissenbaum, H. 2000. "Defining the Web: The Politics of Search Engines." *IEEE Computer*, vol. 33 (January), pp. 54–62.

Word cloud generated by Wordle

10

The Future of Sponsored Search

As we go forward, I hope we're going to continue to use technology
to make really big differences in how people live and work.
Sergey Brin,
cofounder of Google [1]

Hopefully, our framing shop's products and services are matched to the desires and needs of the consumer market that our business is targeting, and our products are within the means of our consumers to purchase. However, the consumer market is an ever-shifting target. Technology changes drastically, altering our market analysis. Consumers may consider a product fashionable today but consider it out of fashion tomorrow. They may need a service today, but they may not need it when the context changes tomorrow. Needs of consumers are continually evolving as the array of products change. Competitors enter the market and often make our services obsolete or put price pressures on our business. Rarely does a business have a market to itself for any extended period of time.

These are just some of the many pressures on businesses today.

These concerns are all issues of change that our framing business must deal with to be successful. The technology, the consumer, and the context are in near-continual flux. It is the same with sponsored search, perhaps more so given the rapid pace of change on the Internet. Everything moves in Internet time!

Predicting how technology, consumers, and context will change is fraught with difficulties, pitfalls, and limitations. However, by analyzing some harbingers currently present, we can make some general predictions for where sponsored search might develop in the near future. We examine this possible future by looking at aspects of technology, consumers, and context.

Nonetheless, I believe the sponsored-search model, in pretty much its current form, will be the default keyword advertising model for the foreseeable future, although it will certainly add features and adapt to the ever-changing Internet environment. The core structure appears to be stable in the near term.

This stability is partially due to the type of returns sponsored search is able to provide on the Web and Internet. No other revenue-generating platform currently can maintain the infrastructure of a search engine and related Web sites to the levels that sponsored search can generate. Additionally, no online advertising model has been as effective for so many different types of businesses as sponsored search. Sponsored search can also be effectively integrated with contextual and social advertising, enhancing its potential for longevity.

However, the long-term potential for the future success of sponsored search depends on it continually adding value, both actual and perceived, to its stakeholders. As long as it does this better than the alternatives, its future is generally secured.

Let us first take a quick look at these terms, value and stakeholders. From there, we will examine what changes the future might hold for sponsored search.

Potpourri: Predicting the future is obviously not easy.

Despite this, scientists are trying hard to do it, from predicting short-term events with social media streams to predicting longer-term threshold events. The Internet has aided in this effort with its extreme capacity for data collection.

The problem with predicting the future using data from the past is described by Hume's Problem of Induction [2]. Hume's Problem of Induction questions whether one can predict that any event in the future will occur just because it occurred in the past.

The induction problem entered pop culture via the book, *The Black Swan*, with the title being a classic example of induction from prior data [3]. For many years, it was widely believed that a black swan could not exist, because no European had ever seen one. Therefore, the prediction was that black swans cannot exist. However, black swans do exist, being native to Australia.

Basically, in the end, we cannot prove that something will or will not occur just because it occurred or did not occur in the past. However, this does not mean that we cannot do anything with data.

Scientists have gotten around this touchy point by using data only to disprove something. That is, empirically, we can show that there is evidence to disprove a hypothesis, but we cannot prove a hypothesis is true. The best we can say is that a hypothesis is supported based on the data.

We see this in the warnings in the marketing literature of financial investments – "Past performance is not a guarantee of future success."

There is the related issue of that one cannot use data to prove a negative (i.e., that something does not exist). All we can say from data is that there is no evidence of something.

Value and Stakeholders

In Sergey Brin's quote in the epigraph about using technology to make a difference, there are two concepts that we must define to evaluate whether or not a positive difference is being made. Namely, we must understand value and stakeholders.

Value
Value examines key questions, such as why goods and services are priced as they are, how the price of goods and services evolves, and how to calculate the correct price of goods and services.

Value is a measure, evaluation, or estimate of the nature, quality, ability, extent, or significance of something. It is based on the theory of value.

Value theory encompasses all the economic theories that attempt to explain the exchange worth or price of goods and services. Economically, the value of a product is the estimation by a consumer of that product. Value represents the relationship between perceived benefits relative to the perceived costs of acquiring benefits.

It is often expressed as the equation:

Value = Benefits / Cost

Equation 10.1. Value defined as a ratio of benefits to cost.

However, value has two components: subjective and actual.

- *Actual value* holds that a product or service is worth what similar goods and services are worth.
- *Subjective value* holds that for a product or service to attain economic value above zero, it must be useful in satisfying human wants or desires.

Value is thus a function of consumers' estimations, and relational to other goods and services. Therefore, the subjective value may have little to nothing to do with a product's actual value, instead depending on the product's ability to satisfy customer desires, needs, or requirements. One's view of the value of sponsored search depends on their perspective and priorities.

Stakeholders

Stakeholders are people or organizations that have a vested interest in something, or would be affected by changes to it. There are three types of stakeholders:

1. *Primary stakeholders* are those ultimately affected, either positively or negatively.
2. *Secondary stakeholders* are "intermediaries," that is, persons or organizations who are indirectly affected.
3. *Key stakeholders* have significant influence or importance. Key stakeholders can also belong to the first two groups.

In evaluating a system, businesses typically do a stakeholder analysis, which is the process of identifying the individuals or groups that are likely to affect or be affected by a proposed action. Then, businesses order these stakeholders according to their impact on the action, and the impact the action will have on them. This information is used to assess how the business should address the interests of stakeholders in a project plan, policy, program, or other action.

Value of sponsored-search stakeholders

We can identify the value of sponsored search to the various stakeholders in the system. For the search engines, sponsored search has to continue to generate revenue to pay the bills. The rate of growth during the first decade of existence was truly phenomenal. Most technologies eventually stabilize, so one would expect sponsored search to do so also. However, there are many stable technologies that are solid revenue generators. As long as this is the case, sponsored search will provide value to the search-engine stakeholder.

For the advertisers, including agencies, sponsored search must continue to be an online advertising system that is on par with or better than other advertising channels in terms of achieving results and business objectives. Sponsored search must continue to move products and services effectively and do it in an efficient manner for the business to generate a profit on these products and services. It must do this in absolute terms and also relative to other modes of consumer communication. Sponsored search must be easy to access and establish, at least for the small- and medium-size enterprises (SMEs), or there must be purchasable expertise available, particularly for larger enterprises.

Drivers of Change

For identifying the future, it is helpful to look at current problems, needs, and desires inherent in sponsored search. From this needs-and-problem analysis, you can expect advances in targeting, tracking, analysis, and optimization. You can expect that sponsored-search advertising will develop toward more control by the advertiser. Feature enhancement will continue in sponsored search. In the area of analytics, you will most likely see more nuanced and broader spectrum of analysis. In the marketing domain, consumers will most likely increase the time and money they spend online.

Sponsored search is in flux [4]. There are confluxes of forces, or drivers, that are pushing, molding, and redefining the implementation of sponsored search. Let us now examine the possible future of sponsored search. Probable drivers of change include technology, consumers, and context. We address these as separate entities, but naturally, they are all interconnected.

Technology
Certainly, one driver of change is technology.

Geo-location software. Online check-in software, applications, and features create a remarkably compelling opportunity for brick-and-mortar businesses, especially those with a primarily localized market. With geo-location software, businesses can interact with online customers in a variety of creative ways that can impact sponsored search.

When a customer announces that they are at a store or restaurant by checking in with a geo-location app, the business can shape and mold the customer experience in compelling ways before the customer even buys.

A check-in by itself is of limited value, although it represents a customer in the door. To make check-ins really valuable, businesses need contextual, demographic, and situational data. With this information as feedback, a business, such as our framing shop, can target offers and recommendations in a way not possible with sponsored search in its current form.

Integrating check-in type of software with sponsored search's knowledge of a consumer's desires and needs will give businesses the opportunity to leverage real-time contextual offers, discounts, and advertisements. These offers can directly shape a consumer's behavior before any transaction occurs, which is an amazing convergence of online and offline interactions.

It would be hard to imagine sponsored search not gaining some check-in type capability.

Sponsored-search analytics. With the increased use of check-in and mobile apps, one would expect to see geo-location-based metrics to measure the increase in foot traffic to brick-and-mortar stores based on sponsored-search advertisements, similar to click-to-call metrics now.

Certainly, given the increased availability of consumer data, the future will hold sponsored-search metrics beyond impressions, clicks, and conversions.

For example, the increasingly social aspects of Web sites, such as reviews and consumer comments, will likely lead to sentiment-analysis metrics that measure the tone of consumer comments about a brand or ad. This data can potentially affect how quality score is calculated. Already, sponsored-search platforms are offering searchers and consumers the ability to rate ads, so integration of reviews from other sites cannot be far behind.

With the increase in tracking devices and use of the Web via many devices such as mobile phones, televisions, and navigation systems, advertisers will have simpler ways to measure the combined reach of television, Web, radio, and mobile advertising in an integrated marketing communication (IMC) approach.

One can also foresee sponsored-search metrics that relate to user intentions and mental models in an effort to understand user goals and actions. From this type of data, one can better align advertisements or automatically adjust bids based on a determination of commercial intent.

Development of such techniques will require complex data mining and analysis of user interaction data to identify the strength of associations among user clicks and actions. Current logging, analysis, and mining software can track these interactions.

However, relating them to underlying user models to understand goals and intents, and doing so within an acceptable degree of accuracy, is not currently feasible within the sponsored-search domain. However, in other areas, such as blogging and microblogging [5], great strides have been made in this endeavor.

It is also reasonable for planning tools to improve. For example, we can expect keyword tools that do not rely on just historical data but gather possible keyphrases from forum, blogs, review site comments, product reviews, customer e-mail messages, social media sites, and thesauruses. These will permit advertisers to increasingly speak the language of their customers.

Based on their successes elsewhere, one would anticipate increased use of these techniques within sponsored search to extract the intentions of users and predict Web-searching behaviors.

Click fraud control. Click fraud counterefforts must continue to be improved. As new venues enter the sponsored-search domains, new potentials for click fraud also enter.

Search engines must maintain a critical point of trust. Advertisers will stop using the sponsored system if click fraud worsens beyond some decisive point, just as merchants will flee a geographical area if shoplifting becomes too bad, making profitable operations impossible or transitioning to looting.

Sponsored-search service providers must keep click fraud in check via more sophisticated technologies:

- *Prevention technology* – stop click fraud from happening
- *Detection technology* – catch click fraud once it occurs
- *Adjustment technology and processes* – credit advertisers after click fraud is detected.

This three-part effort of prevention, detection, and adjustment will call for greater transparency, increased communication, and more data sharing between the advertisers and sponsored-search platform providers. More sophisticated technology on the advertiser's side will focus on microadvertising events, alerting them to unusual patterns.

Given that click fraud and related activities have plagued sponsored search and other online advertising initiatives, it is doubtful that it is going away anytime soon. So, we must plan on dealing with it.

Changes to query submission. Probably the technique that most impacts sponsored search is changes to how the SERP is displayed in response to the query. Changing titles on the SERP, for instance from "sponsored results" to "sponsored ads," can have an effect on searching behaviors. Changing small design aspects on the SERP, including lines, graphics, or borders that separate sponsored results from organic results, can change user behavior. Any technology that changes query submission beyond the traditional "enter a query and click submit" will most likely alter searcher behavior.

The aspect of instant search is a good example. Instant search is a technology to make search more targeted and faster. Instant search combines predictive search with a real-time visualization of the results of that search. Instant search predicts what the searcher is searching for, allowing the searcher to not only see results faster, but also see the change in results while still typing.

However, if results are displayed as someone types a query, and these results change with every additional letter typed, then instant search raises questions that strike at the core of sponsored search. Namely, how does one target for terms in transition? So, the keyphrase may be *frames*, but there are potential targets along the way for *f*, *fr*, *fra*, *fram*, and *frame*.

Any change in the query-submission process that alters the display of the SERP will also affect sponsored-search behaviors. As the query is the major expression of need by the searcher, we should expect continued refinements and changes to the query-submission process.

Mobile device and apps. The effect of mobile technology is having a dramatic effect on how Web searching is conducted as well as introducing avenues of search that totally bypass the Web. The increased use of smart phones is having a dramatic effect on searching behavior, and hence a dramatic effect on sponsored search. A user with a mobile phone and appropriate app software can connect directly to e-commerce Web sites. Smart phones hold more personal information than personal computers, including name, number, and location. The increased ability of our devices to know our identities, locations, and desires will continue to affect how people search and therefore how advertisers will structure sponsored-search campaigns.

For example, navigational queries are quite common on Web search engines, but they have a whole new meaning when executed on a mobile phone. A navigational search on a mobile phone may indicate an immediate desire to physically visit a business, for example. A similar issue occurs with product-related searches, with mobile apps existing just for product searches, including bar code readers and price checkers based on location. Similarly, as more and more retailers provide their own apps to searchers, people will be able to associate with brands directly, bypassing search engines and linking consumers directly with business Web sites.

Sponsored-search services will have to adapt to this new mobile-app environment with advertisements on mobile phone platforms and with advertisements that integrate with the brand's own app.

Consumer

Another driver of change for sponsored search is the consumer.

Privacy concerns of online data. With applications such as toolbars and apps on mobile phones, the ability to target consumers will certainly increase. We can already tell quite a bit about a potential mobile searcher [6].

However, there will be some point where consumers, or governments acting as regulatory agencies on their behalf, will draw the line. Although use of data from search and navigation can seem bland (i.e., I search for a book or browse a book Web site and then ads for this and related books start to appear), consumers can get creeped out by an "ad following them around" [7].

Most online consumers want three things concerning online privacy:

1. *Control* – tell the consumer what you are doing and give the consumer the option to opt out (even if opting out means not using the service)
2. *Obscurity* – use the consumer's data mostly in the aggregate to detect trends and overall patterns
3. *Anonymity* – even when the consumer's data is individually isolated, protect and do not reveal the person's identify.

The use of consumer data will continue, especially with the increased use of mobile searching and the greater insight about the searcher that it contains. However, sponsored-search targeting methodologies will have to continually address consumer privacy concerns to avoid major consumer and legal backlash.

Less computer use. With the increased spectrum and availability of access to the Internet, there will be less use of browser-based Web access from a traditional computer. Consumers are increasingly stepping away from their desktop and laptop computers. As mentioned, they are searching from their phones or other devices. However, aspects such as Internet-based television, tablets, and gaming consoles are also Internet access points.

Therefore, advertisers will need to expand their existing desktop-only targeted efforts to these other forms of access. There will be decreased revenue from the Web site on its own, and sponsored search will morph to fill these other forms of access. Mobile sponsored-search campaigns will most likely become the major revenue generators, with Web-based campaigns becoming secondary.

Sponsored-search efforts need to adapt to a different consumer mindset for the mobile environment and non-computer environment. This new environment influences the entire search experience from aims to keywords to factors influencing these choices. For example, mobile search is often used to find the way to a property that the searcher already has in mind. Mobile search is often used by consumers on the move, either walking or in vehicles. Because of this, mobile searches use shorter queries and more navigational ones, so keyphrase selection and bidding strategies change.

Integration of the online/offline worlds. With the proliferation of check-in applications, local deal Web sites, mobile apps, Internet television, and micropayments, the blending of online and offline consumer data is gaining potential. We see this already occurring across services and devices. This integration is creating an increasingly accurate picture of consumers as individuals. Defining where offline ends and online begins is becoming increasingly difficult.

Obviously, the use of apps and Web services on mobile devices will be the source of much of integration. However, computers and eBook readers, along with online databases, are also potential sources. Unfortunately, for marketers, the proprietary layers of this data are often stored inside individual services and applications; however, this data is increasingly shared among applications, usually with the permission of the consumer via the acceptance of third-party applications.

In this melding of offline and online worlds, sponsored-search ads could increasingly incorporate the customer presence and behavior across the entire Web. With much behavior targeting already occurring, the next logical steps are the integration of behavior data from other sources besides searching.

Context

The final driver of change that we'll discuss is the context in which the sponsored-search system operations.

Real-time content. Where once Web users visited a static Web page, people are now confronted with real-time content generated via review sites, blog comments, and status messages from social media sites [8]. Internet users' increased engagement with real-time content [9] opens up interesting avenues for sponsored search, and it will obviously require structural changes.

Real-time content is short-status message postings, sometimes with links to longer documents or multimedia content. Real-time content is typically generated on social networking and media platforms. Real-time content is normally created for the immediate temporal context, to be consumed as soon as produced rather than for archival intentions. Currently, advertising in the real-time content stream is a mix of keyword and contextual advertising, although there is much ongoing experimentation. Potentially, advertising in real-time content streams will use a combination of CPM, CPC, and CPA pricing models.

Many questions concerning how relevant ads are integrated into real-time conversation flow, and on the SERP, still remain. As real-time content is integrated with the SERP, the searcher will be affected, although these effects are as yet undetermined. Real-time search on some of the major social media platforms already rival that of the major search engines. Therefore, one would expect to see sponsored-search-like models also on these searching platforms [9]. These services offer immediately interesting features such as local focus through geo-tagging postings, statuses, and other messages.

Social media. Certainly the growth of social media has and will impact sponsored search. Many social networking sites already have sponsored search integrated within their own advertising services. Soon, we will most likely see ads that are socially enabled, in that potential consumers will be able to share an ad, comment on an ad, and give feedback on an ad. It will increase the move away from advertisers talking to consumers directly and more to a two-way communication channel between a brand and its consumers.

Searchers no longer have the sole expectation of searching to find information for a specific outcome when they go on the Internet, as the growth of interactions with social media shows [10]. As people spend more and more time connecting, sharing, and interacting with the social Web, they expect to interact with what they find in the search results. Time spent with the social Web involves many types of interactions with like-minded individuals in a community or network, one of which is looking for and sharing recommendations. This will be an exciting and challenging venue for sponsored search.

Also, the blending with social media may introduce more push aspects to sponsored search. Keyword advertising is extremely good for converting people who are searching for information into consumers wanting to buy something. So, it is great for harvesting product demand but not particularly good for growing product demand. However, blended with a social element that can grow this demand, sponsored search can be even more effective.

Alternative pricing models. With the proliferation and diversification of sponsored search, from the Web [11] to mobile to real-time searching [9] to social media [10] to location-based services, it would seem that alternative pricing models beyond just CPC will gain popularity. One can see venues where CPM would apply, and in others where CPA seems most reasonable.

With variations in pricing models along access venues, we will probably see more focused and targeted campaigns that may be mimicked across multiple platforms. Already, you can target similar sponsored-search campaigns to either Web or mobile, and even further target mobile campaigns to specific devices.

Foundational Takeaways

- The future of sponsored search depends on providing value to the stakeholders.
- Changes in sponsored search will come from changes in technology, consumers, and context.
- Expected changes will most likely be in the areas of mobile, social, metrics, and local.
- Sponsored search is a people business, and people's behaviors and attitudes are in a continual state of flux.

Relating Theory to Practice

For each of your accounts, ask yourself:

- What additional sponsored-search metrics would you deem most appropriate?
- Is geo-location software a technology that can impact your client's business model? If so, how will it affect you sponsored-search effort?
- Is click fraud a major concern for your client? What about in the years ahead?
- What change to the query-submission process would most impact the advertisements for your account?
- Is there a place in the mobile-app space for your sponsored-search effort?
- Concerning search privacy, what is the minimal amount of data that you could collect and still reasonably target advertisements?
- Will your sponsored-search effort transition to a mobile searching environment?
- How well does your account integrate with both online and offline consumer activities?
- Is there a place for real-time content in your sponsored-search effort?
- Can social media play a role in achieving your account goals or taking your efforts in new directions?
- Are there alternate pricing models that would be more beneficial in certain contexts?

Conclusion

We see a lot of forces at work on the sponsored-search concept. Intense forces from the mobile-apps area are changing the way people search for information. In this case, consumers are bypassing the Web and going to the Internet for search, and then back to the Web for the actual information.

The use of mobile-app searching goes hand in hand with the increased focus on local search and search with a geographical focus. Mobile-app searching is also tied to the increased use of real-time content and social search, as people want information that is of importance here and now.

These changes will affect sponsored-search analytics, increase personalization, and counter concerns for privacy.

Although click fraud will continue, sponsored-search platforms will continue to combat it. Overall, it will be most likely contained, as advertisers become more selective in their Web site targeting.

Regardless of these changes, the sponsored-search paradigm will be the dominant business model for search engines and the searching components of other major Web sites, including social media services, for the foreseeable future. There is nothing else on the horizon that more fully adds branding, advertising, and marketing value to the variety of stakeholders that sponsored search reaches.

Since 1998, sponsored search has provided the revenue stream to finance the enormous technical infrastructure of the major search engines. As such, sponsored search has shaped the Web as we know it. The Web would be a vastly different place if it were not for sponsored search.

It will be interesting to see where sponsored search takes us in the years ahead. However, for the foreseeable future, the constructs presented in this book might provide some element of continuity for those working in the field.

References

[1] Jennings, P. 2004. "Persons of the Week: Larry Page and Sergey Brin," *ABC News*. Retrieved April 4, 2011, from http://abcnews.go.com/WNT/PersonOfWeek/story?id=131833&page=1

[2] Hume, D. 1910. *An Enquiry Concerning Human Understanding*. Cambridge, MA: P.F. Collier & Son.

[3] Taleb, N. N. 2007. *The Black Swan: The Impact of the Highly Improbable*. New York: Random House.

[4] Brinker, S. 2010. Agile Marketing for Conversion Optimization. (May 24). Retrieved January 26, 2011, from http://searchengineland.com/agile-marketing-for-conversion-optimization-37902

[5] Jansen, B. J., Zhang, M., Sobel, K., and Chowdhury, A. 2009. "Twitter Power: Tweets as Electronic Word of Mouth." *Journal of the American Society for Information Sciences and Technology*, vol. 60(11), pp. 2169–2188.

[6] Jansen, B. J., Zhang, M., Booth, B., Park, D., Zhang, Y., Kathuria, A., and Bonner, P. 2009. "To What Degree Can Log Data Profile a Web Searcher?" *American Society for Information Science and Technology 2009 Annual Meeting*, Vancouver, British Columbia, pp. 1–19.

[7] Helft, M. and Vega, T. 2010. "Retargeting Ads Follow Surfers to Other Sites." *The New York Times* (August 29), p. A1.

[8] Jansen, B. J., Chowdhury, A., and Cook, G. 2010. "The Ubiquitous and Increasingly Significant Status Message." *Interactions*, vol. 17(3) (May–June), pp. 15–17.

[9] Jansen, B. J., Liu, Z., Weaver, C., Campbell, G., and Gregg, M. forthcoming. "Real Time Search on the Web: Queries, Topics, and Economic Value." *Information Processing & Management*.

[10] Jansen, B. J., Sobel, K., and Cook, G. 2011. "Classifying Ecommerce Information Sharing Behaviour by Youths on Social Networking Sites." *Journal of Information Science*, 60(11), 2169–2188.

[11] Jansen, B. J. and Spink, A. 2005. "How Are We Searching the World Wide Web? A Comparison of Nine Search Engine Transaction Logs." *Information Processing & Management*, vol. 42(1), pp. 248–263.

Glossary

Words are but the signs of ideas.
Samuel Johnson,
noted British poet and author credited with
defining the English language [1]

This is a comprehensive glossary developed by leveraging and integrating glossaries from various organizations and terminology from academia, along with my own take on the field's jargon to identify the key practitioner terminology on sponsored search and analytics.

The end results is a combined, value-added glossary that identifies the key terminology of sponsored search from multiple perspectives.

Some of the glossaries that served as references are:

- Advertising Glossary: http://www.advertisingglossary.net/
- Business Dictionary: http://www.businessdictionary.com
- Marketing Terms: http://www.marketingterms.com/dictionary/a/
- MiMi.hu: http://en.mimi.hu/marketingWeb/index_marketingWeb.html
- Quirks eMarketing Glossary: http://www.quirk.biz/resources/glossary/
- Search Engine Dictionary: http://searchenginedictionary.com/
- WebTrendsGlossary:http://www.Webtrends.com/Resources/WebAnalyticsGlossary.aspx
- WebMasterWorld http://www.Webmasterworld.com/glossary/index.htm
- Webopidia: http://www.Webopedia.com/
- WhatIs.com Computer Dictionary: http://whatis.techtarget.com
- Wikipedia: http://www.wikipedia.org/

Naturally, many of these terms and their definitions have floated around the Internet for some time, and in most cases it would impossible to locate the original sources. However, I reference the online source (or academic paper) in which I located the term's definition.

- If the term definition is taken directly from an existing source, I reference it as (Source: [*name of source*]).

- If the core definition is taken from an existing source but I modified it, I state it as such (Source: modified from [*name of source*]).
- In some cases, I have substantially reworked or developed the definition, and in these cases, I provide no source.

With each term, I also provide a reference to the appropriate chapter in the book for you to explore the theoretical aspects of the term (i.e., (see Chapter [chapter number] [chapter subject]).

A/B Testing: testing two variables for a statistically significant influence. In sponsored search, it is typically the process of randomly showing a visitor one version of an ad or landing page (i.e., version A and version B) and tracking differences in behavior for each version. Version A is normally the baseline control design and version B is the independent design. A/B tests are commonly applied to clicked-on ad copy and landing page copy or designs to determine which version drives the more desired result. A/B testing is a method that has been commonly used for years in direct marketing and adopted within the interactive space (Source: modified from Quirk, SEMPO, and WebTrends) (see Chapter 7 analytics).

Abandonment: when a visitor exits or leaves a conversion process on an ad or landing page (Source: modified from WebTrends) (see Chapter 5 customers).

Abort: when a Web server does not successfully transfer a unit of content or ad to a browser. This is usually caused by a user hitting the stop button or clicking on another link prior to the completion of a download (Source: IAB) (see Chapter 5 consumers).

Above the fold: the section of a Web page that is visible on a screen without scrolling. It comes from the newspaper industry, referring to the top fold of the newspaper (Source: modified from SearchEngineDictionary.com and Marketing Terms.com) (see Chapter 4 ads).

Accuracy: the ability of a measurement to match the actual value of the quantity being measured. In statistical terms, accuracy is the width of the confidence interval for a desired confidence level. Accuracy is the foundation on which your marketing analytics should be built (Source: modified from WebTrends) (see Chapter 7 analytics).

Acquisition cost: total cost of an advertising/marketing campaign divided by the number of visitors (this is visitor acquisition cost) or divided by the number of customers (this is customer acquisition cost); an important metric in effective PPC advertising (Source: modified from SearchEngineDictionary.com) (see Chapter 5 consumers).

Acquisition: the point at which a visitor becomes a qualified lead/customer. Generally this is the point where the visitor buys a product or provides contact details and indicates an interest in the product or service. Also refers to the process of gaining customers through the means of different marketing strategies (Source: modified from WebTrends and SearchEngineDictionary.com) (see Chapter 7 analytics).

Action: a specified task performed by a user (Source: modified from Quirk) (see Chapter 7 analytics).

Actionable data: information that allows one to make a decision (Source: modified from WebTrends) (see Chapter 7 analytics).

Active Verb: an action word, usually used in a call to action (CTA) that tells a visitor what to do (Source: Quirk) (see Chapter 4 ads).

Activity audit: independent verification of measured activity for a specified time period. Some of the key metrics validated are ad impressions, page impressions, clicks, total visits, and unique users. An activity audit results in a report verifying the metrics (Source: IAB) (see Chapter 7 analytics).

Ad audience: the number of unique users exposed to an ad within a specified time period (Source: IAB) (see Chapter 7 analytics).

Ad banner: a graphic image or other media object used as an advertisement (Source: IAB) (see Chapter 4 ads).

Ad blocker: software on a user's browser that prevents advertisements from being displayed (Source: IAB) (see Chapter 5 consumers).

Ad blocking: the blocking of Web advertisements, typically the image in graphical Web advertisements (Source: Marketing Terms.com) (see Chapter 5 consumers).

Ad broker: an Internet advertising specialist. Ad brokers act as middlemen between Web site owners with advertising space to sell and advertisers (Source: SearchEngineDictionary.com) (see Chapter 2 model).

Ad campaign audit: an activity audit for a specific ad campaign (Source: IAB) (see Chapter 7 analytics).

Ad centric measurement: audience measurement derived from a third-party ad server's own server logs (Source: IAB) (see Chapter 7 analytics).

Ad click: a click on an advertisement on a Web page, which takes a user to another site (Source: modified from WebTrends) (see Chapter 7 analytics).

Ad copy: the main text of a clickable search or context-served ad. It usually makes up the second and third lines of a displayed ad, between the Ad Title and the Display URL (Source: SEMPO) (see Chapter 4 ads).

Ad display / Ad delivered: when an ad is successfully displayed on the user's computer screen (Source: IAB) (see Chapter 7 analytics).

Ad download: when an ad is downloaded by a server to a user's browser. Ads can be requested, but aborted or abandoned before actually being downloaded to the browser, and hence there would be no opportunity to see the ad by the user (Source: IAB) (see Chapter 7 analytics).

Ad impression: can have multiple meanings depending on the context (Source: IAB) (see Chapter 7 analytics):

- An ad served to a user's browser. Ads can be requested by the user's browser.
- The measurement of responses from an ad delivery system to an ad request from the user's browser, which is filtered from robotic activity and is recorded at a point as late as possible in the process of delivery of the creative material to the user's browser – therefore closest to the actual opportunity to be seen by the user.
- **Ad impression ratio**: click-throughs divided by ad impressions. It is more commonly known as the click-through rate (CTR) (Source: IAB) (see Chapter 7 analytics):

Ad insertion: when an ad is inserted in a document and recorded by the ad server (Source: IAB) (see Chapter 2 model).

Ad inventory: the number of potential page views a site has available for advertising (Source: SearchEngineDictionary.com) (see Chapter 3 model).

Ad materials: the creative artwork, copy, active URLs, and active target sites due to the seller prior to the initiation of the ad campaign (Source: IAB) (see Chapter 4 ads).

Ad network: an aggregator or broker of advertising inventory for many sites. Ad networks are the sales representatives for the Web sites within the network (Source: IAB) (see Chapter 2 model).

Ad recall: a measure of advertising effectiveness in which a sample of respondents is exposed to an ad and then at a later point in time is asked if they remember the ad. Ad recall can be on an aided or unaided basis. Aided ad recall is when the respondent is told the name of the brand or category being advertised (Source: IAB) (see Chapter 7 analytics).

Ad request: the request for an advertisement as a direct result of a user's action as recorded by the ad server. Ad requests can come directly from the user's browser or from an intermediate Internet resource, such as a Web content server (Source: IAB) (see Chapter 7 analytics).

Ad serving: the delivery of ads by a server to an end-user's computer on which the ads are then (Source: IAB) (see Chapter 2 model).

Ad space: the allocated real estate on a Web page of a site in which an advertisement can be placed. Each space on a site is uniquely identified. Multiple ad spaces can exist on a single page (Source: modified from IAB, Marketing Terms.com, and Quick) (see Chapter 2 model).

Ad stream: the series of ads displayed by the user during a single visit to a site (also impression stream) (Source: IAB) (see Chapter 7 analytics).

Ad title: the first line of text displayed in a clickable search or context-served ad. Ad titles serve as ad headlines (Source: SEMPO) (see Chapter 4 ads).

Ad transfers: the successful display of an advertiser's Web site after the user clicked on an ad. When a user clicks on an advertisement, a click-through is recorded and redirects or "transfers" the user's browser to an advertiser's Web site. If the user successfully displays the advertiser's Web site, an ad transfer is recorded (Source: IAB) (see Chapter 7 analytics).

Ad view: when the ad is actually seen by the user. Note this is not measurable today. The best approximation today is provided by ad displays, when a Web page displays an ad (Source: modified from IAB and WebTrends) (see Chapter 7 analytics).

Ad (or Advertisement): the commercial portion of message content for which an advertiser has or will pay when a searcher sees their content after submitting a query in a search engine or Web site search box, which will typically take a searcher to another Web page (Source: modified from SEMPO, IAB, and WebTrends) (see Chapter 4 ads).

Address: a unique identifier for a computer or site online, usually a URL for a Web site or marked with an @ for an e-mail address. Literally, it is how one computer finds the location of another computer using the Internet (Source: IAB) (see Chapter 2 model).

Adjacency: referring to the relationship between words, particularly words used in a search engine query. Search engines typically assign higher value to pages where the search terms appear next to one another (as in the query) than to pages where the search terms are separated by other words (Source: SearchEngineDictionary.com) (see Chapter 4 ads)

Advertiser: the company paying for the advertisement (Source: IAB) (see Chapter 2 model).

Advertising agency: a service business dedicated to creating, planning, and handling advertising (and sometimes other forms of promotion) for its clients. An ad agency is independent from the client and provides an outside point of view to the effort of selling the client's products or services. An agency can also handle overall marketing, branding strategies, and sales promotions for its clients (Source: Wikipedia) (see Chapter 6 BAM!).

Advertising blockade: where one advertiser purchases all advertising outlets at a given point in time or space (see Chapter 4 ads).

Advertising frequency: how often an advertisement is shown (see Chapter 7 analytics).

Advertising network: a service allowing advertising buyers to reach broad audiences relatively easily through run-of-category and run-of-network buys where ads are bought centrally through one company and displayed on multiple Web sites that contract with that company for a share of revenue generated by ads served on their site (Source: modified from Search Engine Watch and Marketing Terms.com) (see Chapter 2 model).

Advertising reach: refers to the total number of different people or households exposed, at least once, to a medium during a given period of time. (Source: Wikipedia) (see Chapter 6 BAM!).

Adware: advertiser-supported software; typically downloaded with other applications such as peer-to-peer file sharing. (Source: Advertising.com) (see Chapter 2 model).

Affiliate marketing: process of revenue sharing where merchants duplicate sales efforts by enlisting other Web sites as a type of outside sales force. In return, the affiliate receives a percentage of sales or some other form of compensation generated by that traffic. Successful affiliate marketing programs result in the merchant attracting additional buyers, and the affiliate earning the equivalent of a referral fee, based on click-through referrals to the merchant site (Source: modified from SEMPO and Quick) (see Chapter 2 model).

Affinity marketing: selling products or services to customers on the basis of their established buying patterns (Source: IAB) (see Chapter 2 model).

Algorithms: sets of rules to solve a problem or some end, typically via the use of some programming language (see Chapter 2 model).

Alternate text: a word or phrase displayed when a user has image loading disabled in their browser or when a user abandons a page by hitting "stop" in their browser prior to the transfer of all images. Also appears as balloon text when a user lets their mouse rest over an image (Source: IAB) (see Chapter 4 ads).

Anchor text: the clickable text part of a hyperlink. The text usually gives visitors or search engines important information on what the page being linked to is about (Source: Search Engine Watch) (see Chapter 2 model).

Anonymizer: an intermediary that prevents Web sites from seeing a user's Internet Protocol (IP) address (Source: IAB) (see Chapter 2 model).

Average Order Value (AOV): amount of revenue generated by an order from a customer (see Chapter 7 analytics).

Applet: a small, self-contained software application that is most often used by browsers to automatically display animation and / or to perform database queries requested by the user (Source: IAB) (see Chapter 2 model).

Applicable browser: any browser an ad will impact, regardless of whether it will play the ad (Source: IAB) (see Chapter 2 model).

ATL (above the line) promotions: are tailored for a mass audience. ATL promotions can establish brand identity, but they are also difficult to measure well (Source: Wikipedia) (see Chapter 4 ads).

Attitude: is a predisposition or a tendency to respond positively or negatively to a certain idea, object, person, or situation. Attitude influences an individual's choice of action and responses to challenges, incentives, and rewards (together called stimuli). Four major components of attitude are (Source: BusinessDictionary) (see Chapter 5 consumer):

- Affective: emotions or feelings
- Cognitive: belief or opinions held consciously
- Evaluative: positive or negative response to stimuli.

Attrition: the erosion of a customer base over time. It is the opposite of customer retention (Source: WebTrends) (see Chapter 5 consumer).

Auction model bidding: is the most popular type of pay-per-click (PPC) bidding. First, an advertiser determines what maximum amount per click they are willing to spend for a keyword. If there is no competition for that keyword, the advertiser pays their bid, or less, for every click. If there is competition at auction for that keyword, then the advertiser with the highest bid will pay one penny more than their nearest competitor. For example, advertiser A is willing to bid up to $0.50; advertiser B is willing to bid up to $0.75. If advertiser A's actual bid is $0.23, then advertiser B will only pay $0.24 per click. It is also referred to as market or competition-driven bidding (Source: SEMPO) (see Chapter 8 auctions).

Audience reach: in the context of search engines, the term refers to the percentage of the total Internet population that uses a particular search engine during a given month. Together with search hours, audience reach is an important measure when calculating the popularity of the different search engines (Source: SearchEngineDictionary.com) (see Chapter 6 BAM! and Chapter 7 analytics).

Audit: third-party validation of log activity and/or measurement process associated with Internet activity/advertising. Activity audits validate measurement counts. Process audits validate internal controls associated with measurement (Source: IAB) (see Chapter 7 analytics).

Auditor: a third-party independent organization that performs audits (Source: IAB) (see Chapter 7 analytics).

Banner ad: an advertisement embedded on a Web page usually intended to drive traffic to a different Web site by linking to the advertiser's site. The Interactive Advertising Bureau (IAB) has created a standard set of banner ad sizes (Medium Rectangle, Rectangle, Leaderboard, Wide Skyscraper) into a set of guidelines called the Universal Ad Package (Source: WebTrends) (see Chapter 4 ads).

Banner blindness: refers to a "condition" among experienced Web users who tend to automatically ignore banner ads, even when the banner ads contain information visitors are actively looking for. Banner blindness is arguably the main cause of low click-through rates in banner advertising (Source: modified from SearchEngineDictionary. com and Marketing Terms.com) (see Chapter 5 customers).

Barter: the exchange of goods and services without the use of cash. The value of the barter is the dollar value of the goods and services being exchanged for advertising. This is a recognized form of revenue under the Generally Accepted Accounting Principles (GAAP) (Source: IAB) (see Chapter 8 auctions).

Behavioral targeting: the practice of targeting and serving ads to groups of people who exhibit similarities not only in their location, gender, or age, but also in how they act and react in their online environment, with the goal of increasing the effectiveness of their campaigns. Behaviors tracked and targeted include Web site topic areas they frequently visit or subscribe to, subjects or content or shopping categories for which they have registered, profiled themselves, or requested automatic updates and information, and so on (Source: modified from SEMPO and IAB) (see Chapter 5 customers).

Beta: a test version of a product, such as a Web site, software, or ad prior to final release (Source: IAB) (see Chapter 2 ads).

Bias: inclination or preference that influences (but ought not to) one's judgment from being balanced or even-handed. Prejudice is bias in pejorative sense (Source: Business Dictionary) (see Chapter 5 customers).

Bid: the maximum amount of money that an advertiser is willing to pay each time a searcher clicks on an ad. Bid prices can vary widely depending on competition from other advertisers and keyword popularity (Source: SEMPO) (see Chapter 8 auctions).

Bid boosting: a form of automated bid management that allows you to increase your bids when ads are served to someone whose age or gender matches your target market (Source: modified from SEMPO) (see Chapter 8 auctions).

Bid management software: software that manages PPC campaigns automatically, called either rules-based (with triggering rules or conditions set by the advertiser) or intelligent software (enacting real-time adjustments based on tracked conversions and competitor actions). Both types of automatic bid management programs monitor and change bid prices, pause campaigns, manage budget maximums, and adjust multiple keyword bids based on CTR, position ranking, and more (Source: SEMPO) (see Chapter 8 auctions).

Bonus impressions: additional ad impressions above the commitments outlined in the approved insertion order (Source: IAB) (see Chapter 2 model).

Bot: software that runs automatically without human intervention. Typically, a bot is endowed with the capability to react to different situations it may encounter. Two common types of bots are agents and spiders. Bots are used by companies like search engines to discover Web sites for indexing. Short for robot (Source: IAB) (see Chapter 2 model).

Bounce: a visitor whose behaviors are classified within the bounce rate (see Chapter 7 analytics).

Bounce rate: refers to the percentage of people that immediately exit or do not progress beyond the entry page within a certain time limit (Source: modified from Quirk and WebTrends) (see Chapter 7 analytics).

Brand: distinctive name or trademark that identifies a product or manufacturer. A symbol (name, logo, symbols, fonts, colors), a slogan, and a design scheme representing a company. Brand is often developed to represent implicit values, ideas, and even personality (Source: modified from Quirk and SEMPO) (see Chapter 6 BAM!).

Brand awareness: a measure of how quickly a brand is recognized or called to mind (Source: Quirk) (see Chapter 6 BAM!).

Brand evangelist: one who lives and breathes a brand, and is capable of spreading the word far and wide (Source: Quirk) (see Chapter 6 BAM!).

Brand lift: a measurable increase in consumer recall for a specific, branded company, product, or service. For example, brand lift might show an increase in respondents who think of Dell for computers, or Wal-Mart for "every household thing" (Source: SEMPO) (see Chapter 6 BAM!).

Brand messaging: creative messaging that presents and maintains a consistent corporate image across all media channels, including search (Source: SEMPO) (see Chapter 6 BAM!).

Brand reputation: the position a company brand occupies (Source: SEMPO) (see Chapter 6 BAM!).

Brand terrorist: one who attacks a brand, normally an industry rival or dissatisfied customer (Source: Quirk) (see Chapter 6 BAM!).

Branding: a brand is a customer experience represented by a collection of images and ideas; often, it refers to a symbol such as a name, logo, slogan, and design scheme. Brand recognition and other reactions are created by the accumulation of experiences with the specific product or service, both directly relating to its use, and through the influence of advertising, design, and media commentary. A brand often includes an explicit logo, fonts, color schemes, symbols, and sound that may be developed to represent implicit values, ideas, and even personality (Source: modified from SEMPO) (see Chapter 6 BAM!).

Branding strategy: is the attempt to develop a strong brand reputation on the Web to increase brand recognition and create a significant volume of impressions (Source: SEMPO) (see Chapter 6 BAM!).

Browser: has a couple of meanings depending on the context (Source: IAB) (see Chapter 2 model):

- The visitor views more pages on your Web site after the landing page.
- A software program that can request, download, cache, and display documents available on the World Wide Web.

BTL (below the line) promotions: are targeted at individuals according to their needs or preferences. BTL can actually lead to a sale, and BTL promotions are highly measurable, giving marketers valuable insights into their return on investment (ROI) (Source: Wikipedia) (see Chapter BAM!).

BtoB/B2B (**Business-to-Business**): businesses whose primary customers are other businesses (Source: IAB) (see Chapter 6 BAM!).

BtoC/B2C (**Business-to-Consumer**): businesses whose primary customers are consumers (Source: IAB) (see Chapter 6 BAM!).

Business intelligence: business practices that foster customer care, loyalty, and/or customer support. Also refers to a category of software and tools designed to gather, store, analyze, and deliver data in a user-friendly format to help organizations make more informed business decisions (Source: modified from WebTrends and IAB) (see Chapter 6 BAM!).

Button: can have a couple of meanings depending on the context (Source: IAB) (see Chapter 2 model):

- clickable graphic that contains certain functionality, such as taking one someplace or executing a program
- buttons can also be ads. See iab.net for voluntary guidelines defining specifications of button ads.

Buying funnel: refers to a multistep process of a consumer's path to purchase a product: from awareness, to education, to preferences and intent, to final purchase. Also called the Buying Cycle, Buyer Decision Cycle, and Sales Cycle (Source: SEMPO) (see Chapter 5 customer).

Buzz: online excitement and word of mouth surrounding a certain brand or incident (Source: Quirk) (see Chapter 6 BAM!).

Caching: the storage of Web files for later reuse at a point more quickly accessed by the end-user. (Source: Marketing Terms.com) (see Chapter 2 model).

Call to Action (CTA): a phrase written to motivate the reader to take a specific action and is usually situated at the bottom of a page. These actions can include signing up for a newsletter, contacting the company, or booking a holiday (Source: Quirk) (see Chapter 4 ads).

Campaign analysis: a feature that tracks activity originating from a marketing campaign, so you can compare your campaigns and evaluate their effectiveness. Campaigns are tracked using a query parameter on the marketing campaign landing page (Source: WebTrends) (see Chapter 7 analytics).

Campaign integration: planning and executing a paid search campaign concurrently with other marketing initiatives, online, offline, or both. More than simply launching simultaneous campaigns, true paid search integration takes all marketing initiatives into consideration prior to launch, such as consistent messaging and image, driving offline conversions, supporting brand awareness, increasing response rates, and contributing to ROI business goals (Source: SEMPO) (see Chapter 7 analytics).

Campaign strategist: the person who is responsible for making the objectives of a campaign a reality, by any means necessary (Source: modified from Quirk) (see Chapter 7 analytics).

Cannibalism: in marketing, situation where the sales of a new (introduced as an extension of an established brand) or differently branded product eat into the sales of other products within the same line. If the total sales revenue of that product line increases, then the line extension is justifiable. However the danger of weakening the main brand remains (Source: BusinessDictionary) (see Chapter 6 BAM!).

Cascading style sheets (CSS): a data format used to separate style from structure on Web pages (Source: Marketing Terms.com) (see Chapter 2 model).

Channel: (1) a band of similar content; (2) a type of sales outlet (also known as channel of distribution), for example retail, catalog, or e-commerce. (Source: IAB) (see Chapter 6 BAM!).

Click: the visitor sees your ad and clicks it (see Chapter 7 analytics).

Click bot: a program generally used to artificially click on paid listings within the engines in order to artificially inflate click amounts. (Source: SEMPO) (see Chapter 2 model).

Click fraud: the act of generating invalid clicks on an ad that occurs in pay-per-click online advertising when a person, automated script, or computer program imitates a legitimate user of a Web browser clicking on an ad, for the purpose of generating a charge per click without having actual interest in the target of the ad's link (Source: modified from WebTrends and Quick) (see Chapter 7 analytics).

Click paths: the pattern of clicks as well as the entry and exit points of a user's interaction with a Web site (Source: Quirk) (see Chapter 7 analytics).

Click potential: the expected percent change in click-throughs in relation to rank 1. This factor represents the combined impact of changes in impressions and click-through rate by rank (see Chapter 7 analytics).

Click tracking: using scripts to track the number of clicks it takes to enter or exit a Web site. This can also be used to shield a link from being picked up as a back link to another site (Source: Quirk) (see Chapter 7 analytics).

Clicks and mortar: a business that has both online trading capabilities and physical stores located offline (Source: Quirk) (see Chapter 2 model).

Clicks: (1) metric that measures the reaction of a user to an Internet ad. There are three types of clicks: click-throughs; in-unit clicks; and mouseovers; (2) the opportunity for a user to download another file by clicking on an advertisement, as recorded by the server; (3) the result of a measurable interaction with an advertisement or keyword that links to the advertiser's intended Web site or another page or frame within the Web site; (4) metric that measures the reaction of a user to linked editorial content. See iab.net for ad campaign measurement guidelines (Source: IAB) (see Chapter 7 analytics).

Click-stream: (1) the electronic path a user takes while navigating from site to site, and from page to page within a site; (2) a comprehensive body of data describing the sequence of activity between a user's browser and any other Internet resource, such as a Web site or third-party ad server (Source: IAB) (see Chapter 7 analytics).

Click-through: the action of following a link within an advertisement or editorial content to another Web site or another page or frame within the Web site. Reported as a 302 redirect at the ad server and should filter out robotic activity (Source: IAB) (see Chapter 7 analytics).

Click-through lift: the increase in CTR resulting from a change (see Chapter 7 analytics).

Click-through rate (CTR): the rate (expressed in a percentage) at which users click on an ad. This is calculated by dividing the total number of clicks by the total number of ad impressions. CTR is an important metric for Internet marketers to measure the performance of an ad campaign (Source: Search Engine Watch) (see Chapter 7 analytics).

Click-within: similar to click down or click. More commonly, however, click-withins are ads that allow the user to drill down and click while remaining in the advertisement, not leaving the site on which they are residing (Source: IAB) (see Chapter 7 analytics).

Client: A computer or software program that contacts a server to obtain data via the Internet or another network. Internet Explorer, Outlook, and other browsers and e-mail programs are examples of software clients (Source: IAB) (see Chapter 2 model).

Client-initiated ad impression: one of the two methods used for ad counting. Ad content is delivered to the user via two methods: server-initiated and client-initiated. Client-initiated ad counting relies on the user's browser for making requests and formatting and redirecting content. For organizations using a client-initiated ad counting method, counting should occur at the publisher's ad server or third-party ad server, subsequent to the ad request or later in the process. See server-initiated ad impression (Source: IAB) (see Chapter 7 analytics).

Client-side: transactions that take place before information is sent to the server (Source: Quirk) (see Chapter 2 model).

Client-side tracking: client-side tracking entails the process of tagging every page that requires tracking on the Web site with a block of JavaScript code. This method is cookie-based (available as first- or third-party cookies) and is readily available to companies who do not own or manage their own servers (Source: SEMPO) (see Chapter 7 analytics).

Close: indicates that the user clicks or otherwise activates a close control that fully dispatches the ad from the player environment. May not apply to nonoverlay ads (Source: IAB) (see Chapter 7 analytics).

Competitive: to have good enough value to compete against commercial rivals (Source: Quirk) (see Chapter 6 BAM!).

Competitive analysis: as used in SEO, CA is the assessment and analysis of strengths and weaknesses of competing Web sites, including identifying traffic patterns, major traffic sources, and keyword selection (Source: SEMPO) (see Chapter 6 BAM!).

Concept search: a search for documents related conceptually to a search term, rather than for documents that actually contain the search term itself (Source: SearchEngineDictionary.com) (see Chapter 3 keywords).

Consumer: is a broad label for any individuals or households that use goods and services generated within the economy (see Chapter 5 customers).

Consumer packaged goods (CPG): typically consumable goods, including food and beverages, footwear and apparel, tobacco, and cleaning (see Chapter BAM!).

Content integration: advertising woven into editorial content or placed in a contextual envelope. Also known as "Web advertorial" (Source: IAB) (see Chapter 6 BAM!).

Content network: networks that serve paid search ads triggered by keywords related to the page content a user is viewing, in exchange for a share of the revenue generated by those ads. For example: Google AdSense or the Yahoo Publisher Network (Source: modified from Search Engine Watch and SEMPO) (see Chapter 2 model).

Content targeting: an ad-serving process in Google and Yahoo! that displays keyword triggered ads related to the content or subject (context) of the Web site a user is viewing. Contrast to search network servers, in which an ad is displayed when a user types a keyword into the search box of a search engine or one of its partner sites (Source: SEMPO) (see Chapter 2 model).

Contextual ads: existing contextual ad engines deliver text and image ads to nonsearch content pages. Ads are matched to keywords extracted from content. Advertisers can leverage existing keyboard-based paid search campaigns and gain access to a larger audience (Source: IAB) (see Chapter 4 ads).

Contextual advertising: advertising that is automatically served or placed on a Web page based on the page's content, keywords, and phrases rather than on based on a query (Source: modified from SEMPO and Quirk) (see Chapter 4 ads).

Contextual distribution: the marketing decision to display search ads on certain publisher sites across the Web instead of, or in addition to, placing PPC ads on search networks (Source: SEMPO) (see Chapter 2 model).

Contextual link ads/inventory: to supplement their business models, certain text-link advertising networks (like Google) have expanded their network distribution to include "contextual inventory." Most vendors of "search engine traffic" have expanded the definition of Search Engine Marketing to include this contextual inventory. Contextual or content inventory is generated when listings are displayed on pages of Web sites (usually not search engines) where the written content on the page indicates to the ad server that the page is a good match to specific keywords and phrases. Often this matching method is validated by measuring the number of times a viewer clicks on the displayed ad. These ads typically do not perform as well as traditional text ads on search engines, but the lower cost justifies the expense (Source: WebTrends) (see Chapter 2 BAM!).

Contextual search campaigns: a paid placement search campaign that takes a search ad listing beyond search engine results pages and onto the sites of matched content Web partners (Source: SEMPO) (see Chapter 2 model).

Contextual search: a search that analyzes the page being viewed by a user and gives a list of related search results (Source: SEMPO) (see Chapter 2 model).

Conversion: to describe the primary measurable events, advertisers use to gauge the effectiveness of their advertising campaigns. An action that signifies a completion of a specified activity. For many sites, a user converts if they buy a product, sign up for a newsletter, or download a file. The conversion rate is the percentage of visitors who do convert. Cookie deletion can have an impact on your conversion rate because if a cookie is being systematically deleted, repeat visitor rates will be undercounted and new visitor rates will be overcounted, thus skewing the conversion rate metric by which you analyze your site's overall effectiveness (Source: modified from WebTrends) (see Chapter 7 analytics).

Conversion action: the desired action you want a visitor to take on your site. Includes purchase, subscription to the company newsletter, request for follow-up or more information (lead generation), download of a company free offer (research results, a video, or a tool), and subscription to company updates and news (Source: SEMPO) (see Chapter 7 analytics).

Conversion cost: total cost-per-sale, calculated by dividing the total cost of an advertising campaign by the number of resulting sales. For example, if $1,000 is spent on an advertising campaign and that campaign results in 20 sales, the conversion cost-per-sale is $50 ($1,000 / 20). That means it costs $50 to generate one sale (Source: SearchEngineDictionary.com) (see Chapter 7 analytics).

Conversion funnel: the series of steps that move a visitor toward a specified conversion event, such as an order or registration signup. Related to the buying funnel (Source: modified from WebTrends) (see Chapter 5 customer).

Conversion point: conversion points are the points at which your customers have completed a specific action on your Web site. Common conversion points are: Newsletter sign up: the "thank you for subscribing" page, Order/Sale: the "thank you for your order" page, Download: the "Your download is complete" page (Source: SearchEngineDictionary.com) (see Chapter 7 analytics).

Conversion potential: the expected percent change in conversions in relation to rank 1. This factor combines the effects of traffic volume and changes in conversion rates by rank (see Chapter 7 analytics).

Conversion rate: the percentage of site visitors that deliver the most wanted response (MWR). The number of visitors who convert (take a desired action at your site) after clicking through on your ad, divided by the total number of click-throughs to your site for that ad. Conversion rates are measurements that determine how many of your prospects perform the prescribed or desired action step (Source: modified from SEMPO and SearchEngineDictionary.com) (see Chapter 7 analytics).

Cookie: information stored on a user's computer via a browser by a Web site for the purpose of identifying that browser during audience activity and between visits or sessions (Source: modified from Marketing Terms.com and IAB) (see Chapter 2 model).

Cookie buster: software that blocks the placement of cookies on a user's browser (Source: IAB) (see Chapter 2 model).

Copy testing: a specialized field of marketing research. It is the study of television commercials prior to airing them and is defined as research to determine an ad's effectiveness based on consumers' responses to the ad. It covers all media including print, TV, radio, the Internet, and so on (see Chapter 4 ads).

Cost: valuation in terms of money of (1) effort, (2) material, (3) resources, (4) time and utilities consumed, (5) risks incurred, and (6) opportunity forgone in production and delivery of a good or service. All expenses are costs, but not all costs (such as those incurred in acquisition of an income-generating asset) are expenses (Source: BusinessDictionary) (see Chapter 6 BAM!).

Cost of acquisition (COA): how much it costs to acquire a conversion (desired action), such as a sale (Source: SEMPO) (see Chapter 7 analytics).

Cost per action (CPA): a form of advertising where payment is dependent on an action that a user performs as a result of the ad. The action could be making a purchase, signing up for a newsletter, or asking for a follow-up call. An advertiser pays a set fee to the publisher based on the number of visitors who take action. Many affiliate programs use the CPA model (Source: Search Engine Watch) (see Chapter 7 analytics).

Cost per click (CPC): the cost or cost-equivalent pay per click-through. Also called Pay per Click (PPC). A performance-based advertising model where the advertiser pays a set fee for every click on an ad. The majority of text ads sold by search engines are billed under the CPC model (Source: modified from Search Engine Watch and Marketing Terms.com) (see Chapter 7 analytics).

Cost-per-Customer: the cost an advertiser pays to acquire a customer (Source: IAB) (see Chapter 7 analytics).

Cost-per-lead (CPL): cost of advertising based on the number of database files (leads) received (Source: IAB) (see Chapter 7 analytics).

Cost per order (CPO): the dollar amount of advertising or marketing necessary to acquire an order. Calculated by dividing marketing expenses by the number of orders. Also referred to as CPA (Cost per Acquisition) (Source: modified from SEMPO) (see Chapter 7 analytics).

Cost-per-sale (CPS): the advertiser's cost to generate one sales transaction. If this is being used in conjunction with a media buy, a cookie can be offered on the content site and read on the advertiser's site after the successful completion of an online sale (Source: IAB) (see Chapter 7 analytics).

Cost per targeted thousand impressions (CPTM): implying that the audience one is trying to reach is defined by particular demographics or other specific characteristics, such as male golfers age 18–25. The difference between CPM and CPTM is that CPM is for gross impressions whereas CPTM is for targeted impressions (Source: IAB) (see Chapter 7 analytics).

Cost per thousand (CPM): an ad model that charges advertisers every time an ad is displayed to a user, whether the user clicks on the ad or not. The fee is based on every 1,000 ad impressions (M is the Roman numeral for 1,000). Most display ads, such as banner ads, are sold by CPM. This term is heavily used in print, broadcasting, and direct marketing (Source: modified from Search Engine Watch and WebTrends) (see Chapter 7 analytics).

Cost-per-transaction (CPT): the dollar amount of advertising or marketing necessary to acquire an order. Calculated by dividing marketing expenses by the number of orders. Also referred to as CPA (Cost per Acquisition) (Source: modified from SEMPO) (see Chapter 7 analytics).

Count: raw figures captured for analysis. These are the most basic Web analytics metric (Source: Quirk) (see Chapter 7 analytics).

Count audit: see *activity audit* (Source: IAB) (see Chapter 7 analytics).

Crawler: a software program that visits Web pages to build indexes for search engines. See also spider, bot, and intelligent agent (Source: IAB) (see Chapter 2 model).

Creative: for the purposes of Web analytics, "creative" describes the characteristics of a marketing activity, such as color, size, and messaging – for example, a "Buy Now" graphic (Source: WebTrends) (see Chapter 4 ads).

Creatives: unique words, design, and display of a paid-space advertisement. In paid search advertising, creative refers to the ad's title (headline), description (text offer), and display URL (clickable link to advertiser's Web site landing page). Unique creative display includes word emphasis (boldfaced, italicized, in quotes), typeface style, and, on some sites, added graphic images, logos, animation, or video clips (Source: SEMPO) (see Chapter 4 ads).

Cross marketing: marketing other products or services to an existing customer. Cross marketing enhances the ability of generating further sales. Also known as Cross Selling (Source: Quirk) (see Chapter 6 BAM!).

Cross selling: selling an additional product or service to an existing customer (see Chapter 6 BAM!).

Crowd sourcing: taking a task that would conventionally be performed by a contractor or employee and turning it over to a typically large, undefined group of people via an open call for responses (Source: IAB) (see Chapter 6 BAM!).

Customer: a person who buys or uses goods or services. A person with whom a business must deal (Source: Quirk) (see Chapter 5 customers).

Customer acquisition cost: the cost associated with acquiring a new customer (Source: Marketing Terms.com) (see Chapter 7 analytics).

Customer life cycle: the progressive steps a customer goes through when purchasing, using, or considering a product or service (Source: Quirk) (see Chapter 6 BAM!).

Customer segment: a powerful aspect of relationship marketing in which you target a subsection or group of customers who share a specific trait or set of behaviors. See also *demographics* and *psychographics* (Source: WebTrends) (see Chapter BAM!).

Data: information that has been translated into a form that is more convenient to move or process (see Chapter 7 analytics).

Dayparting: the ability to specify different times of day, or day of week, for ad displays as a way to target searchers more specifically. An option that limits serves of specified ads based on day and time factors (Source: SEMPO) (see Chapter BAM!).

Demographics: common characteristics used for population or audience segmentation, such as age, gender, household income, and the like. The physical characteristics of human populations and segments of populations often used to identify consumer markets. Demographics can include information such as age, gender, marital status, education, and geographic location. See also *psychographics* (Source: modified from WebTrends and IAB) (see Chapter 6 BAM!).

Description: in the context of the search engines, the description refers to the descriptive text accompanied by a title and URL in the search results page. Some search engines take this description from the meta description whereas most generate their own from the page content. Directories often ask for a description when you submit your page (Source: SearchEngineDictionary.com) (see Chapter 4 ads).

DIKW: Data, Information, Knowledge, and Wisdom, a hierarchy of understanding this overloaded term – information (see Chapter 7 analytics).

Display advertising: a form of online advertising where an advertiser's message is shown on a destination Web page, generally set off in a box at the top or bottom or to one side of the content of the page (Source: IAB) (see Chapter BAM!).

Display URL: the Web page URL that one actually sees in a PPC text ad. Display URL usually appears as the last line in the ad; it may be a simplified path for the longer actual URL, which is not visible (Source: SEMPO) (see Chapter 4 ads).

Distribution network: a network of Web sites (content publishers, ISPs) or search engines and their partner sites on which paid ads can be distributed. The network receives advertisements from the host search engine, paid for with a CPC or CPM model (Source: SEMPO) (see Chapter 6 BAM!).

DIY: Do It Yourself (see Chapter 2 model).

Drop shipper: a company that fulfills the order for another seller (see Chapter 6 BAM!).

Dynamic ad insertion: the process by which an ad is inserted into a page in response to a user's request. Dynamic ad placement allows alteration of specific ads placed on a page based on any data available to the placement program. At its simplest, dynamic ad placement allows for multiple ads to be rotated through one or more spaces. In more sophisticated examples, the ad placement could be affected by demographic data or usage history for the current user (Source: IAB) (see Chapter 2 model).

Dynamic ad placement: process by which an ad is inserted into a page in response to a user's request; dynamic ad placement allows alteration of specific ads placed on a page based on any data available to the placement program (Source: IAB) (see Chapter 2 model).

Dynamic content: Web site content generated automatically, usually from a database and based on user actions/selections. Dynamic content typically changes at regular intervals, for example, daily or each time the users reload the page. SERPs are dynamically generated pages, changing depending on user input (Source: SearchEngineDictionary.com) (see Chapter 2 model).

Dynamic IP address: an IP address (assigned by an ISP to a client PC) that changes periodically (Source: IAB) (see Chapter 2 model).

Dynamic keyword bidding: process by which keyword bids are varied per term according to user behavior, competitor activity, time of day, day of week, and so on (Source: Advertising.com) (see Chapter 8 auctions).

Dynamic keyword insertion: in sponsored search advertising, this allows keywords used in searches to be inserted into advert copy (Source: modified from Quirk) (see Chapter 4 ads).

Dynamic rotation: delivery of ads on a rotating, random basis so that users are exposed to different ads and ads are served in different pages of the site (Source: IAB) (see Chapter 2 model).

East: the ads on the right side as the searcher is facing the SERP. Also known as the right rail (see Chapter 4 ads).

E-commerce: conducting commercial transactions, specifically the process of selling products or services, on the Internet where goods, information, or services are bought and sold (Source: modified from SEMPO and IAB) (see Chapter 6 BAM!).

Editorial review process: a review process for potential advertiser listings conducted by search engines, which checks to ensure relevancy and compliance with the engine's editorial policy. This process could be automated, using a spider to crawl ads, or it could be human editorial ad review. Sometimes it is a combination of both. Not all PPC Search Engines review listings (Source: SEMPO) (see Chapter 4 ads).

Effective Cost Per Thousand (eCPM): acronym for a hybrid Cost-Per-Click (CPC) auction calculated by multiplying the CPC by the click-through rate (CTR), and multiplying that by one thousand. (Represented by: (CPC x CTR) x 1000 = eCPM.) This monetization model is used by Google to rank site-targeted CPM ads (in the Google content network) against keyword-targeted CPC ads (Google AdWords PPC) in their hybrid auction (Source: SEMPO) (see Chapter 7 analytics).

Electronic payment: issuance and receipt of payment via the Internet (Source: Quirk) (see Chapter 2 model).

eMarketing: the process of marketing a brand using the Internet (Source: Quirk) (see Chapter 6 BAM!).

eMarketing strategist: together with the Marketing Managers, the eMarketing Strategists know where and how to effectively position a brand online (Source: Quirk) (see Chapter 6 BAM!).

Entry page: refers to any page within a Web site that a user employs to "enter" the Web site. Also see *Landing Page* (Source: SEMPO) (see Chapter 2 model).

Exact match: if not for partial matching, fuzzy matching, collaborative filtering, and stemming, search engines would only return exact matches. A search for "power" would only return documents containing the exact term, not documents containing variations or related terms like powerful and strength (Source: SearchEngineDictionary. com) (see Chapter 3 keywords).

Exposure: the showing of an ad to a searcher (see Chapter 4 ads).

Eye-tracking studies: studies to track the eye movements of Web page readers in order to understand reading and click-through patterns (Source: modified from SEMPO) (see Chapter 4 ads).

Eyeballs: slang term for audience; the number of people who view a certain Web site or advertisement (Source: IAB) (see Chapter 6 BAM!).

Fast-moving consumer goods (FMCG): products that are sold quickly at relatively low cost (see Chapter 6 BAM!).

First-price auction: an auction in which the bidder who submitted the highest bid is awarded the object being sold and pays a price equal to the amount bid (see Chapter 8 auctions).

Fold: an imaginary line across the browser below which a user has to scroll to see content not immediately visible when a Web page loads in a browser. Ads or content displayed above the fold are visible without any end-user interaction. Monitor size and resolution determine where on a Web page the fold lies. All your critical or most important information should lie above the fold to ensure maximum exposure and to entice the user to read more (Source: modified IAB and Quirk) (see Chapter 4 ads).

Frequency: the number of occurrences of a repeating event per unit time. The number of times an ad is delivered to the same browser in a single session or time period. A site can use cookies to manage ad frequency. Average frequency is the average of frequencies of all the visitors during the reporting period. Frequency is a retention metric and is part of RFM (recency, frequency, monetary) analysis (Source: modified from IAB and WebTrends) (see Chapter 5 customers).

Frequency cap: restriction on the amount of times a specific visitor is shown a particular advertisement. Frequency caps are present to limit the number of times we are exposed to the same online advert (Source: Marketing Terms.com and Quirk) (see Chapter 2 model).

Full-service digital agency: an online adverting agency offering products and services in the full range of online marketing (see Chapter 6 BAM!).

Geographical targeting: delivery of ads specific to the geographic location of the searcher. Geo-targeting allows the advertiser to specify where ads will or will not be shown based on the searcher's location, enabling more localized and personalized results (Source: Search Engine Watch) (see Chapter 6 BAM!).

Goal: the defined action that visitors should perform on a Web site (Source: Quirk) (see Chapter 5 customers).

Googlebot: Google uses several user-agents to crawl and index content in the Google.com search engine. Googlebot describes all Google spiders. All Google bots begin with "Googlebot." For example, Googlebot-Mobile crawls pages for Google's mobile index, Googlebot-Image crawls pages for Google's image index (Source: Search Engine Watch) (see Chapter 2 model).

Gross exposures: the total number of times an ad is served, including duplicate downloads to the same person (Source: IAB) (see Chapter 2 model).

Gross rating points (**GRPs**): an acronym used in advertising to measure the size of an audience reached by a specific media vehicle or schedule (see Chapter 6 BAM!).

Guerilla marketing: unconventional marketing intended to get maximum results from minimal resources (Source: Marketing Terms.com) (see Chapter 6 BAM!).

Head terms: search terms that are short, popular, and straightforward (e.g., "helicopter skiing"). These short terms are called "head terms" based on a bell-curve distribution of keyword usage that displays the high numbers of most-used terms at the "head" end of the bell-curve graph (Source: SEMPO) (see Chapter 3 keywords).

Heat map: a data visualization tool that shows levels of activity on a Web page in different colors. Reds and yellows show the areas of the most activity and blues and violets the least (Source: Quirk) (see Chapter 4 ads).

Heuristic: a way to measure a user's unique identity. This measure uses deduction or inference based on a rule or algorithm, which is valid for that server. For example, the combination of IP address and user agent can be used to identify a user in some cases. If a server receives a new request from the same client within thirty minutes, it is inferred that a new request comes from the same user and the time since the last page request was spent viewing the last page. Also referred to as an inference (Source: IAB) (see Chapter 7 analytics).

Hierarchy of effects: a concept related to the manner in which advertising supposedly works; it is based on the premise that advertising moves individuals systematically through a series of psychological stages such as awareness, interest, desire, conviction, and action (see Chapter 6 BAM!).

Hit: the request or retrieval of any item located within a Web page. For example, if a user enters a Web page with five pictures on it, it would be counted as six "hits." One hit is counted for the Web page itself and another five hits count for the pictures. Webmasters use hits to measure their servers' workload. Because page designs and visit patterns vary from site to site, the number of hits bears no relationship to the number of pages downloaded, and is therefore a poor guide for traffic measurement (Source: modified from SEMPO and IAB) (see Chapter 7 analytics).

Home page: the page designated as the main point of entry of a Web site (or main page) or the starting point when a browser first connects to the Internet. Typically, it welcomes visitors and introduces the purpose of the site, or the organization sponsoring it, and then provides links to other pages within the site (Source: IAB) (see Chapter 2 model).

Host: any computer on a network that offers services or connectivity to other computers on the network. A host has an IP address associated with it (Source: IAB) (see Chapter 2 model).

House ad: self-promotional ad a company runs on their own site/network to use unsold inventory. Revenues from house ads should not be included in reported revenues (Source: modified from Marketing Terms.com and IAB) (see Chapter 2 model).

Human information processing: theory that deals with how people receive, store, integrate, retrieve, and use information (see Chapter 3 keywords).

Hybrid pricing: pricing model based on a combination of a CPM pricing model and a performance-based pricing model. See *CPM pricing model* and *performance-based pricing model* (Source: IAB) (see Chapter 6 BAM!).

Hyperlink: a clickable link (e.g., on a Web page or within an e-mail) that sends the user to a new URL when activated (Source: IAB) (see Chapter 2 model).

Hypertext: any text that contains links connecting it with other texts or files on the Internet (Source: IAB) (see Chapter 2 model).

IAB: Interactive Advertising Bureau (http://www.iab.net) (Source: WebTrends) (see Chapter 6 BAM!).

Impression: a single instance of an online advertisement being displayed (Source: Marketing Terms.com) (see Chapter 7 analytics).

Impression fraud: the act of deliberately generating impressions of an advert without the intention of clicking on the advert. The result is a reduction in click-through rate, which can affect Quality Score in PPC advertising (Source: Quirk) (see Chapter 7 analytics).

Inbound link: an inbound link is a hyperlink to a particular Web page from an outside site, bringing traffic to that Web page. Inbound links are an important element that most search engine algorithms use to measure the popularity of a Web page (Source: Search Engine Watch) (see Chapter 2 model).

Incentivized traffic: visitors who have received some form of compensation for visiting a site (Source: Marketing Terms.com) (see Chapter 2 model).

Information: in general, raw data that has been verified to be accurate and timely, is specific and organized for a purpose, is presented within a context that gives it meaning and relevance, and leads to an increase in understanding and decrease in uncertainty. The value of information lies solely in its ability to affect a behavior, decision, or outcome. A piece of information is considered valueless if, after receiving it, things remain unchanged (Source: BusinessDictionary) (see Chapter 2 keywords).

Information access: the findability of information regardless of format, channel, or location (Source: AIM) (see Chapter 3 keywords).

Information asymmetry: an imbalance of information in a marketplace (see Chapter 5 customers).

Information foraging theory: theory that applies the ideas from optimal foraging theory to understand how human users search for information. The theory is based on the assumption that, when searching for information, humans use "built-in" foraging mechanisms that evolved to help our animal ancestors find food. Importantly, better understanding of human search behavior can improve the usability of Web sites or any other user interface (Source: Wikipedia) (see Chapter 3 keywords).

Information overload: refers to the difficulty a person can have understanding an issue and making decisions that can be caused by the presence of too much information (see Chapter 5 customers).

Information retrieval: a field of study related to information extraction. Information retrieval is about developing systems to effectively index and search vast amounts of data (Source: SearchEngineDictionary.com) (see Chapter 3 keywords).

Information scent: cues related to the desired outcome (see Chapter 3 keywords).

Information searching: refers to people's interaction with information-retrieval systems, ranging from adopting search strategy to judging the relevance of information retrieved (see Chapter 3 keywords).

Insertion: actual placement of an ad in a document, as recorded by the ad server (Source: IAB) (see Chapter 2 model).

Insertion order: purchase order between a seller of interactive advertising and a buyer (usually an advertiser or its agency) regarding the insertion date(s), number of insertions in a stated period, ad size (or commercial length), and ad placement (or time slot). In effect, it is a purchase order and is issued typically through an advertising agency or a media representative (Source: modified from IAB) (see Chapter 2 model).

Integrated marketing communications (IMC): the coordination and integration of all marketing communication tools, avenues, functions, and sources within a company into a seamless program that maximizes the impact on consumers and other end-users at a minimal cost (see Chapter 6 BAM!).

Integrated results listing: multiple results from federated content collections shown on the same SERP (see Chapter 4 ads).

Interactive advertising: all forms of online, wireless, and interactive television advertising, including banners, sponsorships, e-mail, keyword searches, referrals, slotting fees, classified ads, and interactive television commercials (Source: IAB) (see Chapter 6 BAM!).

Internal page impressions: Web site activity that is generated by individuals with IP addresses known to be affiliated with the Web site owner. Internal activity associated with administration and maintenance of the site should be excluded from the traffic or measurement report (Source: IAB) (see Chapter 7 analytics).

Internet marketing: marketing efforts done solely over the Internet. This type of marketing uses various online advertisements to drive traffic to an advertiser's Web site. Banner advertisements, pay per click (PPC), and targeted e-mail lists are often methods used in Internet marketing to bring the most value to the advertiser.

Internet marketing is a growing business mainly because more and more people use the Internet every day. Popular search engines such as Google and Yahoo have been able to capitalize on this new wave of advertising (Source: BusinessDictionary) (see Chapter 6 BAM!).

Inventory: the number of ads available for sale on a Web site (Source: IAB) (see Chapter 2 model).

Invisible Web: a term that refers to the vast amount of information on the Web that is not indexed by search engines. (Source: Search Engine Watch).

IP Address: an abbreviation for Internet Protocol address, it is a unique combination of numbers assigned to individual electronic devices or networks that communicate over the Internet. Basically, it is a trackable address for any computer, and it can be used to localize results. The Internet Assigned Numbers Authority (IANA) oversees global IP address allocation. The format of an IP address is a 32-bit numeric address, written as four numbers separated by periods. Each number can be zero to 255. For example, 1.160.10.240 could be an IP address (Source: SEMPO and Wikipedia) (see Chapter 2 model).

KEI analysis: Keyword Effectiveness Indicator. It is designed to measure and quantify the quality and worth of a search term (Source: Quirk) (see Chapter 7 analytics).

Key performance indicators (**KPIs**): metrics used to quantify objectives that reflect the strategic performance of your online marketing campaigns. They provide business and marketing intelligence to assess a measurable objective and the direction in which that objective is headed (Source: SEMPO) (see Chapter 7 analytics).

Keyphrase: words that are utilized by search engine advertisers to link to query terms (see Chapter 3 keywords).

Keyword: a specific word or combination of words that a searcher might type into a search field. Includes generic, category keywords, industry-specific terms, product brands, common misspellings and expanded variations (called *Keyword Stemming*), or multiple words (called *Long Tail* for their lower CTRs but sometimes better conversion rates). All might be entered as a search query. For example, someone looking to buy coffee mugs might use the keyword phrase "ceramic coffee mugs." Also, keywords that trigger ad network and contextual network ad serves are the auction components on which PPC advertisers bid for all Ad Groups/Orders and campaigns (Source: SEMPO) (see Chapter 3 keywords).

Keyword density: the number of times a keyword or keyword phrase is used in the body of a page. This is a percentage value determined by the number of words on the page, as opposed to the number of times the specific keyword appears within it. In general, the higher the number of times a keyword appears in a page, the higher its density. This, divided by the total number of words that appear on a page, gives you a percentage. The higher the better, but not too high (Source: modified from SEMPO and Quirk) (see Chapter 4 ads).

Keyword frequency: the number of times a keyword or keyphrase appears on a Web site (Source: Quirk) (see Chapter 4 ads).

Keyword marketing: putting your message in front of people who are searching using particular keywords and keyphrases (Source: Marketing Terms.com) (see Chapter 6 BAM!).

Keyword rankings: this term refers to where the keywords/phrases targeted by your SEO efforts rank among the search engines. If your targeted terms do not appear on the first three pages, start worrying (Source: Quirk) (see Chapter 4 ads).

Keyword research: the process of researching what searchers are actually searching for and the analysis of which keywords yield the highest return on investment (ROI). Copy optimization revolves around the selection of the best keywords/keyphrases (Source: modified from Quirk and Marketing Terms.com) (see Chapter 3 keywords).

Keyword stemming: to return to the root or stem of a word and build additional words by adding a prefix or suffix or pluralizing. The word can expand in either direction and even add words, increasing the number of variable options (Source: SEMPO) (see Chapter 3 keywords).

Keyword stuffing: generally refers to the act of adding an inordinate number of key-word terms into the HTML or tags of a Web page (Source: SEMPO) (see Chapter 4 ads).

Keyword tag: refers to the META keywords tag within a Web page. This tag is meant to hold approximately eight to ten keywords or keyword phrases, separated by commas. These phrases should be either misspellings of the main page topic or terms that directly reflect the content on the page on which they appear. Keyword tags are sometimes used for internal search results as well as viewed by search engines (Source: SEMPO) (see Chapter 4 ads).

Keyword targeting: displaying pay-per-click search ads on publisher sites across the Web (see also *Contextual Networks*) that contain the keywords in a context adver-tiser's Ad Group (Source: SEMPO) (see Chapter 2 model).

Lag: the delay between making an online request or command and receiving a response. See *latency* (Source: IAB) (see Chapter 2 model).

Landing page/Destination page: the Web page at which a searcher arrives after clicking on an ad. When creating a PPC ad, the advertiser displays a URL (and speci-fies the exact page URL in the code) on which the searcher will land after clicking on an ad in the SERP. Landing pages are also known as "where the deal is closed," as it is landing page actions that determine an advertiser's conversion rate success (Source: SEMPO) (see Chapter 4 ads).

Latency: 1) time it takes for a data packet to move across a network connection; 2) visible delay between request and display of content and ad. Latency sometimes leads to the user leaving the site prior to the opportunity to see. In streaming media, latency can create stream degradation if it causes the packets, which must be received and played in order, to arrive out of order (Source: IAB) (see Chapter 2 model).

Lead: a potential customer (Source: Quirk) (see Chapter 5 customers).

Lead generation: fees advertisers pay to Internet advertising companies that refer qualified purchase inquiries (e.g., auto dealers that pay a fee in exchange for receiving a qualified purchase inquiry online) or provide consumer information (demographic, contact, and behavioral) where the consumer opts into being contacted by a marketer (e-mail, postal, telephone, and fax). These processes are priced on a performance basis (e.g., cost per action, lead, or inquiry) and can include user applications (e.g., for a credit card), surveys, contests (e.g., sweepstakes), or registrations (Source: IAB) (see Chapter 6 BAM!).

Link: a clickable connection between two Web sites. Formally referred to as a hyperlink. If you click on the link, you will be taken to that page (Source: modified from IAB and Quirk) (see Chapter 2 model).

Link bait: editorial content, often sensational in nature, posted on a Web page and submitted to social media sites in hopes of building inbound links from other sites (Source: Search Engine Watch) (see Chapter 4 ads).

Link building: the process of getting quality Web sites to link to your Web site to improve search engine rankings. Link-building techniques can include buying links, reciprocal linking, or entering barter arrangements (Source: Search Engine Watch) (see Chapter 2 model).

Listing: a series of results shown on a SERP (see Chapter 4 ads).

Load time: the length of time it takes for a page to open completely in the browser window (Source: Quirk) (see Chapter 2 model).

Log analyzer: software that provides information about a site's visitors, activity statistics, accessed files, click-through paths, and other analytical data based on the user's behavior (Source: Quirk) (see Chapter 7 analytics).

Log file: a file that records transactions that have occurred on the Web server. Some of the types of data collected are: date/time stamp, URL served, IP address of requestor, status code of request, user agent string, and previous URL of requestor. Use of the extended log file format is preferable (Source: IAB) (see Chapter 7 analytics).

Log file analysis: the analysis of records stored in the log file. In its raw format, the data in the log files can be hard to read and overwhelming. There are numerous log file analyzers that convert log file data into user-friendly charts and graphs. A good analyzer is generally considered an essential tool in SEO because it can show search engine statistics such as the number of visitors received from each search engine, the keywords each visitors used to find the site, visits by search engine spiders, and so on (Source: SEMPO) (see Chapter 7 analytics).

Logarithmic chart: a chart for which the price scale (usually on the vertical axis) is skewed so that a given distance always represents the same percentage change in price rather than the same absolute change in price (as is the case for a linear chart). In other words, the distance from 1 to 10 is the same as the distance from 10 to 100 on a logarithmic chart, but the latter distance is ten times greater on a linear chart (Source: BusinessDictionary) (see Chapter 3 keywords).

Long tail: keyword phrases with at least three, sometimes four or five, words in them. These long-tailed keywords are usually highly specific and draw lower traffic than shorter, more competitive keyword phrases, which is why they are also cheaper.

Oftentimes, long-tailed keywords, in aggregate, have good conversion ratios for the low number of click-throughs they generate (Source: SEMPO) (see Chapter 3 keywords).

Long-tailed keywords: keyword phrases with at least two or three words in them. (Source: SEMPO) (see Chapter 3 keywords).

Long-Term Value or Life-Time Value (LTV): metric used to describe the value a specific customer has over the life of their relationship with you (Source: WebTrends) (see Chapter 6 BAM!).

Marketing: Management process through which goods and services move from concept to the customer. As a philosophy, it is based on thinking about the business in terms of customer needs and their satisfaction. As a practice, it consists in coordination of four elements called 4P's: (1) a product, (2) its price, (3) distribution to a place, and (4) development of a promotion (Source: BusinessDictionary.com) (see Chapter 6 BAM!).

Marketing mix: the four elements businesses need to consider for the success of their marketing efforts: product, price, place, and promotion. The focus and strategy that is placed on each one is entirely dependent on the goals of the marketing strategy (Source: Quirk) (see Chapter 6 BAM!).

Marketing performance management (MPM): drives stronger customer relationships and higher life-time value based on a framework of established goals, consistent metrics, and constant optimization across the entire marketing organization and across every customer touch point (Source: WebTrends) (see Chapter 6 BAM!).

Marketing plan: a written document detailing the actions necessary to achieve marketing objectives (Source: Quirk) (see Chapter 6 BAM!).

Match: A match occurs when a document in the search engine's index contains terms entered as part of the query. The matching documents, simply called matches, are then displayed on the SERP. It is worth noting that search engines have different criteria for deciding when a document is a match. Most search engines only require that one word in the query match one word in the document. Some search engines (like Google) require all words to appear in the document before that document is considered a match (Source: SearchEngineDictionary.com) (see Chapter 2 model).

Media agency: is a company that helps companies communicate with current and potential consumers and/or the general public (Source: Wikipedia) (see Chapter 6 BAM!).

Merchant: this is the owner of the product that is being marketed or promoted. Also referred to as advertiser (Source: Quirk) (see Chapter 6 BAM!).

Meta data: data about information. Information that can be entered about a Web page and the elements on it that provide context and relevancy information to search engines. This used to be an all-important ranking factor (Source: modified from Quirk) (see Chapter 2 model).

Meta tags: information placed in the HTML header of a Web page, providing information that is not visible to browsers, but can be used in varying degrees by search engines to index a page. Common meta tags used in search engine marketing are title, description, and keyword tags (Source: Search Engine Watch) (see Chapter 2 model).

Metrics: a system of parameters or ways of quantitative assessment of a process that is to be measured, along with the processes to carry out such measurement. Metrics define what is to be measured (Source: WebTrends) (see Chapter 7 analytics).

Minimum bid: the least amount that an advertiser can bid for a keyword or keyword phrase and still be active on the search ad network. This amount can vary and is set by the search engine (Source: modified SEMPO) (see Chapter 8 auctions).

Mobile search: an evolving branch of information-retrieval services centered on the convergence of mobile platforms and mobile handsets or other mobile devices. The services allow users to find mobile content interactively on mobile Web sites, and mobile content shows a media shift toward mobile multimedia (Source: WebTrends) (see Chapter 10 future).

Multivariate testing: a test using many variables to determine statistically significant influences on outcomes. A type of testing that varies and tests more than one or two campaign elements at a time to determine the best performing elements and combinations. Multivariate testing can gather significant results on many different components of, for example, alternative PPC ad titles or descriptions in a short period of time. Often it requires special expertise to analyze complex statistical results. (Compare to *A/B Testing*, which changes only one element at a time, alternately serving an "old" version ad and a changed ad.) In search advertising, you might do A/B Split or Multivariate testing to learn what parts of a landing page (background color, title, headline, fill-in forms, design, and images) produce higher conversions and are more cost-effective (Source: modified from SEMPO and Quirk) (see Chapter 7 auctions).

Navigation: the act of moving from location to location within a Web site, or between Web sites, accomplished by clicking on links. Navigation can also refer to the overall structure of the links on the site, comprising the paths available to the visitor (Source: WebTrends) (see Chapter 9 framework).

Negative keywords: filtered-out keywords to prevent ad serves on them in order to avoid irrelevant click-through charges or to refine and narrow the targeting of your keywords. Formatting negative keywords varies by search engine, but they are usually designated with a minus sign (Source: modified SEMPO) (see Chapter 3 keywords).

Network effect: the phenomenon whereby a service becomes more valuable as more people use it, thereby encouraging ever-increasing numbers of adopters (Source: MarketingTerms.com) (see Chapter 2 model).

New visitor: a unique visitor who visits a Web site for the first time ever in the period of time being analyzed (Source: Quirk) (see Chapter 7 analytics).

Nonqualifying page impressions: page impressions that should be excluded from traffic or measurement reports, such as unsuccessful transfers of requested documents, successful transfers of requested documents to a robot or spider, and/or pages in a frame set. See *frames* (Source: IAB) (see Chapter 7 analytics).

North: the advertisements shown at the top of a SERP (see Chapter 4 ads).

Off the page/off-the-page factors/off-the-page criteria: those factors that impact the ranking of a Web page but that are not located on the Web page itself. Inbound links and anchor text are examples of off-the-page factors (Source: SearchEngineDictionary. com) (see Chapter 2 model).

Off-site measurement: when a site forwards its log files to an off-site Web research service for analysis (Source: IAB) (see Chapter 7 analytics).

On-demand: the ability to request video, audio, or information to be sent to the screen immediately by clicking something on the screen referring to that choice (Source: IAB) (see Chapter 2 model).

On-site measurement: when a server has an appropriate software program to measure and analyze traffic received on its own site (Source: IAB) (see Chapter 7 analytics).

Ontology: in the context of search engines, it refers specifically to a file that defines relationships between words (Source: SearchEngineDictionary.com) (see Chapter 2 keywords).

Optimization: marketing technology through which the best possible ad placement is automatically determined based on advertiser and publisher objectives, and varied according to observed performance. Finding an alternative with the most cost-effective or highest achievable performance under the given constraints by maximizing desired factors and minimizing undesired ones. In comparison, maximization means trying to attain the highest or maximum result or outcome without regard to cost or expense. Practice of optimization is restricted by the lack of full information and the lack of time to evaluate what information is available (see bounded reality for details). In computer simulation (modeling) of business problems, optimization is achieved usually by using linear programming techniques of operations research (Source: modified from Advertising.com and BusinessDictionary) (see Chapter 7 analytics).

Opt-in: refers to an individual giving a company permission to use data collected from or about the individual for a particular reason, such as to market the company's products and services. See *permission marketing* (Source: IAB) (see Chapter 6 BAM!).

Opt-out: when a company states that it plans to market its products and services to an individual unless the individual asks to be removed from the company's mailing list (Source: IAB) (see Chapter 6 BAM!).

Organic listings: listings that appear solely because a search engine has deemed it editorially important for them to be included, regardless of payment (Source: SEMPO) (see Chapter 2 model).

Organic results: listings on SERP that were not paid for; listings for which search engines do not sell space. Sites appear in organic (also called "natural") results because a search engine has applied formulas (algorithms) to its search crawler index, combined with editorial decisions and content weighting, that it deems important enough inclusion without payment. *Paid Inclusion Content* is also often considered "organic," even though it is paid advertising, because paid inclusion content usually appears on SERPs mixed with unpaid, organic results (Source: SEMPO) (see Chapter 2 model).

Organic search: the listings generally found on the left-hand side of a SERP and not influenced by direct financial payments. These listings are results based on factors such as keyword relevancy within a Web page. SEO is used to boost success (Source: Quirk) (see Chapter 2 model).

Page: unit of content (so downloads and Flash files can be defined as a page). A document having a specific URL and comprised of a set of associated files. A page may contain text, images, and other online elements. It may be statically or dynamically generated. It may be made up of multiple frames or screens, but should contain a designated primary object that, when loaded, is counted as the entire page (Source: modified from Quirk and IAB) (see Chapter 2 model).

Page display: when a page is successfully displayed on the user's computer screen (Source: IAB) (see Chapter 2 model).

Page impression: a measurement of responses from a Web server to a page request from the user's browser, which is filtered from robotic activity and error codes and is recorded at a point as close as possible to the opportunity to see the page by the user. See http://www.iab.net for ad campaign measurement guidelines (Source: IAB) (see Chapter 7 analytics).

Page jacking: theft of a page from the original site and publication of a copy (or near-copy) at another site (Source: Marketing Terms.com) (see Chapter 2 model).

Page request: the opportunity for an HTML document to appear on a browser window as a direct result of a user's interaction with a Web site (Source: IAB) (see Chapter 2 model).

Page view: request to load a single HTML page (Source: Marketing Terms.com) (see Chapter 2 model).

PageRank (PR): the Google technology developed at Stanford University for placing importance on pages and Web sites. At one point, PageRank (PR) was a major factor in rankings. Today it is one of hundreds of factors in the algorithm that determines a page's rankings (Source: SEMPO) (see Chapter 2 model).

Paid Inclusion: refers to the process of paying a fee to a search engine in order to be included in that search engine or directory. Also known as guaranteed inclusion. Paid inclusion does not impact rankings of a Web page; it merely guarantees that the Web page itself will be included in the index. These programs were typically used by Web sites that were not being fully crawled or were incapable of being crawled, due to dynamic URL structures, frames, and other factors (Source: SEMPO) (see Chapter 2 model).

Paid listing: a listing on a SERP achieved through outbidding competitors (as in PPC). The term is sometimes also used to refer to keyword-targeted advertisements, where the advertiser pays the search engine a fixed amount to have its ad shown on the SERP for a specific keyword (Source: SearchEngineDictionary.com) (see Chapter 2 model).

Paid placement: advertising program where listings are guaranteed to appear in response to particular search terms, with higher ranking typically obtained by paying more than other advertisers (Source: SEMPO) (see Chapter 2 model).

Paid search: placing ads for products or services on SERPs (listings appear at the top of the page and on the right-hand side) and on content sites across the Internet. These ads are typically small snippets of text linked to merchandise pages (Source: Quirk) (see Chapter 2 model).

Palming off: to misrepresent inferior goods of one producer as superior goods made by a reputable, well-regarded competitor in order to gain commercial advantage and promote sales (see Chapter 6 BAM!).

Parameters: these are located in the URL immediately after a question mark and followed by an equal sign and a return value, known as name=value (Source: WebTrends) (see Chapter 2 model).

Pass-along rate: the percentage of people who pass on a message or file (Source: Marketing Terms.com) (see Chapter BAM!).

Path: a path is the click pattern a visitor uses as they traverse through multiple pages (Source: WebTrends) (see Chapter 2 model).

Pay per call: a model of paid advertising similar to Pay Per Click (PPC), except advertisers pay for every phone call that comes to them from a search ad, rather than for every click-through to their Web site landing page for the ad. Often costs higher than PPC advertising, but valued by advertisers for higher conversion rates from consumers who take the action step of telephoning an advertiser (Source: SEMPO) (see Chapter 2 model).

Pay per click (PPC): online advertising payment model in which payment is based solely on qualifying click-throughs (Source: Marketing Terms.com) (see Chapter 2 model).

Pay-per-click model: the most common payment method, although others are also utilized, such as pay-for-impression, pay-per-action, and pay-per-call (see Chapter 2 model).

Pay-per-click search engine (PPCSE): search engine where results are ranked according to the bid amount and advertisers are charged only when a searcher clicks on the search listing (Source: Marketing Terms.com) (see Chapter 2 model).

Pay per impression: an advertising pricing model in which advertisers pay based on how many users were served from their ads (Source: IAB) (see Chapter 2 model).

Pay per lead (PPL): online advertising payment model in which payment is based solely on qualifying leads (Source: Marketing Terms.com) (see Chapter 2 model).

Pay per sale (PPS): online advertising payment model in which payment is based solely on qualifying sales (Source: Marketing Terms.com) (see Chapter 2 model).

Payment threshold: the minimum accumulated commission an affiliate must earn to trigger payment from an affiliate program (Source: Marketing Terms.com) (see Chapter 2 model).

Perceived marginal utility: gratification received from consuming the next unit of a good (see Chapter 6 BAM!).

Performance pricing model: an advertising model in which advertisers pay based on a set of agreed-on performance criteria, such as a percentage of online revenues or delivery of new sales leads. Examples are CPA, CPC, CPL, CPO, CPS, and CPT (Source: IAB) (see Chapter 2 model).

Performance-based advertising: advertising model in which the advertiser pays based on results achieved (Source: Advertising.com) (see Chapter 2 model).

Permission marketing: marketing centered on getting customer's consent to receive information from a company (Source: Marketing Terms.com) (see Chapter 6 BAM!).

Persistent cookie: cookies that remain on a client's hard drive until they expire (as determined by the Web site that set them) or are deleted by the end-user (Source: IAB) (see Chapter 2 model).

Personal Experience Factor (PEF): the customer's interaction with a Web site, ad, or brand (Source: WebTrends) (see Chapter BAM!).

Personas: these are "people types" or subgroups that encompass several attributes such as gender, age, location, salary level, leisure activities, lifestyle characteristics, marital/family status, or some kind of definable behavior. Useful profiles for focusing ad messages and offers to targeted segments (Source: SEMPO) (see Chapter 5 customers).

Platform: the type of computer or operating system on which a software application runs, (e.g., Windows, Macintosh or Unix) (Source: IAB) (see Chapter 2 model).

Pop-under ad: an ad that displays in a new browser window behind the current browser window (Source: Marketing Terms.com) (see Chapter 2 model).

Pop-up ad: an ad that displays in a new browser window (Source: Marketing Terms. com) (see Chapter 2 model).

Portal: a site featuring a suite of commonly used services, serving as a starting point and frequent gateway to the Web (Web portal) or a niche topic (vertical portal) (Source: Marketing Terms.com) (see Chapter 2 model).

Position: in PPC advertising, position is the placement on a search engine results page where your ad appears relative to other paid ads and organic search results. Top-ranking paid ads (high-ranking ten to fifteen results, depending on the engine) usually appear at the top of the SERP and on the "right rail" (right-side column of the page). Ads appearing in the top slots or "north" are known as premium positions. Paid search ad position is determined by confidential algorithms and quality score measures specific to each search engine. However, factors in the engines' position placement under some advertiser control include bid price, the ad's CTR, relevancy of your ad to searcher requests, relevance of your click-through landing page to the search request, and quality measures search engines calculate to ensure quality user experience (Source: modified from SEMPO) (see Chapter 4 ads).

Position preference: a feature in sponsored search systems enabling advertisers to specify in which positions they would like their ads to appear on the SERP. Not a position guarantee (Source: modified from SEMPO) (see Chapter 8 auctions).

Potential customer: a consumer that may become but is not yet a customer (see Chapter 5 customers).

Power laws: mathematical relationship between two quantities. When the frequency of an event varies as a power of some attribute of that event (e.g., its size), the frequency is said to follow a power law (see Chapter 3 keywords).

PPC advertising: acronym for Pay-Per-Click Advertising, a model of online advertising in which advertisers pay only for each click on their ads that directs searchers to a specified landing page on the advertiser's Web site. PPC ads may get thousands of impressions (views or serves of the ad); however, unlike more traditional ad models billed on a CPM (Cost-Per-Thousand-Impressions) basis, PPC advertisers only pay when their ad is clicked on. Charges per ad click-through are based on advertiser bids in hybrid ad space auctions and are influenced by competitor bids, competition for keywords, and search engines' proprietary quality measures of advertiser ad and landing page content (Source: SEMPO) (see Chapter 6 BAM!).

PPC management: the monitoring and maintenance of a Pay-Per-Click campaign or campaigns. This includes changing bid prices, expanding and refining keyword lists, editing ad copy, testing campaign components for cost effectiveness and successful conversions, and reviewing performance reports for reports to management and clients, as well as results to feed into future PPC campaign operations (Source: SEMPO) (see Chapter 2 model).

Process audit: third-party validation of internal control processes associated with measurement. See *audit* (Source: IAB) (see Chapter 7 analytics).

Profiling: the practice of tracking information about consumers' interests by monitoring their movements online. This can be done without using any personal information, but simply by analyzing the content, URLs, and other information about a user's browsing path/click-stream (Source: IAB) (see Chapter 5 customers).

Profit: money made from a product/service after expenses have been accounted for (Source: Quirk) (see Chapter 2 model).

Prospect: the visitor who reaches an intent-to-transact page (for example, a page with a shopping cart or a form) (see Chapter 5 customers).

Protocol: an established method of exchanging data over the Internet (Source: WebTrends) (see Chapter 2 model).

Publisher: an individual or organization that prepares, issues, and disseminates content for public distribution or sale via one or more media (Source: IAB) (see Chapter 2 model).

Purchase point: a point in time or location where sales are made (see Chapter 2 model).

Quality score: basis for measuring the quality of keywords and determining minimum PPC bids. This score is calculated by measuring a keyword's click-through rate, ad text relevancy, the keyword's historical performance, and the quality of the landing page (Source: Quirk) (see Chapter 4 ads).

Query: a series of terms entered by a searcher into a search engine. The keyword or keyword phrase a searcher enters into a search field, which initiates a search and results in a SERP with organic and paid listings (Source: SEMPO) (see Chapter 3 keywords).

Query length: the number of terms in a query (see Chapter 3 keywords).

Query parameter: an individual piece of a query string consisting of a parameter name and a value for the parameter (Source: WebTrends) (see Chapter 3 keywords).

Rank: a measure of which position an ad is in the SERP listings. How well positioned a particular Web page or Web site appears in search engine results. For example, if you rank at position #1, you are the first listed paid or sponsored ad. If you are in position #18, it is likely that your ad appears on the second or third page of search results, after seventeen competitor paid ads and organic listings. Rank and position affect your click-through rates and, ultimately, conversion rates for your landing pages (Source: SEMPO) (see Chapter 4 ads).

Ranking: in search, ranking is used to describe the relative position of a Web page in the SERPs (Source: Quirk) (see Chapter 4 ads).

Rational actor: a value-maximizing unit in the sense that, with respect to the actor's own values and preferences, the actor makes choices in such a way as to maximize outcomes (see Chapter 5 customers).

Reach: the estimated number of individuals in the audience. The size of the audience reading, viewing, hearing, or interacting with a message in a given period of time. Reach can be understood as either an absolute number or a fraction of a population (Source: WebTrends) (see Chapter 6 BAM!).

Real time: events that happen live at a particular moment. When one chats in a chat room, or sends an instant message, one is interacting in real time (Source: IAB) (see Chapter 2 model).

Recency: the number of days since a visitor's most recent visit during a reporting period. See also *frequency* (Source: WebTrends) (see Chapter 5 customers).

Referral fees: fees paid by advertisers for delivering a qualified sales lead or purchase inquiry (Source: IAB) (see Chapter 2 model).

Referral link: the referring page or referral link is a place from which the user clicked to get to the current page. In other words, because a hyperlink connects one URL to another, in clicking on a link the browser moves from the referring URL to the destination URL. Also known as source of a visit (Source: IAB) (see Chapter 2 model).

Relative conversion rate: The expected change in conversion rate in relation to rank 1 (see Chapter 7 analytics).

Relevance: describes how pertinent, connected, or applicable something is to a given matter. The measure of the accuracy of the search results; in other words, it is a measure of how close the documents listed in the search results are to what the user was looking for (Source: SearchEngineDictionary.com) (see Chapter 4 ads).

Repeat visitor: unique visitor who has accessed a Web site more than once over a specific time period (Source: IAB) (see Chapter 7 analytics).

Research shopper: research shopper phenomenon, which is the tendency of some consumers to research the product in one channel (e.g., the Web) and then purchase it through another channel (e.g., a store) (see Chapter 5 customers).

Results: the listings shown on a SERP in response to a query (see Chapter 2 model).

Return on advertising (ROA): the revenue generated by advertising spent (see Chapter 7 analytics).

Return on advertising spending (ROAS): represents the dollars earned per dollars spent on the corresponding advertising (Source: Internet Marketing Glossary) (see Chapter 2 model).

Return on investment (ROI): the amount of money an advertiser earns from its ads compared to the amount of money the advertiser spends on ads (Source: Search Engine Watch) (see Chapter 7 analytics).

Return visitor: a unique visitor who is not a new visitor to the site (Source: Quirk) (see Chapter 7 analytics).

Return visits: the average number of times a user returns to a site over a specific time period (Source: IAB) (see Chapter 7 analytics).

Revenue: yield of income from a particular source (Source: Quirk) (see Chapter 2 model).

Revenue per thousand impressions (RPI): yield from the display of 1,000 advertisements (see Chapter 7 analytics).

Revenue per search (RPS): yield from the submission of one query to a search engine by a searcher (see Chapter 2 model).

Revshare/revenue sharing: a method of allocating per-click revenue to a site publisher and click-through charges to a search engine that distributes paid ads to its context network partners, for every page viewer who clicks on the content site's sponsored ads. A type of *site finder's fee* (Source: SEMPO) (see Chapter 2 model).

Right rail: the advertisements along the right side of the search engine results page. Also known as east. The common name for the right-side column of a Web page. On a SERP, the right rail is usually where sponsored listings appear (Source: modified from SEMPO) (see Chapter 4 ads).

ROI timelag: the period from when advertising dollars are spent and when revenue is generated (see Chapter 2 model).

Sample: in statistics, a subset of a universe whose properties are studied to gain information about that universe (Source: IAB) (see Chapter 7 analytics).

Sampling: in statistics, the selection of individual observations intended to yield knowledge about a population, especially for the purposes of statistical inference (Source: WebTrends) (see Chapter 7 analytics).

Scenario analysis: a report showing the amount of activity at each step of a defined scenario, plus conversion rates for each transition from step to step as well as for the whole process. Examples of scenarios are check-out, registration, or application sequences (Source: WebTrends)

Score: search engines usually arrange search results from the most relevant to the least relevant (as determined by the search engine's algorithm). To rank documents, the search engine assigns a score to each page, and those with the highest scores are listed first. Most search engines simply give the maximum score to the most relevant document and score all other relevant documents relative to that document. Others compare all documents to a theoretically perfect document. The score of a Web page therefore refers to its relevance as perceived by a specific search engine (Source: SearchEngineDictionary. com) (see Chapter 2 model).

Screen real estate: the area of pixels on a SERP (see Chapter 2 model).

Search: the process of finding information on the Internet using search engines (Source: modified from Quirk) (see Chapter 3 keywords).

Search advertising: an advertiser bids for the chance to have their ad display when a user searches for a given keyword. These are usually text ads, which are displayed above or to the right of the algorithmic (organic) search results. Most search ads are sold by the PPC model, where the advertiser pays only when the user clicks on the ad or text link (Source: Search Engine Watch) (see Chapter 2 model).

Search box: where the searcher enters the query on the search engine Web page (see Chapter 2 model).

Search engine: a program that indexes documents and then attempts to match documents by relevancy to the users' search requests (Source: Marketing Terms.com) (see Chapter 2 model).

Search engine listing: the listing of pages on the search engine results page (SERP) (Source: Quirk) (see Chapter 2 model).

Search engine marketing (SEM): the act of marketing a Web site via search engines, whether this be improving rank in primarily purchasing paid listings (PPC management), but also organic listings (search engine optimization), or a combination of these and other search engine-related activities (i.e., affiliate programs, shopping feeds, or link development). An Internet marketing method that focuses on purchasing ads that appear on the result pages of search engines such as Google. Many search engines offer ways for individuals or businesses to purchase ads that typically appear above or to the right of the content on the search result pages. Typically, the higher the fee one offers to pay for an ad, the higher the ad will appear on the page, depending on how much competition there is to appear on that page. Depending on the agreement, one may pay a flat fee for a given length of time, or may pay a given fee for each click that they receive to their ad (Source: modified from WebTrends and BusinessDictionary) (see Chapter 2 model).

Search engine optimization (SEO): the act of altering a Web site so that it does well in the organic, crawler-based listings of search engines. In the past, has also been used as a term for any type of search engine marketing activity, although now "search engine marketing" is more commonly used as an umbrella term. It refers to the process of improving traffic to a given Web site by increasing the site's visibility in search engine results. Web sites improve search engine optimization by improving content, making sure that the pages can be indexed correctly, and ensuring that the content is unique. Going through the search engine optimization process typically leads to more traffic for the site because the site will appear higher in search results for information that pertains to the site's offerings (Source: modified from WebTrends and BusinessDictionary) (see Chapter 2 model).

Search engine positioning (SEP): synonymous with SEO, search engine positioning is the act of altering a Web site to perform well in organic or natural search results (Source: WebTrends) (see Chapter 2 model).

Search engine results page (SERP): the page searchers see after they have entered their query into the search box. This page lists several Web pages related to the searcher's query, sorted by relevance. Increasingly, search engines are returning blended search results, which include images, videos, and results from specialty databases on their SERPs (Source: Search Engine Watch) (see Chapter 2 model).

Search engine spam: excessive manipulation to influence search engine rankings, often for pages that contain little or no relevant content (Source: Marketing Terms. com) (see Chapter 2 model).

Search engine submission: the act of supplying a URL to a search engine in an attempt to make a search engine aware of a site or page (Source: Marketing Terms. com) (see Chapter 2 model).

Search funnel: movement of searchers, who tend to do several searches before reaching a buy decision, which works from broad, general keyword search terms to narrower, specific keywords. Advertisers use the search funnel to anticipate customer intent and develop keywords targeted to different stages. Also refers to potential for switches at stages in the funnel when, for example, searchers start with keywords for a desired brand but switch to other brands after gathering information on the category (Source: SEMPO) (see Chapter 5 customers).

Search marketer: Whether in SEO, PPC, or both, a search marketer uses search engines to sell products, channel traffic, and heighten brand awareness (Source: Quirk) (see Chapter 6 BAM!).

Search marketing agency: an advertising agency that provides SEM services (see Chapter 6 BAM!).

Search personalization: the ability to personalize SERPs based on personal profile information, settings, or location (IP address) (Source: WebTrends) (see Chapter 10 future).

Search query: the word or phrase a searcher types into a search field, which initiates search engine results page listings and PPC ad serves. In PPC advertising, the goal is to bid on keywords that closely match the search queries of the advertiser's targets (Source: SEMPO) (see Chapter 3 keywords).

Search results: the documents returned by a search engine in response to a query. Also see *SERP* (Source: SearchEngineDictionary.com) (see Chapter 2 model).

Search terms: words entered by the searcher. Search engines will then look for these words in their index and return matching results. Also known as search query (Source: Quirk) (see Chapter 3 keywords).

Searcher: a person engaged in information searching (see Chapter 5 customers).

Searching: exploration of the Web by following one interesting link to another, usually with a definite objective and a planned search strategy. In comparison, surfing is exploration definite in objective but not in strategy, and browsing is exploration without a definite objective or search strategy (Source: BusinessDictionary) (see Chapter 3 keywords).

Second-price auction: an *auction* in which the bidder who submitted the highest bid is awarded the object being sold and pays a *price* equal to the *second* highest bid (see Chapter 8 auctions).

Secondary research: collection of existing research data (Source: Quirk) (see Chapter 7 analytics).

Segment: a grouping of customers, defined by Web site activity or other data that can be used to target them effectively (Source: WebTrends) (see Chapter 6 BAM!).

Sell-through rate: the percentage of ad inventory sold as opposed to traded or bartered (Source: IAB) (see Chapter 2 model).

Server-side: transactions that take place on the server (Source: Quirk) (see Chapter 2 model).

Server-side tracking: the process of analyzing Web server log files. Server-side analytic tools make sense of raw data to generate meaningful reports and trends analysis (Source: SEMPO) (see Chapter 2 model).

Session cookies: these are temporary and are erased when the browser exits at the end of a Web-surfing session (Source: IAB) (see Chapter 2 model).

Session duration: the period that a session lasts (see Chapter 2 model).

Session IDs: dynamic parameters, such as session IDs generated by cookies for each individual user. Session IDs cause search engines to see a different URL for each page each time that they return to recrawl a Web site (Source: SEMPO) (see Chapter 2 model).

Search session length: the number of queries in a session (see Chapter 2 model).

Session: several meanings depending on context (Source: modified from IAB) (see Chapter 7 analytics):

- A sequence of Internet activity made by one user at one site. If a user makes no request from a site during a thirty-minute period of time, the next content or ad request would then constitute the beginning of a new visit.
- A series of transactions performed by a user that can be tracked across successive Web sites. For example, in a single session, a user may start on a publisher's Web site, click on an advertisement, and then go to an advertiser's Web site and make a purchase.
- A sequence of queries submitted by a searcher in one period of interaction with a search engine and around a similar topic.

Sessionization: this is the process for creating a session. Sessionization methods are ways in which you can define a session. Web analytics solutions have multiple sessionization methods such as cookies, IP Address, IP+ Agent, and so on. These methods tell the Web analytics system how they should count a series of page requests from the same individual or browsing machine (Source: WebTrends) (see Chapter 7 analytics).

Shopping bot: intelligent agent that searches for the best price (Source: IAB) (see Chapter 2 model).

Shopping search/feeds: shopping search engines allow shoppers to look for products and prices in a search environment for rapid and easy comparison. Premium placement can be purchased on some shopping search indices via XML feeds (Source: WebTrends) (see Chapter 3 keywords).

Signal processing theory: deals with operations on or analysis of signals, in either discrete or continuous time, to perform useful operations on those signals (see Chapter 7 analytics).

Simple reaction time (SRT): time it takes to react to stimuli (see Chapter 4 ads).

Site optimization: the act of modifying a site to make it easier for search engines to automatically index the site and hopefully result in better placement in results (Source: modified from IAB) (see Chapter 2 model).

Site-targeted ads: site targeting lets advertisers display their ads on manually selected sites in the search engine's content network for content or contextual ad serves. Site-targeted ads are billed more like traditional display ads, per 1,000 impressions (CPM), and not on a Pay-Per-Click basis (Source: SEMPO) (see Chapter 4 ads).

Skip word: a word that often appears in a page's copy or content but has no significance by itself. Examples of skip words are: and, the, of, etc. (known in academia as stop words) (see Chapter 2 model).

SKU: Stock Keeping Units (Source: WebTrends) (see Chapter 6 BAM!).

SMEs: subject matter experts (see Chapter 6 BAM!).

Social media: a category of sites that is based on user participation and user-generated content. They include social networking sites like LinkedIn or Facebook, social bookmarking sites like Del.icio.us, social news sites like Digg or Reddit, and other sites that are centered on user interaction (Source: Search Engine Watch) (see Chapter 10 future).

Software as a service (SaaS): sometimes referred to as "software on demand," it is software that is deployed over the Internet and/or is deployed to run behind a firewall on a local area network (LAN) or personal computer. With SaaS, a provider licenses an application to customers either as a service on-demand, through a subscription, on a "pay-as-you-go" basis, or (increasingly) at no charge. This approach to application delivery is part of the utility-computing model where all of the technology is in the "cloud" accessed over the Internet as a service (Source: Wikipedia). (see Chapter 2 model).

South: the ads at the bottom of a SERP (see Chapter 4 ads).

Space: location on a page of a site in which an ad can be placed. Each space on a site is uniquely identified. There can be multiple spaces on a single page (Source: IAB) (see Chapter 2 model).

Spam: any search marketing method that a search engine deems to be detrimental to its efforts to deliver relevant, quality search results. Some search engines have written guidelines on their definitions and penalties for spam. Examples include doorway-landing pages designed primarily to game search engine algorithms rather than meet searcher expectations from the advertiser's clicked-on ad; keyword stuffing in which search terms that motivated a click-through are heavily and redundantly repeated on a page in place of relevant content; attempts to redirect click-through searchers to irrelevant pages, product offers, and services; and landing pages that simply compile additional links on which a searcher must click to get any information. Determining what constitutes spam is complicated by the fact that different search engines have different standards, including what is allowable for listings gathered through organic methods versus paid inclusion (referred to as spamdexing), whether the listing is from a commercial or research/academic source, and so forth (Source: modified from SEMPO and Webmaster) (see Chapter 2 model).

Spam filter: software built into e-mail gateways as well as e-mail client applications designed to identify and remove spam (Source: IAB) (see Chapter 2 model).

Spamming: refers to a wide array of techniques used to "trick" the search engines. These tactics generally are against the guidelines put forth by the search engines. Tactics such as Hidden Text, Doorway Pages, Content Duplication, and Link Farming are but a few of many spam techniques employed over the years (Source: SEMPO) (see Chapter 2 model).

Spend: the amount of money spent on an advertising effort (see Chapter 8 auctions).

Spider: a program that crawls through the Web, visiting Web pages to collect information to add to or update a search engine's index. The major search engines on the Web all have such a program, which is also known as a "crawler" or a "bot" (Source: Search Engine Watch) (see Chapter 2 model).

Splash page: a branding page before the home page of a Web site (Source: Marketing Terms.com) (see Chapter 2 model).

Sponsored links: the paid search results on a SERP (Source: Quirk) (see Chapter 2 model).

Sponsored listing: a term used as a title or column head on a SERP to identify paid advertisers and distinguish between paid and organic listings (Source: modified from SEMPO) (see Chapter 2 model).

Sponsored results: advertisements on a SERP (see Chapter 2 model).

Sponsored search analytics: collecting, measuring, analyzing, and reporting keyword advertising data for purposes of monitoring, understanding, and optimizing search engine marketing (see Chapter 7 analytics).

Sponsorship: association with a Web site in some way that gives an advertiser some particular visibility and advantage above that of run-of-site advertising (Source: IAB) (see Chapter 6 BAM!).

Stakeholder: a person or organization with an interest (a "stake") in how a resource is managed (Source: Quirk) (see Chapter 9 framework).

Static ad placement: ad-serving approach through which ad placement is not altered based on performance factors commonly employed for sponsorships (i.e., ad placement does not vary according to resulting clicks or conversions, time of day, etc) (Source: Advertising.com) (see Chapter 2 model).

Static keyword bidding: bidding approach through which term bids are not altered based on performance factors (i.e., bidding does not vary according to resulting clicks or conversions, time of day, etc) (Source: Advertising.com) (see Chapter 8 auctions).

Statistical validity: the degree to which an observed result, such as a difference between two measurements, can be relied on and not attributed to random error in sampling or in measurement. Statistical validity is important to the reliability of test results, particularly in multivariate testing methods (Source: modified from UsabilityFirst.com and SEMPO) (see Chapter 7 analytics).

Stickiness: a measure used to gauge the effectiveness of a site in retaining individual users. Stickiness is usually measured by the duration of the visit or the amount of time spent at a site over a given time period (Source: modified from Marketing Terms.com and IAB) (see Chapter 7 analytics).

Stop word: a word that appears on a Web page that will stop a search engine from indexing that Web page (see Chapter 2 model).

Submission: the act of submitting a Web site to search engines and search directories. For some search engines, this is performed simply by typing in the absolute home page URL of the Web site you wish to submit. Other engines and directories request that descriptions of the Web site be submitted for approval (Source: SEMPO) (see Chapter 2 model).

Target audience: the intended audience for an ad, usually defined in terms of specific demographics (age, sex, income, etc.), product purchase behavior, product usage, or media usage (Source: IAB) (see Chapter 6 BAM!).

Targeting: determining one's niche marketing audience by narrowly focusing ads and keywords to attract a specific, marketing-profiled searcher and potential customer. You can target to geographic locations (geo-targeting), by days of the week or time of day (dayparting), or by gender and age (demographic targeting). Targeting features vary by search engine. Newer ad techniques and software focus on behavioral targeting based on Web activity and behaviors that are predictive for potential customers who might be more receptive to particular ads (Source: modified from SEMPO and Quirk) (see Chapter 6 BAM!).

Taxonomy: a set of agreed-on principles according to which information can be stored more logically in an information-retrieval system. The term is used in science to describe the classification of natural elements (Source: SearchEngineDictionary. com) (see Chapter 3 keywords).

Term: a series of characters, typically a word, used in a search query (see Chapter 3 keywords).

Term frequency (TF): a measure of how often a term is found in a collection of documents. TF is combined with inverse document frequency (IDF) as a means of determining which documents are most relevant to a query. TF is sometimes also used to measure how often a word appears in a specific document (Source: SearchEngineDictionary.com) (see Chapter 3 keywords).

Term length: the number of characters in a term (see Chapter 3 keywords).

Text ad: advertisement using text-based hyperlinks (Source: Marketing Terms.com) (see Chapter 4 ads).

Textual ad impressions: the delivery of a text-based advertisement to a browser. To compensate for slow Internet connections, visitors may disable "auto load images" in their graphical browser. When they reach a page that contains an advertisement, they see a marker and the advertiser's message in text format in place of the graphical ad. Additionally, if a user has a text-only browser, only textual ads are delivered and recorded as textual ad impressions (Source: IAB) (see Chapter 7 analytics).

The Google Golden Triangle: triangle that extends from the top of the results over to the top of the first result, then down to a point on the left side at the bottom of the "above the fold" visible results where most searchers examine when looking at a SERP (see Chapter 4 ads).

Three-hit theory: a theory that proposes that the optimum number of exposures to an advertisement to induce learning is three: one to gain consumers' awareness, a second to show the relevance of the product, and a third to show its benefits (see Chapter 4 ads).

Time spent: the amount of elapsed time from the initiation of a visit to the last audience activity associated with that visit. Time spent should represent the activity of a single cookie browser or user for a single access session to the Web site or property (Source: IAB) (see Chapter 7 analytics).

Time-to-convert: is calculated as the period from when a visitor clicks on an ad to when the visitor completes a purchase [2] (see Chapter 7 analytics).

Title tag: an HTML meta tag with text describing a specific Web page. The title tag should contain strategic keywords for the page, because many search engines pay special attention to the title text when indexing pages. The title tag should also make sense to humans because it is usually the text link to the page displayed in search engine results (Source: Search Engine Watch) (see Chapter 2 model).

Touch point: an opportunity to interact with a consumer in a buying cycle when consumers are open to influence (see Chapter 5 customers).

Tracking: measuring the effectiveness of a campaign by collecting and evaluating statistics (Source: Quirk) (see Chapter 7 analytics).

Trademarks: distinctive symbols, pictures, or words that identify a specific product or service, received through registration with the U.S. Patent & Trademark Office. Tier I search engines generally prohibit the use of trademarks in advertisements if the bidder is not the legal owner (Source: modified from SEMPO) (see Chapter 6 BAM!).

Traffic: number of hits or visits a Web site receives during, usually, a twenty-four-hour period. Retailing: Number of shoppers that pass through a shopping area, mall, or store during the business hours. Refers to the number of visitors a Web site receives. It can be determined by examination of Web logs (Source: SEMPO) (see Chapter 7 analytics).

Traffic analysis: the process of analyzing traffic to a Web site to understand what the visitors are searching for and what is driving traffic to a site (Source: SEMPO) (see Chapter 7 analytics).

Unduplicated audience: the number of unique individuals exposed to a specified domain, page, or ad in a specified time period (Source: IAB) (see Chapter 6 BAM!).

Uniform Resource Locator (URL): location of a resource on the Internet. A means of identifying an exact location on the Internet (Source: modified from Marketing Terms.com and WebTrends) (see Chapter 2 model).

Unique selling proposition (USP): what makes one's product or service better, or different, from the competition (see Chapter 6 BAM!).

Unique user: unique individual or browser that either has accessed a site (see unique visitor) or has been served unique content and/or ads such as e-mail, newsletters, interstitials, and pop-under ads. Unique users can be identified by user registration or cookies. Reported unique users should filter out bots. See http://www.iab.net for ad campaign measurement guidelines (Source: IAB) (see Chapter 7 analytics).

Unique visitor: a unique user who accesses a Web site within a specific time period. See *unique user* (Source: IAB) (see Chapter 7 analytics).

Unique visitors (UV): refers to a measure captured by some Web analytics solutions that track the interaction a single user has with a Web site over time (Source: WebTrends) (see Chapter 7 analytics).

Universal search: also known as blended or federated search results. Universal search pulls data from multiple databases to display on the same page. Results can include images, videos, and results from specialty databases like maps and local information, product information, or news stories (Source: Search Engine Watch) (see Chapter 2 model).

Universe: total population of audience being measured (Source: IAB) (see Chapter 7 analytics).

User: an individual with access to the Web (Source: IAB) (see Chapter 7 analytics).

User agent: fields in an extended Web server log file identifying the browser and platform used by a visitor (Source: WebTrends) (see Chapter 2 model).

User agent string: a field in a server log file that identifies the specific browser software and computer operating system making the request (Source: IAB) (see Chapter 2 model).

User-centric measurement: Web audience measurement based on the behavior of a sample of Web users (Source: IAB) (see Chapter 7 analytics).

User session: a period of activity (all hits) for one user of a Web site. A unique user is determined by the IP address or cookie. Typically, a user session is terminated when a user is inactive for more than thirty minutes (Source: WebTrends) (see Chapter 7 analytics).

Value propositions: a customer value proposition is the sum total of benefits a customer is promised to receive in return for his or her custom and the associated payment (or other value transfer). A customer value proposition is what is promised by a company's marketing and sales efforts and then fulfilled by its delivery and customer service processes (Source: SEMPO) (see Chapter 6 BAM!).

View: often used as a synonym for impression (Source: IAB) (see Chapter 7 analytics).

Viewer: person viewing content or ads on the Web. There is currently no way to measure viewers (Source: IAB) (see Chapter 7 analytics).

Visit: a single continuous set of activity attributable to a cookie browser or user (if registration-based or a panel participant) resulting in one or more pulled text and/or graphics downloads from a site. A visit is an interaction a unique visitor has with a Web site over a specified period of time or activity. In most cases, if a visitor has left a site or has not executed a click-within thirty minutes, the visit session will terminate (Source: modified from IAB and WebTrends) (see Chapter 7 analytics).

Visit duration: the length of time the visitor is exposed to a specific ad, Web page, or Web site during a single session (Source: IAB) (see Chapter 7 analytics).

Visitor: individual or browser that accesses a Web site within a specific time period (Source: IAB) (see Chapter 7 analytics).

Visitor session: interaction by a site visitor. The session ends when the visitor leaves the site (Source: WebTrends) (see Chapter 7 analytics).

Wear-in: pertains to the notion that consumers often must be exposed to an ad more than once before the ad has any discernible positive effects (see Chapter 4 ads).

Wear-out: pertains to the notion that after consumers have been exposed to an ad repeatedly, the ad may lose its effectiveness and may actually produce negative effects (see Chapter 4 ads).

Web 2.0: a phrase that refers to a supposed second generation of Internet-based services. These usually include tools that let people collaborate and share information online, such as social networking sites, wikis, communication tools, and folksonomies (Source: Search Engine Watch) (see Chapter 2 model).

Web analytics: site analytics essential to the success of any Web site. They provide you with information detailing how visitors are interacting with your site as well as how successful your supporting eMarketing techniques are on your site's performance. Data for the analysis is mined using specialized software (we use

ClickTracks!). Site analytics provide you with a comprehensive and insightful analysis of your Web site as well as an insight into what needs to be done to ensure even greater success (Source: Quirk) (see Chapter 7 analytics).

Web page: an html, pdf, or other formatted single page on a Web site (see Chapter 2 model).

Web record: all the information a search engine can display about a particular Web page in response to a query. In other words, search engines do not index actual pages. When a page is "indexed," the search engine adds a snapshot-like "Web record" to its index. The Web record contains only the information the search engine is interested in (content) rather than the entire page. The contents of Web records obviously differ from one search engine to another, depending on what each search engine considers important to rank pages accurately (Source: SearchEngineDictionary.com) (see Chapter 7 analytics).

Web server logs: most Web server software, and all good Web analytics packages, keeps a running count of all search terms used by visitors to your site. These running counts are kept in large text files called Log Files or Web Server Logs, useful for developing and refining PPC campaign keyword lists (Source: SearchEngineDictionary. com) (see Chapter 7 analytics).

Web site: the virtual location (domain) for an organization's or individual's presence on the Web (Source: IAB) (see Chapter 2 model).

Weighting: the technique search engines use to compare the relevance of different documents to a query. Search engines effectively "weigh" different pages based on things like the occurrence of keywords in the title in order to list documents in order from most to least relevant (Source: SearchEngineDictionary.com) (see Chapter 2 model).

What if: a type of analysis that allows an end-user to pose hypothetical situations against their data to model or predict outcomes (Source: WebTrends) (see Chapter 7 analytics).

Word-of-mouth: information that is passed between people, as opposed to messages from a company to people (Source: Quirk) (see Chapter 6 BAM!).

Year over year (**YOY**): the means of comparing data from one year to the next. For example, to compare online holiday retail revenue from last year to this year (see Chapter 6 BAM!).

Yield: the percentage of clicks versus impressions on an ad within a specific page. Also called ad click rate (Source: IAB) (see Chapter 6 BAM!).

Yield management: yield and revenue management is the process of understanding, anticipating, and influencing advertiser and consumer behavior to maximize profits through better selling, pricing, packaging, and inventory management while delivering value to advertisers and site users (Source: IAB) (see Chapter 6 BAM!).

Zipf's principle of least effort: an information-seeking client will tend to use the most convenient search method (see Chapter 3 keywords).

References

[1] Johnson, S. 1755. "Johnson, Preface to the Dictionary." In *A Dictionary of the English Language*. London: Johnson. Retrieved April 4, 2011, from http://ethnicity.rutgers.edu/~jlynch/Texts/preface.html

[2] Brooks, N. 2006. "Repeat Search Behavior: Implications for Advertisers." *Bulletin of the American Society for Information Science and Technology*, vol. 32(2), pp. 16–17.

Index